Praise for *Creative Colleges* by Elaina Loveland

"Creative fields of study thrive in collaborative learning environments that capture the passion of the students from that community. Navigating the labyrinth of colleges in search of those inclusive, creative communities is a daunting task and *Creative Colleges* is a noble companion throughout that journey. By helping students map out each step in the selection, application, and academic process, Elaina Loveland curates an essential tool for anyone considering an arts education."

—Dr. José Antonio Bowen, PhD, president, Goucher College, former dean, Meadow School of the Arts, Southern Methodist University

"Put aside the rankings, the phone book–size guides, and the glossy ads. *Creative Colleges* is the resource with the right approach to the college search for the creative student. This book will help you know yourself, know what's out there, and find the right match where you will cultivate your talents, grow, and prosper."

—Bradford R. MacGowan, EdD, former college/career counselor, Newton North High School, Massachusetts

"Navigating the college search and admissions process just got easier for talented artists. *Creative Colleges* answers those frequently asked questions: What is the difference between a liberal arts and a professional degree? How can I make my audition or portfolio stand out in the admissions process? How can I creatively finance an undergraduate education? A must-read for students committed to the arts or writing and seeking the best fit in their college choice."

—Jenifer L. Blair, EdD, director of college counseling and advising at South Carolina Governor's School for Science and Math, former associate vice provost for enrollment management, University of Baltimore

"Students who want to pursue the creative arts face all the usual challenges of the college search process, plus additional stresses, requirements, and questions specific to their artistic goals. Elaina Loveland, with her expertise both in college admission issues and arts education, brings together excellent advice for 'creative applicants' bewildered by all the college options they face. Her view of this area of the college-transition world is clear-eyed and very helpful."

"Elaina Loveland has crafted a book that takes seriously the way creativity flows through the lives of college-seeking students who are interested in the arts. Loveland offers a wealth of guidelines and resources for these students, bolstered by a multitude of quoted 'takes' on art schools and education. Readers hear from college and arts academy administrators, faculty, and students who describe how they decide to admit students, how they teach their classes, and how they finally chose which school to attend. The message throughout is, 'Know yourself, love your art, and find the school that will support your growth.' Refreshingly, what we don't get is any sense that some art practices and life paths are superior to others. Loveland includes information for music students, dramatists, dancers, writers, and artists who want to teach. And in my favorite section, she reminds creative students who decide not to major in art that, at their core, they will 'always be an artist' and stresses that this quality can be nourished forever and will enhance their lives. This is a helpful and generous book that will be useful to any imaginative student who is considering post-secondary education in the arts. I recommend it."

"This is a guide that has been long overdue. The information is solid and presented in a way that is easy to understand. I think this will be a valuable resource, especially to those counselors and parents who may not have personal experience in the arts. The inclusion of interviews with students who are visual and performing arts majors provides a very personal insight that is often hard to find. It's wonderful to have a guidebook that is more than facts and figures and rankings. This gets to the heart of the issues faced by creative students as they try to find that special place that will help them realize their potential."

Creative COLLEGES

FINDING THE BEST PROGRAMS FOR ASPIRING
ACTORS, ARTISTS, DESIGNERS, DANCERS,
MUSICIANS, WRITERS, AND MORE

ELAINA LOVELAND

Published by Sourcebooks, Inc.
P.O. Box 4410, Naperville, Illinois 60567-4410
(630) 961-3900
Fax: (630) 961-2168
www.sourcebooks.com

Originally published as *Creative Colleges* in 2005, 2008, 2010, 2013 in the United States of America by SuperCollege LLC.

The Library of Congress has cataloged the fourth edition as follows:
Loveland, Elaina C.
Creative colleges : a guide for student actors, artists, dancers, musicians and writers / by Elaina Loveland. -- Fourth edition.
pages cm
"Author of 'Creative careers.'"
1. Arts--Vocational guidance--United States. 2. Schools--United States--Admission. 3. Universities and colleges--United States--Admission. I. Title. II. Title: Guide for student actors, artists, dancers, musicians, and writers.
NX503.L68 2013
700.71'173--dc23

Printed and bound in the United States of America.
DR 10 9 8 7 6 5 4 3 2 1

To my family—you are the closest to my heart.

Contents

Acknowledgments   x

Introduction   xii

Chapter 1: The Creative Student's College Search   1

The Artistic Component in the Admissions Process   1

Doing Your Research   2

The Campus Visit   3

Standardized Tests   3

Financing Your Education   4

Have a College-Cost Talk with Your Parents   5

Federal Aid and the FAFSA   5

Artistic Scholarships   7

Part-Time Work   8

The Double Major: Studying the Arts and Another Discipline   9

Creative Students Not Majoring in the Arts   10

Chapter 2: Frequently Asked Questions   11

Chapter 3: Colleges for Actors   24

Types of Drama Programs   24

How to Decide Between a Conservatory Program and a Traditional College Program   26

Concentrations in a Drama Major   27

For Aspiring Musical Theater Majors   28

Film, Television, and Cinema   32

Drama Auditions   32

The Portfolio for Prospective Design and Production Majors   34

Drama Program Philosophy   34

Evaluating Drama Programs   37

Actor Interview, Essay, Application Questions, and Résumé   40

Sample Drama Curriculum   52

Profiles of Selected Drama Programs   58

Comprehensive List of Colleges with Drama Programs   95

Chapter 4: Colleges for Artists and Designers   104

Identifying the Type of Art Student You Are   104

Types of Art Programs   106

Art Program Philosophy   107

Concentrations in Art Degrees   107

The Freshman "Foundation" Year   108

Graphic Design Programs   111

The Artistic Portfolio   116

National Portfolio Days   118

Evaluating Art Programs   118

Artist Statement, Essays, Portfolio, and Résumé   123

Sample Art Curriculum   130

Profiles of Selected Art and Design Programs   136

Comprehensive List of Colleges with Art and Design Programs   179

Chapter 5: Colleges for Dancers   191

Types of Dance Programs   191

College Options: Dancing without a Dance Major   195

Dance Auditions   196

How They Stack Up: Comparing College Dance Programs   205

Dancer Essay, Application Questions, and Résumés   207

Sample Dance Curriculum   217

Profiles of Selected Dance Programs   219

Comprehensive List of Colleges with Dance Programs   252

Chapter 6: Colleges for Musicians   255

Types of College Music Programs   255

Types of Music Degrees   258

Music Specialties   259

Music Auditions   259

Evaluating College Music Programs   263

Preparing for Your Audition: Suggestions for Prospective Music Majors   268

Musician Artist Statement, Essay, Repertoire List, and Résumé   276

Sample Music Curriculum   284

Profiles of Selected Music Programs   288

Comprehensive List of Colleges with Music Programs   327

Chapter 7: Colleges for Writers   338

Types of Creative Writing Programs   338

Writing Portfolios   341

What to Expect in a Creative Writing Workshop   342

Finding a Writing Community   342

Evaluating Creative Writing Programs   343

Creative Writing and the "Real World"   346

Writer Essays and Résumés   349

Sample Creative Writing Curriculum   355

Profiles of Selected Creative Writing Programs   357

Comprehensive List of Colleges with Writing Programs   383

Chapter 8: The Next Step   389

Making the Most of Your Creative College Experience   389

Exploring the Local Arts Community   390

Study Abroad Opportunities   390

Internships   391

Exploring Career Choices after Graduation   392

Appendix   395

Index   398

About the Author   401

Acknowledgments

This book would not have been possible without the love and support of many people who are very dear to me. I want to thank them:

* My husband and daughters, for their support and understanding the dedication it takes to work on a book such as this.
* My mother, Christina Loveland, for driving me to ballet throughout my childhood.
* My father, Dr. Fred Loveland, for being the first to encourage me to write a book at age thirteen.
* My brother, Marcus Loveland, for showing me infinite support and encouragement in all of my endeavors—you are the best brother a person could have.
* The late Robert Liddy, who ignited my passion for writing and who graciously read my very first writings.
* Jari Poulin, my first serious ballet teacher, who taught me the joy of dance.
* The faculty of the Goucher College dance department.
* Madison Smartt Bell, who gave me my first glimpse of the writing life.
* Susan Gossling Walters, for hiring me for my first writing "gig."
* Shanda Ivory, for giving me a chance to merge my interests in higher education and writing at the National Association for College Admission Counseling.
* My colleagues and friends at the National Association for College Admission Counseling.

* Sharon Ritchey, who assisted me with the inordinate amount of research that this project required—I could not have done it without you!

* My readers Julie Bogart, Christine Graziano, Shanda Ivory, and Dani Kehoe, who provided valuable suggestions on drafts of this manuscript.

* Jenifer Blair, José Bowen, Barbara Elliott, Bradford MacGowan, Keith Todd, and Therese Quinn, who kindly read this book in advance and provided me with beautifully written praise.

* All the students, faculty members, and admissions professionals who took the time to speak to me about their experiences for this book.

* And to all of my friends not mentioned here by name who have shared wonderful memories with me over the years—you know who you are.

Introduction

If you are reading this book, then you know your search for the perfect college is unique. Additionally, the application process for enrollment in a creative field of study is decisively different from that of other students. It is not only your academic grades, teacher recommendations, and SAT scores that are important, but it is also the artistic part of your application that can determine your admittance to a particular school or department dedicated to a specific art. If you are an actor, artist, dancer, musician, or writer, your artistic talent—whether presented as an audition or artistic portfolio—probably counts as much as, if not more than, the rest of your application.

Because you are an artist, you need a better-than-average college guide—a book that will allow you to find the school of your dreams and help you prepare for the artistic component of your college application as well as for your career. You might also have other special needs, such as pursuing academic interests outside your artistic talent. In this case, you need to find a college that has both an excellent department that will help you master your craft and more traditional academic courses that will broaden your horizons.

This college guide is your answer. It has separate sections for each field of artistry, and it lists the programs that are available to you. Using this book will help you find the school and degree plan that are right for you.

You'll find stories of real students just like you throughout the book whose experiences you can learn from. Why did they choose their colleges? Did they stay with their intended majors? Were they satisfied with their college choices? Answers to these questions and more lie ahead.

Choosing the Right College for You

Why is choosing the right college such a big decision? The truth is that it's the first major decision you make that will impact the rest of your life. Where you go to school, whom you meet, how much you pay for your degree, and what you study will likely influence other choices you will make down the road.

Graduation from *college*—as opposed to from high school—is the start of the rest of your life. Choosing the college you will attend is the beginning of a journey to becoming the person you will be.

Perhaps more important than choosing the right college is choosing the right college *for you*. Not for your parents. Not for your friends. Not because you think it's more "practical" to go to one college than another. You have to live in your own shoes after college, and when you make your monthly student loan payment (which you may not be thinking about now, but you will probably have one), you want it to be for an experience you'll remember fondly and not one you might regret.

If you are passionate about an artistic discipline, it's important to pursue it now. Chances are, college will be the only time in your life that you don't have rent or a mortgage, grocery bills, or a car payment. Financially, you will never be more free. This is the time to pursue your dreams, because you are not financially committed to anything but your education. You have four years to do whatever you want—choose how you spend that time wisely.

Don't worry if you are torn between your artistic passion and a practical voice in your head that says to do something else. There are plenty of colleges out there that can provide you with solid training in your artistic interests as well as academic studies. On the other hand, you can also attend a college where you can fully immerse yourself in your art. Either way, you will be able to continue to do what you love. In the following pages, you may find the way to your destiny.

EXPLANATION OF COLLEGE DATA SOURCES

Nearly 1,100 surveys were sent to colleges and universities offering creative degrees across the United States. Results were compiled, and the author then selected programs to be highlighted in extended program listings for each discipline based on the strengths of the programs. Reference listings were compiled from information provided by institutions, institutional websites, and the National Center of Education

Statistics data. Profiles describe undergraduate programs only; some institutions also have graduate programs.

DEGREE ABBREVIATIONS

- BA—bachelor of arts
- BFA—bachelor of fine arts
- BM—bachelor of music
- BS—bachelor of science

EXPLANATION OF COST LEGEND

In the sections of this book with in-depth profiles of college profiles, the following legend is used to show tuition costs.

	PUBLIC	PRIVATE
$$$$	More than $13,500	More than $49,000
$$$	$11,001–$13,500	$45,001–$49,000
$$	$9,000–$11,000	$40,000–$45,000
$	Less than $9,000	Less than $40,000

Price categories are based on current tuition and fees and do not include room, board, transportation, and other expenses. Please note that for public institutions, the cost range shown is based on in-state tuition rates; out-of-state tuition rates are higher, and in some cases, considerably so.

CHAPTER

1

The Creative Student's College Search

Selecting a college is a difficult decision for any student. There is so much to consider—location, number of students, quality of education, campus life, and much more. For creative students like you, the decision can be even more complicated. In addition to the usual factors, you should consider how well the college will prepare you for a professional career in the arts, how you may select a double major including the arts, or even how you can participate in the arts while majoring in a different subject. That's a *lot* to have running through your mind!

You have several options. You might decide to attend a professional training school or conservatory that will prepare you for a career in your discipline. If you haven't decided that you'd like to pursue a professional career, or if you want to explore academic subjects during college as well, you can consider a university or liberal arts college.

Right now, you are probably asking, "But how do I know which school is right for me?" This chapter will help guide you through some self-analyzing. It's for all types of creative students—actor, artist, dancer, musician, or writer. You'll want to take time to consider what campus setting you'd thrive in best.

The Artistic Component in the Admissions Process

Unlike many of your college-bound peers, as an artist you have a different angle on the college application process. For many of you, college may be the final step in preparing for a professional career. Also, the selection of your college is not just a choice for the next four years, because where you attend can have a profound impact on whether or not you will have a professional career in the arts.

The artistic component of admissions to college affects you in another way as well. Not only do you have to prepare college applications like any other student—by obtaining teacher recommendations, writing an essay, and possibly taking standardized tests (depending on where you apply)—but you also have to prepare the artistic component, which can be an audition or a portfolio. Many independent art schools, conservatories, and artistically competitive liberal arts colleges and universities view your audition or portfolio as one of the more important components—if not *the* most important—of your college application. Because the artistic component of your college search will likely be a critical factor in your admissions result, you can't be prepared enough for your audition or for creating your artistic portfolio. But not to worry—these are addressed in detail in the chapters for specific arts disciplines.

Doing Your Research

One of the most important things in making the best college choice is to *do your research*! This is especially true for student artists. You have already spent a substantial amount of time pursuing and mastering your art so you can reach your fullest potential. Finding the right college program to advance your training to the next level may be the last step in the process of becoming the artist you want to be.

Other questions you'll need to start thinking about include geography. Do you want to stay close to home? Does it matter? Would you like to live in a particular region of the country?

Campus size is an important factor, because it can have a lot to do with your comfort level. Do you want to know most everyone on campus or in your department? Then smaller might be better for you. Do you want to interact with graduate students and never meet the same person twice? If this is the case, a larger school might be right up your alley.

Consider what you want your college years to be like. If you want the traditional trappings of college life—like sporting events or Greek life—then maybe a more conventional atmosphere like a university or college would suit you better than a professional school.

This book can help you, but there are also several other ways to find the information that you need. (See the appendix for publications and Internet sites that can assist in your college search.) The National Association for College Admission Counseling hosts

Performing and Visual Arts College Fairs across the country each year. At these events, you can learn about various schools and programs and ask admissions officers questions. A trip to a college fair is a great first step in narrowing down what you want in a school.

The Internet has made it easier than ever before to find out details about specific college programs. Visiting school or department websites that interest you can give specific details about that school's offerings and help you determine if you'd enjoy being a student there.

If you determine a list of programs you are interested in, you can also use social media to engage more with the institution to determine if it has the right "feel" you want before visiting a campus in person. You can follow colleges or specific departments on Facebook or on Twitter. Also, some institutions offer the chance to chat online with college admissions officers to learn more about their programs as well.

The Campus Visit

If you decide a school merits serious consideration as one of your college options, you need to talk to people on campus—students, professors, and office personnel can be the ultimate source of information. Of course you can talk by phone, but talking in person is even better.

For most creative students, the campus visit can be paired with an audition or a portfolio review, which is usually part of the admissions process for students of the performing arts. However, if you live a long way from a school you like, you may be able to audition via videotape or send in your portfolio for review without visiting.

While a campus visit can give the best insight into whether or not you would enjoy being a student there, the admissions office might be willing to arrange a phone interview to answer any questions. Ask if you can talk to a few students on the phone to learn more about their experiences. Getting a student's perspective of campus life can help you determine if the school would be a good fit for you.

Standardized Tests

As you probably know, most four-year colleges and universities require your results from either the SAT or the ACT. However, some conservatory arts programs do not require these tests. Check with the admissions office of any institution you are considering to find out if you are required to take one of these exams.

If you plan to apply to a wide range of artistic programs—including conservatories, liberal arts colleges, and universities—you will need to take at least one of these standardized tests. Liberal arts colleges and universities almost unilaterally require test scores as one of the key factors in admissions decisions, and your application will not be considered without a test score. You should plan to take one of the college entrance exams during your junior year of high school, or at the very latest the fall of your senior year.

Test preparation books and free sample tests are available at collegeboard.com for the SAT and at act.org for the ACT. You can get a feel for this type of exam by taking the practice tests offered. If you are still nervous about taking your college entrance exam, or if you have trouble setting your own study schedule, consider working with a study group or taking a test preparation course from a reputable company like Kaplan or the Princeton Review.

Although many schools permit you to submit either SAT or ACT scores, you may want to take both tests. One test format may be better for you than the other, and as a result, your score on one of them may be higher.

Even if you plan to apply to conservatory-based college programs or professional training schools that usually don't require standardized test scores, you should consider taking a standardized test anyway. If, at the last minute, you decide a conservatory or professional arts program is not for you, and you want to apply to a liberal arts college or university artistic program instead, you'll need standardized test scores to apply. If you don't have them as a backup, you may have to defer college for a year so that you can take the test required for admission to one of these schools. The same logic applies to having an SAT or ACT score on your transcript in the event of a transfer to another program or school. Having test scores under your belt affords you many more college options if you discover a program isn't right for you and you want to transfer. Just look at college entrance exams as "insurance" if you change your mind at any point in the admissions process or once you have already enrolled in college.

Financing Your Education

Weighing the cost is no small factor in making your final decision. At first, consider colleges purely from an educational point of view. Ask yourself, "Does this college offer what I need?" Narrow your choices to a short list of favorites. Then add in the cost factor, as it can be quite significant in making your final decision. Although many professional schools, colleges, and universities offer substantial financial aid packages—including grants, scholarships, and loans—these are not always enough. Only you and your family can decide how much is too much.

If your parents are willing to help you pay for your college education, consider yourself lucky. The cost of higher education is substantial, and parents' support can make an enormous difference in your life after college. Parental support can eliminate or reduce debt that you might otherwise incur due to taking out loans to pay college tuition.

Have a College-Cost Talk with Your Parents

Before you get ahead of yourself and count on your parents (or legal guardians) to share your college expenses, find out just how much they are willing or able to contribute. Just because your parents have said they will pay for college—or help you pay for it—does not mean they have the resources to pay for 100 percent of it. Realistically, they may not be able to pay as much as they promise. It's very important to sit down and have an open, honest discussion about the financial aspect of college. Find out the following:

- ★ How much of your college expense do your parents plan to provide?
- ★ How much do they expect you to contribute?
- ★ Will there be a need to take out loans?
- ★ Will they pay for all four years of an undergraduate program?
- ★ Will they give you additional money for books, clothes, and recreation?
- ★ Are they considering the fact that college costs tend to rise each year with tuition increases and that the possibility exists for decreased financial aid, since funding varies from year to year?

Federal Aid and the FAFSA

For many students, the greatest source of financial aid for higher education is the federal government. To be considered for federal grant and loan programs—including Stafford loans and Pell grants—students must file a Free Application for Federal Student Aid (FAFSA). The earliest you can apply is January 1, so make it your New Year's resolution to complete it as soon as possible. Because colleges and universities determine financial aid packages on a rolling basis, it is most advantageous for you to file the FAFSA as soon as possible after the January 1 deadline in the year you plan to attend college. Completing the FAFSA earlier may increase your chances of getting a better financial aid package. You have to file the FAFSA each year you want financial aid.

After filing the FAFSA, you will receive a student aid report (SAR), which determines how much money you and your family should anticipate paying for your college expenses. The expected family contribution (EFC) listed is what college financial aid offices use to determine how much you and your family will have to pay toward your education. The EFC is based on income and the assets belonging to you and your parents.

If your parents aren't willing or able to pay the EFC or can pay only a portion of it, you—the student—are responsible for the cost, unless you meet the very narrow guidelines of being an "independent" student. There are only a few ways that students can be separated from their parents financially for consideration as independent students. You must be one of the following:

* ★   a student at least twenty-four years of age;
* ★   a student pursuing a graduate degree;
* ★   an orphan or ward of the court;
* ★   a veteran of the U.S. Armed Forces; or
* ★   a married student or a person with dependent children or other dependents who live with the student and who receive more than half of their support from the student.

You can see why it's so important to have a frank conversation with your parents about college costs. Unless you fit the independent student status each year, you will still need their income figures to report on the FAFSA, and each year, your financial aid package will be based on those numbers. Obtaining parental support for college costs and agreeing how much both they and you will contribute to the expense is critical in making the best financial plan for college, a plan that is likely to span the entire four years of your education. And keep in mind that many students do not finish college in four years. Some degree plans or certain college programs (like picking up an education certification credential) can stretch your college years past the traditional four. Other possibilities, like switching majors, also can make college take longer. So if you think an extra semester or a fifth year might be a possibility, you may want to consider that in your financial plan as well.

Once you have been accepted, colleges will send financial aid packages that outline what your family is expected to contribute and the level of aid offered by the school. When you receive these financial aid packages, you will have a much better picture of what the cost of college will be. It is important to remember that at most higher educational institutions, tuition and room and board costs traditionally rise each year, so the estimated amounts that you are given will be only for your freshman year. To plan for the cost of your entire education, you will have to make some estimates of what the remaining three years will cost given the impact of inflation and other factors.

If you feel that you are due more financial aid than you are offered, you can ask for a reassessment with the financial aid office. This doesn't always bring success, but it is worth a try. If you are an excellent student, if you have exceptional artistic ability (such as might be indicated by obtaining one of the school's artistic scholarships), or if you have extenuating financial circumstances, it will be easier to plead your case to the financial aid office. And don't forget that each year is a new year. If costs are rising to the point where you or your family can't pay the tuition, or if your financial situation has changed, you can revisit the financial aid office and ask them to reassess your package.

Artistic Scholarships

For talented creative students, a number of colleges and universities offer special scholarships based on artistic ability. Favoring college programs that offer such scholarships is a good way to narrow your search if you are considering a number of schools. In most cases, competing for artistic scholarships is part of either the portfolio review process for visual arts students or the audition process for performing arts students.

Even if a school doesn't offer artistic scholarships, it's important not to rule it out immediately. The availability of artistic scholarships should be *one factor* in your decision-making process, but not the *only* one. It is best to apply for as many artistic scholarships as you can to investigate all your options. Remember that there are also scholarships offered by arts organizations not affiliated with specific colleges. When the time comes to decide which school to attend, sit down with all the information including funding from an artistic scholarship, your financial aid package, your firsthand experience visiting the college, and detailed information about the degree programs. Then decide where to go from there.

Part-Time Work

Working while in school requires some time management, but it's possible. These days, more and more students work part-time to supplement the cost of their education. As part of your financial aid package, you may be eligible for the federal work-study program, which allows you to find a job on campus. If you are lucky, you may be able to find a job within your department. This way, not only will you earn money to pay for expenses, but you will also gain valuable experience in your field that you can put on your résumé.

Gaining employment experience off campus is also an option; wages might be slightly higher than in federal work-study programs, and making contacts off campus can be helpful in seeking internships later in your college career. If you do take the plunge to get a part-time job in the "real world," it may be beneficial to find a job related to your field of study. The experience could be invaluable when looking for that first job after graduation from college. Here are some ideas:

ART STUDENTS

* Work at an art gallery or museum.
* Work at a local arts organization.
* Teach art to children.
* Try to sell your art, whether it's a painting, illustration, or graphic design work.

DRAMA STUDENTS

* Work at a local professional theater company.
* Find out if you can get paid to assist with local high school plays and musicals.
* If you live in a major metropolitan area, see if you can land any acting work, if your program allows you to accept outside acting work. Related acting work could be performing for a commercials or events such playing the role of a flapper for a 1920s corporate event or a Disney princess for a child's birthday party.
* Try to work part-time at a local casting agency.

DANCE STUDENTS

★ Teach dance to children at a local dance studio.

★ Work at a local dance company.

★ Work at a dance supply store.

MUSIC STUDENTS

★ Work at a local symphony or opera company.

★ Teach music to children.

★ Work at a music supply store.

CREATIVE WRITING STUDENTS

★ Work at a local publishing company or newspaper.

★ Work at a local literary arts organization.

★ Tutor high school students in writing.

Remember to keep things in balance, no matter how rewarding your on-campus or off-campus job may be. You must remain focused on your studies, limiting your job to about fifteen hours a week. You'll want to make your education the top priority, followed by work, and still fit in time for a social life.

The Double Major: Studying the Arts and Another Discipline

Should you decide to combine studying another discipline with an arts degree, keep in mind that you can most easily attain a double major by pursuing a bachelor of arts (BA). Because professional degree programs such as a bachelor of fine arts (BFA) or bachelor of music (BM) dedicate most of their requirements to the arts curriculum itself, there is little room for taking electives for another major if you want to graduate in four years. However, if you don't mind staying in school for an extra year, it may be possible to add another major or do a dual degree, such as a BFA in art and a BA in art history. The key is to plan your academic studies early in your college career.

Creative Students Not Majoring in the Arts

What if, after doing some serious soul searching, you decide that despite your talent, you don't see a future professional career in the arts as your path in life? That's fine. You are still a creative student and will still be a creative person. Everyone is different, and although you might have what it takes to become a professional artist, that doesn't mean that is necessarily right for you. Only you can make that decision. You can still study the arts in college; it just might not be your sole focus.

Perhaps you are a creative student who has decided that you want to pursue a more academic route after high school. That's okay! You can still enjoy the benefits of the creative departments on a college campus. You may consider a double major or a minor in an artistic discipline. Also, don't forget the contributions you can make with your creative side beyond an academic setting. You can always offer your talents to the community. You can participate in arts-related organizations or do artistic work on your own for personal satisfaction.

If you have spent much of your childhood and teenage years pursuing an art form, it will never be lost, even if you don't continue your studies in college. It is part of who you are! You can always pick up where you left off, even though there may be no professional career as the ultimate goal. You can return to studying your art later in life or share your love of the arts with others. At your core, you will always be an artist.

CHAPTER

Frequently Asked Questions

In the previous chapter, you learned the importance of visiting college campuses and speaking with students directly. There is no substitute for seeing and hearing with your own eyes and ears.

In this chapter, you'll have the opportunity to hear directly from admissions officers at conservatories and arts and music colleges. While it's still important for you to conduct your own research, this roundtable will give you the perspectives of four different admissions officers about deciding whether to attend a conservatory or arts college, how to approach the admissions process, and how to pay for your education.

What is different about the admissions process for artistic students, compared with students pursuing a traditional college experience?

The main difference in the admission process is that it is designed to demonstrate the students' commitment to their art form. They have to display the depth and breadth of their experience in the visual or performing arts, in addition to their academic achievement.

—*Barbara Elliott, director of enrollment planning, Pennsylvania College of Art and Design, former dean of enrollment management, The University of the Arts*

The biggest difference between the two is the focus on the individual on an artistic level. For example, many traditional college admissions processes evaluate a student's ability based on numbers: GPA, test score, school rank, etc.—sometimes with or without an in-person interview or personal assessment. Our institution requires an in-person audition for all majors, allowing our faculty to assess the student on an individual basis, considering their talent and preparation, but also their potential, passion, and fit within our creative community. In fact, we do not even require test scores, further focusing on the individual in the performing arts admission process.

—Brian Calhoon, director of admissions, Boston Conservatory at Berklee

For a student who is applying to the arts, in addition to academic records, arts colleges ask for an audition or a portfolio as part of the admission process.

—Carol Kim, vice president of strategic enrollment management, The New School

The major difference is that the audition is the primary criterion for admission. We review supplementary materials like SAT scores, an artistic résumé, and writing samples, but the audition is by far most important.

—Thomas Novak, interim president, provost,
and dean at the New England Conservatory

What factors should students consider when preparing to study a creative discipline in college?

The greatest consideration is commitment. Students need to ask themselves, "Is this really what I want to do?" To ensure that they have firsthand experience and are prepared for the demands that will be placed on them at the college level, students should take as many art courses during their high school years as possible. When you come to a conservatory, there is a significant level of achievement that is expected in order to begin the program.

—Barbara Elliott, director of enrollment planning, Pennsylvania College of Art
and Design, former dean of enrollment management, The University of the Arts

Having a skill at a creative discipline is not enough. You must have a passion for the craft to sustain you on your path towards a career. There will be challenges, and there are no guarantees, like any career path. Talent is helpful, but without discipline and a commitment to improve and a drive to maintain your art, you won't go far.

—Brian Calhoon, director of admissions, Boston Conservatory at Berklee

Students have to be aware that this is what they really want to do with their lives—it is something they cannot live without. In music and dance, in particular, an applicant should have a lot of training already. Usually these students have been practicing their art from about age eight or ten. For visual arts and theater, this is a little more flexible.

—*Carol Kim, vice president of strategic enrollment management, The New School*

The primary factor is the possibility of studying with a certain primary teacher in college. The relationship between a student and a professor in college, especially in music, is a special one.

—*Thomas Novak, interim president, provost,
and dean at the New England Conservatory*

What benefits should creative students look for in considering a college?

Who will be teaching you? Faculty or graduate teaching assistants? Are they practicing professionals in their field? Find out what types of arts events are held on campus. What type of access does the institution have with the greater arts community? Look at the facilities. For dancers, find out what types of floors you'll be dancing on. For visual arts students, look to see if the facilities are being well used and if the equipment looks well maintained.

—*Barbara Elliott, director of enrollment planning, Pennsylvania College of Art
and Design, former dean of enrollment management, The University of the Arts*

First and foremost, you should choose a college that feels right when you visit. Finding the right fit is the most important, even more than an institution's prestige or shiny new facilities. Other factors to look for are if you have a connection with a particular faculty member, if the school provides ample performance opportunity throughout the degree program (not just [for] upperclassmen), and if the school provides the opportunity to be creative in your path. For example, is the school strict in its training, or is there stylistic variety to allow you to be a versatile musician/dancer/actor?

—*Brian Calhoon, director of admissions, Boston Conservatory at Berklee*

Students should look into the faculty, class size, and mentorship opportunities with faculty. Looking at facilities is especially important in the arts. Will you have access to the darkroom or practice rooms at all times? Other questions to ask are: How many performing opportunities are available? Do art students get to participate in both group and solo exhibitions?

—*Carol Kim, vice president of strategic enrollment management, The New School*

The main benefit to look for is who might be teaching. Make sure teachers are of a high caliber. A lot of good facts and nuts and bolts about a school can be found on the Web, but this is not enough. In addition to sending a viewbook to prospective students, we also send a CD and DVD of students' performances. This is more of what our type of ideal student is looking for in evaluating schools.

—*Thomas Novak, interim president, provost, and dean at the New England Conservatory*

How important are standardized tests in the admissions process for artistic students?

Standardized tests play a role, but they are not central to the admission process. They help to corroborate an academic record that is strong; their role becomes more significant when there are weaknesses in the academic record. Strong test scores can balance an academic record that may be unimpressive because the student focused on his or her primary interests—the arts. Test scores are also helpful in placing a student within the liberal arts curriculum, especially in courses such as first-year writing.

—*Barbara Elliott, director of enrollment planning, Pennsylvania College of Art and Design, former dean of enrollment management, The University of the Arts*

Not important at all at our institution. The Boston Conservatory at Berklee does not require tests, only English language tests for international students.

—*Brian Calhoon, director of admissions, Boston Conservatory at Berklee*

We do not require standardized tests. We don't believe the scores are an indicator of how well a student will do at our school.

—*Carol Kim, vice president of strategic enrollment management, The New School*

Standardized test scores are of small importance, but there is a minimum requirement that is pretty modest. For international students, the TOEFL [Test of English as a Foreign Language] test is important.

—*Thomas Novak, interim president, provost,*
and dean at the New England Conservatory

How competitive are auditions and portfolio requirements?

Auditions are extremely important and competitive. Although auditions happen before academic review at my institution, the application needs to be complete before the audition. If the audition committee recommends the student for admission based on the performance, the applicant then undergoes academic review.

Portfolio requirements for the visual arts are also competitive. The portfolio review helps us to ensure that incoming students have the necessary skills and visual experiences needed to successfully participate in the first-year program. If an applicant presents a portfolio that demonstrates potential and commitment but does not have the skill and breadth of experience needed to ensure success, the admission committee may recommend or require the university's summer PREP program as a prerequisite for admission.

—*Barbara Elliott, director of enrollment planning, Pennsylvania College of Art*
and Design, former dean of enrollment management, The University of the Arts

They are quite competitive. We average admitting a little less than a third of the students who apply.

—*Thomas Novak, interim president, provost,*
and dean at the New England Conservatory

How can students best prepare for auditions and portfolios?

In terms of portfolio development, ideally you will have been taking art classes during high school. In the summer between 11th and 12th grades, you should revisit the work you have done throughout high school and select several to redo as a senior for your college admission portfolio. You might also consider taking a pre-college summer program in the arts to further develop your experience and skill. It's important to work closely with your art teacher during the first semester of your senior year to round out your final portfolio presentation. Ultimately, you want to present twelve to fifteen strong pieces. And be sure to photograph your work either digitally or in slide format.

For music, dance, and theater applicants: practice, practice, practice. Work with your teacher to select performance pieces that will meet audition requirements of the colleges you think you'd like to attend. Try to identify your pieces during the spring of your junior year so you have the summer to learn them and the fall to really hone your performance.

—*Barbara Elliott, director of enrollment planning, Pennsylvania College of Art and Design, former dean of enrollment management, The University of the Arts*

Students really need to look closely at the requirements of each individual school. Find out the philosophy of each school. Our philosophy and beliefs are different than a lot of schools. Our "best fit" applicant shows that they understand the school's philosophy by demonstrating it through the portfolio or audition process.

—*Carol Kim, vice president of strategic enrollment management, The New School*

Practice. Practice. Practice.

—*Thomas Novak, interim president, provost, and dean at the New England Conservatory*

Are student interviews recommended?

I recommend them. We love to meet our applicants in person. The format for the interview differs depending upon whether the candidate is a visual or performing arts applicant. Performing artists will have an informal discussion with their audition committee; the visual artists' interview occurs during the portfolio review.

—*Barbara Elliott, director of enrollment planning, Pennsylvania College of Art and Design, former dean of enrollment management, The University of the Arts*

Depending on if they are required. We hold individual auditions that include a brief interview. Whenever possible, we encourage students to audition on campus, but we also provide regional audition sites in select cities around the country and abroad. When visiting a school, it is encouraged to schedule sample private lessons with one or more faculty. Finding a compatible teacher is an essential part of a performing arts education.

—*Brian Calhoon, director of admissions, Boston Conservatory at Berklee*

Student interviews are part of the audition process [for performing arts applicants], but not for other students (like those in the visual arts).

—*Carol Kim, vice president of strategic enrollment management, The New School*

There is no formal interview process. Faculty may wish to speak to a student at his or her audition.

—*Thomas Novak, interim president, provost, and dean at the New England Conservatory*

How can students get the best teacher recommendations?

We only require one recommendation. It helps to give a broader sense of who the applicant is if there is information from a guidance counselor or from a teacher outside of their artistic discipline. However, many applicants choose to ask their art or music teacher to write on their behalf, and that's fine too. No matter who you want to write the recommendation, ask them early in the process. Ask them if they have the time to write a recommendation and tell them when it needs to be submitted. And always send a thank-you note afterward.

—Barbara Elliott, director of enrollment planning, Pennsylvania College of Art and Design, former dean of enrollment management, The University of the Arts

Recommendations are simply another way for our faculty and admissions team to learn more about the student, their skill and potential, as well as their personality. Find recommenders who can provide more insight into the student in an honest, constructive way.

—Brian Calhoon, director of admissions, Boston Conservatory at Berklee

We require two letters of recommendation. One should be from a teacher who knows the student on an artistic level.

—Carol Kim, vice president of strategic enrollment management, The New School

We require an artistic recommendation. We prefer that it is from a student's private music teacher. They have the best knowledge of a student's potential.

—Thomas Novak, interim president, provost, and dean at the New England Conservatory

What advice can you give students about writing an admissions essay or artist's statement? What is the difference between the two?

Do not send your first draft. Writing an essay or an artist's statement must be approached as a project. Make sure you answer the question that was posed. Double-check grammar and structure with your English teacher and get feedback from others whose opinions you value. Our question is, "How would your best friend describe you?" We use a question like this because we want to get a good sense of who a person is, in addition to being an artist. No matter the topic, make sure the final product reflects that you've taken the time and effort to do your best.

—Barbara Elliott, director of enrollment planning, Pennsylvania College of Art and Design, former dean of enrollment management, The University of the Arts

Be genuine. Don't write or tell a story you think an admissions office or faculty would want to hear, but instead share an honest story from your past or passion. Tell us why it is you do what you do. For our institution, they are one and the same.

—*Brian Calhoon, director of admissions, Boston Conservatory at Berklee*

An artist's statement is different than an admission essay in that it asks who the students are and how they found themselves as artists. It asks how they see art being a part of their lives and what they want to do with their art.

—*Carol Kim, vice president of strategic enrollment management, The New School*

Some schools have a specific topic required for writing an essay. Our requirement is that students send in any piece of writing. About a third to half of students write about why they are a musician and what they hope to accomplish, but they do this on their own accord. It will not make or break an admission decision.

—*Thomas Novak, interim president, provost,
and dean at the New England Conservatory*

What advice do you have for students in preparing an artistic résumé?

Start taking notes of all of your activities as early as your freshman year of high school. Take photos of your experiences—exhibits you've had, stage sets you've worked on—so that you remember them. Then, during your senior year, pull out the notes and select the best activities and most notable accomplishments from your list. Don't forget to include volunteer work and jobs that you've held.

—*Barbara Elliott, director of enrollment planning, Pennsylvania College of Art
and Design, former dean of enrollment management, The University of the Arts*

Start early! If you wait until your senior year to compile all the artistic things you've done in recent years, it will be a challenge to remember everything. Keep a running list of events you've done, from extracurricular activities to private instruction and performances of note. Résumés should fit on one page, so pick items that best represent your training and the artist you are today. No need to include less significant experiences, or those more than four years in the past.

—*Brian Calhoon, director of admissions, Boston Conservatory at Berklee*

Be honest. We want to have accurate expectations of what the student can do artistically.

—*Carol Kim, vice president of strategic enrollment management, The New School*

Our biggest piece of advice is that we don't want a five-page résumé. We give specific instructions about what should be in the résumé.

—*Thomas Novak, interim president, provost,*
and dean at the New England Conservatory

What are some of the best sources of financial aid for artistic students?

By and large, probably the best source of financial aid is the schools where you're applying. However, you should also look for aid in every possible avenue outside of the colleges for private scholarships. Use the Internet and search scholarship websites. Be sure to file for federal and state financial aid.

—*Barbara Elliott, director of enrollment planning, Pennsylvania College of Art*
and Design, former dean of enrollment management, The University of the Arts

For us, the audition is also your application for merit/talent-based scholarship. Determine what the school uses to determine merit awards. Is it talent/audition-based? Is it academic? Many performing arts colleges do not award academic scholarships, only talent-based scholarships.

—*Brian Calhoon, director of admissions, Boston Conservatory at Berklee*

Most private music schools have financial aid available, and it is largely driven by the audition. Probably the thing I'd recommend most is that students complete the required documentation for financial aid consideration by the deadline. We encourage students to research other sources of funding—like [scholarships] from their local area, scholarships for minorities, and scholarships for playing a particular instrument.

—*Thomas Novak, interim president, provost,*
and dean at the New England Conservatory

What advice do you have for students who are considering both arts conservatories and traditional liberal arts colleges and universities?

You really have to spend time on different types of campuses. Also, you have to do some serious soul searching and ask yourself, "What is really important to me?" To go to a conservatory, you have to want to live and breathe your art form. Ask yourself what balance you want in college. At a school like The University of the Arts, two-thirds of your studies will be your art. At a more traditional campus, the balance would probably be one-third in your art and two-thirds in general education requirements and electives. Another thing to consider is that conservatories do not have the traditional trappings of other schools, like sports activities and Greek life. If sports and fraternity life are important to you, a traditional college campus might be a better fit.

—*Barbara Elliott, director of enrollment planning, Pennsylvania College of Art*
and Design, former dean of enrollment management, The University of the Arts

How passionate are you about your art? The biggest difference between conservatory and college curriculums [is] in the number of credit hours/time spent in your major/art. Learn the difference between a Bachelor of Arts and a Bachelor of Music or Bachelor of Fine Arts. Also, if you wish to study a greater variety of academic courses (or double major/minor), then a university may be best for you. If you are fully dedicated and focused on your art, and have less desire to study other academic areas, then a conservatory will fit.

—*Brian Calhoon, director of admissions, Boston Conservatory at Berklee*

This is a very individual question. They really need to do their research. Many times it depends on what a student's expectations are about college life. They need to have a clear idea about what they want. If they don't know, an arts school is probably not the place for them.

—Carol Kim, vice president of strategic enrollment management, The New School

It really depends on what the student is looking for. There is a valid argument for both sides. One says students should have conservatory training to have a more focused college experience studying and pursuing their art almost exclusively. The other says students might benefit from a more broad-based academic experience in a more traditional campus setting. I'd tell students to investigate each college program as much as they can and trust their gut instincts.

—Thomas Novak, interim president, provost,
and dean at the New England Conservatory

What advice do you have for students whose parents are apprehensive about allowing them to pursue an arts degree?

We live in a new economy that is based on the ability to be creative. If you are creative and disciplined, you can succeed. Although there's no guarantee that comes with any degree, a program that provides you with professionally focused education and training will enable you to be among the best in your chosen field. The potential for successes is pretty high.

—Barbara Elliott, director of enrollment planning, Pennsylvania College of Art
and Design, former dean of enrollment management, The University of the Arts

For those students who are lucky enough to have found their passion, it is important to foster that. It is also important to identify different definitions of success for your student. Pursuing a career path primarily for financial security may not fit a student's definition of success, resulting in a loss of satisfaction or lack of personal fulfillment. Following a passion must be coupled with a dedication to making a career out of that passion, being creative and open to where the path may lead you. Many students start an arts degree with one idea of success, and through their study that definition may change, and they find themselves along another path. These are the choices that lead to personal and professional fulfillment.

—*Brian Calhoon, director of admissions, Boston Conservatory at Berklee*

Parents should try to be as supportive as possible... Students find their own way to do what they want. It is a misconception among many parents that if they send their child to an arts school, he or she won't get a good education. Many arts schools have a substantial liberal arts curriculum. Finally, I can't stress enough that students really need to do their research. It is their responsibility, and visiting the schools is the best way to make a final choice.

—*Carol Kim, vice president of strategic enrollment management, The New School*

Parents often wonder, "Is my child going to be successful?" if they study the arts in college. But the truth is, there is no guarantee that any other major is going to make them successful either. Many parents think that going to a traditional campus will give their child more options in life, but this is not necessarily true. With a conservatory education, parents should remember that students can use the skills they acquire in the arts in other fields as well. The discipline that is required to study the arts carries over to almost anything else.

—*Thomas Novak, interim president, provost,*
and dean at the New England Conservatory

Colleges for Actors

Whether you dream of joining the Screen Actors Guild or earning a Tony Award, you need to ask yourself, what kind of actor are you? Stage? Broadway? Television? Film? The answer to this question can be the first step in determining where you want to study acting after high school. Regardless of what type of actor you want to be, there is a program out there for you. All it takes is some research to start. This chapter will help you look more deeply at yourself as an actor and find out what higher education environment and degree are ideal for the next step toward your future.

Types of Drama Programs

FOUR-YEAR DEGREES

Luckily for actors, the majority of colleges and universities in the United States offer a degree in drama and have student performing ensembles. However, the wide array of options may seem overwhelming, and this can make it difficult to narrow down where you want to study. The most common option is a four-year bachelor's degree. All types of schools—theater conservatory programs, liberal arts colleges, and universities—offer this degree plan. The trick is deciding which bachelor's degree in what setting you want.

The bachelor of fine arts, or BFA, fulfills most of the degree requirements with drama courses. This degree is considered a professional degree in drama and is the most intensive in terms of studying the discipline. Approximately two-thirds of coursework is in the drama department, and the remaining one-third is in general education taken outside the department. Professional drama conservatory programs almost always grant the BFA degree.

The bachelor of arts, or BA, is a major just like any other in the college or university, although the student's focus is primarily on drama. Drama majors take the same number of drama courses as a history major would take history courses. Approximately one-third of the studies for this degree plan are in the drama department, and the remaining two-thirds are general education requirements or electives. Although the BA is less rigorous in terms of professional drama training, there are usually a comparable number of performing opportunities. The BA allows for some flexibility in your coursework, with the option of taking several electives outside the drama department or of picking up a double major or minor in another field. Liberal arts colleges and universities generally grant the BA.

KJERSTINE
CORNISH COLLEGE OF THE ARTS

Kjerstine already had a taste of what life would be like as a drama major at Cornish College of the Arts when it was time to make her college decision. Before finishing high school, she participated in the Young Actor Institute with the Seattle Children's Theatre, which was held on the Cornish campus.

Kjerstine took a year off after high school, traveled to the Dominican Republic, and got a "real" job, but she says, "I knew I always wanted to do theater," which led her back to Cornish.

Kjerstine describes the Cornish audition as "more intimate than putting on a number and standing in line." As an audition group, they did a warm-up with a movement theater teacher and played actor games to "get everyone's energy level up." Later each student had to recite two monologues: one chosen by the school and one that was his or her choice.

"It is a 'choose your own adventure' kind of school," says Kjerstine. "If you find something unique you want to do, they are willing to listen to you and adapt it to your needs."

Because she is concentrating in performance, Kjerstine thinks the fact that teachers are all working professionals in the Seattle area is advantageous. "They know what's happening in the professional arena."

Like in many arts conservatory programs, Kjerstine's experience focusing on her major requirements started almost as soon as she set foot on campus. "We really dove in headfirst freshman year," she explains. "There was a lot of exploring your emotions and limitations and where you can go with it."

Indeed, by senior year, Kjerstine's limitations have been explored and stretched. She played a man in Shakespeare's *Merry Wives of Windsor*. "The faculty chooses works that bring out the best in the ensemble, and for me, playing a man was a unique opportunity and showed me more of what I can accomplish as an actor," she says.

Hot Tips from Kjerstine

→ Go to the campus with an open mind. There are lessons the faculty are trying to teach you. They are like Yoda in that way—you might not understand it at the time, but you will years later.

→ If you are considering a conservatory, be sure it is what you want—it can be pretty intense.

Recently, Kjerstine landed a paid internship with Book-It Repertory Theatre, which adapts books into plays. She is following several leads for a job after graduation, from trying to break into the indie film scene in Seattle to auditioning for a Shakespeare company in California to considering auditions in Europe. Her ultimate destination, however, is New York or Chicago.

Looking back, Kjerstine believes she made the right choice to attend Cornish. "It has exceeded my expectations," she says.

The bachelor of science, or BS, is the least common degree offered in drama. It is more similar to the BA than to the BFA in most cases. In general, it requires fewer drama-specific courses than a BFA program and nearly the same breakdown of drama courses and general education requirements as a BA program. A college or university that has the drama department as part of a school that is not in the liberal arts (such as in the School of Communication) would normally offer the BS rather than the BA.

How to Decide Between a Conservatory Program and a Traditional College Program

If you want to live and breathe drama and know for certain that your ultimate career goal is to become an actor, director, stage manager, or theater artist, a conservatory program might be a good fit. Because the training is rigorous, there are abundant performing opportunities, and because you are surrounded by fellow theater artists, you'll feel right at home.

TWO-YEAR DEGREES AND PROFESSIONAL CERTIFICATE PROGRAMS

You may have heard of the American Academy of Dramatic Arts or the American Musical and Dramatic Academy. These are not traditional colleges that grant bachelor's degrees. These professional theater conservatory programs grant two-year certificates that are designed to launch you into the real world of professional acting. If you are certain that you want to pursue a professional acting career, attending a professional conservatory is another option available to you after high school. Be careful about making a decision, because outside of the professional acting world, a credential from one of these schools does not have nearly the same weight as a degree from a traditional college or university. This will become important if you are seeking employment in another field.

Fortunately, your education does not have to end with a professional certification program. A number of programs partner with four-year institutions to offer students in two-year professional certification programs the option of continuing their studies. With arrangements such as this, a drama student can earn a bachelor's degree at a neighboring institution during the two years following the professional certification program. The New York campus of the American Musical and Dramatic Academy (AMDA), for example, offers a joint program with New School University for students interested in obtaining a BA after their first two years of study at the AMDA.

Concentrations in a Drama Major

Most college drama programs emphasize performance in their degree programs. There are general education requirements, of course. But as a drama major, you'll also have the opportunity to take other classes within the department in areas such as theater history, improvisation, scene design, stage production, lighting, costuming, and playwriting.

If you are interested in focusing your studies in another area of drama, such as design or production, you may want to investigate the colleges on your list closely. Make sure there are enough classes offered in those areas to satisfy your curiosity or to prepare yourself for a career in those fields after graduation.

Here are some brief definitions to help you as you research:

Performance	The study of acting as a performing art.
Design	The study of theater design, which may include stage and set design as well as costume design.
Film and Television	The study of film and television's history and production; some programs have a specific focus on acting for film and television.
Production	The study of the technical elements of producing plays such as directing and lighting.
Musical Theater	The study of acting incorporating the additional talents of singing and dancing. Think Broadway.

For Aspiring Musical Theater Majors

To study musical theater, you'll need multiple talents: acting, singing, and dancing. Not all drama programs offer musical theater programs. Be proactive in asking the schools you are considering if they offer a minor or a concentration in musical theater. Remember that an important indicator of whether a department is adequate to meet your expectations for studying musical theater is the availability of performing opportunities. In other words, are musicals standard in the department's repertory? Are musicals performed every year or every semester? If a department has some courses in musical theater but does not typically have musical productions, you may not get the learning experience you desire. You may be disappointed if a drama program only performs plays without singing or dancing, so make sure to ask in advance whether musical theater is an integral part of the drama department rather than an elective course or two.

In terms of coursework, prospective musical theater majors should know that their degree programs are structured somewhat differently than a typical drama degree. Besides acting courses, you may have to take private voice lessons, a choral ensemble course, dance technique (which could be ballet, modern, tap, jazz, or dancing for musical theater), as well as courses in music.

RICHARD ISACKES
FORMER CHAIR OF THE DEPARTMENT OF THEATRE AND DANCE, UNIVERSITY OF TEXAS AT AUSTIN

Inside the Department

The University of Texas at Austin has the second-oldest theater department in the United States. With nearly forty faculty members, it is also one of the largest. Unlike many theater programs, UT Austin does not require an audition for admission to the undergraduate program.

"We would like to be the most rigorous academic program focused around the study of theater," asserts Richard Isackes, former chair of the Department of Theatre and Dance.

Isackes emphasizes that UT Austin is not a conservatory program. He says most undergraduate students leave the department for careers other than the professional theater. Isackes explains it this way: "For students who want to just act, this isn't the program for them, but it is perfect for the student who wants a broad intellectual experience."

Some may think a university with a graduate theater program might put undergraduates at a disadvantage for roles, but this is not the case at UT Austin. The department is careful not to put the undergraduate theater program in competition with the graduate theater program.

The ideal student for UT Austin's theater department is quite different than for an acting conservatory. "Our

Expert Tips from Professor Isackes

→ Check the credentials of the faculty.

→ Find out how committed the faculty is to teaching undergraduate students specifically.

→ Ask, "What are the destinations of your students?"

→ Can the program demonstrate what they promise to students? For example, if a program promises you will get to study with top professors during the freshman year, find out if that actually happens.

ONCE YOU GET INTO COLLEGE...

→ Be proactive about getting to know faculty members personally. Stop by and introduce yourself to faculty members in the department during office hours.

→ Take responsibility to engage yourself in that department. Participate in all the activities you can.

ideal student is a smart kid who loves theater and who wants the opportunity to investigate themselves to decide whether or not they want to be a professional actor, a biologist, or a teacher," says Isackes. "Conservatories serve a different type of student."

Unlike some programs, UT Austin does not have a fierce competitiveness among students for the best opportunities in the department.

"Here, we intentionally try to undermine the zero-sum game, meaning if you win someone else has to lose, which is a pretty common attitude," explains Isackes. "We like to think it is possible for everyone to grow together."

Students in the department have done more than act on stage; they have also written plays, created theater companies, written criticism, and created multidisciplinary performances.

NEAL

UNIVERSITY OF NORTH CAROLINA SCHOOL OF THE ARTS

Neal is living proof that arts in education can make a world of difference in some students' lives. While attending a public high school, Neal had lower-than-average grades and was not engaged in his academic life. He decided to attend a performing arts high school for a postgraduate year of study before applying for college. At Idyllwild School for the Arts, Neal found himself in acting. It took him a while, but he had finally found his niche. He is now a senior pursuing a BFA in drama at the University of North Carolina School of the Arts.

"My decision to postpone college was probably the smartest I ever made," he says. "I wanted direction and I liked performing, but I didn't know I could do it as a discipline."

Neal describes his discovery of acting as something that has given him a passion in life. Growing up, Neal says that he was one of those kids who always yearned to be normal but felt somewhat out of place. "I only really felt at home when I was around creative people."

Applying for college acting programs was a daunting experience for Neal. "I didn't know if I was good enough to get into a conservatory and I didn't know if I could get into a regular college because I had a less-than-stellar GPA."

Luckily, Idyllwild prepares its students well. Each year, like several other performing arts secondary schools across the country, the school sends its students to Chicago to audition for college drama programs on one scheduled day. Neal auditioned for twenty-one schools that day—he calls it the "shotgun approach."

"The only school I had ever heard of for acting was Juilliard, and that was my first audition," says Neal. "And I blew it."

Neal says that he benefited from his Juilliard audition experience. To prospective students, he conveys the lesson he learned: "Just because Juilliard is great, it doesn't mean it is the best school for you. It depends on what you think your strengths are."

Neal performed well at the rest of his auditions and got into two schools: Carnegie Mellon and the University of North Carolina School of the Arts.

Ultimately, Neal chose the University of North Carolina School of the Arts because of the way they treated him at the audition and afterward when he was still in the process of making his final college choice. "The response you get from a school—how they do it—is indicative of how they will treat you once you are there," he says.

"They didn't have that common theatrical attitude of superiority," Neal explains. "They were congenial people and down-to-earth. When I visited the school, they were very welcoming. I spoke with the assistant dean and he took an active interest in me."

> ## Hot Tips from Neal
>
> → **Don't do the "shotgun approach" to finding a college—do your research instead.**
>
> → **Look for where you can grow to help your weaknesses.**
>
> → **Know what each school can offer and make sure that is what you want.**
>
> → **Ask yourself if you want to be a big fish in a little pond or a small fish in a big pond.**
>
> → **Go where you think you will be challenged as an actor to be the best you can be.**

At the University of North Carolina School of the Arts, Neal has had roles in *As You Like It*, *The Misanthrope*, *Of Mice and Men*, *Journey's End*, *The Taming of the Shrew*, *Romeo and Juliet*, *A Man of No Importance*, and *Hogan's Goat*.

With a film school on campus, Neal has also had parts in student films, which will bolster his résumé for acting on the big screen.

After graduation, Neal is considering both moving to New York to audition for roles and graduate study at the Yale School of Drama.

"I have to ask myself 'When do I have enough school?'" Neal says. "At this point, I'm salivating to work, but on the other hand, I want to take initiative. If I tried to attend Yale, I'd be forced to make theater happen on my own rather than passively waiting for a role."

Neal's possibilities for the future are wide open. For him, the University of North Carolina School of the Arts was the perfect college fit. He says, "It is a place where you can be nurtured rather than moved along a conveyor belt."

In addition to acting, you usually need to have advanced proficiency in one of the other two talents associated with musical theater: singing or dancing. You probably already know (or you'll soon learn) that casting calls for musicals often specify different audition times for "Actors Who Sing" or "Actors Who Dance." Of course, if you can achieve advanced proficiency in both singing and dancing, you'll have more options after college to consider and may audition for more parts.

Film, Television, and Cinema

Not all college drama programs have an emphasis or concentration particularly geared to students who want to study film or television acting or who want to focus their studies on filmmaking (including documentary filmmaking), scriptwriting, or production. Larger programs are more likely than smaller programs to have course offerings or even degrees in these areas. If television or the big screen is your primary interest, make sure the drama programs you are considering have specialties in these areas. Otherwise, you might be disappointed that you aren't able to get the in-depth study you desire.

If you primarily want to study film and video, such as if you want to become a filmmaker, it is important to note that many colleges and universities have a school of film, which is in a different school or department than a school of drama or theater. For this book, if a large theater program includes courses—or in some instances, an undergraduate degree—in film, it is listed in the college profile section only if the film program is housed in the drama department. This particular book does not focus on film programs or schools of film.

Drama Auditions

Every actor knows how nerve-wracking an audition can be—your performance of a short two-minute monologue can make you or break you in many instances. This is also true for most competitive college drama programs and conservatory programs. The audition for these programs often has more weight in the college admissions process than other components of your application, like your SAT scores or recommendation letters. Because acting is a performance profession, how you deliver a monologue during an audition is key to how faculty members judge your potential to perform in their drama department.

Auditions are organized in two primary ways for admission to postsecondary drama programs: (1) joint audition days whereby students can audition for several different colleges or professional training schools on one day, such as the National Unified Auditions (unified auditions.com); or (2) auditions hosted by individual schools or programs that can be regional or on campus. Whichever type of audition you attend, prepare well by rehearsing until your monologue is so much a part of you that it represents your very best performance.

When contemplating the monologue you will perform, choose something that you can deliver well. You don't want to select something so ambitious that you can't pull it off expertly during the audition. It may be helpful to perform a monologue in which the character learns something or grows as a result of the circumstance you re-create. If your character goes through some type of inner conflict or journey during the monologue, it can give your adjudicators the chance to see that you can show emotion during different segments of the monologue. And emphasizing the most dramatic parts of the monologue at just the right moment will convince the judge that you have that uncanny sense of timing that is necessary for great character portrayals. If you can ask an acting teacher or coach to help you rehearse several monologues in preparation for your college auditions, he or she can guide you into choosing your best monologue for audition day.

Day in the Life of a Drama Major	
10 a.m.	Acting class
11 a.m.	Voice lessons (singing)
12 p.m.	Lunch
1 p.m.	Dance (modern, jazz, ballet, tap)
2 p.m.	Voice for performance (speech)
3 p.m.	Theater history, literature, and criticism
4–6 p.m.	Eat dinner, work on memorizing, reading, homework
6–10 p.m.	Rehearsal
10–11 p.m.	Student theater meetings
11 p.m.–bed	Homework

The Portfolio for Prospective Design and Production Majors

If you are interested in drama but you are not an actor, there are plenty of opportunities to study the technical aspects of theater in college as well. However, rather than an audition being a component of your college application process, you may need to prepare a portfolio. Preparing a portfolio for studying theater design and production is much like preparing an artist's portfolio. Here is a list of what you should include in your design or production portfolio:

★ Photographs of sets, props, or costumes you've designed. If you've done design for scenery, you may also want photos to illustrate lighting arrangements you've designed. If you created set models before designing sets, you can send photos of these as well.

★ Drawings of sets, props, or costumes before you created the finished products. Sketches can give adjudicators insight into your creative process and show that you've taken precise time and care in planning your designs from the original idea through completion.

★ Miscellaneous paperwork such as notes that show your planning process, and schedules for rehearsals or materials like lighting cue sheets that show the technical side of stage design. And don't forget to include your résumé!

Drama Program Philosophy

You might not realize it now, but there are many different ways to approach acting. Because of this, every college acting program follows its own teaching philosophy. When researching your acting training opportunities after high school, it's important to find the exact philosophy of the college's drama department.

Some drama programs follow a certain method of acting. You may have heard of "The Method," which is an acting technique that Lee Strasberg developed based on the principles of Constantin Stanislavsky in the early twentieth century. This acting technique emphasizes preparing for roles by looking inward to find the "believable truth" of a scene. Strasberg popularized his version of Stanislavsky's system in the United States.

Another popular acting technique is Meisner Technique. It is also based on Stanislavsky's teachings but the training is somewhat different. Actors participate in repetition exercises that focus on behavioral communication as the heart of the technique.

SARAH
NORTHWESTERN UNIVERSITY

The saying goes, "The apple doesn't fall far from the tree," and in the case of Sarah Graber, a theater major at Northwestern University, it is definitely true. Mom is an artist. Dad is a musician. Sarah also chose the arts; she started acting seriously in high school.

Between her junior and senior years of high school, Sarah attended the National High School Institute (NHSI) in theater at Northwestern University—and that is how she became familiar with the university in the first place. This intensive summer program exposed Sarah to broader aspects of theater besides acting; she was able to learn about theater history, scenic design, and playwriting. The experience made a lasting impression.

"It was the first time I was surrounded by incredibly talented people who were as passionate and dedicated as I was in theater," recalls Sarah. "I saw how beautiful the campus was and met the professors, and that made my decision about college easier."

The location of Northwestern, on the outskirts of Chicago, was appealing to Sarah when she considered colleges. The Windy City is known for an active and prestigious professional theater community.

Hot Tips from Sarah

FOR YOUR AUDITION...
- ➜ Give it your best.
- ➜ Know your monologue well.
- ➜ Keep a positive outlook.
- ➜ Show energy and enthusiasm.

WHEN YOU GET ON CAMPUS...
- ➜ Get involved with as many activities as possible.
- ➜ Get your face known—don't just be another student.
- ➜ Challenge yourself in whatever ways you can.
- ➜ Do more than you think you can—push yourself.

"As a student, it is such a delight to be in a place where the theater scene is so accessible," she says. "So many theater professionals have ties to Northwestern. It's a good connection base to have."

Sarah credits Northwestern for doing a great deal to help promote their students to the professional theaters in the Chicago area. They know that experience is the best way to get them prepared for the working world after graduation.

The college has career sessions and brings in casting directors, agents, and photographers. For seniors, there is Senior Showcase, in which Chicago casting directors come to campus one day to see the senior class perform. The casting directors also receive the headshots and résumés of students. Sarah says, "If nothing else, they at least have your credentials for opportunities in the future."

Besides her academic studies, Sarah discovered a way to gain real-life exposure to theater through employment. To help pay for college expenses, she has a federal work-study position on campus. What's even better is that Sarah found a one-of-a-kind paying position as an assistant to the chair of the theater department. As part of her job, Sarah does a variety of things from making photocopies to assisting with research projects and preparing for professional theater conferences.

Sarah is more than happy with her college choice. "I love it," she says. "It's a great place to be and one of the best choices I think I've made."

Some acting programs may emphasize one technique over another. They might have teachers who use various methods, or they may be neutral in terms of which techniques they teach. The kind of actor you are—and which teaching techniques make you comfortable—may make a difference in your choice of a college drama program where you will feel at home. Be sure to research the acting philosophy of each program you are considering. This will allow you to discover how you might fit in and how happy you might be with the school.

Figuring out a drama program's philosophy is also important to prospective drama majors who are involved with other aspects of the art besides performance. If you want to study theater history, stage production, or drama education, determining the program's philosophy toward teaching in those areas is just as important as it is for an actor. For instance, to study theater history, you'll want to know if a program concentrates on twentieth-century theater history or provides a broad overview either from Ancient Greece or Shakespeare until today. Or to become a drama teacher, you'll need to find out which courses in the drama department and which general education courses you'll need. The department's philosophy will determine whether these courses are specifically geared to future drama teachers or whether they are separate courses in the school of education for prospective teachers in any field.

COLLEGES FOR ACTORS   37

Evaluating Drama Programs

After several auditions, college drama programs may start to look the same to you. But it is important to remember that they are not. To narrow down your college choices and make the final decision, investigate several aspects of a program by talking to faculty members and students. Remember that current students can give the most candid information about what the college acting life is really like. Be sure to examine all the aspects of each school's program. Here are some general areas of thought to help you get started:

- *Performance opportunities.* How many are there per semester? What is the percentage of the students in the program who are normally cast? Is there a wide range of performance opportunities, from classics to contemporary plays?
- *Faculty.* Are the faculty working actors, playwrights, or stage designers? The best faculty have extensive experience in the field and are often still practicing artists. Do they have industry contacts? Do they have advanced education like master of fine arts degrees (MFAs)?
- *Facilities.* What are the facilities like? How many spaces are there for productions? Is there a black-box theater? What sort of rehearsal space is available?
- *Industry guests.* Does the program invite industry guests like casting agents and directors in to speak to students? If so, when and how often? Can contacts be made for internships or professional acting jobs at these events?
- *Alumni.* Where are the school's acting alumni now? Are they professional actors or playwrights? Are they working in the field? How many are full-time actors and part-time actors? Do a large number of alumni belong to a professional association such as the Screen Actors Guild-American Federation of Television and Radio Artists (SAG-AFTRA)?

JUDD
NEW YORK UNIVERSITY TISCH SCHOOL OF THE ARTS

Growing up in Salt Lake City, Judd Harvey always knew he wanted to do musical theater but felt like he was "in the dark."

"I was probably the only one in my neighborhood who wanted to pursue acting beyond high school," he says.

It wasn't until he moved to San Francisco at the end of his high school years that he felt more at home with his goal of acting professionally. At the advice of his college counselor, he auditioned for Tisch School of the Arts. He recalls her words of wisdom: "It's one thing to study acting, but it is really a hands-on learned profession."

Judd realized that there is no place where theater thrives more than New York. "Being in New York, it happens in the environment…both in and outside the classroom," he says. That's how he decided it was where he wanted to be. It was by happenstance that Judd ended up focusing on experimental theater rather than musical theater. He auditioned for the musical theater studio placement and describes his audition as "frightening." But Judd remembers what calmed his nerves and made the audition much more comfortable. "A woman stood up and said 'Tisch is a great school. There are a lot of great schools. This will not make or break you as an actor. If you want to work as an actor, you'll work as an actor,'" he says.

As part of his audition, Judd sang a song and performed a monologue from the play *Free Will and Wanton Lust* by experimental playwright Nicky Silver. Coincidentally, Judd later flew to Denver to see a play called *The Laramie Project* by Moisés Kaufman, who is a Tisch School of the Arts alumnus. They met afterward, and Kaufman told Judd, "You need to be in experimental theater." The audition faculty must have had the same instincts, because when Judd was accepted into Tisch, he was placed in the experimental studio program.

The drama program at Tisch requires students to attend their studio classes three days a week from 9:30 a.m. to 5:30 p.m.; the other two days are reserved for academic classes at New York University.

His NYU roommates sometimes poked fun at Judd for studying acting, but he says that he was in class more than anyone else. "One of the most demanding parts of studying acting is that you are required to be emotionally, physically, and mentally invested 100 percent of the time. In traditional academic classes, sometimes students can sit in the back and zone out if they are having an off day. With acting, this isn't possible."

Adjusting to life in New York was a little daunting to Judd when he first arrived at Tisch. "New York can be intimidating, and it is easy to feel invisible," he recalls. "What saved me was the small, tight group of people looking out for each other in the studio program. At NYU, they break it down. You aren't just a student, you are a student of the Tisch School, then you are a member of the drama program, and then further, you are a member of whichever studio program you belong to. In the end, your family consists of the other thirty-one students in your studio."

For Judd and a lot of other students, attending Tisch was a financial concern. His parents agreed to pay for the first two years of school and during the first year, he worked part-time. He says. "I know a lot of talented students who have left due to the cost."

"NYU is a money-making machine. To Tisch, I matter. To NYU, I'm a number," he explains. "When I had concerns about coming back for my senior year, I talked to everyone. I had my teachers from Tisch writing letters to the financial aid office on my behalf—there was an overwhelming show of support to help me out."

Between his sophomore and junior years, Judd left school for a year to work full-time to save money. During that year, Judd traveled to Kenya, looking in on a place he had already visited at age sixteen when he helped build a school in a small village. This time, a humanitarian organization sent Judd over for a year to be a coordinator. He taught English and math and set up an after-school drama program. "It was a life-changing experience," he says.

After his year in Kenya, Judd had serious concerns about whether he'd be able to return to Tisch. But all the work he had done to get support from the school for his financial situation had paid off. Much to his delight, Judd received the Ron Howard Scholarship, which would cover the expenses of his senior year. A few years ago, film director Ron Howard's daughter attended Tisch, and then Howard set up a scholarship fund to help one talented senior each year. Judd had been chosen as that senior.

When Judd returned to school, he had to reevaluate whether he still wanted to be an actor, because his experience in Kenya had such an impact on him. He started taking courses in Africana studies and made it a second major. One of his professors, Awan Amka from Ghana, pointed out that it didn't have to be "either or." He could do acting and also pursue his interest in social issues in Africa.

Hot Tips from Judd

→ If you are wondering about how much emphasis you want in acting and how much you want in academic coursework, find a program that wants you to be a well-educated artist and that enables you to take liberal arts courses as well.

→ Becoming an actor has very little to do with the school you attend. It really is more important how committed you are. Find out what you are committed to the most and go for it.

Judd is now interested in a growing field called theater for development, which places theater in an educational context to teach others about real-life problems. For example, the field involves activities like creating plays to raise awareness about social issues such as AIDS or genocide.

Judd's senior performance thesis merges his experimental studio training and interest in Africana studies. He did a solo performance incorporating his experiences visiting Rwanda and observing the consequences of genocide while he was in Africa during his year off. After he graduates, he wants to go back to Rwanda to educate others with theater for development—which interestingly, is right in line with his interest in experimental theater.

At Tisch, Judd found himself transformed from a musical theater actor, to an experimental actor, to an actor and theater-for-development activist. He sums it up as "an amazing experience."

INTERVIEW WITH A THEATER DESIGN STUDENT

Laura is a student in the BFA in Scene Design, which is a concentration in the School of Design & Production at the University of North Carolina School of the Arts.

When did your interest in drama begin?

I was always a very outgoing child, so while my siblings did sports and kept to themselves, my parents signed me up for a summer performing arts camp. It grew into being Sarah Brown in *Guys and Dolls Jr.* during middle school and later being a "regular" at my community theater in South Carolina. More than anything I loved the experience, the people, and the bonding moments it created. I started not to care as much about what role I received as long as I got to be a part of it all. This was a clue that performing and being a Broadway actress was not my dream. However, I still dreamt of being a Disney Channel star, but what child doesn't?

How did you know you wanted to study design and production rather than performance?

Yes, performing was a love of mine, and all the relationships and fantastical experiences that came along with it; however, visual arts was a big family thing. I remember watching my mom draw and color with my siblings and I as children, begging her to draw us a pot of gold at the end of the rainbows we made. She used to make cards that she painted and sold at a local farmers market every Saturday morning. My dad is the greatest at Fred Flintstone and Barney Rubble drawings, and my brother, who is four years older, has always inspired me. Due to all these influences and my constant growing love for art, painting and drawing became a priority right next to performing. I soon became aware of how I could marry my love for both art and theater by becoming a scenic artist.

Why did you choose to attend UNCSA? What made that program stand out to you?

UNCSA is one of the two schools in the country that has a concentration specifically in scenic painting. My parents live in South Carolina, so North Carolina was very convenient, and when looking more into the program and the professors, I could not lose. Howard Jones [Director of Scenic Art/Scene Painting] is a mastermind when it comes to not only painting, but also design and technical direction. He knows all the tricks of the trade and is constantly five steps ahead. To have him as my advisor is the greatest blessing. Also the size of the school, making the student-to-teacher ratio small, allows every student to have a priceless relationship with every professor.

Have you been able to do any internships that will help your future career? What other real-world opportunities have you had during your undergraduate studies?

Yes, internships and other summer jobs are highly encouraged at our school. In fact, the design and production program holds a job fair every February where the students get a chance to interview with more than forty companies for a potential job. They even hold a Q&A session where the students can stand up and ask for résumé, cover letter, and interview advice. For the past two summers I have had the pleasure of working at Flat Rock Playhouse as first an intern, and this past summer as a staff painter. Real-world opportunities are graciously given by professors and honestly at the mention of our school name. My roommate and I had a chance to paint a mural at the Downtown Perk market last year due to the owner knowing our school had amazing painters; this led to other open doors as the community witnessed our work. Professors ask students for help with their outside projects, such as with model making, painting renderings, or focusing lights, and in return the student is usually paid and given professional credit.

What are your future career goals after you graduate?

I love theater, but I also have a passion for the film world. Being the only one in my family interested in theater, I was not exposed to it; however family movie night was definitely a thing—thus the Oscars are way more familiar to me than the Tonys. To paint for one of the future sequels of *Pirates of the Caribbean* would be a dream. Traveling is a big goal; fortunately it usually coincides with being a scenic artist. I'm going out of the country for the first time this spring break, and it will definitely will not be my last. I love the thought of moving from one place to another with a backpack on my back, a suitcase in one hand, and a paintbrush in the other. My roommate and I also run a nonprofit organization called Art4Purpose where we create pieces of artwork, sell them, and 75 percent of the money goes to a fighting cause. My career goal would definitely have Art4Purpose tied into it.

What advice do you have for other students who want to study design and production in college? How can they choose the right program? What will make them successful in the program itself once they are accepted?

Look into your professors! Check out their résumé, portfolio, and the work they do. Does it inspire you? Look at the production value from pictures, and question how many productions are put on each year. When touring the campus, as embarrassing and inconvenient as you may feel, ask the upperclassmen what the schedule is like and what their responsibilities are. Once accepted, the key to success is to never truly feel accepted. Constantly prove yourself. If one is truly pushing and challenging [oneself], that person should never feel completely safe. Questioning yourself shows growth. Growth brings answers. Answers [are] what people seek, making you invaluable.

Sample Admissions Essay

Footprints

I had just begun the seventh grade when I was invited to audition for the world premiere of a new play to be produced in San Francisco. A week later, I got the part. I'd be Roy, the son who spends most of the play coming to understand his relationship with his past and with his mother, the only other character in the play.

The process of bringing this professional production to life on the Magic Theater stage taught me about myself in ways I'd never experienced before. Not at school. Not at home. Not even in the almost twenty-five shows in which I'd already performed.

The character I played was transformed night after night in the same predetermined and dramatic way. He always did what the script said he should do. My own personal changes were otherwise. Unscripted. Subtle.

The play, called *Wyoming*, was written by Barry Gifford, author of *Wild at Heart* and *Lost Highway*. "Wyoming is a vast open space," Barry told me, "where Roy's headed to rediscover who he is. I created this young character on paper," he continued. "Your job now is to bring him to life on stage."

The changes in me had mostly to do with the expectations of others. I was no longer treated as a child actor. I was treated instead as an actor, period. I was expected to be a part of the team that made the entire undertaking work. Others older than I were counting on me to do my job professionally; this wasn't children's theater anymore. I was expected to show up on time. To know my lines. To remember everything I'd already been taught. And to be ready to continue learning more.

I quickly became a valued member of the team (although I was still the only member not yet old enough to drive). And while nobody else may have noticed, I saw myself changing. I welcomed criticisms and questions. I worked harder than I'd ever worked before. My trust in my ideas and opinions grew stronger. And all the while I was able to manage all the other aspects of my life—most notably, everything having to do with the seventh grade.

On opening night, seven weeks after the original audition, the play was greeted with enthusiastic applause and great reviews. The entire team had succeeded in creating a *Wyoming* that no audience had ever visited before. And I had succeeded in leaving my footprints on the Magic Theater stage. I'd made my mark. I'd exceeded the team's expectations. And I'd exceeded my own.

I'd succeeded in creating a new character onstage, but when the run of the play ended, so did he; Roy was just a memory.

I, of course, continued on.

Just a little differently than before.

Sample Application Questions

From New York University's Tisch School of the Arts

Please tell us about something you did last Sunday afternoon (or the Sunday before that or the Sunday before that...)

Ten Sundays ago, I was wiping nonstop sweat off the back of my neck, the result of lugging suitcases and cartons up the stairs of Weinstein Hall. The hauling and the heat and the humidity would have been unbearable if I weren't preparing to spend the next four weeks in the Tisch Summer High School Program. I'd been looking forward to this day for three months, ever since I learned I'd been accepted.

Ten Sundays ago, I was also doing a lot of unpacking, working to make myself a new home at NYU. The unpacking, of course, made me sweat even more.

And I itched. Which is why, when I retrieved my octopus-shaped head massager from the middle of an overstuffed duffle bag, I got a welcome hint of relief. I knew there was a reason I'd brought that thing along.

So that was my very full Sunday ten Sundays ago: sweating, unpacking, and massaging my head. All to get ready for what I knew would be an incredible month.

Today, ten Sundays ago seems like yesterday. And the month proved to be much more than incredible.

Apart from the New York City location, please tell us what other aspects make you feel NYU will be a good match for you.

This past summer, as a student in the Tisch Summer High School Program, I was fortunate enough to taste a little of the NYU experience. And while I'd be lying if I were to say that New York City, itself, was merely a backdrop to this experience, in fact the city was hardly what mattered most.

I received training at Tisch that I'd never received anywhere else. I developed relationships and a sense of community more quickly there than anywhere else. Very early in the program, I knew I belonged.

Most of this happened inside the walls of NYU rather than on the streets of New York. Relocate NYU to downtown Biloxi, and I'd still be applying. Because after what I've already experienced, I can't imagine a curriculum and a faculty more suited to preparing me for my future in musical theater. It's one thing to hear a guidance counselor say that NYU has one of the best theater programs in the country. It was quite something else for me to be even a small part of that program and to experience that reality for myself.

(Oh, and please don't take the relocation idea too seriously. I'm sure Biloxi is a fine place, but in the end there really is something unique and defining and completely engaging about New York City.)

What led you to select your anticipated academic program and/or NYU school/college, and what interests you most about your intended discipline?

"There is beauty in perfect moments."

My vocal performance teacher told me that. And, he continued, "No matter how many times you see a triple axel, when it's done perfectly it is beautiful."

I chose CAP21 as my anticipated program because it seems to be among the richest places to discover and to strive for perfect moments.

These moments, in my experience, are subtle. And fleeting. And infrequent. They might happen in a rehearsal hall or during a performance. Maybe it's the tilt of a head or the arching of an eyebrow. Maybe it's taking an extra beat before reciting a line. Maybe it's helping a fellow performer reach a little higher.

These are the moments when the director finally cracks a small smile. Or when the audience rises together to applaud the performance. These are the moments that add inches to my self-esteem.

I live for these moments. I watch for them. I work for them. I use them to help me grow as a performer and as a person.

From what I've experienced at NYU's CAP21 program this past summer, I cannot imagine an environment richer with opportunities for my pursuit of musical theater's perfect moments.

Please explain how you decided which extracurricular activity on your list was the most important to you.

I love sports. I can't spend enough time with friends. Or my guitar. Or my family. I see every movie that comes to town. And there are few parties that I'm not in the middle of.

I enjoy reading. And writing. And public speaking. I'm a good teacher, especially for developmentally disabled students.

I'm interested in so much about the world. But I'm truly passionate about only one thing: musical theater.

Musical theater is what I've been dreaming about since I can remember having dreams. It's what I think about practically all the time, whether I'm in a rehearsal hall or an algebra class. It is more than my pursuit. It is my passion.

And it is my future.

SAMPLE ADMISSIONS RÉSUMÉ

Theater

Date	Production	Role	Theater Company	Director
3/15	AIDA	Radames	CMTSJ	Kevin Hauge
3/14	Little Shop of Horrors	Seymour	CMTSJ	Kevin Hauge
11/13	Translations	Owen	Bellarmine Prep	Tom Allesandri
8/13	The Who's Tommy	Lead Dancer	CMTSJ	Kevin Hauge
8/13	Seven Ages of Bob	Bob	Edinburgh Fringe Fest.	Peter Canavese
3/13	Smokey Joe's Cafe	Singer	CMTSJ	Kevin Hauge
8/12	Joseph...Dreamcoat	Pharaoh	SCCMT	Lisa Boiko
7/12	Footloose	Bickle	CMTSJ	Kevin Hauge
5/12	Joseph...Dreamcoat	Joseph	CMTSJ	Mark Phillips
3/12	Jekyll & Hyde	Soloist/Newsboy	CMTSJ	Kevin Hauge
1/11	The Laramie Project	Aaron Kreifels	Bellarmine Prep	Tom Allesandri
7/11	Once Upon A Mattress	Sir Harry	CMTSJ	Doug Santana
6/11	Her Lightmess	Ensemble	San Jose Repertory	Polly Mellon
5/11	Hello Dolly	Louie Waiter	CMTSJ	Heather Stokes
3/11	School House Rock	Bartlett	CMTSJ	Ian Leonard
11/10	The Secret Garden	Colin	Sunnyvale Players	Elizabeth Neipp
9/10	Bread of Winter	Greg	Bay Area Playwright Fest.	Arturo Catri
7/10	Barnum	Barnum	SJCMT	Shannon Self
4/10	Wyoming	Roy	Magic Theater	Amy Glazer
2/10	Wind in the Willows	Rat	SJCMT	Doug Santana
12/09	Big	Young Josh	SJCMT	Kevin Hauge
7/09	Dames at Sea	Swabby	SJCMT	Mike Czymanski
5/09	Phantom	Young Phantom	SJCMT	Heather Stokes
2/09	The Wizard of Oz	Wizard/Marvel	SJCMT	Doug Santana

5/08	*Thru the Looking Glass*	Ben	Traveling Jewish Theater	Amy Glazer
4/08	*The Neighborhood Kids*	Singer/Dancer	SJCMT	Kevin Hauge
7/07	*Pulse: The Rhythm of Life*	Thomas	SJCMT	Kevin Hauge
6/07	*Romeo & Juliet*	Sean Potpan	TheatreWorks	Robert Kelly
5/07	*The Who's Tommy*	Young Tommy	SJCMT	Kevin Hauge
3/07	*Harm's Way*	Boy	Stanford Univ. Drama	Rebecca Groves
10/06	*The Secret Garden*	Colin	SJCMT	Gary DeMattei
11/06	*Emperor's New Clothes*	Stitch the Tailor	SJCMT	Doug Santana
3/06	*Cabaret*	Hitler Youth	TheatreWorks	Robert Kelly
12/05	*Three Musketeers*	D'Artagnan	SJCMT	Joe O'Keefe

Training

Summer 2016 NYU, Tisch School of the Arts, CAP21, Musical Theatre Program

2014–2015 Marie Stinnet Dance

2011–2014 Conservatory of Performing Arts, San Jose Children's Musical Theater

Film/TV/CD

Short Film, lead actor, *The Face*, Face Pictures

TV Documentary, lead actor, *The Making of Pulse*, PBS, Annette Bening, Host

Student Film, lead actor, *Get Reel*, Children's International Film Festival Winner

Feature Film, ensemble actor, *Garage Sale*, Red Rocket Productions

Regional Commercial, lead actor, "Grandcell Battery"

Regional Radio Spot, lead actor, "Peapod.com"

Pilot, *ZAP!*, ZDTV

Music

Borderline Rock Band, lead singer (10, 11)

Original Cast Recording CD of *Pulse: The Rhythm of Life* (Musical)

Demo CD for *Salaam Bombay* (Musical)

Neighborhood Kids, Touring song and dance troupe

Athletics

Lacrosse (10, 11)

Intramural (9, 10, 11)

Volunteer/Community Service

Morgan Center for developmentally disabled young adults (9, 10, 11)

San Jose Children's Musical Theater Summer Program (9, 10)

Work Experience

Host, *Real Science*, (National PBS Series) (9, 10, 11)

Counselor, Conservatory of Performing Arts, CMTSJ Theater Camp (9, 10)

Travel

Edinburgh Fringe Festival, American High School Theatre Festival 2016 (11)

New York City, Summer Theater Bonanza (8, 9, 10)

Clubs/Activities

Sanguine Humours Improv. Team, Bellarmine HS Prep (9, 10, 11)

Jewish Society, President, Bellarmine High School Prep (9, 10, 11)

African American Club, Bellarmine High School Prep (10)

Battle of the Bands, Bellarmine High School Prep (10, 11)

KEVIN KUHLKE
PROFESSOR AND FORMER CHAIR, DEPARTMENT OF DRAMA, NEW YORK UNIVERSITY TISCH SCHOOL OF THE ARTS

Audition Spotlight

The Department of Drama at New York University Tisch School of the Arts has an audition tour across the country with approximately 250 audition sessions. During the course of the tour, faculty and staff at Tisch see 2,500 to 3,000 students.

Like most conservatory-model programs, the audition is an important component of a prospective drama major's college application.

"The artistic component is the first criterion in the admission process," explains Kevin Kuhlke, chair of the Department of Drama. "Faculty recommend students who they would like to join the program to the NYU admissions office. Not only do [students] have to do well in the audition, but they must also have a strong academic record to meet NYU's requirements."

However, what makes studying acting at Tisch unique among other college acting programs is that the academic aspect of the program is as important as the artistic training. As a result, students get the best of both worlds: a conservatory acting program and a liberal arts education.

"The level and depth of close reading, research, critical thinking, and argumentative writing required in the academic theater studies component of our curriculum is much more developed than any other program that I know of in the country," says Kuhlke.

Also, students applying to Tisch should know that the required interview is given as much weight as the artistic audition in the admissions process.

"In other words, a prospective student may be extremely talented, but if they exhibit no intellectual curiosity during the interview process, chances are they will not be seen as a good fit for the program," explains Kuhlke.

Tips from a Theater Production and Design Professor

John Coyne, Director of Scenic Design, School of Design and Production University of North Carolina School of the Arts (UNCSA)

What advice do you have for high school students aiming for acceptance into a design and production program? And how can they choose which program is right for them?
The most important thing is that students apply to a program that will challenge them and let them grow in an area they are passionate about. And while we do have students whose area of study may shift while enrolled, most come to us fairly certain of the area they want to study and eventually work within the industry.

Some students know they want to study theater, but perhaps they don't know that they ultimately want to go into the production side vs. the performing side (or maybe they don't know the specialty within production that they want to study). What is your advice on helping students want to go into theater professionally to choose the specialty they want to study?

Students really should study the area that excites them the most. But it is often a hard decision, and sometime students aren't ready for that commitment yet. Some programs, like UNCSA, are a conservatory setting and are best for students who know the areas they want to pursue. Other programs are more general and allow students to explore multiple areas as part of the program. When researching colleges, students should keep in mind the type of program they are looking for and really make sure the college offers that. Another thing to keep in mind is the faculty at any given college. Students want to study with faculty members who are experts and working in their field. If, for example, you want to study Scene Design and there is not a faculty member working in that area professionally or recently, or there is only one faculty member in that area—the school may not be the best fit for you.

What skills do students need to be good students in a design and production program?
Students come to us with a wide range of experience from high school. And we certainly will work with the students to build the skills they need. But the common skills we have found that help students succeed are a passion for their work, strong curiosity about their chosen area of study and the industry as a whole, an ability to collaborate with a team, and good time management skills.

The University of North Carolina School of the Arts has a design and production program that has many different specialty areas at the undergraduate level (lighting, costume design, sound technology, etc.). Please share how this and (and other aspects of your program) make UNCSA unique at the undergraduate level.
Most programs do not offer as many areas of specialty as we do, so it is exciting to watch students learn about all of these areas at UNCSA. Many are learning about the many facets of this industry for the first time when they attend UNCSA: the professional standards that are expected in the industry across all disciplines, and the collaborative nature of our industry. Because of this and through their production classes, students are ready to work directly in their career choice after they get their degree without additional classes, degrees, or internships.

Can you describe the difference between different areas in your program? For example, what is the difference between scene design and scene painting?
Scene Design is responsible for developing the visual look, mood, and function for the stage of

any production they are working on, be it drama, musicals, opera, or dance. Scene designers work with the director and other designers to figure out the conceptual approach and specific design elements, including what any painted elements might look like. The scenic painter brings their skill and expertise to executing the painted elements in the scene design.

As the director of the Scene Design program, what courses do you teach? What are the favorite courses among students in your program?

I teach Hand Drafting for Design, Scenic Design at various levels, and Advanced Model-Making focusing on technology such as laser-cutting and 3D printing. I also teach a Plein-Air Watercolor class. And of course I teach Production, which for scene designers is advising students on their design assignments for realized productions. I love teaching all levels of students, but my favorite classes are the Scene Design courses. It's where my students' individual artistic "voice" or style starts to emerge, and I enjoy helping them discover that.

Would you also be able to describe what attributes a student needs to be successful in a program focused on Scenic Design?

Of course, students who have the talent and drive to make creative work both independently and collaboratively usually do well in our Scene Design Program. Again, students who display curiosity and a good work ethic will be successful at UNCSA.

How can students prepare in high school for design and production training at the college level?

Any classes they can take in art, design, theater history, and theater production are useful and help them build a portfolio they will show during college interviews. Also, it is helpful if they can spend time working with a local theater company or designer to get an insight into the industry and how it works. But we also like to see students who pursue other interests as well, be it music, history, or even community service—these types of interests usually make them a better designer, as they have more to draw from as a designer.

What have some of the recent alumni in your program accomplished?

Our Design and Production alumni are working across the country, on Broadway shows and in regional theaters, on plays, dances, and opera. Many go on to work in film and television commercial design. We have found they have the necessary skills, abilities, and temperament to be successful in many of the different areas within the entertainment industry and are able to start pursuing their career immediately after graduation.

Sample Drama Curriculum*

University of North Carolina School of the Arts the School of Drama
Drama Credits and General Education Requirements

BFA DEGREE TOTAL: 132 CREDITS

Drama Course Total: 96 credits
DLA Course Total: 36 credits

	Year One, Fall/Spring	Credits per Semester		Total Credits
DEP 1011	Technical Theatre for Drama I	1	-	1
DEP 1020	Technical Theatre Practicum	-	1	1
DRA 1151, 1152	Acting IA & IB	2	2	4
DRA 1161, 1162	Voice & Speech IA & IB	2	2	4
DRA 1171, 1172	Movement IA & IB	2	2	4
DRA 1183, 1184	Special Techniques IA & IB	2	2	4
DRA 1185, 1186	Applied Techniques IA & IB	1	1	2
DRA 5599	Intensive Arts	1	-	1
ENG 1101, 1102	Composition I & II	3	3	6
	Liberal Arts Elective	3	-	3
MAT/SCI	Math or Science Elective*	-	3	3
YEAR ONE TOTAL		**17**	**16**	**33**
	Year Two, Fall/Spring	Credits per Semester		Total Credits
DRA 2251, 2252	Acting IIA & IIB	2	2	4
DRA 2261, 2262	Voice & Speech IIA & IIB	2	2	4
DRA 2264, 2265	Singing Class IIA & IIB	2	2	4
DRA 2271, 2272	Movement IIA & IIB	2	2	4
DRA 2283, 2284	Special Techniques IIA & IIB	2	2	4
DRA 2285, 2286	Applied Techniques II A & II B	2	2	4
DRA 5599	Intensive Arts	1	-	1
HUM 2101	Self, Society, and Cosmos	3	-	3

HUM 21XX	Paths to the Present (choose one course)	-	3	3
PSY/PHI	Psychology or Philosophy Elective	3	-	3
	Liberal Arts Elective	-	3	3
YEAR TWO TOTAL		**19**	**18**	**37**

Year Three, Fall/Spring		Credits per Semester		Total Credits
DRA 3351, 3352	Acting IIIA & IIIB	2	2	4
DRA 3361, 3362	Voice & Speech IIIA & IIIB	2	2	4
DRA 3371, 3372	Movement IIIA & IIIB	2	2	4
DRA 3383, 3384	Special Techniques IIIA & IIIB	2	2	4
DRA 3364, 3365	Studio Singing IIIA & IIIB	2	2	4
DRA 3341, 3342	Rehearsals & Performance IIIA & IIIB	2	2	4
DRA 5599	Intensive Arts	1	-	1
THH 2101, 2102	Theatre History I & II	3	3	6
HUM/HIS	Humanities or History Elective	3	-	3
LIT 29XX	Dramatic Literature	-	3	3
YEAR THREE TOTAL		**19**	**18**	**37**

Year Four, Fall/Spring		Credits per Semester		Total Credits
DRA 4441, 4442	Rehearsal & Performance IV A & IV B	12	12	24
DRA 5599	Intensive Arts	1	-	1
YEAR FOUR TOTAL		**13**	**12**	**25**

*This sample curriculum is reprinted with permission. The course schedule shown here is representative of courses for a drama major. Each institution has slightly different emphases and requirements, and students are advised to investigate the curriculum at each program they apply to.

Sample Drama Curriculum*

Stage Management

BFA DEGREE TOTAL: 134 CREDITS

DEP Course Total: 98 credits

Liberal Arts Course Total: 36 credits

Year One, Fall/Spring		Credits per Semester		Total Credits
DEP 1000	Production	4	4	8
DEP 1001, 1002	Introduction to Theatrical Production I & II	1	1	2
DEP 1111, 1112	Drawing I & II	2	2	2/4
Student Choice of DEP 1112 or DEP 1123 in Spring				
DEP 1121, 1123	Color and Design I & II	2	2	2/4
DEP 1131	Drafting for the Theater I	2	—	2
DEP 1912	Introduction to Stage Management	—	2	2
DEP 3024	3D Design for the Theatrical Designer	—	2	2
DEP 5599	Intensive Arts	1	—	1
ENG 1101, 1102	Composition I & II	3	3	6
	Liberal Arts Elective	3	—	3
MAT/SCI	Math/Science	—	3	3
YEAR ONE TOTAL		**18**	**17**	**35**
Year Two, Fall/Spring		Credits per Semester		Total Credits
DEP 2000	Production	5	5	10
DEP 2371	Introduction to Lighting Design	—	3	3
DEP 2921, 2922	Stage Management IA & IB	3	3	6
DEP 2513	Introduction to Scene Design	2	—	2
DEP 2613	Introduction to Costume Design	2	—	2
DEP 5599	Intensive Arts Projects	1	—	1
HUM 2101	Self, Society, and Cosmos	3	—	3
HUM 21XX	Paths to the Present (choose one course)	—	3	3
PSY/PHI XXXX	Psychology/Philosophy Elective	—	3	3
YEAR TWO TOTAL		**16**	**17**	**33**

Year Three, Fall/Spring		Credits per Semester		Total Credits
DEP 3000	Production	6	6	12
DEP 3931, 3932	Stage Management IIA & IIB	3	3	6
DEP 3942	Theater Management Survey	2	–	2
	Arts Elective**	–	3	3
DEP 5599	Intensive Arts	1	–	1
TTH 2102, 2102	Theater History I & II	3	3	6
LIT 29XX	Dramatic Literature Elective	3	3	6
YEAR THREE TOTAL		**18**	**18**	**36**

Year Four, Fall/Spring		Credits per Semester		Total Credits
DEP 4000	Production	6	6	12
DEP 3952	Directing	3	–	3
DEP 4941, 4942	Senior Stage Management Seminar I & II	3	3	6
	Arts Elective**	2	3	5
DEP 5599	Intensive Arts	1	–	1
HUM/HIS XXXX	Humanities/History Elective	–	3	3
YEAR FOUR TOTAL		**15**	**15**	**30**

This sample curriculum is reprinted with permission. The course schedule shown here is representative of courses for a drama major. Each institution has slightly different emphases and requirements, and students are advised to investigate the curriculum at each program they apply to.

** Arts elective credits may be fulfilled using any course offered through the School of Design and Production or School of Filmmaking with Arts advisor's approval.*

Sample Drama Curriculum*

Scene Design

BFA DEGREE TOTAL: 131/132 CREDITS

DEP Course Total: 96/98 credits

Liberal Arts Course Total: 36 credits

Year One, Fall/Spring		Credits per Semester		Total Credits
DEP 1000	Production	4	4	8
DEP 1001, 1002	Introduction to Theatrical Production I & II	1	1	2
DEP 1111, 1112	Drawing I & II	2	2	4
DEP 1121, 1123	Color and Design I & II	2	2	4

DEP 1131, 1132	Drafting for the Theater I & II	2	2	4
DEP 5599	Intensive Arts	1	—	1
MAT/SCI XXXX	Math/Science	—	3	3
ENG 1101, 1102	Composition I & II	3	3	6
	Liberal Arts Elective	3	—	3
	YEAR ONE TOTAL	**18**	**17**	**35**

Year Two, Fall/Spring		Credits per Semester		Total Credits
DEP 2000	Production	5	5	10
DEP 2211	Foundations of Scene Painting I	3	—	3
DEP 2412	Stagecraft	—	3	3
DEP 2511, 2512	Scene Design IA & IB	3	3	6
DEP 3103	Scenic Rendering	—	1	1
DEP 3153	Model Building	1	—	1
DEP 5599	Intensive Arts Projects	1	—	1
HUM 2101	Self, Society, and Cosmos	3	—	3
HUM 21XX	Paths to the Present (choose one course)	—	3	3
ARH 1101, 1102	Art History I & II	3	3	6
	YEAR TWO TOTAL	**19**	**18**	**37**

Year Three, Fall/ Spring		Credits per Semester		Total Credits
DEP 3000	Production	6	6	12
DEP 1143	CAD Drafting for Design	3	—	3
DEP 31XX	Studio Skills Series*	—	1	1
DEP 3511, 3512	Scene Design IIA & IIB	3	3	6
DEP 5599	Intensive Arts	1	—	1
TTH 2102, 2102	Theater History I & II	3	3	6
HUM/HIS XXXX	Humanities/History Elective	—	3	3
	YEAR THREE TOTAL	**16**	**16**	**32**

Year Four, Fall/Spring		Credits per Semester		Total Credits
DEP 4000	Production	6	6	12
DEP 2371 or DEP 2613	Introduction to Lighting Design or Introduction to Costume Design	— —	3/2	3/2
DEP 4511, 4512	Scene Design IIIA & IIIB	3	3	6
DEP 5599	Intensive Arts	1	—	1

LIT 29XX	Dramatic Literature Elective	3	—	3
PSY/PHI XXXX	Psychology/Philosophy Elective	—	3	3
	YEAR FOUR TOTAL	**13**	**14/15**	**27/28**

*DEP 31XX Studio Skills Series requirement can be fulfilled with any of the following courses:

FALL SEMESTER		SPRING SEMESTER	
DEP 3104	Studio (Figure)	DEP 3103	Scenic Rendering
DEP 3114	Studio (Architecture)	DEP 3115	Digital Rendering
DEP 3163	Advanced Model Building	DEP 3133	Portraiture
DEP 3193	Digital Graphics	DEP 3173	Advanced Drafting
		DEP 3183	Adv. Mechanical/Perspective Drawing
		DEP 3024	3D Design for the Theatrical Designer

*This sample curriculum is reprinted with permission. The course schedule shown here is representative of courses for a drama major. Each institution has slightly different emphases and requirements and students are advised to investigate the curriculum at each program they apply to.

DRAMA PROGRAMS

Profiles of Selected Programs

Northeast / 59

Southeast / 73

Midwest / 77

West / 85

Comprehensive List of Colleges with Drama Programs

By State / 95

Northeast

BOSTON CONSERVATORY
AT BERKLEE

8 Fenway
Boston, MA 02215

Phone: (617) 912-9137
Website: bostonconservatory.berklee.edu
Email: admissions@bostonconservatory.edu

Tuition: $$
Campus student enrollment (undergraduate):
563

Degree(s): BFA
Areas of study: Musical Theater, Contemporary Theater
Audition requirement: Yes
Scholarships available: Yes
Number of faculty: 42
Number of majors and minors: 271
Department activities: Students perform regularly throughout the year in Boston Conservatory's fully produced theater productions, which are presented four times per year on the school's mainstage. In addition, students perform regularly in master classes with renowned guest artists, in recital, in faculty- and student-directed studio theater productions, and also in performances that showcase seniors and grads, live and digitally, in Boston and New York City. Whether studying musical theater or contemporary theater, the curriculum for all students includes core components of theater performance training: acting, speech, dance, theater movement, voice, musicianship, directing, stagecraft, and theater history and foundations. Every aspect of the conservatory's theater training focuses on helping students achieve professional readiness for a lifelong career in the performing arts, and offers professional grooming and skills for auditions and cold readings, repertoire development, interviewing skills and business skills, including how to manage agents, casting directors, managers, and contracts.

Prominent Alumni:
Adam Hetrick—Editor in Chief of *PlaybillOnline*
Adam Souza—Music Supervisor for *Wicked* (second national tour) and *Kinky Boots* national tour
Alysha Umphress—Broadway actor
Angela Christian—Broadway actor
Anne Nathan—Broadway actor
Austin Lesch—Broadway actor
Austin Regan—Assistant Director for Broadway's *American Idiot* and *On a Clear Day*
Bud Weber—Broadway actor
Chad Kimball—Broadway actor; Tony Award nominee
Constantine Maroulis—Broadway actor; Tony Award nominee; *American Idol* finalist
Danielle Williamson—Broadway actor
Eddie Korbich—Broadway actor
Emily Ferranti—Broadway actor
Erin Davie—Broadway actor
Jack Noseworthy—Broadway and film actor
Jason Michael Snow—Broadway actor
Jennifer Simard—Broadway actor
Joe Machota—Head of the Theater Department at the Creative Artists Agency
Josh Grisetti—Broadway actor; Theatre World Award winner; Drama Desk, Outer Critics Circle, Lucille Lortel, and Drama League Award nominee
Katharine McPhee—*Scorpion* (CBS); *Smash* (NBC); *American Idol* finalist
Kimiko Glenn—*Orange Is the New Black* (Netflix Original); Broadway actor
Laura Dreyfuss—Broadway actor
Laura Marie Duncan—Broadway actor
Matthew Wall—Broadway actor
Natalie Toro—Broadway actor
Nick Adams—Broadway actor/dancer; Broadway.com Audience Choice Awards winner
Nick Christopher—Broadway actor (*Hamilton*)
Noah Racey—Broadway dancer, choreographer
Stephanie Umoh—Broadway actor
Westin Wells Olson—Broadway actor
Will Blum—Broadway actor

BOSTON UNIVERSITY

School of Theatre
855 Commonwealth Avenue
Room 470
Boston, MA 02215

Phone: (617) 353-3390
Website: bu.edu/cfa
Email: theatre@bu.edu or design@bu.edu

Tuition: $$$$
Campus student enrollment (undergraduate): 16,496

Degree(s): BFA
Concentrations: Acting, design, directing, stage management, theater arts, production
Audition/portfolio requirement: Yes. Audition for acting and theater arts. Portfolio for design, production, and stage management.
Scholarships available: Yes
Number of faculty: 14 in performance and 13 in design and production.
Number of applicants accepted into the department per year: 850 to 950 undergraduate applicants; 125 accepted (65 students usually matriculate)
Department activities: The Professional Theatre Initiative (PTI), designed to link students to a network of professional theaters throughout the U.S., including the Huntington Theatre Company (in residence), the New Play Initiative (NPI), and the Boston Center for American Performance (BCAP), the professional extension of the School; the InCite Arts Festival, which provides seniors in all BFA programs the opportunity to showcase their work for professional audiences New York City each spring. Study abroad in London in conjunction with the London Academy of Music and Dramatic Arts. Dual degrees available. Minor in dance.

Prominent Alumni:

Jason Alexander—Tony Award–winning actor, *Seinfeld*

Michael Chiklis—stage, TV, and film star; Emmy Award winner for *The Shield*
Ginnifer Goodwin—actress, *Once Upon a Time* and *He's Just Not That into You*
Julianne Moore—actress; star of *Nine Months*, *Boogie Nights*, *End of the Affair*, *Safe*, *Hannibal*, *Far from Heaven*, *The Hours*, among others

CARNEGIE MELLON UNIVERSITY

School of Drama
Purnell Center for the Arts
5000 Forbes Avenue
Pittsburgh, PA 15213

Phone: (412) 268-2407
Website: cmu.edu/cfa/drama
Email: undergraduate-admissions@andrew.cmu.edu

Tuition: $$$$
Campus student enrollment: 6,203

Degree(s): BFA
Concentrations: Acting, musical theater, design (costume, light, scenery, sound, video and media), directing, dramaturgy, production technology and management (production management, stage management, technical direction)
Audition/portfolio requirement: Yes
Scholarships available: Yes
Number of faculty: 50
Number of majors and minors: 240 majors and minors
Percentage and number of applicants accepted into the department per year: Approximately 2,800 students apply each year. The BFA program accepts 12–14 actors, 12–14 music theater students, 4–6 directors, 4–6 dramaturgs, 24 production technology and management and design students per year. The acceptance rate is 3 percent.

Prominent Alumni:

Holly Hunter

Ted Danson

Patrick Wilson

Billy Porter

Zachary Quinto

Megan Hilty

Leslie Odom Jr.

Renee Elise Goldsberry

Christian Borle

Matt Bomer

Josh Gad

Leigh Silverman—director

Josh Harmon—playwright

Denée Benton—actor, Broadway

Many successful actors in television and film and on Broadway, Off Broadway, and in regional theaters. Successful theater design alumni include Robert Perdziola (Metropolitan Opera, Santa Fe Opera, etc.), Ann Roth (Oscar winner for movies and Broadway), Joe Steward, and John Shaffner.

FORDHAM UNIVERSITY

Theatre Program
113 W. 60th Street
New York, NY 10023

Phone: (212) 636-6338
Website: fordham.edu/theatre
Email: fordhamtheatre@gmail.com

Tuition: $$$
Campus student enrollment (undergraduate): 1,931

Degree(s): BA in theater
Concentrations: Performance, playwriting, design and production, directing
Audition/portfolio requirement: Yes (Audition and interview in New York City, Chicago, and Los Angeles in January and February of each year. Interview only [D & P, Directing, Playwriting] in NYC.)
Scholarships available: Yes. Students can compete for President's and Dean's Scholarships granted by the university, which begin at $7,500. Artistic Merit Scholarships are granted to incoming students based on audition/interview, beginning at $5,000. The Denzel Washington Endowed Scholarship is available to one exceptional undergraduate theater student annually, covering full tuition, room and board.

Number of faculty/staff: 9 full-time, numerous part-time. All full-time and adjunct faculty are working theater professionals. Prominent adjunct faculty include Jackie Sibblies Drury and Steven Skybell. A Denzel Washington Endowed Chair in Theatre is appointed each fall semester, teaching one course in their specialty and participating in the Theatre Program community. Past chairs have included Phylicia Rashad, Joe Morton, JoAnne Akalaitis, and Kenny Leon.

Percentage of applicants accepted into the program per year: 10%

Department activities: Four mainstage and 15–20 studio productions each year; Annual Distinguished Guest Speaker series; opportunities for study abroad to Moscow Art Theatre and various programs in England, Italy, and Australia; Host for Acting Training Symposium, Beyond Orientalism: A Public Forum on Race and Identity in Theatre, National Graduating Class Conference, and other panels featuring distinguished artists and speakers; national audition tour each January and February, well-attended Senior Showcase and Design Show for graduating seniors.

Prominent Alumni:

Denzel Washington—Oscar-winning actor
Patricia Clarkson—actor
Annie Parisse—actor, *Law and Order*, *Prelude to a Kiss*, *Person of Interest*, *Vinyl*
John Benjamin Hickey—Tony Award–winning actor
Taylor Schilling—actor, *The Lucky One*, NBC's *Mercy*, *Orange is the New Black*
John Ort—previous head of East Coast casting for ABC
John Johnson—Broadway producer.

THE JUILLIARD SCHOOL

60 Lincoln Center Plaza
New York, NY 10023–6588

Phone: (212) 799-5000 x223
Website: juilliard.edu
Email: admissions@juilliard.edu

Tuition: $$
Campus student enrollment: 530 undergraduate; 894 total

Degree(s): BFA, Artist Diploma in Playwriting
Concentrations: Acting or playwriting
Audition/portfolio requirement: Yes
Scholarships available: Yes
Number of faculty: 64 including guest directors and part-time faculty
Number of majors and minors: 70 acting, 10 playwriting
Number of acting applicants accepted into the department per year: 2,000 apply and 18 are accepted
Department activities: Six fully staged productions featuring the graduating class per year; biweekly readings and workshops of new plays.

Prominent Alumni:

David Auburn, playwright, best known for his 2000 play *Proof*, which won the 2001 Tony Award for Best Play, as well as the 2001 Pulitzer Prize for Drama. He adapted it into a film, which was released in 2005. Auburn has been awarded the Helen Merrill Playwriting Award and a Guggenheim Fellowship. Following *Proof*, he wrote the screenplay for the movie *The Lake House*, released by Warner Bros. in 2006.

Christine Baranski, actress and recipient of an Emmy Award and two Tony Awards.

Jessica Chastain, actress and film producer, actress and film producer. Golden Globe Award recipient and Academy Award nominee. Best known films are *The Help* and *Interstellar*.

Viola Davis, actress, numerous roles in film (such as *Solaris*, *Syriana*, and *The Help*) and television, most recently ABC's *How to Get Away with Murder* Katori Hall, playwright, *The Mountaintop*.

Val Kilmer, actor best known for roles in *Top Gun*, *The Doors*, *Willow*, *Tombstone*.

Kevin Kline, actor. Recipient of an Academy Award and two Tony Awards. Best known for roles in *Sophie's Choice*, *The Big Chill*, *A Fish Called Wanda*, *Dave*, *The Hunchback of Notre Dame*, *The Ice Storm*, *In & Out*.

David Lindsay-Abaire, playwright, lyricist and screenwriter. He received the Pulitzer Prize for Drama in for his play *Rabbit Hole*, which also earned several Tony Award nominations.

Laura Linney, actress with four Emmy Awards and two Golden Globe Awards as well as a three-time Academy Award and three-time Tony Award nominee. Notable films include *Primal Fear*, *Absolute Power*, *You Can Count on Me*, *The Life of David Gale*, *Love Actually*, *Mystic River*, *The Squid and the Whale*, *The Nanny Diaries*.

Anthony Mackie, actor best known for roles in *8 Mile*, *The Hurt Locker*, *Captain America: The Winter Soldier*.

Kevin Spacey, actor with both a Tony Award and Academy Award. Best known for roles in films such as *The Usual Suspects*, *Seven*, *L.A. Confidential*, *American Beauty*, *Pay It Forward*, *Superman Returns*, and most recently the Netflix original series *House of Cards*.

Danielle Brooks, actress best known for her role as Tasha "Taystee" Jefferson on the Netflix original series *Orange Is the New Black*, and for her Tony Award–nominated portrayal of Sofia in the 2015 Broadway production of *The Color Purple*.

Branden Jacobs-Jenkins, playwright. He won the 2014 Obie Award for Best New American Play, for his plays *Appropriate* and *An Octoroon*. His play *Gloria* was a finalist for the 2016 Pulitzer Prize for Drama. He is also a 2016 MacArthur Fellow.

Alexander Sharp, a Tony Award-winning English actor.

Oscar Isaac, actor known for roles in *Inside Llewyn Davis*, *A Most Violent Year*, *Ex Machina*, *The*

Nativity Story, Star Wars: The Force Awakens, X-Men: Apocalypse, and in the HBO miniseries *Show Me a Hero.*

Adam Driver, actor best known for his role on HBO's *Girls* and for playing the villain Kylo Ren in *Star Wars: The Force Awakens,* a role which he is set to reprise in the future Star Wars films.

Beau Willimon, playwright and screenwriter; creator of the Netflix original series *House of Cards.*

KEAN UNIVERSITY

Department of Theatre
VE 410, 1000 Morris Avenue
Union, NJ 07083

Phone: (908) 737-4420
Website: kean.edu
Email: theatre@kean.edu

Tuition: $$
Campus student enrollment: 15,221

Degree(s): BA, BFA
Concentrations: Performance, Design and Technology and General Theater Studies, Theater Education with K–12 certification.
Audition/portfolio requirement: Yes, for entrance and retention in BFA programs. Also used as assessment tool for BA students.
Scholarships available: Yes. Department scholarships include renewable full-tuition waivers for promising freshmen, and several other merit- or need-based awards.
Number of faculty: 7 full-time, 10 part-time
Number of majors and minors: 135 majors, 25 minors
Department activities: Mainstage production series, three to four per year; student-directed series, one to two per year; student directed workshops, up to 16 per year; Equity theater in residence; cabaret performance series at least once per semester.

Prominent Alumni:

Shayne Miller—director of PR and press relations, Paper Mill Playhouse

Sara Leone—actor, Theatre Works

Amy Hadam Gilbert—AEA Stage Manager

Danny Douress—AEA Stage Manager

Jeff Ronan—actor, NYC BATS Theatre

Jason Gillis—education department, Paper Mill Playhouse

Dusty Ballard—teaching artist, George Street Playhouse

Tim Regan—actor, Theatre Works

Cara Ganski—actor, Growing Stage

Darin Carlton—lighting and stage technician, Alliance Theatre

Ernio Hernandez—writer, *Playbill* online

Amanda Davis—stage manager, George Street Playhouse

Joe Regan—New York cabaret pianist

Kelly Wasilishen—actor, national tour

Aimee Eckert—associate editor, *Entertainment Design* magazine

Terri Muuss—actor

Joe Bevilaqua—writer, actor, National Public Radio

Maria Balboa—project manager, Prop N Spoon (Broadway prop house)

Katie Venezia—project manager, Prop N Spoon

LONG ISLAND UNIVERSITY, CW POST CAMPUS

School of Performing Arts
Department of Theatre, Dance & Arts Management
720 Northern Boulevard
Brookville, NY 11548

Phone: (516) 299-2900
Website: liu.edu/post
Email: post-enroll@liu.edu

Tuition: $
Campus student enrollment: 4,429

Degree(s): BA, BFA

Concentrations: Acting, arts management, design and production, directing and playwriting, musical theater, theater arts

Audition/portfolio requirement: Audition required for theater, dance, and music; Art Department requires portfolio for transfer students only.

Scholarships available: Yes

Number of faculty: 34

Number of majors and minors: 60

Department activities: The Post Theatre Company has three to four mainstage performances, plus thesis projects, and the Post Student Theatre Association presents two performances a year.

MARYMOUNT MANHATTAN COLLEGE

Department of Theatre Arts
221 East 71st Street
New York, NY 10021

Phone: (212) 774-0767
Website: mmm.edu
Email: theatre@mmm.edu

Tuition: $
Campus student enrollment: 1,800

Degree(s): BA, BFA

Concentrations: BFA in Acting; BA in Theatre Arts (Theatre Performance, Musical Theatre, Design & Technical Production, Directing, Producing & Management, Theatre History, Performance & Digital Media, and Writing for the Stage). Minors in Arts for Communities, Drama Therapy and Arts Management.

Audition/portfolio requirement: Yes

Scholarships available: Yes. $1,000–$10,000, Theatre Arts Awards, in addition to Academic Awards and need-based grants.

Number of faculty: 20 full-time, 60 part-time

Number of majors and minors: 450

Percentage and number of applicants accepted into the department per year: 1,300 audition per year, 1 in 6 admitted to the

College are also offered admission to Theatre Arts, 76% offered admission to Theatre Arts attend MMC

Department activities: Seven mainstage productions per year; three are musicals. Twelve to 20 student directed projects each year in the 50-seat Box Theatre. Fall and spring advanced playwriting projects, fall and spring 24-hour play festival, and fall and spring advanced film projects. Specialized senior-year courses: Auditioning for Musicals, Professional Preparation: Musical Theatre, the Business of Acting, and the Senior Showcase, where students are seen by agents and casting directors.

Prominent Alumni:

Melissa Rauch—series regular on *The Big Bang Theory* (television)

Annaleigh Ashford—2015 Tony Award (Best Featured Actress in a Play), *Sylvia, You Can't Take it With You, Kinky Boots, Rent, Hair, Wicked,* and *Legally Blonde* (Broadway), *The Rocky Horror Picture Show/2016* and *Masters of Sex* (television)

Laverne Cox—*Rocky Horror Picture Show/2016* and *Orange Is the New Black* (television)

Emmy Raver Lampman—*Hamilton, A Night with Janis Joplin, Jekyll and Hyde,* and *Hair* (Broadway), *Wicked* (national tour), *The SpongeBob Musical* (regional/pre-Broadway)

Adrienne Warren—2016 Tony nominee (Best Featured Actress in a Musical), *Shuffle Along* and *Bring It On,* the Musical (Broadway), *Dreamgirls* (national tour)

Brian Avers—*The Father, Rock'n'Roll,* and *The Lieutenant of Inishmore* (Broadway)

Reggie Bythewood—screenwriter, *Get on the Bus* (directed by Spike Lee), *Dancing in September, Biker Boyz, Notorious, One Night in Vegas* (screenplay and director)

Ta'rea Campbell—*Aida* and *Little Shop of Horrors* (Broadway), *Sister Act* (national tour)

Bashirrah Creswell—*Lion King* (Broadway)

Timothy Douglas—former associate artistic director, Actors Theatre of Louisville

Ryan Kasprzak—*So You Think You Can Dance*

(television), dance captain for *Billy Elliot* (Chicago), *Cut to the Chase* (off-Broadway)

Dan Bittner—*The Vertical Hour* (Broadway), *The House in Town* (off-Broadway), and films *Farragut North*, *Adventureland*, *Law Abiding Citizen*, *The Producers: The Movie Musical*, *The Last Girl on Earth*, *Coda*

Moira Kelly—*Chaplin*, *The West Wing*, *The Cutting Edge*, *Little Odessa*, *Entertaining Angels*, *Law and Order*

Debra Ann Byrd—producing artistic director, Take Wing and Soar Productions at The National Black Theatre

Eric Palladino—*ER*, *Over There* (television)

Nick Sanchez—*Rent*, *Tarzan*, *Mary Poppins* (Broadway)

Manny Perez—*El Cantante*; *Illegal Tender*; *Yellow, Pride and Glory*; *Rockaway* (film); *Third Watch*, *Law and Order* (television)

Kelly Coffield—*Field of Dreams*, *Jerry Maguire*, *Little Man* (film); *In Living Color*, *Law and Order* (television)

MONTCLAIR STATE UNIVERSITY

Department of Theatre and Dance, Theatre Division
1 Normal Avenue
Upper Montclair, NJ 07043

Phone: (973) 655-7000
Website: montclair.edu/arts/theatre-and-dance

Tuition: $
Campus student enrollment (undergraduate): 16,336, as of spring 2016

Degree(s): BA and BFA
Concentrations: Acting, musical theater, production and design, theater studies, minor in musical theater. Bachelor of Fine Arts (BFA) in Theatre—Acting Concentration.
Audition requirement: Yes
Scholarships available: Yes.
Cento Amici Award (Theatre & Dance)

Choreographic Excellence Award
Danceaturgy Award
Department of Theatre & Dance Service Award
Doris Bianchi Senior Award
Jeanne Wade Heningburg Award
Joseph F. Bella Production/Design Award
Linda Roberts Outstanding Senior Dance Award
Marc Mattaliano Theatre Award
Mary Ann Peins Dance Scholarship
MSU Dance Education Award
MSU Dance Spirit Award
Outstanding Performer Award
Senior BFA Acting Award
Wycoff Award

Number of faculty: 15 full-time, 45 part-time (Department of Theatre and Dance)
Numbers of majors and minors: 255 majors, 67 minors
Percentage and number of applicants accepted into the department per year: Approximately 17%; 324 applied, 58 accepted
Department activities: Department of Theatre and Dance students learn acting, dance, theater studies, and theater production with imminent faculty and visiting professionals. The Theatre programs are rigorous, conservatory-based programs of study that prepare students for a careers in theater and film, musical theater, and stage performance. Our location just 14 miles west of Manhattan puts students just minutes away from Broadway productions, world-class dance performances, and career-building internships. There are many study-abroad programs as well opportunities to work and perform in our exceptional performance and teaching facilities—from the state-of-the-art Alexander Kasser Theater to fully equipped dance studios, a 2,000-seat amphitheater; and the intimate L. Howard Fox Theatre.

Prominent Alumni:
Olivia Polci (BFA 2015)—Ensemble (Elphaba understudy) on the first national tour of *Wicked*
Ari Frenkel—roles on HBO's *Silicon Valley* and TNT's *Rizzoli & Isles*

Nicholas Alesander Rodrigues—national tour, *Sister Act*

Josh Dela Cruz—Disney's *Aladdin* (Broadway)

Rob McClure—*Something Rotten, Noises Off, Honeymoon in Vegas, Chaplin, Avenue Q* (Broadway)

Carlos Gonzales—*On Your Feet* at the Marquis Theater, NYC

Wilson Mendieta—*Man of La Mancha, Bombay Dreams* (Broadway)

MUHLENBERG COLLEGE

Department of Theatre and Dance
Trexler Pavilion for Theatre and Dance
Muhlenberg College
Allentown, PA 18104

Phone: (484) 664-3330
Website: muhlenberg.edu
Email: richter@muhlenberg.edu

Tuition: $$$
Campus student enrollment (undergraduate): 2,200

Degree(s): BA
Campus student enrollment: 2,200
Concentrations: Acting, directing, design/technical theater, performance studies, stage management, full dance major and complete musical theater training
Audition/portfolio requirement: No, recommended but not required
Scholarships available: Yes; Baker Talent Grants and Muhlenberg Talent Scholarships range from $1,000 to $4,000.
Number of faculty: 23 full-time, 12 part-time
Number of majors and minors: 250 theater majors/100 dance majors and minors; there is no theater minor
Percentage and number of applicants accepted into the department per year: Accepts about 40% of applicants, about 70 new

students in the theater major each year and 20 students in the dance major
Department activities: Six major theater productions (at least one musical), 25–40 workshop productions, three summer musical productions, three school touring productions. Three major dance concerts, two informal dance concerts.

Prominent Alumni:
David Masenheimer (1981)—Equity actor, *Les Miserables, Side Show, Ragtime, Scarlet Pimpernel* (Broadway)

Neil Hever (1982)—program director of WDIY, Lehigh Valley Public Radio

John Speredakos (1984)—professional actor in theater, film, and television. Film credits include *The Roost, Wendigo, Rules of Engagement, School Ties*. TV credits: *Brewster Place, Return to Lonesome Dove, Sirens, Kojak, Law and Order, Law and Order: Special Victims Unit*. Broadway and national tour credits: *A View From the Bridge, Death of a Salesman*. MFA: Mason Gross School of the Arts

John Hessler (1990, MFA in stage lighting)—University of Wisconsin, staff member—ETC corporation

Anthony Azizi (1990)—*McHale's Navy, Tomcats, Desert Son, For Richer or Poorer* (film); *24, The Shield, Dragnet, Threat Matrix, JAG, Commander in Chief, Desperate Housewives, Lost* (TV)

Kam Cheng (1991)—Equity actor, *Miss Saigon, The King and I* on Broadway

Frankie Grande (2005)—Equity actor, *Mamma Mia, Rock of Ages* on Broadway

George Psomas (2005)—Equity actor, *South Pacific, Fiddler on the Roof* on Broadway

Nicholas Carriere (2003)—Equity actor, Scar in national tour of *The Lion King*

Madison Ferris (2014)—Equity actress, Laura in *The Glass Menagerie* with Sally Field as Amanda (Broadway)

NEW YORK UNIVERSITY TISCH SCHOOL OF THE ARTS

Department of Drama
721 Broadway
Third Floor South
New York, NY 10003

Phone: (212) 998-1850
Website: drama.tisch.nyu.edu
Email: tisch.drama.ug@nyu.edu

Tuition: $$$$
Campus student enrollment (undergraduate):
3,163 (Tisch)

Degree(s): BFA
Concentrations: Acting, musical theater, directing, production design, and theatrical management
Audition/portfolio requirement: Yes
Scholarships available: Yes, vary from year to year. Alec Baldwin Drama Scholarship (amount varies).
Number of faculty: Approximately 350
Number of majors and minors: 259 (university-wide)
Number of applicants accepted into the department per year: 500 students, approximately
Department Activities: 150+ shows each year

Prominent Alumni:
Deborah Aquila (1980 BFA UD)—casting agent, vice president of casting for Deborah Aquila Casting and Paramount Pictures Feature casting
Alec Baldwin (1994 BFA UD)—actor, appeared in *30 Rock*, *The Edge*, *Mercury Rising*, *The Juror*, *The Hunt for Red October*, among others
Rachel Bloom (2209, BFA UD)—Golden Globe Award for acting, *Crazy Ex-Girlfriend*
Ismael Cruz Cordova (2009, BFA UD)—*Ray Donovan*, *Sesame Street*, named one of 25 "Leaders of the Future" by *Latino Leaders* Magazine
Thais Francis (2012, BFA UD)—winner of 2016 *Essence* Magazine Short Film Contest for

producing/writing/directing/starring in *Late Expectations*
Lucy Alibar (2005 BFA UD)—actor/writer, cowrote the Academy Award–nominated *Beasts of the Southern Wild*
Lisa Gay Hamilton (1985 BFA UD)—actor, appeared in ABC drama *The Practice*; appeared in the films *Jackie Brown* and *The Last Breath* as well as the Broadway production of *The Valley Song*
Jessica Hecht (1987 BFA UD)—actress, appeared on Broadway in *The Last Night of Ballyhoo*; recurring roles on *The Single Guy* and *Friends*
Kristen Johnston (1989 BFA UD)—actress, appeared on *Third Rock from the Sun*; received the 1997 Emmy for Best Supporting Actress in a Comedy Series
Richard Lagravenese (1980 BFA UD)—screenwriter/director

SALEM STATE UNIVERSITY

Theatre and Speech Communication
352 Lafayette Street
Salem, MA 01970

Phone: (978) 542-6290
Website: salemstate.edu
Email: admissions@salemstate.edu

Tuition: $$
Campus student enrollment: 9,215

Degree(s): BA, BFA
Concentrations: BA in theater performance, technical; BFA in theater performance, design, technical and stage management; 4+1 Theatre Education Program
Audition/portfolio requirement: Yes. Audition/portfolio as part of application review for the BFA Program. Students who do not initially apply to the BFA program may do so during freshman year. Audition and portfolio review required for accepted BFA students every semester to remain in program. No audition/portfolio review is required for the BA program.

Scholarships available: Yes; Presidential Arts Scholarship, which covers in-state tuition.

Number of faculty: 12 full-time, 13 part-time (adjunct)

Number of majors and minors: 165 majors, 20 minors

Percentage and number of applicants accepted into the department per year: 62% of students who applied in 2015 were accepted; 85 students were accepted in 2015–2016.

Department activities: Four department productions per year. First-year lab presentation for all first-year students. Two Student Theatre Ensemble productions each year. Participates in Kennedy Center American College Theater Festival at the local, regional, and national levels. Additional workshops with guest artists, staged readings, and playwriting group.

Prominent Alumni:

Tracee Chimo—Broadway actress

Derek DeGregorio—Broadway stage manager

Paul Melendy—TV, industrials, stage actor

Thomas Silcott—*Bring in 'da Noise* national and international tours and *Criminal Minds: Beyond Borders*

Kathy St. George—Broadway actress

Nancy McNulty, Thomas Silcott, and Stephen Laferriere won the National Irene Ryan Scholarship at the Kennedy Center

SYRACUSE UNIVERSITY

College of Visual and Performing Arts
202 Crouse College
Syracuse, NY 13244

Phone: (315) 443-2769
Website: vpa.syr.edu
Email: admissu@syr.edu

Tuition: $$
Campus student enrollment (undergraduate): 14,566

Degree(s): BFA, BS

Concentrations: BFA: Acting, theater design and technology, musical theater, stage management. BS: Drama, with a featured track in theater management.

Audition/portfolio requirement: Yes, auditions required for acting and musical theater, portfolios for stage management and theater design and technology, and an interview is required for theater management. Additionally, musical theater requires submission of an online pre-screen. For all other programs, an online submission or Skype interview may be arranged in lieu of a live audition/interview.

Scholarships available: Yes, based on a combination of need, artistic merit, and academic merit. All financial aid is awarded by the University financial aid office, not through the drama department.

Number of faculty: 22 full-time, 33 part-time

Department activities: The department shares its home with Syracuse Stage, a professional (LORT) theater company that is the leading professional theater company in the Central New York region. Advanced students may audition for and perform in Syracuse Stage productions and may earn Equity Membership Candidate points. Designers, stage managers, and theater management students also participate as assistants to professional designers, stage managers, and key staff members for Syracuse Stage, earning professional credits as part of their undergraduate training. Internships with the Stage are available in all areas of production. Productions include faculty- and professional guest–directed plays and musicals, a musical coproduced with Syracuse Stage, and a children's tour, also coproduced with the Stage and performed and stage managed by drama students. Productions in the Loft Theatre include both faculty- and student-directed shows. There is a student producing organization, the Black Box Players. All Star C.A.S.T. (Community Actors & Students' Theater) is a community-based program that provides an opportunity for drama students to serve (under faculty guidance) as facilitators of weekly theater workshops for members of the Syracuse community with developmental disability. Many other projects, such as cabarets and new play workshops, including student-written work, are part of the yearly activities. Wednesday Lab is an opportunity for alumni and visiting artists to host a lecture or workshop for students in the drama department. Off-campus programs include study abroad at the SU center and the Globe Theatre in London, Rose Bruford College, Sorkin Week in L.A., and the Tepper Semester in NYC.

Prominent Alumni:

Actors:

Jessie Mueller

Patti Murin

Josh Young

Reid Scott

Taye Diggs

Vera Farmiga

Frank Langella

Neal McDonough

Julia Murney

Jerry Stiller

Vanessa Williams

Design/technology:

Charles Kirby

Cory Pattak

Martin Vreeland

Laurent Linn

Jason Strangfeld

Producers, writers, agents, managers, casting directors and other professionals:

Aaron Sorkin

Arielle Tepper Madover

Hank Unger and Michael Rego (The ARACA Group)

David Tochterman

Evan Weinstein

Lauren Port

UNIVERSITY OF THE ARTS

College of Performing Arts

Ira Brind School of Theater Arts

320 South Broad Street

Philadelphia, PA 19102

Phone: Toll-free (800) 616-2787 or (215) 717-6030

Website: uarts.edu

Email: admissions@uarts.edu

Tuition: $$

Campus student enrollment (undergraduate): 1890

Degree(s): BFA

Concentrations: Acting; Directing, Playwriting + Production; Musical Theater; Theater Design + Technology; Film Design + Production

Audition/portfolio requirement: Yes

Scholarships available: Yes; range from $8,000 to full tuition

Number of faculty: 105 full-time faculty university-wide; 8-to-1 student-faculty ratio

Number of majors and minors: Over 50 undergraduate programs university-wide; theater students may minor in other disciplines including music, fine art, and design

Percentage and number of applicants accepted into the department per year: More than 100 new students enroll each year in the School of Theater; acceptance rates vary year to year, and program to program.

Department activities: The School of Theater Arts stages 10 to 12 productions per year; 3 or 4 of these are musicals. Courses in audition techniques, acting for the camera, stage combat, and the business of the theater are available.

Prominent Alumni:

Jared Leto—*Fight Club; Girl, Interrupted*

Kate Flannery—*The Office*

Ana Ortiz—*Ugly Betty*

KaDee Strickland—*Private Practice*

LaChanze—Tony Award for *The Color Purple*

Cornelius Jones Jr.—*The Lion King*

Tallia Brinson—*Rent, Dreamgirls*

Kelli Barrett—*The Royal Family, Rock of Ages*

Heather Donahue—*The Blair Witch Project*

Lukas Poost—*Shrek*

Alyssa DiPalma—*American Idiot*

Rory Donovan—*Young Frankenstein*

THE HARTT SCHOOL/ UNIVERSITY OF HARTFORD

Theatre Division

200 Bloomfield Avenue

West Hartford, CT 06117–1599

Phone: (860) 768-4465

Website: hartford.edu/hartt

Email: harttadm@hartford.edu

Tuition: $

Campus student enrollment (undergraduate): 5,246

Degree(s): BFA

Concentrations: Actor training, musical theater

Audition/portfolio requirement: Yes

Scholarships available: Yes

Number of faculty: 20

Department activities: The Hartt School annually presents at least 4 musicals and 10 non-musicals. The musical theater program boasts a faculty of professional voice teachers and vocal coaches who also maintain studios in New York City; each vocal studio has its own weekly master class. Emphasis is also placed on sight-reading. Acting classes for both programs are identical until the senior year, when the music theatre students participate in "scene to song" classes. The actor training students spend 6–8 weeks studying Shakespeare in Birmingham, England, during the spring semester of their junior year. The Theatre Division presents new plays and musicals yearly and has a partnership in training with Tony

Award–winning regional theaters Hartford Stage Company and Goodspeed Musicals.

Prominent Alumni:

Marin Ireland

Kier O'Donnell

Renee Feder

Steve French

Kyle Wrentz

Carrie Brown

UNIVERSITY OF NEW HAMPSHIRE

Department of Theatre and Dance

Paul Creative Arts Center

30 Academic Way

Durham, NH 03824

Phone: (603) 862-2919

Website: cola.unh.edu/theatre-dance

Email: admissions@unh.edu

Tuition: $$$$

Degree(s): BA

Concentrations: Acting, dance, musical theater, general theater, design and theater technology, secondary theater education, youth drama, youth drama for special education. Minors: Musical theater, theater, dance, youth drama.

Audition/portfolio requirement: Auditions are required for acting, musical theater, and dance. Portfolio Review/Interview requested for design and theater technology.

Scholarships available: Yes, more than $34,000 awarded by UNH Theatre and Dance Department each year

Number of faculty: 15

Number of majors and minors: 100 majors, 70 minors

Department activities: Mainstage theater productions (five productions per year); UNH Dance Company (two productions per year); studio musical (one production per year);

undergraduate prize play competitions (up to three winning produced plays selected each year); Summer Theatre Camp; touring troupes (three productions per year) by The Little Red Wagon (professional summer tour) and ArtsReach (spring tour); school field trip opportunities to matinees and Drama Days; after-school theater workshops; Teacher Short Courses for professional development; student showcases (eight per year); Mask and Dagger (student theater company); WildActs (Student Theatre for Social Justice); Anna Zornio Memorial Children's Playwriting Competition (endowed sponsor, national competition every four years); New England Theatre Conference (annual participation); Kennedy Center American College Theatre Festival (annual participation, region 1).

Prominent Alumni:

Mike O'Malley—actor, Fox series *Glee*, ABC series *Yes, Dear*

Marcy Carsey—TV producer, co-owner of The Carser-Werney Co., responsible for *The Cosby Show*, *Roseanne*

Michael Graziadei—CBS daytime drama *The Young and the Restless*

Maryann Plunkett—Tony Award, 1987, various Broadway productions and film roles

Gary Lynch—lead Broadway actor and various on/off Broadway productions and national tours

David Leong—top 10 fight masters and choreographers in world; stage and film, New York, Los Angeles, Broadway, London; Chair of Theatre Department at Virginia Commonwealth University

Suzanne Cornelius—associate producer for *Sesame Street*

Ed Trotta—award-winning screen and stage actor

Brian Sutherland—Broadway actor and various on/off Broadway productions and national tours

Gene Lauze—Star Dresser for Broadway Across America's *Beauty and the Beast*

Kristen Vermilyea—actor, NBC series *Third Watch* and *Law and Order* and HBO's *The Sopranos*

WESTERN CONNECTICUT STATE UNIVERSITY

Theatre Arts Department
181 White Street
Danbury, CT 06810

Phone: (203) 837-8258
Website: wcsu.edu/theatrearts
Email: mcdanielp@wcsu.edu

Tuition: $
Campus student enrollment (undergraduate): 5,298

Degree(s): BA
Concentrations: Performance, design/tech, management, drama studies, musical theater, education
Audition/portfolio requirement: Yes for BA in musical theater
Scholarships available: Yes (limited)
Number of faculty: 5 full-time, 21 part-time (adjuncts and guest artists)
Number of majors and minors: 150 majors, 5 minors
Department activities: In addition to course work, the program includes productions of musicals, straight plays, children's theater, one-acts, and new plays. There is a New York Showcase each May, Edinburgh Festival productions every other summer, internships available at regional and New York theaters, Club productions, an a cappella group, several trips to NY venues on Broadway and off Broadway, workshops with industry professionals, active participation in USITT, as well as opportunities in related arts and entertainment projects.

WESLEYAN UNIVERSITY

Theater Department
275 Washington Terrace
Middletown, CT 06459

Phone: (860) 685-2950
Email: theater@wesleyan.edu

Tuition: $$$$
Campus student enrollment (undergraduate): 2,897

Degree: BA in theater
Courses offered: Acting, playwriting, documentary performance: theater and social justice, theater history, directing, introduction to costume design, lighting design for theater, production
Artistic portfolio requirement: No
Number of faculty: 2 tenured, 1 tenure track, visitors varying from 7 to 10 per academic year
Department activities: Two fully produced faculty-directed productions each year; Center for the Arts/Theater Department collaborative program called "Outside the Box" brings professional touring productions and guest lecturers with coordinating residency activities for students. Wesleyan University has preapproved study abroad programs with a focus on theater at the British American Drama Academy in London and a Moscow Art Theatre Semester.

Prominent Alumni:

Lin-Manuel Miranda (2002)—composer, lyricist, actor
Maria Santana (1998)—CNN anchor and correspondent
Doug Berman (1984)—radio producer
Laura Walker (1979)—president and CEO, New York Public Radio
Rob King (1984)—senior vice president, *SportsCenter*
Lynn Chen (1998)—actor
Santigold (1997)—musician
Daniel Handler (1992)—writer
Ariel Levy (1996)—writer
Joss Whedon (1987)—creator, producer, director, writer
Bradley Whitford (1981)—actor
Michael Bay (1986)—actor

YALE UNIVERSITY

Theater Studies Program
220 York Street, Room 102
New Haven, CT 06511

Phone: (203) 432-1310
Website: yale.edu/theaterstudies
Email: Nathan.roberts@yale.edu

Tuition: $$$$
Campus student enrollment (undergraduate): 5,532

Degree(s): BA
Concentrations: Theater studies
Audition/portfolio requirement: No
Number of faculty: 30
Number of majors and minors: 30–50
Percentage and number of applicants accepted into the department per year: Any student accepted by Yale may enter the department.
Department activities: Students must fulfill a senior requirement, which is either a senior seminar or a senior project. Senior projects may take the form of directing or writing a play, performing a role, or writing a critical essay. Performance projects are in addition to the essay. Senior projects may take the form of directing, designing, or writing a play; performing a role; choreographing a dance; or writing a critical essay.

Southeast

CATAWBA COLLEGE

Theatre Arts Department
2300 West Innes Street
Salisbury, NC 28144

Phone: (704) 637-4770
Website: catawba.edu/academic/theatrearts
Email: cdzink@catawba.edu or
eahoman@catawba.edu

Tuition: $
Campus student enrollment (undergraduate):
1,270 (final as of fall 2015)

Degree(s): BFA, BA, BS
Majors: Theater arts, musical theater, theater arts administration, theater arts education
Audition/portfolio requirement: Yes
Scholarships available: Yes; performance awards up to $5,000; Burnet Hobgood Theatre Arts Scholarship for full tuition (by invitation only); McCorkle Scholarship up to full tuition (by invitation only).
Number of faculty: 12
Number of majors and minors: Approximately 44 majors and 24 minors
Percentage of applicants accepted into the department per year: 2016: 68.3% 2015: 53.4%
Department activities: Multiple productions (12–15) with up to 300 performance roles and 250 tech roles.

Prominent Alumni:
Pen Chance (2015)—resident actor and production assistant, Charleston Stage Company, Charleston, SC
Maggie Saunders (2015)—resident actor, Charleston Stage Company, Charleston, SC
Jesse Siak (2012)—associate director of education, Charleston Stage Company, Charleston, SC
Aaron Ganas (2009)—working on an MPA in Public and Nonprofit Management and Policy at New York University
Michael Lasris (2008)—actor/company manager/resident choreographer/academy principal at Midtown Arts Center, Ft. Collins, CO
Mary Alice Nichols (2011)—program coordinator for the Institute for Educators & Teaching Artists at Alliance Theatre, Atlanta, GA
Kara Procell (2013)—stage management and production assistant, Alliance Theatre, Atlanta, GA
Brooke Beall (2013)—scenic artist, Alliance Theatre, Atlanta, GA
Jodye Carroll (2013)—MFA directing candidate, University of Southern Mississippi
Anthony Johnson (2005)—AEA, Off-Broadway actor, most recently Harbor Lights Theatre Co, Staten Island
Amanda Lederer (2010)—AEA, Off-Broadway actor, member Strangemen and Co., NYC
Daniel Hines (2008)—AEA actor, Guthrie Theatre (MN); national tour: *Memphis: the Musical*
Eleanor Withrow (2010)—Cofounder with Amber Hughes (2010), Town Theatre Company, Seattle WA
Justin Dionne (2008)—former managing artistic director, Lee Street Theatre Company, Salisbury, NC; current MFA Theatre Arts Administration candidate, Florida State University
Robin Elizabeth Tynes (2012)—cofounder with Carmen Bartlett (2010), and managing artistic director, Three Bone Theatre, Charlotte, NC
Gerald "Jerry" Archer (2014)—entertainment technician, Walt Disney World
David Loehr (2007)—resident actor, literary manager, dramaturg
Sean "Shaggy" Sears (2004)—cofounder with Liam Macik (2005), Throughline Theatre Company, Pittsburgh, PA
Meredith Fox (2007)—assistant professor of Theatre Arts and coordinator of Musical Theatre, Catawba College
Jasika Nicole Pruitt (2002)—Fox television series *Fringe*
Amy Guenther (2007)—PhD candidate (ABD), Theatre History, Theory, Criticism, University of Texas at Austin

NOVA SOUTHEASTERN UNIVERSITY

College of Arts, Humanities, and Social Sciences
Department of Performing and Visual Arts
3301 College Avenue
Fort Lauderdale, FL 33314–7796

Phone: (954) 262-8094
Website: cahss.nova.edu
Email: markdunc@nova.edu

Tuition: $
Campus student enrollment (undergraduate):
Nearly 4,000

Degree(s): BA
Concentrations: Art and design (concentrations in graphic design and studio act), arts administration, communication, dance, music (concentrations in performance and commercial music), and theater (concentrations in acting for stage and screen, musical theater, and design and technical production). Minors are also available in arts administration, communication, dance, film, graphic design, and theater.
Audition/portfolio requirement: No
Scholarships available: Yes
Number of faculty: 8 full-time
Department activities: Each year, the college at Nova Southeastern University presents outstanding productions in theater, music, and dance, as well as a variety of visual arts exhibitions. These performances and events serve as co-curricular opportunities for students to gain practical experience, and provide the community with a local resource for educational—and entertaining—performing and visual arts presentations. Classes and productions are held on campus, within the college's Performing and Visual Arts Wing. This state-of-the-art home for creative expression includes a 230-seat performance theater; a 100-seat black box theater; scene and costume shops; a dance studio; orchestra, choral and music practice rooms; technology labs; art studios for painting, drawing, sculpture, ceramics, and graphic design; and Gallery 217, which hosts a variety of exhibitions throughout the year.

LOYOLA UNIVERSITY NEW ORLEANS

Department of Theatre Arts and Dance
6363 St. Charles Avenue
New Orleans, LA 70118

Phone: (504) 865-3840
Website: cmfa.loyno.edu/theatre
Email: drama@loyno.edu

Tuition: $
Campus student enrollment (undergraduate):
2,691

Degree(s): BA
Concentrations: Theater arts, theater arts/ musical theater, theater arts with minor in business administration
Audition/portfolio requirement: Yes. Admission to the Department of Theatre Arts and Dance requires every candidate to complete a satisfactory performance and/or portfolio audition in addition to normal university admission. This audition also serves as a basis of consideration for awarding talent scholarships.
Scholarships available: Yes
Number of faculty: 6 full-time, 2 part-time
Number of majors and minors: 60 majors and 16 minors
Percentage and number of applicants accepted into the department per year: Varies based on annual need of department
Department activities: Loyola University Theatre Productions, four per academic year. The Senior One-Act Festival is directed by members of the senior class. The number of productions can vary, with the fall festival averaging four one-acts and the larger spring festival with 8 to 12 one-acts.

Prominent Alumni:

Brian Schrader (2009)—production manager, Jefferson Performing Arts Center

James Moore (2006)—freelance lighting designer and electrician

Kelly Brooks (2001)—Equity stage manager

Chris Delhomme (1997)—public relations coordinator, *E! Entertainment Network*

Mike O'Connell (1998)—appearing at the Comedy Club in Los Angeles

Lucy Ramos (1992)—member, Nuestro Nuevo Teatro company, Puerto Rico

Ryan Rillette (1995)—artistic director, Southern Rep Theatre

Marlene Sharp (1992)—director of development, Renaissance-Atlantic Films

Susan Shaughnessy (1972)—head of performance, University of Oklahoma School of Drama

NEW WORLD SCHOOL OF THE ARTS

Theater Division
300 NE 2nd Avenue
Miami, FL 33132

Phone: (305) 237-3541
Website: nwsa.mdc.edu
Email: nwsainfo@mdc.edu

Tuition: $
Campus student enrollment: 448

Degree(s): BFA
Concentrations: Theater or musical theater
Audition/portfolio requirement: Yes
Scholarships available: Yes, merit scholarships available in varying amounts
Number of faculty: 7 full-time, 14 adjunct
Number of majors and minors: 67
Number of applicants accepted into the department per year: 30–40 freshmen per year

Prominent alumni:
Tyrone Davis—actor, The Classical Theatre of Harlem

Yara Martinez—actor, *The Unit*
Meredith Zealy—actor, *The Notebook*
Katie Finneran—actor, *Bloodline*
Edson Jean—*The Adventures of Edson Jean,* winner of the American Black Film Festival and playing on HBO

UNIVERSITY OF CENTRAL FLORIDA

Theatre UCF, part of the UCF School of Performing Arts
12488 Centaurus Blvd.
Orlando, FL 32816–2372

Phone: (407) 823-2862
Website: theatre.ucf.edu
Email: theatre@ucf.edu

Tuition: $
Campus student enrollment (undergraduate): 60,767

Degree(s): BFA, BA, theater minor, dance minor.
Majors: Acting, musical theater, stage management, design and technology, theater studies
Audition/portfolio requirement: Audition or interview for BFA, interview for BA
Number of faculty: 36
Department activities: Eight to ten productions per year, including musicals, plays, student-produced one-act festivals, dance, and a large arts festival. Theatre UCF has artistic partnerships with Walt Disney World, the Orlando Repertory Theatre, and the Orlando Shakespeare Theater.

UNIVERSITY OF MEMPHIS

Department of Theatre & Dance
144 Theatre Communication Building
Memphis, TN 38152–1350

Phone: (901) 678-2523
Website: memphis.edu/theatre
Email: theatre@memphis.edu

Tuition: $$
Campus student enrollment (undergraduate): 16,639

Degree(s): BFA
Concentrations: Performance, design and technical production, musical theater
Audition/portfolio requirement: Musical theater for acceptance. Audition/portfolio review after freshman year for performance and design/technical.
Scholarships available: Yes, three talent scholarships available each year for incoming BFA students cover full tuition for four years; other scholarships range from $500 to $3,500.
Number of faculty: 14
Number of majors and minors: 111 majors, 22 minors
Percentage of applicants accepted into the department per year: 100%; 25% for musical theater
Department activities: Six shows per season, and many directing projects performed on Tuesdays and Thursdays throughout the year in school's Lunchbox Series. A lab theater is available for students to use for in-class and extracurricular projects.

Prominent Alumni:
John Dye
Michael Jeter
Miles Potter

UNIVERSITY OF NORTH CAROLINA SCHOOL OF THE ARTS

School of Design and Production
Office of Admissions
1533 South Main Street
Winston-Salem, NC 27127

Phone: (336) 770-3290
Website: uncsa.edu
Email: admissions@uncsa.edu

Tuition: $
Campus student enrollment (undergraduate): 856 (includes all five conservatories)
Audition/portfolio requirement: Yes
Scholarships available: Yes
Degree(s): BFA, Undergraduate Arts Certificate
Concentrations: costume design and technology, lighting, scene design, scene painting, scenic technology, sound design, stage management, stage properties, and wig and makeup design. More than 150 courses are offered each year, covering virtually every area of theatrical design, technical theatre and management.
Number of faculty: 34 plus guest artists
Department activities: Eight to ten major productions, six to seven workshop productions, special workshops. In partnership with UNCSA's Schools of Drama, Music, and Dance, the School of Design and Production produces more than 25 separate theater, dance, and opera events each year, totaling nearly 100 individual performances, all of which are student designed, produced, promoted, and managed.

Prominent Alumni:
Michael Clark—projection designer, *Jersey Boys* on Broadway
Charlie Morrison—lighting designer, North American and European tours
Paul Tazewell—costume designer, Broadway's *Hamilton* and TV's *The Wiz Live!*
Angela Hays—executive director, North Carolina Theatre Conference
Al Crawford—lighting director, Alvin Ailey American Dance Theater
Clay Benning—sound designer, Alliance Theatre (Atlanta)

Midwest

DENISON UNIVERSITY

Department of Theatre
100 W. College
Granville, OH 43023

Phone: (740) 587-6231
Website: denison.edu/theatre
Email: sundin@denison.edu

Tuition: $$$
Campus student enrollment (undergraduate):
2,200

Degree: BA
Audition/portfolio requirement: No
Scholarships available: Denison practices need-blind admissions and provides financial aid for 98 percent of its students. Additional scholarships are available beginning with the sophomore year for theater majors. Amounts vary widely. Some are need-based, some are awarded by audition, and some by faculty decision.
Number of faculty: 5
Number of majors and minors: 40 majors, 10 minors
Percentage and number of applicants accepted into the department per year: Any student accepted by Denison is eligible to declare a theater major.
Department activities: The department produces four mainstage theater productions each academic year. Enrollment in theater classes and participation in theatrer productions is open to students at all levels and from all disciplines.

Prominent Alumni:
Susan Booth—artistic director of Alliance Theatre Company in Atlanta
Michael Eisner—former CEO of The Disney Company

Sharon Siegel Carr—Tony-winning Broadway producer
Carl Moellenberg—Tony-winning Broadway producer
Playwrights:
Jonathan Reynolds
Jeffrey Hatcher
José Rivera
Actors:
Steve Carell
Jennifer Garner
Hal Holbrook
John Davidson
Richard Roland
Hollis Resnik
John Schuck

DEPAUL UNIVERSITY

The Theatre School
2350 N Racine Avenue
Chicago, IL 60614

Phone: (773) 325-7999
Website: theatre.depaul.edu/
Email: theatreadmissions@depaul.edu

Tuition: $
Campus student enrollment (undergraduate):
16,498

Degree(s): BFA
Concentrations: Acting, costume design, costume technology, dramaturgy/criticism, lighting design, playwriting, scenic design, sound design, stage management, theater arts, theater management, theater technology
Audition/portfolio requirement: Yes for acting applicants. Interview required for all other majors other than acting (specific portfolio requirements for each major).
Scholarships available: Yes. All applicants are automatically eligible and evaluated for scholarships, and all admitted students receive scholarships. Scholarships can range between $10,000

and $30,000 per year and are automatically renewable for up to four years.

Number of faculty: 28 full-time, 68 part-time

Number of majors and minors: 330

Percentage and number of applicants accepted into the department per year: 12%; incoming class for each year of 92 undergraduate students

Department activities: The theatre school's production season includes 40 productions each year in a variety of types and sizes of venues from October through May. The Wrights of Spring Festival is an annual three-week playwriting festival to celebrate work of BFA playwriting students. The New Playwrights Series features the world premiere of a play written by a current theatre school student or recent graduate, selected by the theatre school faculty. In 2013, The Theatre School moved to a new 165,000-square-foot facility that includes all need classrooms, labs, shops and two new performance spaces—a 250-seat thrust stage and a 100-seat flexible theatre.

Prominent Alumni:

Kevin Anderson (BFA)—Brooklyn on Broadway

Gillian Anderson (BFA)—*The X-Files*

Scott Ellis (BFA)—associate artistic director of Roundabout Theatre in New York City, producing director of *Weeds*

Judy Greer (BFA)—*Arrested Development, Cursed, The Village*

Joe Mantegna (BFA)—*Valentine's Day, The Simpsons, Criminal Minds*

John C. Reilly (BFA)—*Chicago, The Aviator, The Hours, Step Brothers, Walk Hard: The Dewey Cox Story*

ROOSEVELT UNIVERSITY

The Theatre Conservatory
Chicago College of Performing Arts
430 South Michigan Avenue
Chicago, IL 60605

Phone: (312) 341-6735

Website: roosevelt.edu/ccpa

Email: ccpaadmissions@roosevelt.edu

Tuition: $

Campus student enrollment (undergraduate): 3,239

Degree(s): BFA

Concentrations: Acting, Musical Theater—Voice, Musical Theater—Dance

Audition/portfolio requirement: Yes

Scholarships available: Yes

Department activities: Numerous showcase and mainstage performances, as well as the opportunity to audition for productions in the city of Chicago. Students receive academic credit for interning at Chicago's professional theaters.

NORTHERN ILLINOIS UNIVERSITY

School of Theatre and Dance
Northern Illinois University
1425 W Lincoln Hwy.
DeKalb, IL 60115

Phone: (815) 753-1334

Website: niu.edu/theatre/

Email: theatreinfo@niu.edu

To schedule an audition, please contact: aperrella@niu.edu or stantondavis@hotmail.com.

Tuition: $$

Campus student enrollment (undergraduate): 14,079

Degree(s): BA, BFA

Concentrations: Acting, Design, Technology, Theater Studies

Audition requirement: Yes (for acting, design, and technology)

Number of faculty: 22

Number of majors and minors: 150

Percentage and number of applicants

accepted into the department per year: Varies

Department activities: Over 80 performances of at least 12 productions per year, industry showcases, on campus workshops by business professionals. The School of Theatre and Dance at Northern Illinois University provides intensive artistic and academic training for students preparing for careers in theater and theater-related areas. The course of study is rigorous and realistic, designed to develop, challenge, and broaden the skills and attitudes of all theater students, but especially the highly motivated student who takes responsibility for his or her own growth. Our principles are simple. Students perform publicly all four years of the program. Our students have a strong work ethic and commitment to excellence, but also the ability to work as an ensemble and treat other artists with respect—this is not only fostered but required. We emphasize in collaboration and NOT competition!

NORTHWESTERN UNIVERSITY

Department of Theatre
1949 Campus Drive
Evanston, IL 60208

Phone: (847) 491-3170
Website: communication.northwestern.edu/theatre
Email: ug-admission@northwestern.edu

Tuition: $$$$
Campus student enrollment (undergraduate): 8,000

Degree(s): BA, BS
Concentrations: Acting, design and stage management, music theater, playwriting. Additional intensive modules: Acting for Screen, Children and Communication, Devising and Adaptation, Music Theater Choreography, Playwriting, Theater for Young Audiences, Theater Management, and Theatrical Design.
Audition/portfolio requirement: No

Scholarships available: No; financial aid is based solely on need, and Northwestern meets 100 percent of demonstrated need for all students.
Number of faculty: 48
Number of majors and minors: 150+ majors and minors
Percentage and number of applicants accepted into the department per year: One in nine
Department activities: The department has as many as 40 productions per year.

Prominent Alumni:
Warren Beatty (1959)—actor, Academy Award–winning producer
Heather Headley (1997)—Tony Award–winning actress, star of *Aida*, *Lion King*, and *The Color Purple* on Broadway, Grammy-nominated R&B singer
Charlton Heston (1945)—Academy Award–winning actor
Julia Louis-Dreyfus (1982)—Emmy Award–winning actress, *Seinfeld* and *Veep*
David Schwimmer (1988)—actor
Anna Gunn (1990)—two-time Emmy Award–winning actress for *Breaking Bad*
Brian d'Arcy James (1990)—three-time Tony Award–nominated actor for *Sweet Smell of Success*, *Shrek the Musical*, and *Something Rotten*; starred in *Spotlight*, the 2016 Best Picture Oscar winner
John Logan (1983)—Tony Award–winning playwright, *Red*, and multi-Oscar nominated scriptwriter, *The Last Samurai*, *The Aviator*, *Hugo*
Seth Meyers (1996)—actor, Emmy Award–winning writer for SNL, host of NBC's *Late Night with Seth Meyers*
Jason Moore (1993)—Tony Award–winning director, *Avenue Q*, film director, *Pitch Perfect*
Megan Mullally (1981)—two-time Emmy-winning actress, *Will and Grace*
Dermot Mulroney (1985)—actor, *My Best Friend's Wedding*, *August: Osage County*
Greg Berlanti (1994)—Emmy-nominated TV and film writer/producer, *Everwood*, *Dawson's Creek*, *Political Animals*

Michael Greif (1981)—Tony Award–nominated director, *Rent* and *Grey Gardens*

John Cameron Mitchell (1985)—actor, writer, and director, *Hedwig and the Angry Inch*

Ana Gasteyer (1989)—stage, film, and television actress, *Saturday Night Live*, *Suburgatory*, Netflix's *Lady Dynamite*

Zach Gilford (2004)—actor, starred in the NBC drama *Friday Night Lights*

Stephen Colbert (1986)—comedian, writer, producer, actor, media critic, and television host, *The Late Show with Stephen Colbert* on CBS

Stephanie D'Abruzzo (1993)—Tony Award–nominated actress, *Avenue Q*

Lily Rabe (2004)—stage and television actress, Tony Award–nominated for *The Merchant of Venice*; on television, the FX anthology series *American Horror Story* and lead actress on ABC's *The Whispers*

audience; students prepare all the different facets of these productions.

Prominent Alumni:

Jay Harnick—artistic director for TheatreWorks, one of the nation's largest touring companies

Jerry Orbach—portrayed Lennie Briscoe on *Law and Order*; starred in a dozen Broadway productions, including *Chicago, Carnival,* and *Promises, Promises* (for which he won a Tony); film credits include *Prince of the City* and *Dirty Dancing*

Lawrence Wilker—president of the Kennedy Center

Greg Vinkler—lead actor at Chicago Shakespeare and Steppenwolf

Ang Lee—Academy Award–winning director of such films as *The Wedding Banquet, Eat Drink Man Woman, Sense and Sensibility, The Ice Storm,* and *Crouching Tiger, Hidden Dragon*

UNIVERSITY OF ILLINOIS-URBANA CHAMPAIGN

Department of Theatre
4–122 Krannert Center for the Performing Arts
500 South Goodwin
Urbana, IL 61801

Phone: (217) 333-2371
Website: theatre.illinois.edu
Email: theatre@illinois.edu

Tuition: $$$$
Campus student enrollment (undergraduate): 32,579

Degree(s): BFA
Concentrations: Acting; design, technology, and management; theater studies
Audition/portfolio requirement: Yes
Scholarships available: Yes
Number of faculty: 16 full-time, 2 part-time
Department activities: The department produces five or six productions each year for a large

UNIVERSITY OF MICHIGAN

Theatre & Drama Department
Walgreen Drama Center
1226 Murfin Avenue
Ann Arbor, MI 48109–1212

Phone: (734) 764-5350
Website: theatre.umich.edu
Email: theatre.info@umich.edu

Tuition: $$$$
Campus student enrollment (undergraduate): 28,000

Degree(s): BA, BFA
Concentrations: Performance (acting or directing), Design and Production, Theatre Arts
Audition/portfolio requirement: Yes
Scholarships available: Yes, for returning students
Number of faculty: 29
Department Activities: Five mainstage productions per year

Prominent Alumni:

Darren Criss—*Glee* (TV), *Smitten!* (film), *Transformers: Robots in Disguise* (TV), *Hedwig and the Angry Inch* (Broadway)

David Alan Grier—stand-up comedian, *The Wiz! Live*, *Comedy Bang! Bang!*

James Earl Jones—*Gin Game* (Broadway) *The Lion Guard: Return of the Roar* (film) *The Great White Hope*, *Field of Dreams*, *Cry the Beloved Country*

Christine Lahti—*Leaving Normal*, *The Blacklist*, *The Doctor*, *Housekeeping*, *Chicago Hope*

Richard Winkler—producer: *Something Rotten*, *Hand to God*, *King Charles II*, *Vanya and Sonya and Masha and Spike*

Matthew Letscher—*The Flash*, *Castle* (TV); *The Mask of Zorro*, *Gods and Generals*, NBC's *Good Morning, Miami*

Margo Martindale—*August: Osage County* (film); *The Americans*, *The Boss*, *The Good Wife* (TV)

Gilda Radner—*Saturday Night Live*, *The Woman in Red*

UNIVERSITY OF MICHIGAN-FLINT

Department of Theatre & Dance
303 E. Kearsley St.
Theatre 238
Flint, MI 48502

Phone: (810) 762-6522
Website: umflint.edu/theatre
Email: lfriesen@umflint.edu or newport@umflint.edu

Tuition: $
Campus student enrollment: 8,289

Degree(s): BA, BFA, BS
Concentrations: Performance, Design & Technology, Dance, Theater, and Musical Theater
Audition/portfolio requirement: Yes for scholarships
Scholarships available: Yes. For majors in both theater and dance, scholarships range from $500 to $1,000 per semester.

Number of faculty: 9 full-time, 4 part-time, 3 staff members (Costume Shop, Scene Shop, Office Administrator)
Number of majors and minors: 106
Department activities: Four mainstage productions a year, including one musical and one dance concert. One to three black-box shows a year. A number of student-initiated performances each year.

Prominent Alumni:

Erin Darke—New York–based actress

Ammar Daraiseh—a long list of Hollywood Credits, SAG, AFTRA

Steve Carpenter—Washington, D.C. actor/director

Janet Haley—Michigan Shakespeare Associate Artist

Ernie Gilbert—Nickelodeon art director

Ben Motter—Metropolitan Opera, NYC, lighting and automation specialist

Sean Michael Welch—playwright

Tony Guest—actor, professor at Oakland University

Cameron Knight—actor, professor at DePaul University

UNIVERSITY OF MINNESOTA

Theatre Arts & Dance Department
580 Rarig Center
330 21st Ave South
Minneapolis, MN 55455

Phone: (612) 625-6699
Website: cla.umn.edu/theatre/
Email: theatre@umn.edu

Tuition: $$$$
Campus student enrollment (undergraduate): 28,945

Degree(s): BA in Theater Arts, BFA in Acting, BA and BFA in Dance, BA Theater
Concentrations: Performance Creation, Design and Technology, History/Literature, and Social Justice. No tracks/concentrations in dance;

emphasis on contemporary dance in a global context through performance, choreography, and dance studies.

Audition/portfolio requirement: BFA Acting, BFA and BA Dance. BA Theater has no audition requirement.

Scholarships available: Yes, both in Theater and in Dance

Number of majors and minors: Theater program: majors, BA, 107; minors, 15; BFA 75. Dance program: approximately 90 majors (combined BA and BFA Dance); no dance minor.

Number of faculty: 36

Department activities: Many opportunities including University Theatre, Open Stage, Peers Arts Quarter Collective, Student Dance Coalition, workshops, guest lectures, many community opportunities, university bands, choirs, orchestras, and clubs.

UNIVERSITY OF MINNESOTA, MORRIS

Theatre Arts
Division of the Humanities
600 East 4th Street
Morris, MN 56267

Phone: (320) 589-6035 or (888) 866-3382
Website: academics.morris.umn.edu/theatre
Email: admissions@morris.umn.edu

Tuition: $
Campus student enrollment (undergraduate): 1,856

Degree(s): BA
Concentrations: Theater Arts: acting, directing, design/technical, teaching licensure in dance and theater arts
Audition/portfolio requirement: No
Scholarships available: Yes. Many university scholarships awarded to incoming students based on academic achievements; theatre scholarships: Alice McCree Scholarship; George Fosgate Scholarship.

Number of faculty: 4
Number of majors and minors: 26 majors, 6 minors

Department activities: The department usually produces three shows a year: one in the fall semester, one in the early part of spring semester and a children's show late in the spring semester. Meiningens, Morris's student theater organization, also produce one or two shows a year. Auditions are limited to UMM students, but all UMM students are encouraged to audition. Qualified students frequently direct and design discipline productions. As a capstone theater experience, theater majors undertake a personalized senior project with a faculty advisor in their area of interest. Students also perform and design at the many community theaters in the region and have directed productions at the local high school.

Prominent Alumni:
Matt Lefbevre has been a costume designer at the Guthrie Theatre for numerous productions; as well as an associate professor of Theatre at the University of Minnesota Twin Cities campus.

NEBRASKA WESLEYAN UNIVERSITY

Theatre Arts
5000 Saint Paul Avenue
Lincoln, NE 68504

Phone: (402) 465-2395
Website: theatre.nebrwesleyan.edu
Email: theatre@nebrwesleyan.edu

Tuition: $
Campus student enrollment (undergraduate): 1,500

Degree(s): BA, BFA
Concentrations: Acting, directing, musical theater, design and technology, theater education
Audition/portfolio requirement: Auditions are for scholarship consideration and acceptance

into the BFA programs. A portfolio is required for prospective design and technology majors.

Scholarships available: Yes

Number of faculty: 5 full-time, 7 adjunct and part-time

Number of majors and minors: 105

Percentage and number of applicants accepted into the department per year: There is no fixed percentage or number accepted into the program annually.

Department Activities: Ten to 14 faculty-directed main season shows in three performing venues, 30–40 student-directed shows, guest artists from Broadway and other professional theater companies around the country work with students approximately once a month. Student organizations include Wesleyan Theatre Company. While this is a 92 percent BFA program, study abroad experience is encouraged. With so many performances, students perfect their audition techniques and engage in all aspects of production work, equipping them with valuable skills for post-bachelor's education or direct entrance into the industry.

OTTERBEIN UNIVERSITY

Department of Theatre & Dance
1 South Grove St
Westerville, OH 43081

Phone: Admission: (614) 823-1500 or toll-free (800) 488-8144; Theatre and Dance: (614) 823-1657

Website: otterbein.edu/theatre

Email: auditions@otterbein.edu

Tuition: $

Campus student enrollment: 2,800

Degree(s): BA, BFA, dance minor

Concentrations: Acting, musical theatre, musical theatre with dance concentration, theatre, theatre design/technology

Audition/portfolio requirement: Yes (interview for DT and BA)

Scholarships available: Yes. Range from $500–6,000. Talent awards and are based upon audition, portfolio review, or interview.

Number of faculty: 11 full-time theater faculty, 2 part-time; 3 full-time dance faculty, 6 part-time.

Number of majors and minors: 111 theater majors (no theater minors); 20 dance minors (no dance major).

Percentage and number of applicants accepted into the department per year: A class of 32 — 8 in musical theater, 8 in acting, 8 in design/technology, and 8 in the BA program — selected from approximately 600 applicants.

Department activities: The Department of Theatre and Dance produces six productions, including at least two musicals and one dance concert each academic year. Otterbein Summer Theatre produces three productions per season, including one musical. (Summer Theatre is a paid professional experience for Otterbein students.)

Prominent Alumni:

Dee Hoty (1974). Musical theatre actress. Three-time Tony award–nominated actress. Broadway credits include *City of Angels* (Alaura Kingsley/Carla Haywood), *Will Rogers Follies* (Betty Blake), *Footloose* (Vi Moore), *Mamma Mia!* (Donna Sheridan)

David Robinson (1978). Costume designer. *Confessions of a Teenage Drama Queen*, *Zoolander*, *Meet Joe Black*

Tonye Patano (1983). Television/movie actress. Most notable production *Weeds* (Heylia Jones)

TJ Gerckens (1988). Lighting designer. 2002 Drama Desk Award winner for design for Broadway's *Metamorphoses*

Rachael Harris (1990). Television actress, most notable productions include *Notes from the Underbelly* (Cooper), *Fat Actress* (Kevyn Shecket), *The Daily Show*, among others

Steve Sakowski: (2003). Lighting designer and technician. Recently named one of the "top 10 lighting designers under 30" by *Lighting Dimensions* magazine

Jeremy Bobb (2004). Stage actor. Recent Broadway credits include *Is He Dead?* (Phelim O'Shaughnessey), *Translations* (Doalty). TV/Film: *The Knick, House of Cards, Hostages*

Mandy Bruno (2004)—television actress, Marina on *Guiding Light*

Daniel Everidge (2006)—musical theater actor, Roger in Broadway production of *Grease*

Molly Camp (2009)—Broadway: *The Heiress*

Cory Michael Smith (2010)—Broadway: *Breakfast at Tiffany's*; Off Broadway: *The Whale, Cock,* TV/Film: *Carol, Gotham* (Edward Nygma), *Olive Kitteridge*

Josie Roberts (2005)—Broadway: *Grinch, Rock of Ages*

Jordan Donica (2016)—Broadway: *The Phantom of the Opera* (Raoul)

Lili Froehlich (2013)—Broadway: *CATS*

OHIO NORTHERN UNIVERSITY

Department of Theatre Arts
525 S. Main Street
Ada, Ohio 45810

Phone: (419) 772-2049
Website: onu.edu/theatre
Email: Laurie Bell, chair, l-bell@onu.edu

Tuition: $
Campus student enrollment (undergraduate): 2,401 (Fall 2015)

Degree(s): BA, BFA, dance minor, arts administration minor, theater minor
Concentrations: Theatre, musical theater, international theater production
Audition/portfolio requirement: Auditions are required for entrance into the BFA program in musical theater and theater production. Auditions are not required for the BA in theater or dance minor but are required for Talent Award consideration.

Scholarships available: Yes. Theatre Talent Awards, Presidential Scholarships, Trustee Scholarships, Deans Scholarships, and Faculty Scholarships.
Number of faculty: 3 full time, 4 adjuncts (Fall 2015)
Number of majors: 70
Percentage and number of applicants accepted into the department per year: 72%; acceptance of 120–125 new majors each year
Department activities: International guest artists, study abroad and international touring opportunities. Students have studied abroad at Queen Margaret College in Edinburgh, Scotland; Glasgow Caledonian University in Glasgow, Scotland; Queensland University of Technology in Australia; National Academy of Singing and Dramatic Art in New Zealand; National Institute of Dramatic Arts in Australia; University of Cape Town in South Africa. Students have also interned at the Estonia Ministry of Culture; the Byre Theatre in St. Andrews, Scotland; the Mull Theatre in Mull, Scotland; and University of Salford, Manchester, England. Occasionally, ONU travels abroad with its theater and dance productions.

Prominent Alumni:
Alumni/students have interned at McCarter Theatre in Princeton, NJ; Cleveland Play House; Alley Theatre in Houston; Weston Playhouse in Weston, VT; Actors Theatre of Louisville, KY; Houston Grand Opera; Glimmerglass Festival in Cooperstown, NY.; Santa Fe Opera in Santa Fe, NM; Atlanta Theatre of the Stars (national touring company); Walt Disney World in Orlando, FL; Imagination Stage in Bethesda, MD, Center Stage in Baltimore, MD; Goodman Theatre in Chicago; MFA at Yale.

WITTENBERG UNIVERSITY

Department of Theatre and Dance
P.O. Box 720
Springfield, Ohio 45501

Phone: (937) 327-7464
Website: wittenberg.edu/academics/thdn.html
Email: cgeorges@wittenberg.edu or
admission@wittenberg.edu

Tuition: $
Campus student enrollment (undergraduate):
1,865

Degree(s): BA
Concentrations: Theater, technical theater, performance; minors in theater, technical theater, dance
Audition/portfolio requirement: No
Scholarships available: Yes; range from $500 to half tuition
Number of faculty: 5
Number of majors and minors: 36 majors, 25 minors
Department activities: Three mainstage productions and one dance concert annually; ten to 14 student-directed productions and one student-produced dance concert annually.

Prominent Alumni:
Chris Conte—Vari-Lite Lighting Company, Emmy Award–winning team, Salt Lake City Olympics
Catherine Cox—actress and Tony nominee; performed in *Oh, Coward, Barnum, Baby, Footloose*
George Izenour—theater architect
Peter Kluge—CEO, Impact Artists Group, Hollywood management agency
Tim Jebsen—executive director, Midland Community Theatre, Midland, Texas
James Rebhorn—actor, *The Book of Daniel, Law and Order, Boston Legal, Coma, The Odd Life of Timothy Green, Homeland, My Cousin Vinny, Stone Mountain*
Dan Stroeh—National Student Playwriting Award 2001, Kennedy Center American College Theatre Festival
Andy Wedemeyer—general foreman, set construction, *Spiderman I* and *II*

West

ARIZONA STATE UNIVERSITY

School of Film, Dance and Theatre
Herberger College of Fine Arts
P.O. Box 872002
Tempe, AZ 85287–2002

Phone: (480) 965-5337
Website: herbergerinstitute.asu.edu
Email: theatre@asu.edu

Tuition: $$
Campus student enrollment (undergraduate):
41,828

Degree(s): BA
Concentrations: Performance and movement, digital culture (theater, film, interdisciplinary arts, and performance), theater (acting, design, and production), film (film and media production, filmmaking practices), dance, dance education
Audition/portfolio requirement: No
Scholarships available: Yes
Number of faculty: 43 full-time plus 22 part-time and numerous guest artists
Number of majors and minors: 225 theater, 420 film
Department activities: Annually, the school produces five mainstage theater productions, four second stage workshops, eight to 16 readings of new work, three major film festivals and screenings, eight-plus dance concerts, and more than 50 special events, including speaker series and private showings. Four student organizations in theater, dance, and film produce another full slate of events each year.

Prominent Alumni:
David Saar—artistic director, Childsplay
Ron May—artistic director, Stray Cat Theatre
Matthew Watkins—artistic director, Orange Theatre

Katherine Harroff—artistic director, Circle Circle Dot Dot

Triste Baldwin—playwright

Jose Cruz Gonzales—playwright

Howard Burkons—filmmaker

CALIFORNIA INSTITUTE OF THE ARTS

School of Theater

24700 McBean Parkway

Valencia, CA 91355

Phone: (661) 255-1050

Website: theater.calarts.edu

Email: admissions@calarts.edu

Tuition: $$$

Campus student enrollment (undergraduate): 946

Degree(s): BFA

Concentrations: Acting, Design & Production (with specializations available in costume, scenic, sound, lighting, and technical direction), and Stage Management.

Audition/portfolio requirement: Yes, a portfolio is required for Design & Production and Stage Management. A live audition is required for the program in Acting.

Scholarships available: Yes. All students are eligible for merit scholarships. Additional financial aid is also available.

Number of faculty: 56

Number of majors and minors: 8 majors are available for undergraduate students within the School of Theater.

Percentage of applicants accepted into the department per year: 33%

Department activities: Eight to 12 fully produced performances annual, plus three to five workshop processes, as well as opportunities for professional work through the Center for New Performance. Students also have ample opportunities to share and create student-generated work.

Prominent Alumni:

Don Cheadle (1986)—Golden Globe–winning and Academy Award–nominated actor (*House of Lies, Flight, Hotel Rwanda, Crash, Traffic, Out of Sight, Ocean's 11*)

Ed Harris (1975)—Golden Globe–winning and Academy Award–nominated actor and director (*Game Change, Pollock, The Hours, A Beautiful Mind, The Truman Show, Apollo 13, The Right Stuff*)

Kevin Adams (1986)—Tony and OBIE Award–winning lighting and scene designer (*Spring Awakening, Next to Normal, Passing Strange, American Idiot, The 39 Steps, Hedwig and the Angry Inch*)

Condola Rashad (2008)—Tony-nominated stage and screen actress (*Stickfly, Ruined, Steel Magnolias, Sex and the City 2, Smash*)

Alison Brie (2004)—film and television actress

CHAPMAN UNIVERSITY

College of Performing Arts

Department of Theatre

One University Drive

Orange, CA 92866

Phone: (714) 744-7087

Website: chapman.edu/copa/theatre/index.aspx

Email: tdoffice@chapman.edu

Tuition: $$$$

Campus student enrollment (undergraduate): 6,000

Degree(s): BA, BFA

Concentrations: Broad-based BA degree in theater, with an area of study in theater technology or theater studies. Second, the pre-professional BFA degree in theater performance, and third, the interdisciplinary BFA in screen acting offered cooperatively with the Dodge College of Film and Media Arts.

Courses offered: Performance techniques, technical theater, and theater studies

Audition requirement: Audition for students

interested in the BFA degrees in theater perfor-mance or screen acting, or by interview/portfolio review for prospective students interested in the BA degree, in the theater studies or theater technology areas of study.

Number of faculty: 18

Department activities: The Henry Kemp-Blair Shakespeare Festival is an annual event hosted in the spring by Chapman University's Department of Theatre.

CORNISH COLLEGE OF THE ARTS

Performance Production Department
1000 Lenora Street
Seattle, WA 98121

Phone: (800) 726-ARTS
Website: cornish.edu
Email: admission@cornish.edu

Tuition: $
Campus student enrollment (undergraduate): 720

Degree(s): BFA
Concentrations: Lighting, costume, scenic, or sound design, stage management, or technical direction
Portfolio requirement: Yes
Scholarships available: Yes
Number of faculty: 5 Performance Production faculty
Number of majors/students in depart-ment: 48 (2015–16)
Number of applicants accepted into the department per year: Cornish has expanded admission in this department over the past two years, and approximately 20 slots are now avail-able annually.
Department activities: Unlike other colleges, Cornish's Performance Production Department operates separately from its Theater Department. Students are encouraged to work in all areas of

the visual and performing arts, from designing/running shows for Dance, Music, or Theater to providing support for outside exhibitions and events. Cornish Playhouse at Seattle Center is a union (IATSE) performance space and work there can help students qualify for union membership.

Prominent Alumni:

Colleen Atwork—costume designer (took Art at Cornish College of the Arts)
David Brack
Sarah Nietfield
Kat Stromberger
Shelby Choo—USITT scholarship winner

CORNISH COLLEGE OF THE ARTS

Theater Department
1000 Lenora Street
Seattle, WA 98121

Phone: (800) 726-ARTS
Website: cornish.edu
Email: admission@cornish.edu or theater@cornish.edu

Tuition: $
Campus student enrollment (undergraduate): 720

Degree(s): BFA
Concentrations: Acting, musical theater, and original works
Audition requirement: Yes
Scholarships available: Yes
Number of faculty: 32 theater faculty
Number of majors/students in department: 185 (2015–16)
Number of applicants accepted into the department per year: Cornish has approxi-mately 60 slots available annually for freshmen and transferring students.
Department Activities: Cornish's Theater Department produces 14 shows annually including

a fall cabaret and a spring musical. Students are also encouraged to create their own shows. Theater has three performance spaces: Raisbeck Hall's Skinner Theater, Cornish Playhouse at the Seattle Center, and the Alhadeff Studio at the Cornish Playhouse. Additional rehearsal and black box spaces are available on campus. Collaboration with other performing and visual arts departments is encouraged.

Prominent Alumni:

Brendan Fraser—movie star

Courtney Sale—artistic director

Lady Rizo—cabaret star

Jinkx Monsoon—performer

Don Darryl Rivera—Broadway performer

Ramiz Monsef—playwright/actor

NORTHERN ARIZONA UNIVERSITY

University Theatre Department

P.O. Box 6040

Flagstaff, AZ 86011

Phone: (928) 523-3731

Website: cal.nau.edu/theatre

Email: theatre@nau.edu

Tuition: $$

Campus student enrollment: total 29,031 (statewide); Flagstaff Mountain campus only 21,107

Degree(s): BS, BA, theater minor

Concentrations: Performance, theater studies, design/technology

Audition/portfolio requirement: No audition required for admission to the department. An audition or interview is required for entrance into two major emphases: theater performance and design/technology majors.

Scholarships available: Yes; full and partial theater activity tuition waivers, various donor scholarships, amounts vary from year to year; auditions

and interviews every March, paperwork deadline March 1 of each year.

Number of faculty: 10

Department activities: Four mainstage productions, one or two guest artist productions, numerous Second Stage (student-driven) productions a year, and rentals which include dance productions designed to give design/technology students the opportunity to work with different lighting and sound experiences.

SOUTHERN METHODIST UNIVERSITY

Meadows School of the Arts

Division of Theatre

P.O. Box 750356

Dallas, TX 75275–0356

Phone: (214) 768-3217

Website:

smu.edu/Meadows/AreasOfStudy/Theatre

Email: theatre@smu.edu

Tuition: $$$$

Campus student enrollment (undergraduate): 6,391

Degree(s): BFA

Concentrations: Acting or theater studies

Audition/portfolio requirement: Yes

Scholarships available: Yes. Academic merit scholarships available through SMU admissions process. Artistic merit scholarships available based on audition or portfolio evaluation. Scholarship amounts vary.

Number of faculty: 24

Number of majors and minors: 75 majors, no minors

Percentage and number of applicants accepted into the department per year: 20% of applicants are accepted with a target matriculation of 10%. Approximately 300 students audition.

Department activities: New Visions, New Voices (student-written/directed play festival),

Fountain Show, Femme Fest, Men Fest, Buffet Combat Theatre, 8 additional mainstage theater productions plus about 15 student studio productions through SMUST (SMU Student Theatre).

Prominent Alumni:

Amy Acker

John Arnone

Kathy Bates

Brian Baumgartner

Powers Boothe

Tim DeLuca

Katie Featherston

Harry Ford

Lauren Graham

Austin Hébert

Debra Monk

Patricia Richardson

Wrenn Schmidt

Regina Taylor

Stephen Tobolowsky

SOUTHERN OREGON UNIVERSITY

Department of Theatre Arts

1250 Siskiyou Boulevard

Ashland, OR 97520

Phone: (541) 552-6346

Website: sou.edu/theatre/

Email: theatre@sou.edu

Tuition: $

Campus student enrollment (undergraduate): 5,421

Degree(s): BA, BFA, BS

Concentrations: BA/BS include theater generalist, performance, lighting, set, sound, and costume design, costume construction, technical theater, stage management, Shakespeare studies minor. BFA includes performance, lighting, set, sound and costume design, costume construction, technical theater, stage management.

Audition/portfolio requirement: Yes for BFA in all concentrations, no for BA or BS in theater arts.

Scholarships available: Yes; range from $1,000 to $5,000 for current theater majors.

Number of faculty: 11

Number of majors and minors: 290 majors

Percentage and number of applicants accepted into the department per year: 70 admitted, which is 60% of those applying to the program.

Department activities: Three major productions for the mainstage (including one dinner theater production); three to four smaller productions for the center stage and showcases.

Prominent Alumni:

Tyler Burrell—actor

David Ivers—artistic director, Utah Shakespeare Festival

Joel David Moore—actor

R. Michael Miller—head of design, Rutgers University

Kim Rhodes—actress

Josh Marquette—hair and makeup design

Jeremy Lee—sound designer

James Bryant—rigging and special effects

Arlan J. Vetter—production design

David Weberg—sound engineer

TEXAS CHRISTIAN UNIVERSITY

Department of Theatre

P.O. Box 297510

Fort Worth, TX 76129

Phone: (817) 257-7625

Website: theatre.tcu.edu

Email: theatre@tcu.edu

Tuition and Fees: $$

Campus student enrollment: 10,323 (8,894 undergraduate; 1,429 graduate)

Degree(s): BA, BFA

Concentrations: Acting, design, musical theater, production, theater studies

Audition/portfolio requirement: No for BA, yes for scholarships and BFA

Scholarships available: Yes

Chancellor's Scholarship: Full tuition

Nordan Fine Arts Scholarship $15,625

Lou Miller Canter Scholarship $2,500

Mel and Katy Dacus Musical Theatre Scholarship $2,100

TCU Fine Arts Guild Scholarship $3,850

Activity Grants $2,000–12,000

Mary Hawn Scholarships $2,500

OMIT: Humphreys Foundation Scholarships

Forrest Newlin Memorial Scholarship $1,500

Ann Bradshaw Stokes Scholarships $2,550

Clay & Kristen Hicks First Nighters Scholarship $4,900

Mary Scriven & J. William Haley Scholarship $2,370

Theatre Production Grants $2,000–5,000

Number of faculty: 13

Number of majors and minors: 120 majors (90 BFA, 30 BA)

Number of applicants accepted into the department per year: 300 applicants; approximately 35 accepted for BFA

Department activities: Four Main Stage Series theater productions, two Studio Series theater productions, two Kaleidoscope Series theater productions (often coproductions with local professional theaters); Alpha Psi Omega, USITT Student Chapter.

Prominent Alumni:

Betty Buckley

Frederic Forrest

Dennis Burkley

Carman Lacivita

David Coffee

UNIVERSITY OF CALIFORNIA, LOS ANGELES

School of Theater, Film and Television

102 East Melnitz Hall

Box 951622

405 Hilgard Avenue

Los Angeles, CA 90095

Phone: (310) 206-2736

Website: tft.ucla.edu

Email: info@tft.ucla.edu

Tuition: $$$

Campus student enrollment (undergraduate): 29,585

Degree(s): BA

Concentrations: Acting, animation, cinema and media studies, cinematography, costume design, digital media, directing, film, lighting design, musical theater, playwriting, producing, production design, scenic design, screenwriting, television, theater

Audition/portfolio requirement: Yes

Scholarships available: Yes

Number of faculty: 41 (in both the Dept. of Theater and the Dept. of Film, Television and Digital Media)

Number of Students with Declared Majors (Theater): 276

Number of Students with Declared Minors (Theater): 113

Number of Students with Declared Majors (Film, Television, and Digital Media): 96

Number of Students with Declared Minors (Film, Television, and Digital Media): 201

Department activities: Students can participate in 12+ theater productions and 200+ student films a year.

Prominent Alumni:

Ana Lily Amirpour

Dustin Lance Black

Jack Black

Carol Burnett

Francis Ford Coppola

James Dean

Susan Egan

Marielle Heller

David Koepp

Justin Lin

Frank Marshall

Jim Morrison

Alexander Payne

Tim Robbins

Thomas Schumacher

Darren Star

Ben Stiller

George Takei

Gore Verbinski

UNIVERSITY OF CALIFORNIA, SANTA BARBARA

Department of Theater and Dance
Santa Barbara, CA 93106–7060

Phone: (805) 893-3241
Website: theaterdance.ucsb.edu
Email:
theaterdance-ugradadv@theaterdance.ucsb.edu

Tuition: $$$$
Campus student enrollment (undergraduate):
23,495

Degree(s): BA in theater, BFA in acting, BA and BFA in dance, minors in production and design and theater
Concentrations: Design, directing, playwriting, theater and community, theater studies
Audition/portfolio requirement: Yes
Scholarships available: Yes. In 1975, a yearly playwriting competition with cash awards was established by the late Sherrill C. Corwin, then chairman of the board of Metropolitan Theatres Corporation. Prizes are given in categories including best full-length play, best one-act play, best full-length screenplay, best short film or television script, and original choreography. The Matthew Alan Plaskett Memorial Scholarship Fund was established in memory of Matthew Plaskett (1967–1987). The scholarship is open to male students in either the dance or dramatic art major with an interest in musical theater at UCSB. The annual scholarship is awarded based on academic achievement, talent, and potential for a performance career. Preference will be given to incoming freshman or continuing sophomores. The Robert G. Egan Memorial Fund was established in memory of Robert G. Egan (1945–2000) to provide scholarship support annually for an undergraduate student who shows promise of exemplifying a similarly wide range of talents, both academic and artistic. Additional scholarships include the Stanley Glen Scholarship in Dramatic Arts for juniors in the BFA acting emphasis, Patricia Sparrow Dance Scholarship for BFA dance students, Alice Condodina Dance Performance Award for dance majors, Rona Sande Award, Tonia Shimin Award for Promising Dance Artist, Carol M. Press and Nicolas Tingle Awards for Promising Dance Scholar and Dance History, Drama and Dance Association Scholarships, Dilling Yang Fellowship in Dramatic Art.
Number of faculty: 26
Number of majors and minors: 224 majors

UNIVERSITY OF CALIFORNIA, RIVERSIDE

Department of Theatre, Film and Digital Production
900 University Avenue
Riverside, CA 92521

Phone: (951) 827-3343
Website: theatre.ucr.edu
Email: paadvising@ucr.edu

Tuition: $$$$
Campus student enrollment (undergraduate):
18,607

Degree(s): BA
Concentrations: Acting, technical theatre,

literature, playwriting, screenwriting, filmmaking, theater minor

Audition/portfolio requirement: No

Scholarships available: Yes; Chancellor's Performance Award, up to $2,500

Number of faculty: 9

Number of majors and minors: 118 majors, 9 minors

Department activities: Students are able to practice acting in faculty-directed shows, student productions and class presentations. Special projects and studies are offered for advanced students to produce an original work or to study in more depth acting, directing, scenic design, playwriting, or filmmaking.

UNIVERSITY OF COLORADO AT BOULDER

Department of Theatre and Dance
Theatre Division
261 UCB
Boulder, CO 80309–0261

Phone: (303) 492-7355
Website: colorado.edu/theatredance/theatre
Email: thtrdnce@colorado.edu

Tuition: $$$$
Campus student enrollment: 30,789 total graduate and undergraduate

Degree(s): BA, BFA
Concentrations: Design technology and management, performance, musical theater, and theater
Courses offered: Acting, foundations, history and development of theater, costume technologies, lighting, production practicums, makeup design, illustration and rendering, audition techniques, voice and movement for the stage, musical theater repertory, sound design, professional orientation
Audition requirement: No, for BA applicants; yes for musical theater BFA

Scholarships available: Yes,
Number of faculty: 10 tenure-track professors and 4 full-time instructors
Number of majors and minors: 150 majors, 38 minors
Percentage of applicants accepted into the department per year: 100%
Department activities: During the academic year, THDN produces an average of 20 complete productions: theater (13) and dance concerts (7). In addition to approximately 100 departmental performances a year, students are involved in events are produced by Colorado Shakespeare Festival, OnStage (the student performing arts group), CU Dance Connection, Performers without Borders, Senior Showcase (an audition preparation trip to New York or Los Angeles), various improvisation troupes and a cappella choirs.

UNIVERSITY OF HAWAII AT MANOA

Department of Theatre and Dance
1770 East-West Road
Honolulu, HI 96822

Phone: (808) 956-7677
Website: manoa.hawaii.edu/liveonstage/
Email: theatre@hawaii.edu

Tuition: $$$
Campus student enrollment (undergraduate): 14,126

Degree(s): BA
Concentrations: Theater
Audition/portfolio requirement: No
Scholarships available: No
Number of faculty: 17
Number of majors and minors: 50 majors, 15 minors

Prominent Alumni:
Stan Egi
Georgia Engel

Randall Duk Kim
John Phillip Law
Bette Midler

UNIVERSITY OF TEXAS AT AUSTIN

Department of Theatre and Dance
300 E. 23rd Street
Austin, TX 78705

Phone: (512) 471-5793
Website: theatredance.utexas.edu/undergrads
Email: inquiry@mail.utexas.edu

Tuition: $$
Campus student enrollment (undergraduate):
39,619

Degree(s): BA theater and dance, BFA theater studies (teaching), BFA dance, BFA acting
Concentrations: BA in theater and dance with the following focus tracks: music theater, performance, media and design/technology, dance; BFA acting; BFA theater education; BFA dance
Audition/portfolio requirement: Yes
Scholarships available: Yes. Generous scholarships available for BFA acting, BFA dance, and BA music theater track; some limited scholarships for other BA students during matriculation
Number of faculty: More than 50
Number of majors and minors: 400 majors
Percentage and number of applicants accepted into the department per year: 41.6% in theater education; 30% in dance; 10% in acting
Department Activities: Six mainstage productions a year (including Dance Repertory Theatre, department's dance company, and theater performances), New Works Festival every other year.

Prominent Alumni:
Marcia Gay Harden
Tommy Tune
Robert Schenkkhan

UNIVERSITY OF SOUTHERN CALIFORNIA

School of Dramatic Arts
1029 Childs Way
Los Angeles, CA 90089–0791

Phone: (213) 821-2744
Website: dramaticarts.usc.edu
Email: admissions@sda.usc.edu

Tuition: $$$$
Campus student enrollment (undergraduate):
19,000

Degree(s): BA, BFA, MFA
Concentrations: Acting, design, sound design, technical production, and stage management
Audition/portfolio requirement: Yes for BFA, interview for BA
Scholarships available: Yes. A number of merit-based scholarships up to full tuition are available from the university, and a number of talent-based scholarships are available from the department for second-year and graduate students.
Number of faculty: 64
Department activities: Approximately 20 productions per year.

Prominent Alumni:
Forrest Whitaker
LeVar Burton
Swoosie Kurtz,
Danny Strong
Patrick Adams
Troian Bellisario
James Lesure
Todd Black
Deborah Ann Woll

WILLAMETTE UNIVERSITY

Department of Theatre
900 State Street
Salem, OR 97301

Phone: (503) 370-6222
Website: willamette.edu/cla/theatre/
Email: theatre-info@willamette.edu

Tuition: $$$
Campus student enrollment: 1,901

Degree(s): BA
Concentrations: Acting; Design; Stage Management; Performance Studies.
Audition/portfolio requirement: No for admission, yes for scholarship consideration
Scholarships available: Yes, with interview and/or audition; average scholarship varies from $2,000 to $5,000.
Number of faculty: 6 full-time; 3 adjunct
Number of majors and minors: 31 majors; 12 minors
Percentage and number of applicants accepted into the department per year: 6 to 10 applicants accepted each year
Department activities: Four mainstage theater productions, one dance concert, an opera coproduced with the department of music, and one solo performance.

WHITMAN COLLEGE

Theatre Department
Harper Joy Theatre
345 Boyer Avenue
Walla Walla, WA 99362

Phone: (509) 527-5279
Website: whitman.edu/academics/departments -and-programs/theatre-and-dance/dance
Email: admission@whitman.edu

Tuition: $$$
Campus student enrollment: 1,500

Degree(s): BA
Concentration: Theatre
Audition/portfolio requirement: No

Scholarships available: Yes. The President's Scholarship in Theatre is a talent-based award based on the audition and portfolio. Winners receive a four-year renewable scholarship covering their full computed financial need, from $2,500 to $55,000.
Number of faculty: 6
Number of majors and minors: 22
Percentage and number of applicants accepted into the department per year: 100% seeking admission to the department; 50% seeking admission to the college
Department activities: Whitman produces eight major productions each year. Any student, regardless of major, may participate in the theater productions.

Prominent Alumni:
Kaliswa Brewster (2005)—actor
Christa Scott-Reed (1994)—actor
Dan Donohue (1988)—actor
Patrick Page (1985)—actor
Dirk Benedict (1967)—actor
Adam "Batman" West (1951)—actor
John Moe (1990)—humorist/broadcaster
Nagle Jackson (1958)—director/playwright

Drama Programs by State

Programs with an asterisk (*) are accredited by the National Association of Schools of Theatre.

ALABAMA
Alabama State University*
Athens State University
Auburn University*
Birmingham–Southern College
Huntingdon College
Jacksonville State University*
Judson College
Samford University*
Spring Hill College
Stillman College
University of Alabama*
University of Alabama at
   Birmingham*
University of Mobile
University of Montevallo
University of South Alabama

ALASKA
University of Alaska Anchorage
University of Alaska Fairbanks

ARIZONA
Arizona State University
Grand Canyon University
Northern Arizona University
University of Arizona*

ARKANSAS
Arkansas State University*
Arkansas Tech University
Harding University
Henderson State University
Hendrix College
John Brown University
Lyon College
Ouachita Baptist University

Southern Arkansas University
University of Arkansas
University of Arkansas at Little
   Rock*
University of Arkansas at Pine Bluff
University of Central Arkansas*
University of the Ozarks

CALIFORNIA
American Academy of Dramatic
   Arts, Hollywood*
American Conservatory Theater
American Film Institute
   Conservatory
American Musical and Dramatic
   Academy, Los Angeles*
Azusa Pacific University
Biola University
California Institute of the Arts*
California Lutheran University
California State Polytechnic
   University, Pomona
California State University,
   Bakersfield
California State University, Chico*
California State University,
   Dominguez Hills*
California State University, Fresno*
California State University,
   Fullerton*
California State University,
   Hayward
California State University, Long
   Beach*
California State University, Los
   Angeles
California State University,
   Monterey Bay
California State University,
   Northridge*
California State University,
   Sacramento*
California State University, San
   Bernardino*

California State University, San
   Marcos
California State University,
   Stanislaus*
Chapman University*
Claremont McKenna College
Columbia College Hollywood
Concordia University
Dell'Arte International School of
   Physical Theatre*
Design Institute of San Diego
Fresno Pacific University
Humboldt State University
Loyola Marymount University*
Notre Dame de Namur University
Occidental College
Pacific Union College
Pepperdine University
Pitzer College
Point Loma Nazarene University
Pomona College
Saint Mary's College of California
San Diego State University*
San Francisco State University*
San Jose State University*
Santa Clara University
Scripps College
Sonoma State University
Stanford University
University of California, Berkeley
University of California, Davis
University of California, Irvine
University of California, Los
   Angeles*
University of California, Riverside
University of California, San Diego
University of California, Santa
   Barbara
University of California, Santa Cruz
University of La Verne
University of the Pacific
University of Redlands
University of San Diego
University of San Francisco

University of Southern California
Vanguard University of Southern
    California*
Westmont College

COLORADO
Adams State University
Colorado Christian University
Colorado College
Colorado Mesa University
Colorado State University
Fort Lewis College
Metropolitan State University of
    Denver*
Naropa University
University of Colorado at Boulder
University of Colorado Denver
University of Denver
University of Northern Colorado*

CONNECTICUT
Albertus Magnus College
Central Connecticut State
    University
Connecticut College
Eastern Connecticut State
    University
Fairfield University
The Hartt School/University of
    Hartford*
Sacred Heart University
Southern Connecticut State
    University
Trinity College
University of Bridgeport
University of Connecticut
University of New Haven
Wesleyan University
Western Connecticut State
    University
Yale University

DELAWARE
Delaware State University
University of Delaware

DISTRICT OF COLUMBIA
American University
Catholic University of America
Gallaudet University
Georgetown University
Howard University*
University of the District of Columbia

FLORIDA
Barry University
Bethune-Cookman University
Eckerd College
Flagler College
Florida A&M University
Florida Atlantic University
Florida International University*
Florida Southern College
Florida State University*
Jacksonville University
New World School of the Arts*
Palm Beach Atlantic University
Rollins College
Stetson University
University of Central Florida*
University of Florida*
University of Miami
University of North Florida
University of South Florida*
University of Tampa
University of West Florida

GEORGIA
Agnes Scott College
Armstrong Atlantic State University
Berry College
Brenau University
Brewton–Parker College
Clark Atlanta University
Clayton College and State
    University

Columbus State University*
Emory University
Georgia College & State
    University
Georgia Southern University*
Georgia Southwestern State
    University
Georgia State University
Kennesaw State University*
LaGrange College
Mercer University
Morehouse College
Oglethorpe University
Paine College
Piedmont College
Reinhardt University
Savannah College of Art and Design
Shorter University
Spelman College
State University of West Georgia
University of Georgia*
University of West Georgia*
Valdosta State University*

HAWAII
University of Hawaii at Hilo
University of Hawaii at Manoa

IDAHO
The College of Idaho
Boise State University*
Brigham Young University–Idaho
Idaho State University*
University of Idaho

ILLINOIS
Augustana College
Benedictine University
Bradley University*
Columbia College Chicago
DePaul University
Dominican University
Eastern Illinois University*
Elmhurst College

Eureka College
Greenville College
Illinois State University*
Illinois Wesleyan University
Judson College
Knox College
Lewis University
Loyola University Chicago*
MacMurray College
McKendree College
Millikin University
National-Louis University
North Central College
North Park University
Northeastern Illinois University
Northern Illinois University*
Northwestern University
Principia College
Quincy University
Robert Morris University
Rockford College
Roosevelt University
Southern Illinois University
   Carbondale*
Southern Illinois University
   Edwardsville*
University of Chicago
University of Illinois at Chicago
University of Illinois at Urbana-
   Champaign
Western Illinois University*

INDIANA

Anderson University
Ball State University*
Bethel College
Butler University*
DePauw University
Earlham College
Goshen College
Hanover College
Huntington University
Indiana State University
Indiana University Bloomington*

Indiana University Northwest
Indiana University–Purdue
   University Fort Wayne*
Indiana University–Purdue
   University Indianapolis
Indiana University South Bend
Indiana University Southeast
Indiana Wesleyan University
Purdue University*
Saint Mary-of-the-Woods College
Saint Mary's College
Taylor University
University of Evansville
University of Indianapolis
University of Notre Dame
University of Southern Indiana
Valparaiso University
Vincennes University*
Wabash College

IOWA

Briar Cliff University
Buena Vista University
Central College
Clarke University
Coe College
Cornell College
Dordt College
Drake University
Graceland University
Grand View University
Grinnell College
Iowa State University
Loras College
Luther College
Morningside College
Mount Mercy University
Northwestern College
St, Ambrose University
Simpson College
University of Iowa*
University of Northern Iowa*
Waldorf University
Wartburg College

KANSAS

Baker University
Benedictine College
Bethel College
Emporia State University
Fort Hays State University
Friends University
Kansas State University*
Kansas Wesleyan University
McPherson College
Ottawa University
Pittsburg State University
Southwestern College
Sterling College
Tabor College
University of Kansas
University of Saint Mary
Washburn University
Wichita State University

KENTUCKY

Berea College
Campbellsville University
Centre College
Eastern Kentucky University
Georgetown College
Morehead State University*
Murray State University*
Northern Kentucky University
Thomas More College
Transylvania University
University of the Cumberlands
University of Kentucky*
University of Louisville*
Western Kentucky University*

LOUISIANA

Centenary College of Louisiana
Dillard University
Grambling State University*
Louisiana College
Louisiana State University*
Loyola University New Orleans
McNeese State University

Northwestern State University of
Louisiana*
Southern University and A&M
College
Tulane University
University of New Orleans*

MAINE

Bates College
Bowdoin College
Colby College
University of Maine at Farmington
University of Maine
University of Southern Maine

MARYLAND

Frostburg State University
Goucher College
McDaniel College
Morgan State University
Mount St. Mary's University
Salisbury University
St. Mary's College of Maryland
Towson University*
University of Maryland, Baltimore
County
University of Maryland, College
Park
University of Maryland Eastern
Shore
Washington College

MASSACHUSETTS

Amherst College
Bard College at Simon's Rock
Boston College
The Boston Conservatory at
Berklee
Boston University
Brandeis University
Bridgewater State College
Clark University
College of the Holy Cross*
Emerson College

Fitchburg State College
Hampshire College
Mount Holyoke College
Northeastern University
Regis College
Salem State University*
Smith College
Suffolk University
University of Massachusetts
Amherst
University of Massachusetts Boston
Wellesley College
Westfield State College
Wheaton College
Wheelock College
Williams College

MICHIGAN

Adrian College
Albion College
Alma College
Calvin College
Central Michigan University
Eastern Michigan University
Grand Valley State University
Hillsdale College
Hope College*
Kalamazoo College
Michigan State University
Northern Michigan University
Oakland University*
Olivet College
Saginaw Valley State University
Siena Heights University
University of Detroit Mercy
University of Michigan, Ann Arbor
University of Michigan-Flint
Wayne State University*
Western Michigan University*

MINNESOTA

Augsburg College
Bemidji State University
Bethany Lutheran College

Bethel University
College of Saint Benedict and
Saint John's University
Concordia College, Moorhead
Concordia University, St Paul
Gustavus Adolphus College
Hamline University
Macalester College
Metropolitan State University
Minnesota State University,
Mankato
Minnesota State University,
Moorhead
North Central University
Northwestern College
St. Catherine University
Saint Cloud State University*
Saint Mary's University of
Minnesota
St. Olaf College*
Southwest Minnesota State
University
University of Minnesota, Duluth
University of Minnesota, Morris
University of Minnesota Twin
Cities*
University of St. Thomas
Winona State University*

MISSISSIPPI

Belhaven University*
Jackson State University
Millsaps College
Mississippi College
Mississippi University for Women
University of Mississippi*
University of Southern Mississippi*
William Carey College

MISSOURI

Avila University
Central Methodist University
College of the Ozarks
Culver-Stockton College

Drury University
Evangel University
Fontbonne University
Hannibal-LaGrange University
Lindenwood University
Missouri Southern State University
Missouri State University*
Missouri Valley College
Northwest Missouri State
   University
Rockhurst University
Saint Louis University
Southeast Missouri State
   University*
Southwest Baptist University
Stephens College
Truman State University
University of Central Missouri*
University of Missouri
University of Missouri–Kansas City*
University of Missouri–St. Louis
Washington University in St Louis
Webster University
William Jewell College
William Woods University

MONTANA
Carroll College
Montana State University Billings
Montana State University
Rocky Mountain College
University of Montana, Missoula*
University of Montana Western

NEBRASKA
Chadron State College
Concordia University
Creighton University
Doane University
Hastings College
Midland University
Nebraska Wesleyan University
University of Nebraska–Lincoln*
University of Nebraska at Kearney

University of Nebraska Omaha
Wayne State College

NEVADA
University of Nevada, Las Vegas*
University of Nevada, Reno

NEW HAMPSHIRE
Colby-Sawyer College
Dartmouth College
Franklin Pierce University
Keene State College
Plymouth State University
University of New Hampshire

NEW JERSEY
Bloomfield College
Caldwell College
Centenary University
Drew University
Fairleigh Dickinson University
Kean University*
Montclair State University*
New Jersey City University
Ramapo College of New Jersey
Rider University
Rowan University*
Rutgers University–Camden
Rutgers University–New Brunswick
Rutgers University–Newark
Thomas Edison State University

NEW MEXICO
Eastern New Mexico University
New Mexico State University
Santa Fe University of Art and Design
University of New Mexico*
University of the Southwest

NEW YORK
Adelphi University
Alfred University
American Academy of Dramatic
   Arts, New York*

American Musical and Dramatic
   Academy, New York*
Bard College
Barnard College
City College of New York
Colgate University
College of Staten Island
Columbia University
CUNY, Brooklyn College
Elmira College
Five Towns College
Fordham University
Hamilton College
Hartwick College
Hobart and William Smith
   Colleges
Hofstra University
Hunter College
Iona College
Ithaca College*
Juilliard School
Lehman College
Long Island University, Brooklyn
Long Island University, CW Post
   Campus
Manhattanville College
Marist College
Marymount Manhattan College
Mercy College
Molloy College
Nazareth College
Neighborhood Playhouse School
   of the Theatre*
New York Conservatory for
   Dramatic Arts
New School University
New York University
Niagara University
Pace University
Queens College, City University of
   New York
Sage Colleges
Sarah Lawrence College
Skidmore College

St. Lawrence University
Stella Adler Studio of Acting*
SUNY at Albany
SUNY at Binghamton
SUNY Buffalo State College*
SUNY at Buffalo
SUNY College at Brockport*
SUNY at Fredonia*
SUNY at Geneseo
SUNY at New Paltz*
SUNY at Potsdam*
SUNY at Stony BrookSUNY at Old
    Westbury
SUNY at Oneonta*
SUNY at Oswego*
SUNY at Plattsburgh
SUNY Purchase College
Syracuse University
Vassar College
Wagner College
Wells College
York College, City University of
    New York

NORTH CAROLINA

Appalachian State University*
Barton College
Brevard College
Campbell University
Catawba College
Chowan University
Davidson College
Duke University
East Carolina University*
Elon University
Fayetteville State University
Gardner-Webb University
Greensboro College
Guilford College
High Point University
Lees-McRae College*
Lenoir-Rhyne University
Livingstone College
Mars Hill University*

Meredith College
Methodist College
North Carolina A&T State
    University*
North Carolina Central University*
Pfeiffer University
Queens University of Charlotte
Saint Augustine's University
Salem College
Shaw University
University of North Carolina at
    Asheville
University of North Carolina at
    Chapel Hill
University of North Carolina at
    Charlotte
University of North Carolina at
    Greensboro*
University of North Carolina at
    Pembroke
University of North Carolina
    School of the Arts
University of North Carolina at
    Wilmington
Wake Forest University
Western Carolina University*
Winston-Salem State University

NORTH DAKOTA

Dickinson State University
Minot State University
North Dakota State University*
Trinity Bible College
University of Jamestown
University of North Dakota*

OHIO

Antioch College
Ashland University
Bowling Green State University*
Capital University
Case Western Reserve University
Cedarville University
College of Wooster

Denison University
Heidelberg University
Hiram College
Kent State University*
Kenyon College
Lake Erie College
Malone College
Marietta College
Miami University*
Mount Vernon Nazarene
    University
Muskingum University
Oberlin College
Ohio Northern University
Ohio State University*
Ohio University*
Ohio Wesleyan University
Otterbein University*
University of Akron
University of Cincinnati*
University of Dayton
University of Findlay
University of Mount Union
University of Toledo
Wittenberg University
Wright State University
Youngstown State University*
Xavier University

OKLAHOMA

Cameron University
East Central University
Northeastern State University
Northwestern Oklahoma State
    University
Oklahoma Baptist University
Oklahoma Christian University
Oklahoma City University
Oklahoma State University*
Oral Roberts University
St. Gregory's University
Southeastern Oklahoma State
    University
University of Central Oklahoma

University of Oklahoma*
University of Science and Arts of
  Oklahoma
University of Tulsa

OREGON
Eastern Oregon University
George Fox University
Lewis & Clark College
Linfield College
Pacific University
Portland State University*
Reed College
Southern Oregon University
University of Oregon
University of Portland*
Western Oregon University
Willamette University

PENNSYLVANIA
Albright College
Allegheny College
Arcadia University
Bloomsburg University of
  Pennsylvania*
Bucknell University
California University of
  Pennsylvania*
Carnegie Mellon University
Cedar Crest College
Chatham College
Chestnut Hill College
Cheyney University of
  Pennsylvania
Clarion University of Pennsylvania
DeSales University
Dickinson College
Drexel University
Duquesne University
East Stroudsburg University of
  Pennsylvania
Edinboro University of
  Pennsylvania
Elizabethtown College

Franklin & Marshall College
Gannon University
Geneva College
Gettysburg College
Grove City College
Indiana University of Pennsylvania*
King's College
Kutztown University of Pennsylvania
Lehigh University*
Lock Haven University of
  Pennsylvania
Lycoming College
Mansfield University of Pennsylvania
Marywood University
Messiah College*
Moravian College
Muhlenberg College
Pennsylvania State University*
Pennsylvania State University, Penn
  State Abington
Pennsylvania State University, Penn
  State Altoona
Point Park University
Saint Vincent College
Seton Hill University
Slippery Rock University of
  Pennsylvania*
Susquehanna University
Swarthmore College
Temple University*
The University of the Arts
University of Pennsylvania
University of Pittsburgh*
University of Scranton
Washington & Jefferson College
West Chester University of
  Pennsylvania*
Westminster College
Wilkes University
York College Pennsylvania

RHODE ISLAND
Brown University
Providence College

Rhode Island College
Roger Williams University
Salve Regina University
University of Rhode Island

SOUTH CAROLINA
Anderson University
Charleston Southern University
Coastal Carolina University*
Coker College
College of Charleston*
Converse College
Francis Marion University*
Furman University
Lander University
Limestone College
Newberry College
North Greenville College
Presbyterian College
South Carolina State University
University of South Carolina*
Winthrop University*
Wofford College

SOUTH DAKOTA
Augustana College
Dakota Wesleyan University
University of Sioux Falls
University of South Dakota*

TENNESSEE
Belmont University*
Cumberland University
East Tennessee State University*
Fisk University
Freed–Hardeman University
Lipscomb University
Maryville College
Middle Tennessee State University*
Rhodes College
Sewanee: The University of the
  South
Tennessee State University
Union University

University of Memphis*
The University of Memphis
  Lambuth Campus
University of Tennessee at
  Chattanooga*
University of Tennessee, Knoxville*
University of Tennessee at Martin
Vanderbilt University

TEXAS

Abilene Christian University
Baylor University*
Del Mar College*
East Texas Baptist University
Hardin–Simmons University
KD College Conservatory of Film
  and Dramatic Arts*
Lamar University
McMurry University
Midwestern State University*
Our Lady of the Lake University
Prairie View A&M University
Sam Houston State University
Schreiner University
Southern Methodist University*
Southwestern University
Stephen F. Austin State University*
Sul Ross State University
Tarleton State University
Texas A&M University
Texas A&M University–Commerce
Texas A&M University–Corpus
  Christi
Texas A&M University–Kingsville
Texas Christian University
Texas Lutheran University
Texas Southern University
Texas State University
Texas Tech University*
Texas Wesleyan University
Texas Woman's University
University of Dallas
University of Houston
University of Mary Hardin–Baylor

University of North Texas
University of St. Thomas
University of Texas at Arlington
University of Texas at Austin
University of Texas at El Paso
University of Texas at Tyler
University of Texas–Pan American*
University of the Incarnate Word*
Wayland Baptist University
West Texas A&M University*

UTAH

Brigham Young University*
Southern Utah University
University of Utah
Utah State University
Weber State University

VERMONT

Bennington College
Castleton State College
Johnson State College
Marlboro College
Middlebury College
Norwich University
Saint Michael's College
University of Vermont

VIRGINIA

Averett University
Bluefield College
Bridgewater College
Christopher Newport University*
College of William & Mary
Eastern Mennonite University
Emory and Henry College
Ferrum College
George Mason University
Hampton University
Hollins University
James Madison University*
Longwood University*
Lynchburg College
Mary Baldwin University

Old Dominion University*
Radford University*
Randolph College
Randolph-Macon College
Regent University
Roanoke College
Shenandoah University
Sweet Briar College
University of Richmond
University of Virginia*
University of Virginia's College at
  Wise
Virginia Commonwealth
  University*
Virginia Tech*
Virginia Union University
Virginia Wesleyan College
Washington and Lee University

WASHINGTON

Central Washington University
Cornish College of the Arts
Eastern Washington University
Gonzaga University
Pacific Lutheran University
Saint Martin's College
Seattle Pacific University
Seattle University
University of Puget Sound
University of Washington
Washington State University
Western Washington University
Whitman College
Whitworth College

WEST VIRGINIA

Alderson Broaddus University
Bethany College
Concord University
Davis & Elkins College*
Fairmont State University
West Virginia University*
West Virginia Wesleyan College

WISCONSIN

Beloit College

Cardinal Stritch University

Carroll University

Carthage College

Lawrence University

Marquette University*

Ripon College

University of Wisconsin–Eau Claire

University of Wisconsin–Green
   Bay

University of Wisconsin–La Crosse

University of Wisconsin–Madison*

University of Wisconsin–
   Milwaukee

University of Wisconsin–Oshkosh

University of Wisconsin–Parkside

University of Wisconsin–Platteville

University of Wisconsin–River Falls

University of Wisconsin–Stevens
   Point*

University of Wisconsin–Superior

University of Wisconsin–
   Whitewater*

Viterbo University

Wisconsin Lutheran College

WYOMING

University of Wyoming

Colleges for Artists and Designers

a s an artist or a designer, you are probably used to finding inspiration through your medium. Perhaps you are most moved with a paintbrush, charcoal, or pencil in hand, looking through the eye of a camera, or shaping glass or ceramics. It makes sense then that you want to find a college that can help you develop your artistic abilities. You'll want to find a school with a faculty that can guide and inspire you, adequate facilities, and the opportunities to share your work.

Art students will find that they have numerous and varied choices in college selection—almost every college and university in the United States has an art department! So the choice is up to you: a professional art school, a liberal arts college, a small university, or a large university could offer the art program of your dreams. When you begin the college search process, you may know that you want to study art, but you might not know which kind of art appeals to you most. On the other hand, you may know exactly what kind of art you want to focus on and the kind artist you want to become.

Identifying the Type of Art Student You Are

Early in the college search, it's important to identify which type of art student you are: the art student who still wants to explore art forms before choosing one or two for mastery; or the art student who has chosen a specific focus already.

If you are the "exploring student," you have the widest options available—you can choose almost any art department and take several courses in different art forms, since your college goal is to explore art in general. As you progress in your studies, you will begin to narrow down which types of art are the best for you to pursue in depth.

Suppose that you already have experience with different art courses in high school and in extracurricular courses, and you have decided that you have an affinity for sculpture. As a "focused student," you need to structure your college search process slightly differently. You will have to dig a little deeper in your research and do more investigating among faculty members and admissions officers at prospective schools. You want to be certain the programs you are considering offer enough courses in your area. It's also important to find a program at the level of intense study you need to become a certain type of artist.

If you know you want to be a painter, find out how many faculty members teach painting and how many levels of painting courses are offered. Also research the *kinds* of painting courses offered. Watercolor? Acrylic? Both? If your goal is to become a painter, you will need to have a breadth of courses in all painting forms with multiple painting classes rather than a college that only offers one or two.

SHEA
UNIVERSITY OF THE ARTS, SENIOR

Shea was studying film at the University of Southern California when he realized that living in Los Angeles was overwhelming him. Feeling a strong pull to return to his hometown of Philadelphia, Shea googled *photography* and *Philadelphia.* What he found pleased him—there was a photography program right there in Philly. He could return home and continue his education by earning a BFA degree at the University of the Arts.

Why the switch from film to photography? Shea had discovered that he wanted to be a creative director. "With film, there are so many people involved before getting to the finished product," he says. "With photography, you can be the creative director right away since it's just you—the photographer—creating the work."

As with most college art programs, photography has a foundation year. Shea didn't take any photography courses during the first year of art school. Instead, he enrolled in all types of other courses to get the basics down. During his sophomore year, 90 percent of his classes were photography related.

By senior year, "the ball is in your court," asserts Shea. "The entire senior year is getting you ready to walk out the door to get a job."

Hot Tips from Shea

➜ You have to love what you are getting into.

➜ If you transfer, keep in mind that many credits may not transfer to your new program, which may keep you in school longer and will cost more.

➜ Tuition is costly—if you get a scholarship, consider that institution more seriously.

➜ Make sure you are getting what you are paying for in a program.

➜ Do some serious soul searching to find out what you really want to study before choosing a college.

➜ The cost of attendance is never as cheap as it looks in the acceptance letter—you always have to factor in tuition increases from year to year and extra money for living expenses such as books, clothes, art supplies and recreation.

Shea already had a head start on his photography portfolio that he will use when he looks for employment. When he started volunteering for the National Democratic Committee for the Kerry-Edwards campaign in 2004, the press secretary at the Philadelphia headquarters asked him to do photography for them. His assignments included taking photographs of John Kerry's arrival at the airport, the University of Pennsylvania rally of 40,000 people, and a gathering at an African American church in inner-city Philadelphia.

Last summer, Shea took his skills abroad, becoming a teacher's assistant in the photography program at Cavendish College at the University of London.

"I seem to have done a good job, because they asked me to come back for another summer session," he remarks.

After graduation, Shea would like to specialize in travel photography. "Ideally, I'd like to work for nongovernmental organizations, go to remote areas of the world, and make a difference with my photography. This doesn't pay well, so I'll have to balance that with doing freelance work for magazines."

Types of Art Programs

The most common art degree offered by a professional art school—as well as several colleges and universities—is the BFA. This degree is designed to prepare you to become a professional artist. Approximately three-quarters of your studies will be in art courses, and the remainder will consist of general education requirements.

The BA is most often offered at liberal arts colleges and small universities. The BA is more flexible in terms of courses taken outside of art and usually has more emphasis on art history and art criticism than professional art school courses. The BA can be a good choice if you are not sure you want to be a professional artist one day but still want to consider the possibility while exploring other academic options.

Pursuing a BA usually requires about thirty to forty credits of courses in the art major, and the rest of the coursework is for general education requirements and electives. Double majoring in another field is feasible if you elect to attend a liberal arts college or university and enter a BA program.

Art Program Philosophy

Art programs each have their own approach to teaching art. Some schools are more traditional and focus on the basics in a very structured way, from beginning-level courses to advanced courses. Other schools can be more experimental. One of these is California Institute of the Arts, where students are encouraged to do more exploratory art, push boundaries of their artmaking, and combine art forms.

Because every program is different, it is crucial that you investigate the philosophy of each art program you are contemplating. If you are the kind of student who prefers more structure or who knows that you want to be an art teacher, you'll need a more traditional art program to prepare you for that career. Also, happiness is a key element. When talking to faculty members, compare your art philosophy with theirs. If your expectations mesh with theirs, you'll probably be happy on that campus. But if you find yourself thinking differently, you'd probably be happier elsewhere, and you should continue your search.

Concentrations in Art Degrees

While most students know that they can concentrate in painting or ceramics, there are many more options for college study. Here is an overview of the variety of art forms you can take at the college level:

* Animation
* Art Education
* Art History
* Art Therapy

* Architecture
* Ceramics
* Drawing
* Electronic Media (Web Design)
* Fashion Design
* Fine Arts
* Glass
* Graphic Design
* Illustration

* Industrial Design (such as furniture design, toy design)
* Interior Design
* Jewelry
* Metalsmithing
* Painting
* Photography
* Printmaking
* Sculpture

The Freshman "Foundation" Year

Many prospective college art students don't realize that the freshman year of an art program is different from the traditional freshman year at a college or university. Typically, freshmen majoring in other fields take general education requirements and perhaps one or two introductory courses in their intended major. For the most part, art students are not required to take several general education requirements like math or English composition. Instead, they take a variety of introductory courses in several art forms. This is commonly referred to as the freshman "foundation" year because these courses are designed to provide a common artistic foundation for all the art students in the program. The goal of the foundation year is to ensure that each art student has learned the basics of artmaking so that they can advance their skills and nurture their talent in the remaining three years of higher education.

Sample Coursework for a First Year in Art School

Many art programs require a "foundation year" before a specific art major is selected. Here is an example of a course plan for a first-year art student. This example is from the Rhode Island School of Design (RISD); their first year is known as Experimental and Foundation Studies (EFS). One of the first of its kind, RISD's Experimental and Foundation Studies program began in 1940. It provided a new approach to art education and has since been widely adopted at other colleges of art and design. All first-year students follow the same course of study before they move on to specific art majors as sophomores.

First-year studios

FALL

Drawing I

Design I

Spatial Dyanmics I

WINTER

Non-major studio elective

SPRING

Drawing II

Design II

Spatial Dynamics II

THOMAS LAWSON
DEAN OF THE SCHOOL OF ART CALIFORNIA INSTITUTE OF THE ARTS

What do art schools look for when reviewing prospective student portfolios?
Thomas Lawson, dean of the School of Art at the California Institute of the Arts, states that students have to demonstrate some kind of initiative.

"When we review portfolios, we look for [students'] own work, not so much class work," Lawson explains. "This means that we want to see what students have been doing on their own—their own imaginative work outside of high school classes." Some art programs are more specific than others in what they want to see in a portfolio. At a school like CalArts, which considers itself an experimental environment for artists, ingenuity is key.

"We are not looking for a figure drawing," says Lawson. "We encourage students to experiment in mixed genres—they are young and should be experimenting."

Lawson acknowledges that a lot of parents have some apprehension about supporting their student in their desire to study art in college. "Parents worry about it, but students shouldn't," he says. "Students need to come to terms with it."

The purpose of studying art in college, according to Lawson, is to explore four years of artmaking with the possibility of becoming a professional.

"If students want to teach at a high-school level, there are different skills you need to master, but to be an artist, you need ideas," he says.

A student really needs to know early in the college admissions process whether their ultimate goal is to become a professional artist or to use their skills to teach art in an educational setting. This decision becomes crucial in evaluating different kinds of art programs.

"More traditional art programs, rather than experimental, would be better for students considering teaching art as a career," concludes Lawson.

Expert Tips from Dean Lawson

→ Investigate the priorities of the art school, whether the curriculum is more traditional or more experimental.

→ If your priorities are to spend four years artmaking and exploring art, and you are considering the possibility of becoming a professional artist, an experimental program might be the right fit. But if you feel like you might want to be an art teacher, a more traditional art program would probably be a better fit.

KATERINA
LONG ISLAND UNIVERSITY CW POST CAMPUS

A native of Long Island, Katerina is pursuing a BFA in digital arts and design. Her curriculum includes publishing, Web design, two-dimensional art, and some classes in three-dimensional graphics such as animation.

Katerina asserts that everyone who arrives at art school has come from a different background. "Some students are really well prepared and had advanced-level art classes in high school. Others have only the limited experience of taking a couple of art classes," she explains.

Katerina didn't have to prepare an artistic portfolio for acceptance to her program, but she did so to be considered for a scholarship.

In preparing an artistic portfolio for admissions, Katerina recommends including no more than fifteen pieces. "You don't want to overwhelm the people reviewing your work," she says. "You should also have a mix of samples that shows the breadth of your artistic ability."

"Wherever you go to school, you get out of it what you put into it," Katerina warns. "You have to do a lot of things on your own—you have to go out of your way to make your assignments exceptional."

In comparing art to other disciplines, Katerina says that a lot of students outside the department—and even some art students—have a perception that studying art is easy. But Katerina will tell you this is not the case at all, that art is a lot more work than it might seem. "You are creating a perfect picture, and this could take many more hours than it seems to a person who glances at the finished product. You never know how long it is going to take to make it perfect," she says.

Katerina stresses that the level of commitment you have to improving your art in college is more important than the school you attend. "If you work hard from beginning to end, it doesn't really matter what kind of art school you went to," she explains. "When you are looking for jobs when you finish your degree, it's your portfolio that matters."

Graphic Design Programs

Graphic design programs may have many names. They could be visual design, communications design, or graphic design. Programs that have a heavier emphasis on technology may be called digital arts, digital design, interactive design, or multimedia design. No matter the name of the degree, most graphic design programs use technology in their programs because the profession has evolved, and the silos separating what used to be just print media and electronic media have merged. "Learning to use digital technology is more and more often combined in classes that explore and incorporate the precepts of good design," says Kathleen Creighton, chair of Communication Design at the Pratt Institute. "Design education differs a bit from courses a student might have taken ten years ago primarily in the increasingly interdisciplinary nature of study. There are fewer silos in the profession, and as time passes even those that remain will lessen. To be most effective, and successful, today's designers create and design across disciplines and express their ideas and visualize solutions across media platforms."

Sample Course Descriptions for Graphic Design Programs

Here are some examples of course descriptions in the graphic design BFA at the Rhode Island School of Design to show how design for both print and digital media are part of their program (which is similar to most design programs).

Identity Design

Branding—or the development of an identity and an identity system—is a critical skill for today's designers. Before we can design a brochure or a website or an interface, there must be an identity to frame and influence the medium. Branding as a discipline not only requires the ability to design logos, but to think strategically about a company's ethos and mission. Having thought strategically about ethos or mission positions a designer not only to create an identity and identity system but to influence the way a company or organization conducts all of its communications.

In this course, students will create two identity systems: one for a traditional company and one for a socially constructive campaign. While a traditional identity system is defined as a logo and a set of rules for that logo's application, the goal of this class is to expand upon the ways a brand identity can be expressed through the manipulation of language, materials, and audience expectation/participation.

Graphic Design for the Web

Design is a crucial element in making a website that is accessible, exciting, and effective. This course will look at ways of using fundamental graphic design principles and site design tools necessary to create sites that are strategic, interactive, energetic, and visually imaginative. This course will also explore the rich history of designers, artists, and collectives that have used the Web as a medium in various ways—from Neen sites to Tumblrs to 4chan to Wordpress to Flickr, looking for interesting, novel, and alternative approaches to web design.

Interactive Text: Interactive Sound and Image Emphasis

Presented as fine art practice, this course will introduce the student to narrative and nonnarrative experimentation with language in digital space.

During the course students will be given a number of short-term assignments which will serve as explorations of common themes. Students will also propose a longer-term investigation, which will develop in the form of a semester-long project.

We will explore both analog and digital technologies to develop the concepts presented during the semester, utilizing Final Cut, After Effects, Illustrator, InDesign, Photoshop, Ableton Live, and/or other programs for the production of texts. The course will have an interactive sound and image emphasis. Students will experiment with interactive text, visuals, and audio composition in the digital realm, placing emphasis on the effect and meaning transformation that occurs when texts are combined with visuals and audio material.

The course will balance conceptual concerns related to content and structuring methodologies with artistic expression. Specific aesthetic histories will be explored tracing the use of text in artistic practice, including Concrete Poetry, the texts of Kurt Schwitters, Russian Constructivist posters, Fluxus poetic works, the Dada and Surrealist Word/Image, Magritte, Jenny Holzer, Ed Ruscha, Barbara Kruger, as well as other contemporary practitioners.

Motion Design

This course combines disciplines of graphic design, animation and filmmaking. Through a series of in-studio and multi-week projects, students will create a series of short animated movies that explore the dynamic structure and organization of typography, image, and sound, over time.

From storyboards to final production, students will exercise critical thinking and experimentation as well as develop professional animation and presentation skills.

Short weekly lectures will present historic and current works of influential designers, animators, and directors. Topics of discussion will include storytelling, visual systems, narrative structure, sound, and broadcast design.

Adobe After Effects will be the primary production tool for this class. Through the sequence of assignments, students will become fluent with the software. Students should have some basic After Effects experience and have Creative Cloud installed on their laptops.

Typography I

Typography, the physical shaping of language, resides at the center of the discipline of graphic design. Typography I is the first in a sequence of three courses that covers the fundamentals of typographic practice, both as a technical skill and an expressive medium. This course is an introduction to the basic principles of typography—its theory, practice, technology, and history—through the study of letterforms, page composition, proportion, hierarchy, and contrast.

Web Design

Designing for the Internet requires a solution that embraces the Web as a communication medium while providing for a unique user experience. The goal is to strike a balance between form and function, between visual design and effective communication. This course will cover the latest methods of web design, development, and production including standards-based XHTML, CSS, Javascript, and media integration. From beginners to those with more experience, students will learn the most current techniques for planning, designing, building, and testing a fully functional website start to finish.

Design for Publishing

This course will cover all aspects of designing comprehensive art and photographic books. We will examine the use of type in layouts, editing images, grids, scale, and pacing. Particular attention will be paid to certain elements of design production, including the visual, tactile, and aesthetic qualities of paper, printing, binding, color separation, and advanced techniques in reproduction, namely duotone and three-tone in black and white photography. In the first part of the semester, students will design the layout and the corresponding dust jacket for a photographic book. The material will include a number of original black and white photographs from one of the very well-known French photographers. In the second part of the semester, students will be given the choice between designing a book based on their own interests and completing a book design project using assigned material.

Editorial Design for the Screen

How can you draw on your foundations in graphic design to make reading experiences for the screen? What aspects of the craft translate, and what needs fresh exploration? This class covers basic HTML/CSS, wireframes, and flow diagrams, but it is not about "designing and coding a website." Students will learn to compose dynamic forms, tell engaging stories, and make meaning in digital environments. After experimenting with a series of form-led studies, the course turns to narrative design on screen. What are the components of a story? What are the needs and expectations of digital readers/viewers, and how can we design reading experiences that both serve and stir them? Where is the overlap between reader experience and user experience, between graphic design and product design? The semester's work not only engages the challenges that editorial web designers and digital storytellers in the industry face today, but asserts that designers should continue to rethink and re-assert their practice, whatever the future brings.

SAMPLE COURSES IN AN UNDERGRADUATE DESIGN CURRICULUM

Here are the names of the types of courses offered in a degree for graphic design, communication design, interactive design, or design and technology.

Alternative Design

Book Jacket Design and Beyond

Brand Identity and Branding

Communication Graphic Design

Creating a Subculture Using Screen Printing

Design for Social Change

Design Photo

Designing a Business

Designing a Phenomenon

Editorial Design

Experimental Book Art

Interaction Content Creation and Design

iPad, iPhone, App Design

Motion Graphics

Package It

Packaging Design: Appetite Appeal Food

Packaging

Platforms and Campaigns

Three-Dimensional Design

Toys and Games

Typographic Design

Visual Identity and Multimedia

Visual Literacy

Visual Storytelling: Autobiography through

Visual Language

Website Design

These course titles are offered from the School of Visual Arts.

TIPS ON CHOOSING A GRAPHIC OR DIGITAL ARTS DESIGN PROGRAM

Kathleen Creighton, chair of the Communication Design Department at the Pratt Institute, offers these tips on choosing a graphic design program.

Seek a program with a range of course offerings covering as many facets of communications messaging as possible. Besides the obvious, typography and graphic design courses, it would be important to include classes that cover interaction, motion, sound, information design, illustration, photography, and business. The best programs integrate these areas and have strong conceptual development at their core.

Consider the composition of the faculty—professionals who teach in addition to teaching professionals.

Seek programs that offer opportunities in experiential education, an extremely important component of a design education and one that provides many opportunities for additional field-related knowledge and experience, which is the most helpful in securing employment upon graduation.

The Artistic Portfolio

Whether you are an exploring art student or a focused art student, chances are that you will need to prepare an artistic portfolio as part of your college application. Each institution has different requirements in regard to the portfolio.

For professional art schools, the portfolio review is usually the first part of the admissions process. If your portfolio is not acceptable, your information will not be forwarded to the admissions office. At these schools, the portfolio review bears the most weight on whether or not you'll be accepted. This is because the purpose of a professional art school is to prepare you to become a professional artist, so the ability and creativity you present in the portfolio is of utmost importance. To accompany the portfolio, you may also be required to write an essay or an artist's statement that explains your reasons for wanting to become an artist and attend a particular art school.

In contrast, if you apply to a college or university as a prospective art major, the portfolio review process is secondary to other application components such as good grades, SAT scores, an admissions essay, and teacher recommendations.

Portfolio requirements vary by school, but in most cases, you'll need to show at least ten pieces of different art work in at least two different art forms. Additionally, each school has specific requirements on how to submit work for review. Usually, you will have to submit your portfolio digitally, but some programs still accept mailed portfolios. Few schools require on-campus portfolio reviews, but you may want to request one in conjunction with a campus visit.

It's important to follow the requirements of each school when submitting the portfolio. You want to make the best impression possible, so be sure to follow every last detail of a program's instructions. Ask an art teacher to help you.

If you are having trouble getting your portfolio to have the pizzazz that you know it needs, consider attending a summer art program. You might even be able to attend a summer program at a prospective college or professional art school—there are many postsecondary schools that offer such programs for high school students. Your artistic portfolio should represent your best work, and it should be recent work, not work that is a couple of years old. Artists grow over time, and what you did as a freshman or sophomore in high school probably does not reflect the artist you are today as you are about to enter college.

Here is a list of typical items in a portfolio:

TWO-DIMENSIONAL ART:

*   Drawings (charcoal, collage, ink, pastel, pencil, sketchbooks)
*   Paintings (oil or acrylic)
*   Photography
*   Graphic design (posters from a high school event or advertisements for a school newspaper or yearbook)

THREE-DIMENSIONAL ART:

*   Sculpture (in various materials like clay or metal)
*   Jewelry
*   Ceramics (an item you made on the potter's wheel)
*   Glass (stained glass or blown glass)

ELECTRONIC ART:

*   Animation
*   Film or video production
*   Websites (this may also include interactive media techniques like flash animation)

Depending on the art program's philosophy, you may be able to submit nontraditional or experimental pieces such as graphic novels or performance art.

National Portfolio Days

Throughout the academic year, the National Portfolio Day Association hosts National Portfolio Days across the country. Attending one of these evens should be on the to-do list of every serious art student. The National Portfolio Days, held in approximately thirty-five cities, bring together admissions representatives from college art programs so students have a chance to ask questions about applying to college art programs. You can also use this opportunity to obtain guidance on portfolios. In fact, making use of the opportunity to talk with admissions representatives can be an excellent way to get advice on how to improve your portfolio and determine which type of art program is right for you. Input from the pros could help you narrow down the list of schools you will ultimately apply to. Get more information about the National Portfolio Days at portfolioday.net/.

Week in the Life of a School of the Art Institute of Chicago Student

MONDAY	
7 a.m	Wake up
8 a.m.	Train to school
9 a.m.–4 p.m.	Video 1 with one-hour lunch break
4–10 p.m.	Train home, homework
TUESDAY AND THURSDAY	
9 a.m.–4 p.m.	Sculpture with one-hour lunch break
4–6 p.m.	Free time to do homework and eat dinner
6–9 p.m.	Research studio
WEDNESDAY	
6:30 a.m.	Wake up
7:30 a.m.	Train to school
8a.m.–12:30 p.m.	Work-study at registrar's office
12:30–1 p.m.	Lunch
1–4 p.m.	Art history
4–11 p.m.	Train home, homework
FRIDAY	
8:30 a.m.–4:30 p.m.	Work-study at registrar's office

Evaluating Art Programs

You've made your list of potential schools. Some may be professional art schools. Others may be traditional college campuses. "Now what?" you ask. Just how *do* you shorten that list and finally determine which school you should attend? Good question! Let's discuss some ideas for closing in on the choice that is best for you. Talking to admissions officers, faculty members, and current students can help you get the information you need to make a decision. Don't be shy about asking students their honest opinions—they have the inside scoop and can tell you what being an art student is really like. Asking questions about these aspects of an art program can make all the difference in choosing the best program for you.

THERESE QUINN
FORMER DIRECTOR OF THE BFA WITH EMPHASIS IN ART EDUCATION, SCHOOL OF THE ART INSTITUTE OF CHICAGO

"Unlike many art schools, SAIC accepts a variety of art portfolios for admission consideration," states Therese Quinn, former director of the BFA teacher education program at the School of the Art Institute of Chicago. "In addition to accepting portfolios with traditional work like still-life paintings and figure drawings, the School of the Art Institute encourages submissions of a wide range of other artistic forms such as e-zines and blogs, comic books, and home-produced videos through our nontraditional portfolio option. Our main interest is the development and expression of ideas."

"But what if you want to be an art teacher?" Then SAIC may be just the place for you!

The undergraduate art education

Expert Tips from Professor Quinn

→ Attend the National Portfolio Days early in your high school career to see what types of art schools exist.

→ Investigate current art faculty and make sure they are active in the field in ways that are artistically meaningful to you.

→ Consider class size—the lower the better, which means more individual attention to help you grow as an artist.

→ Consider where the school is located— what resources does the location have to offer you as a student (such as art museums, etc.)?

→ Visit the schools you are considering and make sure you feel comfortable in the campus environment.

→ Remember that alumni don't always represent the current philosophy of the school, so this shouldn't be a deciding factor.

program at SAIC also emphasizes ideas. "We want to educate teachers of art who bring the world into their classrooms and who understand that all teaching is creative and intellectual work," Quinn explains. "We link art and teaching to activism and try to help our students see that art education is fundamentally about changing the world."

Some students know from the beginning that their goal is to be an art teacher after finishing art school. Quinn has her own take on this. "Usually students who aspire to teach art had an inspiring art teacher in high school and want to make teaching part of their experience as an artist," she concludes.

Therese Quinn is currently an associate professor of art history and director of museum and exhibition studies at the University of Illinois at Chicago.

CHRISTOPHER
RHODE ISLAND SCHOOL OF DESIGN

Because Christopher attended an arts magnet high school, his college search was easier because admissions representatives visited the school. And it also helped that Christopher always knew he wanted to do illustration.

In the admissions process for the Rhode Island School of Design, Christopher had to submit a portfolio showing full sheets of slides of his work. He also had to take a drawing test with three drawings—one of his choice, one from an interior space looking out, and a bicycle.

"Illustration is a broad discipline," he says. "I thought studying illustration would force me to study the basics."

"Once you are in school, try to be open-minded," Christopher advises. "A lot of freshman teachers have you doing basic stuff, and it seems like a waste of time. In retrospect, I realize I was being arrogant. The teachers are there for a reason. Try to be humble. Try to figure out what each teacher can offer you."

Throughout his years in art school, Christopher noticed a tremendous difference

Hot Tips from Christopher
→ Visit the schools (that's what really made me decide).
→ See the faculty's work.
→ See the studio spaces.
→ Ask yourself whether you are impressed with the quality of work from both faculty and students.

between being a freshman and a senior. "By the time you are a senior, you should be able to take any assignment and be creative with it and make it work."

Christopher says that there are a lot of places in the art field for use of illustration: designing children's books, web design, character development for animation, sculpting toys and action figures. These are just a few of the options that some of his friends have explored.

Now armed with a BFA in illustration, Christopher is trying to break into freelance editorial work.

Faculty. Are the faculty members professional artists as well as teachers? Have they won awards? Where do they exhibit their work? How many have master of fine arts (MFA) degrees (the highest academic degree for an artist)?

Exhibition Opportunities. What kind of exhibition opportunities are available? Are they open to you both on campus and off campus in the community?

Facilities. Are the facilities well kept? Do they look used, or do they look vacant? What kind of studio space is available to students, and what hours is it accessible? Is the work in both faculty and student studios interesting or intriguing to you? Is there ample exhibition space? Does it seem that exhibitions—both faculty and student—are well attended? Do you see others looking at art while you are visiting the campus?

Alumni. Are alumni making a living as artists? Did they obtain jobs in their chosen artistic concentration? Are they teaching? Are they exhibiting and winning awards? You should try to attend a school where art majors do what you want to eventually do after graduation. If you have a special interest in art education, art history, art criticism, or another field altogether, try to find out what alumni who focused on those areas are doing now.

A consideration for students contemplating a professional art school is the lack of on-campus residences at some schools. As a result, finding a place to live—and figuring where and how you will eat—is up to you. Fortunately, a lot of professional art schools provide assistance to prospective students in finding affordable housing and matching them with roommates if they so desire. If it's important to you to live on campus, make sure this option is available at the professional art school you select. If not, consider a more traditional campus setting. As you plan your finances prior to settling on school choices, include the cost of room and board if you attend a professional art school that does not provide housing. In this situation, you will have to make plans to pay for room and board separately from tuition and it may end up being a substantial out-of-pocket cost.

Day in the Life of an Art Major

6:30 a.m.	Ignore alarm clock
6:55 a.m.	Panic and get ready for 7:30 bus to far end of campus
7:30 a.m.	Take bus to south campus
7:55 a.m.	Attempt to reassemble sculpture that fell only seconds before entering the classroom
8–10 a.m.	Listen and participate in class critique of everyone's work
10:01 a.m.	Bum a ride to the other end of campus from classmate
10:11 a.m.	Enter photo class late because a parking spot was unavailable nearby
10:12–11 a.m.	Free time in darkroom to finish prints. No good ones this time. Nearly chop off finger when opening film canister.
11:01 a.m. –12 p.m.	Class critique on this week's assignment, not enough contrast in black and white prints again.
12:10–1:20 p.m.	Lunch
1:25–3:20 p.m.	Learn the difference between complementary and tertiary colors, receive new assignment in color theory. Must paint four 6″ x 6″ 2D compositions with tertiary color scale for Wednesday.
3:21 p.m.	Contemplate panicking.
3:22–6 p.m.	Homework and free time.
6:05 p.m.	Leave to work on school newspaper.
6:10 p.m.–2 a.m.	Attempt to organize photos and layout for newspaper with only a few articles in on time.
2:10 a.m.	Return to room.
2:30–4 a.m.	Attempt to fall asleep while roommate watches TV, curse roommate's existence silently.
Sometime after 4 a.m.	Fall asleep and be prepared for 8 a.m. class the next morning.

MIKE
SCHOOL OF THE ART INSTITUTE OF CHICAGO

Mike wasn't really thinking about going to college once he finished high school. In fact, he was working at a local movie theater and learned about the School of the Art Institute of Chicago (SAIC) through a friend.

"I had been creating comic books on and off," he comments. "I'd been drawing forever."

When Mike learned about SAIC, he decided that he wanted to go to college after all. "I committed myself to getting in," he explains. Because he couldn't afford the tuition, Mike applied for the fully funded tuition scholarship.

Initially, Mike was accepted to SAIC, but he did not get the coveted scholarship. So he deferred his admission for a year and decided to try again the next year while enrolling in a local community college.

His perseverance paid off. The next year, Mike tried again for the scholarship and got it. Mike's portfolio was multidisciplinary; it combined video, puppetry, and comic books—and it is what earned him the money to attend art school.

Mike's goal is to take as many video classes as he can, and he hopes to do video production someday. "I think it will give me better job prospects in the future," he adds.

The advice Mike has to offer newly enrolled students is to take the first year's curriculum at art school as a preparation year. Mike found that there are a lot of foundation courses before the fun classes start. "During the first year, expect to take classes you might not necessarily enjoy, but do it anyway," he advises.

SAMPLE ARTIST STATEMENT

I paint because I like the feeling of accomplishment when my work is complete. I love mixing colors and placing them where I know they belong. When I paint, I become a master. I become the best painter in the world. I belong to a universe within which I control everything. There is no wrong or right—that is, until someone critiques my work offering suggestions and helping me improve. And this is my goal—to learn more, to experience more and to become the best artist I can be so that I can express my creativity, feel good about my paintings and bring something new to those who view my art.

In life, growing up, there was always one right and then one wrong. I could never grasp this notion because I thought so much out of the box that it was hard for me to get back in. For instance, I never saw purpose in memorizing math equations or memorizing states on a map. I was always the one to suggest that we paint the map onto the wall and then learn from there. As I went through elementary school, my grades kept dropping. It wasn't because I wasn't trying; it was because I couldn't conform to the structured way of their learning system. The school week became a chore and I endured the days only because I could dream about the weekend.

Every Sunday my family and I would visit with my great-grandmother. These were the times I cherished. Though I remember her as a frail, old woman with shaking hands, in her younger days she was one of the most renowned artists in the Chicago area. My great-grandmother's apartment was overrun with canvasses and paint-filled paper. She had closets full of paintings that she just didn't know what to do with. I loved just being with her art; I would look at the pictures from every angle, enjoying the colors and forms and yearning to create paintings of my own. My grandmother would set up markers and paper for me. I always begged to be able to use her paints and brushes, but she never let me play with her expensive art supplies. Because she screeched every time I would breathe close to her brushes, I wanted to play with them even more. All I wanted to do was spread the chilled glob of paint onto the paper, but because it was not mine I couldn't. At that time, I never thought art would be my escape from the world. I struggled getting the red to stick to the flower I so carefully drew next to the random sticks of green I called grass. Art was something I accepted as the norm. It never was special to me because it was something I was constantly surrounded by. Art to me then as a child was like money to a rich man, valuable but not understood.

The more I struggled with my schoolwork, the more my father pushed my art. Naturally, the more my father pushed my artistic future, the more I threw it back into his face. I made myself believe that because I couldn't perform like the rest of the class I couldn't do anything— and "anything" included the art I had grown to love and be good at. It just didn't seem good to me. I stopped drawing, I stopped painting, and I stopped doing anything artistic because I needed to prove to my father that I was better than that. The more I canceled art from my life, the emptier I felt. Without my expressive vent I was lost. Slowly, I came to realize that I am different than most of my peers; I have a different way of learning and a different way of expressing myself. And, slowly I began to realize that my being different is a good thing. Art became what I do. It became my best friend. In life I have gone through some tragedies and some heartbreaks and the only thing that was always there for me was my paintbrush and canvas. It tends to be difficult for me to physically show emotion, and a lot of the time people read me as unemotional. However, I amass my emotions and then illustrate them through my artistic expression. Because I find it satisfying to illustrate my emotions on canvas, I chose to portray my emotional stages as my concentration. I have painted a series of three self-portraits, each series expressing a set of emotions that accompany a particular experience. It is a challenge to paint my own form and it is a challenge to capture my emotions on canvas. My goal is to continually challenge myself with my art so that I can grow and develop in this field.

SAMPLE ESSAY

Home Exam: Essay Describing and Analyzing My Bed

Tears form at the corners of my eyes as my body gets peeled from the warmth and comfort of my bed every morning. I hear my mother's voice: "Karina, it's time to go to school; get up or you'll be late." Her words feel like long, sharp fingernails sliding down a classroom chalkboard. My bed hugs me as my eyes open towards my windows and my head turns towards my clock. The clock reads 6:35; the bright red numbers pierce my virgin eyes. Time to get up and start a day filled with people telling me what to do. I hear my bed crying for me, wanting me to return so we can continue our amazing adventures through my unconscious mind. I look at it from above. Its shape, its feel, its total structure is faultless. The white featherbed that lies across my bed reminds me of sheets of clouds in the sky. My mouth waters with the thought and desire of jumping into its marshmallow softness, but I stop myself, for I know that I must begin my day.

All day I think about the mushy, purple pillows that hold my head during the night and the quilted mattress that firmly supports my back so comfortably. The white picketed headboard, that dear white picketed headboard, which so beautifully and simply brings everything together so well, sits perfectly at a ninety-degree angle from the mattress. My bed is perfectly situated in the center of my bedroom. As I lie with my head towards the ceiling, I can see the world float above me. The sun rises towards my right, and it hits me so peacefully in the morning as if it whispers my name to wake me.

I'm like every other kid in the world. When it comes to cleaning my room I have the tendency to quickly shove everything underneath my bed as if being timed. I have always felt that one might as well make useless space into something useful, so I try my best to do that. As I drop my head from my bed and balance myself with my legs so not to fall, I peer underneath into the "infinite abyss" and find things I never knew I had. Old chewed up socks that my dog once found a liking towards covered in dust bunnies and old mementos I have collected over the years are a few things that were carefully thrown underneath my bed. It's like a world of trash that seems to have developed over the years, but not just any trash—trash that I can't appear to bring myself to throw out. For some reason I have this feeling deep down in my stomach that one day I will in fact need all that valuable and precious junk. Although underneath my bed the floor is cluttered and full of garbage, without it I don't think my bed would be the same. That space underneath my bed describes the very world I live in. The very world that is clearly useless and a waste of space to everyone, but to me, if used correctly, is the very thing that holds everything together.

Sample Essay

I think of important events in my life as photographic images viewed through the lens of a camera. My eyes have been opened to the arts throughout my life, first just a bit like the smallest aperture of a lens and eventually to the point where I have made life decisions based on a clear image through the viewfinder. I want to pursue my passion for the arts; this is a field in which I want to work for the rest of my life.

F-Stop 22...My third birthday party. Painting on the covered walls in my house. Most three-year-olds look at a wall and see a wall; I saw an empty canvas. That's where it all began.

F-Stop 16...The Needlecraft School. Six years old and walking the catwalk as I model my own creations (poodle skirts, ensembles, pajamas and pillows). I patterned and sewed them all on Mrs. Faucet's antique Singer sewing machine, the same model my great-grandmother learned to sew on. While other girls were building their coordination through soccer and ballet, I was building mine through Ease-Stitching and Back-Tacking.

F-Stop 11...The Art Barn. My oil painting finally took to a canvas and no longer to walls and floors. My abilities began to blossom, from tulips and oranges, to vases and grapes. That was my first taste of a still life.

F-Stop 8...Belvoir Terrace. Being accepted to this fine and performing arts program was my first experience with so many artistically competitive girls. Here's where I put my brush to rest and began clicking away. I realized I could capture more through a lens than on a canvas. Photography is an artist's perspective of a true image of a subject whereas painting is the artist's interpretation of that same image.

F-Stop 5.6...Rhode Island School of Design. The curriculum is demanding, in an intoxicating way. It energized my creative juices and confirmed my desire to excel in the arts. My final project was shot at an abandoned funhouse. The eerie feeling that ran through me was exhilarating, knowing there had been life here many years before. I could visualize hundreds of people screaming from excitement. This is where I learned my goal was to present images to thrill and inspire all who appreciate the art of photography.

F-Stop 4…The Montclair Art Museum. My drawings are selected to be featured at a show. It was the first time my artwork was displayed in an art venue. Observing the many expressions of the public critiquing my work was intensely gratifying.

Click…Academy of Art University, San Francisco. Every view in this picturesque city holds the potential to become an expression of art. The setting enabled me to see beauty as it is, yet also allowed me to expand my boundaries. Removing myself from my suburban life and the sameness of everyday living, I broadened my scope and my understanding of more colorful people. This enabled me to become more controversial.

I have always loved to create, working with my hands and eyes. I began to view the world through the eyes of an artist, and now through the lens of my camera.

SAMPLE APPLICATION ESSAY ANSWER

Pratt clearly understands what it takes to properly guide a student who hopes to maintain a successful artistic life style. Art to me is a philosophy, a philosophy that Pratt professes. Pratt proclaims: "The ideal of the fine arts is work done for its own sake. Freed of external constraints, the artist responds only to the internal necessities of creativity: art is pure visual research." Art creates itself. All people are here for is to verbally defend it and enjoy its emotional conclusion. I want to learn everything there is to learn about creative expression. I want to train to be the best in my field, and I want to learn how to share the beauty of art with the rest of the world. After reading Pratt's philosophies, I began to feel like I belonged. I live my life according to the same beliefs Pratt is structured by. I am excited about the varied courses Pratt offers, as well as the methods of study and the ability to explore different media and directions. My dream is to take my artistic love and, with it, help those in need. Eventually, I plan to become an art therapist. I love people, and I love solving and negotiating issues. The fact that Pratt is in the center of New York City is beneficial to me, as it offers the opportunity to visit museums and galleries and to get to know New York's artists on a more personal level. It also encompasses a diverse population, which I know will contribute to my understanding of art and of the world.

SAMPLE INTRODUCTION TO AN ART PORTFOLIO

Hello and welcome to my portfolio! This portfolio represents the work I have done in high school. I created this compilation to document my life at Pacific Crest, my accomplishments, and the challenges I have faced, and to give you an idea of how I would do in a college environment. Because my school does not give letter grades, we create portfolios to display some of the work we have done, extracurricular activities, interests, and the community service projects with which we have been involved.

Pacific Crest Community School is a small, alternative private high school in Portland, Oregon. At Pacific Crest, we choose our own curriculum and receive written evaluations instead of letter grades. We keep all of our work and store it in a portfolio to be presented to parents and teachers at the end of the year. I am sending this portfolio to accompany my college applications as a more complete profile of my accomplishments than provided by a GPA.

I have experienced many adventures during high school. I have taught for five seasons at Outdoor School, a program in which high school students teach sixth graders a natural sciences–based curriculum while living with them in cabins in the forest.

During the summer of my freshman year, I traveled around the world with my family. We started in Poland to visit my father's family, who I see every three or four years. We then flew to Southeast Asia, where in Bali my interest in zoology was indulged as our hotel was just a few yards from the famous Balinese monkey forest. I also was honored to travel on a school trip to Japan for ten days, where I learned about the history, language, and culture of that country.

I became interested in photography during my second year at Pacific Crest. One of my favorite hobbies is taking photos of all different genres, including macro-photography, portrait, city life, and architecture. I also created an online gallery of my photography so that friends and strangers can comment on my art.

I am very passionate about creating art, traveling, and helping the community, which is why, along with creating sections in my portfolio that display my academic achievements, I have areas for my art, my travels, community service, and other extracurricular activities.

I hope that my portfolio conveys to you my academic achievements, my interests, and my personality. I have worked hard in the past four years and am glad that my school allows me to preserve my work and display it in this manner. This collection is the result of four years of hard work, fun, and my love of learning.

Sample Résumé

Karina D.

1 Main Street

Anytown, NY 10000

Phone: (212) 555-1111

Email: karina@me.com

Web portfolio: karinaart@portfolio.com

Extracurricular Activities and Leadership Positions:

Varsity Volleyball, Team Manager, 9, 10, 11

Teacher's Aide, Helped students in special needs program, 9, 10, 11

Theater, Thespian, 9

AWARDS, HONORS, AND SPECIAL RECOGNITION:

Hallelujah Hollywood Art Exhibition 11

City of Hollywood Art and Culture Art Exhibition 9

COMMUNITY SERVICE:

Senior Class President 12

The "Club" Film, literature and religion discussion group, Creativity Leader 12

NCSY Religious youth group, President of Art 10, 11, 12

Varsity Basketball Team Player 9, 10, 11

National Scholastics Art Competition Gold Key Award 11

National Art Honor Society 9, 10, 11, 12

Volunteered with children in Joe DiMaggio Children's Hospital 11, 12

Painted a stool which was auctioned for $150 to benefit Chai Lifeline, a children's cancer fund 11

Group Leader at Beth Torah Day Camp Summer 2015

ART-RELATED JOBS HELD:

Helped organize a $2,000,000 Art Collection Summer 2016

Painted art samples for an arts and crafts catalog 2015–16

Prepared storyboards for a film 2014

SAMPLE ART CURRICULUM*

Maine College of Art

Four-Year Curriculum Overview

YEAR 1: FOUNDATION			
Fall	**Credits**	**Spring**	**Credits**
Two-Dimensional Foundation	3	Two-Dimensional Foundation II	3
Three-Dimensional Foundation	3	Three-Dimensional Foundation II	3
Art History Survey I	3	Art History Survey II	3
Composition and Literature	3	Composition and Literature	3
Studio Elective	3	Studio Elective	3
Tool Technology	1		
	16		15
Total: 31			

YEAR 2: TRANSITION			
Fall	**Credits**	**Spring**	**Credits**
Studio Elective	3	Studio Elective	3
Studio Elective	3	Studio Elective	3
Studio Elective	3	Studio Elective	3
Art History Elective: Non-Western	3	Liberal Arts Elective: Western Hist.	3
Liberal Arts Elective: Western Phil.	3	Liberal Arts Elective	3
	15		15
Total: 30			

YEAR 3: MAJOR			
Fall	**Credits**	**Spring**	**Credits**
Studio Major Courses	9	Studio Major Courses	9
Art History Elective	3	Art History Elective	3
Liberal Arts Elective	3	Liberal Arts Elective	3
	15		15
Total: 30			

YEAR 4: MAJOR			
Fall	**Credits**	**Spring**	**Credits**
Studio Major Courses	9	Studio Major Courses	9
Critical Issues: Art, Theory, Crit.	3	Liberal Arts Elective	3
Liberal Arts Elective	3	Liberal Arts Elective	3
	15		15
Total: 30			
TOTAL CREDITS FOR GRADUATION: 121			

This sample curriculum is reprinted with permission. The course schedule shown here is representative of courses for an art major. Of course, each institution has slightly different emphases and requirements, and students are advised to investigate the curriculum at each program they apply to.

SAMPLE CURRICULUM IN ARTS AND TECHNOLOGY*

The Digital Arts Program at the University of Oregon encourages students to combine new media practice and visual art theory, with strong technical sophistication, a rich sense of visual design, and an ability to articulate themselves as artists.

Degree Requirements

All majors are required to complete the University of Oregon general degree requirements for either a Bachelor of Arts or Bachelor of Science degree in addition to the departmental major requirements listed below.

BA/BS IN DIGITAL ARTS	CREDITS
Surface, Space & Time—ART 115	4 credits
Core Interdisciplinary Laboratory—ART 116	4 credits
Drawing—ART 233	4 credits
Print Media Digital Arts—ARTD 250	4 credits
Time Based Digital Arts—ARTD 251	4 credits
Interactive Digital Arts—ARTD 252	4 credits
History of Art and Architecture	3 credits
Digital Arts Studio—ARTD 300/400 level (up to 12 credits can be 300/400 level Fine Arts studio)	36 credits
	Total: 63 credits

Courses

250 Print Media Digital Arts (4R) Examines application of print media in contemporary visual culture; explores its use in a fine art context. Introduces digital drawing, digital photo editing, and typographic layout to visually communicate expressive concepts. Laboratories, lectures.

251 Time-Based Digital Arts (4R) Explores the notion of time as a medium in relation to contemporary art through which concepts of sequence, narration, scoring, and motion are expressed. Laboratories, lectures.

252 Interactive Digital Arts (4R) Introduces resources that the computer offers the artist. Concentrates on animation, interaction, and the Web as expressive mediums. Laboratories, lectures.

256 Introduction to Production (4) Traditional camera, sound, and lighting techniques in production; nonlinear editing; and key theoretical, historical, and aesthetic approaches to video art.

350 Digital Drawing (4R) Applies technology as a drawing medium to communicate concepts visually. The entire creative process is researched in an experimental studio environment. Prereq: ART 115, 116, 233, ARTD 250, 251, 252.

360 Digital Imaging (4R) Intermediate-level focus on the proper preparation and presentation of digital images for use in print and on screen. Covers color theory. Prereq: ARTD 250, 251, 252. R once for maximum of 8 credits.

361 Introduction to Animation (4) Introduction to principles of animation, timing, sequence; key frames, in-betweens, and metamorphosis. Uses various methods to record and edit animation tests. Prereq: ART 115, 116, 233, ARTD 250, 251, 252.

362 Digital Letterform (4R) Concepts in the history, use, and appreciation of digital typography. Considers issues in communicative power of type and situations where it functions as message. Prereq: ART 115, 116, 233, ARTD 250, 251, 252, 360. R once for a maximum of 8 credits.

378 Multimedia Design I (5R) Introduces multimedia design and authoring; use of motion, duration, and time-based interaction as a means of artistic expression. Students build navigational structures and explore stochastic principles in developing an individual approach to interactivity. Sequence with ARTD 478/578. Prereq: ARTD 350.

379 Introduction to Video Art (4R) Intermediate video-audio production and nonlinear editing, including camera, sound, and lighting techniques. Key theoretical, historical, and aesthetic approaches to time-based art in video and sound are surveyed. Prereq: ART 115, 116, 233; ARTD 250, 251, 252, 350, 360.

411/511 Web Art (5) Involves study and creation of Internet-based artwork. Students engage with conceptual systems of interactivity, scripting, hypermedia in current and developing forms; discussions, short readings. Prereq: ARTD 350.

412/512 Experimental Animation (5) Intermediate to advanced students explore personal creative practice and experiment with film, video, and computer animation techniques. Integrates readings, screening, and discussion with production. Prereq: ARTD 361, 379.

413/513 Emerging Technologies (5) Explores use of emerging technologies in art. Create works using emerging technologies and techniques and explore contemporary artworks, philosophies, and cultural trends. Prereq: ARTD 378 or 416.

415/515 Video Art: Experimental Film (4) Video and sound art practices, from conceptual deconstructions of the film-video apparatus to self-reflexive sociopolitical and/or cultural critique, are examined through short format and video installation. Prereq: ARTD 379.

416/516 Programming for Artists (4R) Introduces students to the basics of computer programming within an art context. Topics include interaction design, web development, and physical computing programming. Prereq: ART 115, 116, 233; ARTD 250, 251, 252.

463/563 Communication Design (4R) Explores the communication of ideas and information through visual means. Introduces design process and principles, visual language, and the art of problem solving in visual communication. Prereq: ARTD 350, 362. R once for maximum of 8 credits.

471/571 3D Computer Imaging (5R) Introduces 3D computer graphic arts: 3D digital space and form, model building, scene composition, surface properties, lighting, and rendering 3D images. Prereq: ARTD 350 or 361. R once for maximum of 10 credits.

472/572 3D Computer Animation (5R) Introduces 3D computer animation arts. Includes time and space in the digital 3D environment, animation concepts and techniques in 3D space, production techniques for various multimedia applications. Prereq: ARTD 471/571. R thrice for maximum of 20 credits.

478/578 Multimedia Design II (5R) Intermediate and advanced multimedia design and authoring. Emphasizes creation of larger, student-directed multimedia projects. Prereq: ARTD 378. R once for maximum of 10 credits.

490 Issues and Practices in Digital Arts (1–5R) Intensive critique, discussion, readings, and presentations. BFA or MFA standing required.

494/594 Advanced Design I (5) Theory, problems, and projects in language, meaning and communication, identity and signification, conceptual invention and creativity, critical analysis. Lectures, projects, critique. Prereq: ARTD 463/563.

This sample curriculum is reprinted with permission. The course schedule shown here is representative of courses for an art major. Of course, each institution has slightly different emphases and requirements, and students are advised to investigate the curriculum at each program they apply to.

Sample Industrial Design BFA Program*

This sample curriculum is provided by the Rhode Island School of Design (RISD). All freshman applicants apply to RISD as opposed to a specific department and begin with a required year of Experimental and Foundation Studies. Students select a major midway through the first year but don't begin those programs until sophomore year.

The program begins sophomore year with skill-based exposure to both traditional and state-of-the-art techniques for visualization. Through the manipulation of wood, metal, paper, and plastic, students begin to understand the unique properties of these materials and the design possibilities inherent in them.

Junior year builds on the skills learned the first year by encouraging students to focus on projects dealing with technology as it applies to products, form and human factors, mechanics and movement, and more.

During senior year, students take advanced design studios, learn more about legal and business practices in the profession and undertake projects that emphasize innovation and the ability to refine formal design issues.

Foundation Studies

FRESHMAN		
Fall	**Winter session**	**Spring**
Drawing I	Non-major studio elective	Drawing II
Design I		Design II
Spatial Dynamics I		Spatial Dynamics II
Liberal Arts courses		Liberal Arts courses
SOPHOMORE		
Fall	**Winter Session**	**Spring**
Wood I	Open elective	Design Principles II
Metal I		History of Industrial Design
Design Principles I		Designing with Solid Works
Liberal Arts elective		Liberal Arts elective
JUNIOR		
Fall	**Winter Session**	**Spring**
Metal II or Wood II	Open elective	Advanced Design: Studio
Special Topic Studios		Open elective
Manufacturing Techniques		Liberal Art elective
Liberal Arts elective		
SENIOR		
Fall	**Winter Session**	**Spring**
Advanced Design: Studio	Open elective	Advanced Design: Studio
Designing with Rhino		Open elective
Open elective		Liberal Arts elective
Liberal Arts elective		

This sample curriculum is reprinted with permission. The course schedule shown here is representative of courses for a student studying industrial design. Of course, each institution has slightly different emphases and requirements, and students are advised to investigate the curriculum at each program they apply to.

ART AND DESIGN PROGRAMS

Profiles of Selected Programs

Northeast / 137

Southeast / 155

Midwest / 160

West / 170

**Comprehensive List of Colleges with
Art and Design Programs**

By State / 179

Northeast

ALFRED UNIVERSITY

School of Art and Design
2 Pine Street
Alfred, NY 14802

Phone: (607) 871-2412
Website: art.alfred.edu
Email: admissions@alfred.edu

Tuition: $$$$
Campus student enrollment (undergraduate):
1,759

Degree(s): BFA, BS
Concentrations: BS in art history and theory;
BFA with concentrations in ceramic art, drawing,
painting, photography, graphic design, print
media, video, sonic art, interactive media or glass
and sculpture.
Artistic portfolio requirement: Yes
Scholarships available: Yes
Number of faculty: 34 full-time, 12 part-time
Number of majors and minors: 368
**Percentage and number of applicants
accepted into the department per year:**
81%; 356 students

CARNEGIE MELLON UNIVERSITY

School of Art
CFA 300—5000 Forbes Avenue
Pittsburgh, PA 15213

Phone: (412) 268-2409
Website: cmu.edu/art/index.html
Email: artscool@andrew.cmu.edu

Tuition: $$$$
Campus student enrollment (undergraduate):
6,049

Degree(s): BFA, Bachelor Humanities and
Arts (BHA), Bachelor of Science and Arts (BSA),
Bachelor of Computer Science and Arts Degree
(BCSA)
Concentrations: Drawing, Painting, Printmaking
and Photography; Sculpture, Installation and
Site-Work; Electronic and Time Based Media;
Contextual Practice.
Courses offered: Drawing, electronic media,
interactive art and computational design, painting,
printmaking, wood, welding, clay, foundry, metals,
mixed media, computer art, video art.
Portfolio requirement: Yes
Number of faculty: More than 30
Department activities: Work by graduating
seniors is showcased in a group exhibition at the
Miller Gallery at the end of the spring semester.

THE COOPER UNION SCHOOL OF ART

30 Cooper Square
New York, NY 10003

Phone: (212) 353-4100
Website: cooper.edu
Email: admissions@cooper.edu

Tuition: $
Note: As of fall 2014, all enrolled students receive
a half-tuition scholarship worth $21,000 annually.
Students demonstrating need receive additional
financial aid to assist with remaining tuition
charges, living costs, books, and supplies. In
addition, students must pay $1,600 in mandatory
student fees.
Campus student enrollment (undergraduate):
873 (278 in the School of Art)

Degree(s): BFA in Fine Arts
Concentrations: Drawing, film, graphic design,
painting, photography, sculpture, video
Artistic portfolio requirement: Yes. In addition, a
home test is required for admission

Scholarships available: Yes. Half tuition for all as of 2014 and additional financial aid based on need.

Number of faculty: 9 full-time faculty, 60 adjuncts

Percentage and number of applicants accepted into the department per year: Approximately 8%, 70 applicants admitted

Prominent Alumni:

Lee Krasner

Alex Katz

Milton Glaser

Paul Thek

Eve Hesse

R. B. Kitaj

Tom Wesselmann

Alex Katz

Thomas Nozkowski

Philip Taaffe

Donald Baechler

Verne Dawson

CORCORAN COLLEGE OF ART AND DESIGN AT GEORGE WASHINGTON UNIVERSITY

500 17th Street NW

Washington, D.C. 20006

Phone: (202) 639-1814; toll-free: (888) CORCORAN

Website: corcoran.gwu.edu/

Email: admissions@corcoran.org

Tuition: $$$$

Campus student enrollment (undergraduate): 11,157

Degree(s): BA, BFA, BA/MA

Concentrations: Digital media design, fine art, fine arts and art history (BA/MA), fine art photography, graphic design, digital media design, interior architecture and design

Artistic portfolio requirement: Yes

Scholarships available: Yes. Dean's Scholarship:

Merit program that awards up to $4,000 for students entering Corcoran's BFA program. Merit awards are available and range from $2,500–16,000 for students entering into the BFA and BA programs. All awards are renewable based on academic performance. Arthur J. Ellis Scholarship: In memory of Arthur J. Ellis, a Washington *Post* photographer for more than 47 years. Ellis scholarships are available to first-time freshmen majoring in photojournalism. Selection is based on review of academic records and portfolios. Awards range from half to full tuition and are distributed over four years. Koenig Trust Scholarship: These are available to first-time freshmen entering in the fall semester. The chairs of each department select recipients based on review of academic records and portfolios. Highest consideration is given to students with minimum GPAs of 3.5. Awards range from half to full tuition and are distributed over four years. Corcoran College of Art + Design Grant: Need-based grants for new and continuing students of up to $7,125. On-Campus Grant: Need-based grants for new and continuing students who reside in Corcoran housing of up to $1,000. Scholastic Art Award: For students named by the National Scholastic jury; at least $1,000.

Number of faculty: 10 full-time

Percentage and number of applicants accepted into the department per year: Moderately selective

Department activities: Senior students exhibit in the Corcoran Gallery. There are year-round exhibitions of work by students, faculty, alumni, and contemporary artists who participate in programs at the college.

Prominent Alumni:

Y. David Chung

Jason Gobbiotti

Tara Donovan

FASHION INSTITUTE OF TECHNOLOGY

Seventh Avenue at 27th Street
New York, NY 10001

Phone: (212) 217-7999
Website: fitnyc.edu

Tuition: $
Campus student enrollment (undergraduate): 9,622

Degree(s): Certificates, Associate of Applied Science (AAS), BS, BFA
Concentrations: For bachelor's degree programs: accessories design, advertising design, advertising and marketing communications, art history and museum professions, computer animation and interactive media, cosmetics and fragrance marketing, direct and interactive marketing, entrepreneurship for the fashion and design industries, fabric styling, fashion business management, fashion design, film and media, fine arts, graphic design, home products development, illustration, interior design, international trade and marketing for the fashion industries, packaging design, photography and the digital image, production management: fashion and related industries, technical design, textile development and marketing, textile/surface design, toy design, visual presentation and exhibition design.

For associate's degree programs: accessories design, advertising and marketing communications, communication design, fashion business management, fashion design, film and media, fine arts, illustration (fashion and general illustration options), interior design, jewelry design (jewelry design and studio options), menswear, photography and related media, production management: fashion and related industries, textile development and marketing, textile/surface design.
Artistic portfolio requirement: Yes
Scholarships available: Yes
Number of faculty: 229 full-time, 738 part-time

Prominent Alumni:
Amsale Aberra
John Bartlett
Stephen Burrows
Francisco Costa
Norma Kamali
Calvin Klein
Michael Kors
Nanette Lepore
Ralph Rucci
Leslie Blodgett—creator, bareMinerals
Nina Garcia—creative director, *Marie Claire*
Edward Menicheschi—chief marketing officer and president, Condé Nast Media Group
Joe Zee—editor-in-chief and executive creative director, Yahoo! Style.

LESLEY UNIVERSITY

College of Art and Design
29 Everett Street
Cambridge, MA 02138

Phone: (888) LESLEY-U or (617) 349-8300
Website: lesley.edu
Email: admissions@lesley.edu

Tuition: $
Campus student enrollment (undergraduate): 1,463

Degree(s): BA, BFA, BS
Majors:
Animation & Motion Media
Art History
Art Therapy
Design
Digital Filmmaking
Fine Arts Illustration
Interactive Design
Photography
Animation & Motion Media/Illustration (5-year)
Art History/Fine Arts (5-year)
Design/Animation & Motion Media (5-year)

Design (BFA)/Business Management (BS)

Design/Fine Arts (5-year)

Design/Illustration (5-year)

Illustration/Fine Arts (5-year)

Photography/Design (5-year)

Artistic portfolio requirement: Yes for BFA programs

Scholarships available: Yes

Number of faculty: Approximately 100 art and design full-time and adjunct faculty

Department activities: Lesley University presents a full program of exhibitions throughout the year. Students may assist in mounting exhibitions, personally meet visiting artists and participate in exhibitions arranged with commercial galleries around Boston. Students have the opportunity for periodic, professional reviews of their portfolios as they advance toward completion of their studies. The spring semester culminates in Critique Week, when all students present their work in small critique groups composed of faculty and peers.

Prominent Alumni:

Caroll Spinney—creator of *Sesame Street* character Big Bird

LYME ACADEMY COLLEGE OF FINE ARTS OF THE UNIVERSITY OF NEW HAVEN

84 Lyme Street

Old Lyme, CT 06371

Phone: (860) 434-5232

Website: lymeacademy.edu

Email: admissions@lymeacademy.edu

Tuition: $

Campus student enrollment (undergraduate): 125

Degree(s): 3-year certificate, BFA

Majors: Painting, sculpture, drawing, illustration

Artistic portfolio requirement: Yes

Scholarships available: Yes. Chandler Scholarships for freshmen and transfers range from $2,000 to full scholarship.

Number of faculty: 21 (Lyme Campus), 268 Faculty University of New Haven

Prominent Alumni:

Jeremy Santiago Horseman earned his BFA from Lyme Academy College in 2013 and after earning his MFA degree, Mr. Horseman has achieved marked success in professional career, including being invited to exhibit in the 2016 International Moscow Biennale for Young Art, multiple solo exhibitions in New York City, Los Angeles, and other national locations.

E. Thurston Belmer is a professional artist in New York City, exhibiting his work in commercial galleries and museums nationally. His work and articles about his work have been featured in numerous publications. His artwork is part of multiple private and museum collections.

Gavin Gardner installed his second commission for Our Lady of Mercy Catholic Church, Potomac, Maryland, on May 27, 2004. Gardner was awarded the Dexter Jones Award by the National Sculpture Society for these reliefs in the summer of 2002.

T. Allen Lawson, who studied at the College in the eighties, designed the 2008 White House Christmas card, which depicts the view from the Truman Balcony, and shows the Washington Monument and Jefferson Memorial in the distance. It is now part of the permanent collection of the White House. Lawson is also widely recognized for his landscape paintings of Wyoming and Maine.

Lynn Jadamec Grayson (BFA, Painting, 2000) is currently working on a project that involves painting tectonic fault lines around the world. She also designs storyboards for commercials and feature films in Hollywood. Her artwork has been featured on television shows and in galleries around the world.

Lisa Nonken (Post-Baccalaureate, Sculpture, 2006) has received numerous awards and recognitions, including residencies at Yaddo, the Vermont Studio

Center and Blue Sky Project. She is presently study-ing in Siena, Italy, where she is a Professor of Fine Arts and working as a program developer for the Siena Art Institute.

Ronnie Rysz (BFA, Painting, 2006) is a prosthetic artist for Alternative Prosthetic Services and, in this capacity, he travels across the continental US creat-ing custom prosthetics for civilians and soldiers alike. Nathan Lewis received his BFA in painting from and has since exhibited both nationally and inter-nationally in museums, galleries, and universities. His work is in private collections in NY, CT, MA, CA, OR, Germany, Russia, and India. His paint-ings have been on the cover of numerous books and journals. His work has been published and reviewed by the *New York Times*, the *New York Press*, *International Artist*, *Fine Art Connoisseur*, *Art in New England*, *Big Red and Shiny*, the *Boston Globe*, and the *Huffington Post*, among others. He is currently a tenured Associate Professor at Sacred Heart University in Fairfield, CT.

LONG ISLAND UNIVERSITY CW POST CAMPUS

School of Visual Arts, Communications and Digital Technologies
Department of Art
720 Northern Boulevard
Brookville, NY 11548

Phone: (516) 299-2900
Website: liu.edu/post
Email: post-enroll@liu.edu

Tuition: $$$$
Campus student enrollment: 4,429

Degree(s): BFA, BA, BS
Concentrations: Art, art education, art history and theory, art therapy, creative art studio, digital arts and design, electronic media, photography
Artistic portfolio requirement: No for admis-sion, yes for scholarships

Scholarships available: Yes; amounts and qualifications vary by department
Number of faculty: 52
Number of majors and minors: 150
Department activities: The Art Students League has various exhibitions throughout year.

MAINE COLLEGE OF ART

522 Congress Street
Portland, ME 04101

Phone: (800) 639-4808, or (207) 775-3052
Website: meca.edu
Email: admissions@meca.edu

Tuition: $
Campus student enrollment (undergraduate): 500 undergraduates

Degree(s): BFA, post-baccalaureate in art education
Majors: Ceramics, digital media, graphic design, illustration, metals and jewelry, painting, photog-raphy, printmaking, sculpture, textile and fashion design, woodworking and furniture design.
Artistic portfolio requirement: Yes
Scholarships available: Yes. Merit awards between $6,000 and $16,500 per year; average is $12,000 per year and 1 full-tuition scholarship per year.
Number of faculty: 22 full-time, 55 part-time. Faculty and visiting artists are professional artists, designers, writers and scholars who have been honored by many foundations and organizations including the National Endowment of the Arts, the Getty Foundation, the Mellon Foundation, the New England Foundation of the Arts and the Haystack Mountain School. Their works are featured in galleries and museums throughout the world and in magazines and journals like *Ceramics Monthly*, *The New Yorker*, and the *Boston Globe*. Each year, MECA hosts well-known artists, designers, writers and other scholars who lecture on their work and contemporary issues in the arts.

Number of majors and minors: 216 students have declared a major. (Majors are declared at the end of a student's sophomore year.) 11 majors and 5 minors.

Department activities: BFA Exhibition, Talent and Merit Exhibition, Thesis Exhibition, numerous student and faculty shows throughout the year. Student clubs and organized activities including, cosplay club, gaming club, contra club, anime club, cycling club, faith community, LGBTQIA group, outdoor adventure, rock climbing club, SK8 collective, ski and snowboard collective, theatrical arts and running club.

Unique art-specific study abroad programs:
China Academy of Art; China Academy of Visual Arts; Hong Kong Baptist University; Hong Kong Burren College of Art; Ireland Studio Art Centers International; Italy AICAD campus mobility program; U.S. and Canada

---

Prominent Alumni:

Ahmed Alsoudani—painter; 2011 Venice Biennale

Vivian Beer—furniture maker; 2016 *Ellen Design Challenge* winner

Greg Dyro—photo lab director, Warner Bros.

Seth Goldenberg—founder and CEO of The Epic Decade

Connie Hayes—painter

David Hutchins—animator; Disney Studios. Academy Award winner for special effects on *Frozen*

Nelson Lowry—animator; Laika Studios

Laurie Lundquist—public artist

John Raimondi—monumental sculptor

Bradly Werley—animator on the *Box Trolls*

Brian Wilk—senior product designer, Hasbro Inc.

MARYLAND INSTITUTE COLLEGE OF ART

Office of Undergraduate Admissions
1300 Mount Royal Avenue
Baltimore, MD 21217–4191

Phone: (410) 225-2222
Website: mica.edu
Email: admissions@mica.edu

Tuition: $$
Campus student enrollment (undergraduate): 1,820

Degree(s): BFA: Animation, architectural design, art history, ceramics, drawing, fiber, film and video, game design, humanistic students, illustration, interactive arts, interdisciplinary sculpture, painting, photography, printmaking, product design. Dual-degree and fifth-year capstone graduate programs: Art education (five-year BFA/MAT), business of art and design (MPS), critical studies (MA), information visualization (MPS), social design (MA).

Concentrations: Studio concentrations can be incorporated into any MICA major. Animation, architectural design, book arts, ceramics, curatorial studies, experimental fashion, film and video, filmmaking, game arts, graphic design, illustration, interactive arts, photography, printmaking, sound art, sustainability and social practice, and theater.

Artistic portfolio requirement: Yes
Scholarships available: Yes
Number of faculty: 297
Department activities: More than 70 student-focused exhibitions in school galleries each year.

Prominent Alumni:

Reuben Kramer (1932)

Betty Cooke (1946)

Mary Miss (1968)

Doug Hall (1969)

Joyce J. Scott (1971)

Nancy Rubins (1974)

Jan Staller (1975)

Jeff Koons (1976)

Donald Baechler (1978)

Lesley Dill (1980)

Jason Dodge (1993)

Naomi Fisher (1998)

Rashawn Griffin (2002)

Shinique Smith (2003)

Baker Overstreet (2004)

Lu Zhang (2004)

Colin Campbell (2004)

Gabriela Bulisova (2005)

MICA has been a top producer of Fulbright scholars among specialty schools over the past five years; other honors earned by recent graduates include the Jacob Javits Fellowship, the Soros Fellowship for New Americans, and the Jack Kent Cooke Fellowship.

MASSACHUSETTS COLLEGE OF ART

621 Huntington Avenue

Boston, MA 02115

Phone: (617) 879-7000

Website: massart.edu

Email: admissions@massart.edu

Tuition: $

Campus student enrollment (undergraduate): 1,646

Degree(s): BFA

Concentrations: Animation, architectural design, art history (see history of art), art teacher education, ceramics, fashion design, fibers, film/video, glass, graphic design, history of art, illustration, industrial design, jewelry and metalsmithing, museum education, painting, photography, printmaking, sculpture, studio education, studio for interrelated media.

Artistic portfolio requirement: Yes

Scholarships available: Yes

Number of faculty: 115 (full time)

Percentage of applicants accepted into the department per year: 70%

Prominent Alumni:

William Wegman (painting)—photographer and painter

Arne Glimcher (painting)—art dealer, founder of Pace Gallery, NYC

Brian Collins (graphic design)—founder and CEO of COLLINS, a marketing and branding firm in NYC

Kelly Wearstler (graphic design)—interior designer, fashion designer and founder of her own lifestyle brand

Nancy Haigh (ceramics)—five-time Academy Award–nominated (won once for *Bugsy*) set designer; most recently worked on *Oz, The Great and Powerful, Moneyball*, and *True Grit*

Exchange Programs:

The MassArt International Exchanges are full immersion programs at one of our reciprocal exchange partner institutions. Students enroll directly in the institution abroad but pay MassArt tuition and fees. Most forms of financial aid apply, but it is important to check with the financial aid office for more information. Because of the immersive nature of these programs, students must be independent-minded. MassArt has reciprocal exchange partnerships with the following institutions:

Australia:

Melbourne University/Victorian College of Art

University of Sydney/Sydney College of Art

India:

Srishti institute of Art, Design and Technology

Israel:

Bezalel Academy of Arts and Design

Italy:

Alchimia, School of Contemporary Jewelry

Japan:

Kyoto University of Art and Design

Osaka Seikei University

Netherlands:

ArtEZ Institute of the Arts

Willem de Kooning Academie

South Korea:

Korea National University of Arts

Spain:

University of Barcelona

Scotland, U.K.:
Edinburgh College of Art
Glasgow School of Art
England, U.K.:
University for the Creative Arts

MONTCLAIR STATE UNIVERSITY

Department of Art and Design
1 Normal Avenue
Upper Montclair, NJ 07043

Phone: (973) 655-7295
Website: montclair.edu/arts/art-and-design/
Email: artsschool@mail.montclair.edu

Tuition: $
Campus student enrollment (undergraduate):
16,336, as of spring 2016

Degree(s):
BFA in Animation/Illustration
BA in Fashion Studies
BFA in Product Design
BA in Visual Arts
BA in Visual Arts with a concentration in Art Education
BA in Visual Arts with a concentration in School and Community Settings
BA in Visual Arts/MAT with Teacher Certification in Art (P–12) & Teacher of Students with Disabilities Certification
BFA in Visual Communication Design
Minor in Fine Art Studio
Minor in Fashion Design
Minor in Fashion Merchandising
Fine Arts Teacher Certification in art Preschool to Grade 12
Concentrations: arts education in school and community settings. Studio specializations: ceramics, drawing, metalwork/jewelry, painting, photography, printmaking, sculpture.
Artistic portfolio requirement: Yes
Scholarships available: Yes:

Ann Chapman Award: $500
Advisory Board Scholarship and Talent Awards: $500–2,000
Cento Amici Scholarship: $1,000–2,000
Don and Judy Miller Scholarship for the Visual Arts: $500–1,500
Fashion Studies Award: $500–9,500
John and Rose Cali Scholarship for the Arts: $1,000
Katherine Hall Fashion Studies Scholarship: $1,250
Ruslink Fashion Studies Award: $1,200
Number of faculty: 23 full-time, 2 part-time
Department activities: Department hosts Master Studio Workshops as well as Art Forum, the MFA Lecture Series and a speakers collaboration with the Montclair Art Museum, each featuring presentations by notable artists, designers, critics and curators. Also sponsored are art clubs such as the Montclair State Art Educator's Club and student-run Gallery 3½ Committee. There are many study-abroad programs as well as opportunities for students to exhibit their work, including an annual show in New York's gallery district for MFA students, and the award-winning George Segal Gallery (on campus) for BFA students. MFA students, furthermore, have worked on projects with notable artists such as Robert Wilson, Robert Whitman, and Fluxus pioneer Alison Knowles in venues including the Alexander Kasser Theater, the Guggenheim Museum, and The Kitchen (in Chelsea).

Prominent Alumni:
William Pope.L—visual and performance artist
Amer Kobaslija—painter

MOORE COLLEGE OF ART AND DESIGN

20th Street and the Parkway
Philadelphia, PA 19103

Phone: (215) 965-4015
Website: moore.edu
Email: enroll@moore.edu

Tuition: $
Campus student enrollment (undergraduate): 450 (all women)

Degree(s): BFA, postbaccalaureate (in art education)
Concentrations/Majors: Animation and game arts, art education, art history, curatorial studies, fashion design, fine arts, graphic design, illustration, interior design, photography and digital arts.
Artistic portfolio requirement: Yes
Scholarships available: Yes, up to $20,000

NEW ENGLAND SCHOOL OF ART AND DESIGN AT SUFFOLK UNIVERSITY

75 Arlington Street
Boston, MA 02116

Phone: (617) 573-8785
Website: suffolk.edu/nesad
Email: admission@suffolk.edu

Tuition: $

Degree(s): BFA, certificate
Concentrations: Graphic design BFA certificate, interior design BFA, Fine Arts BFA
Artistic portfolio requirement: Yes, but alternative pathway available
Scholarships available: Yes
Number of faculty: 16 full-time, 28 part-time
Number of majors and minors: 206 students enrolled with an UG or CTU major or minor
Department activities: Includes all Suffolk University activities in addition to student exhibitions, gallery, museum and design firm visits, collaborations with our Business School and College students on a large variety of projects.

Prominent Alumni:
Kodiak Starr (BFA Graphic Design, 2002)—White House Creative Director, 2010–2014

Silvi Naci (BFA Fine Arts & Graphic Design, 2011)—Assistant Gallery Director, Samson Projects, Boston
Andrea Dabrilla (BFA Fine Arts, 2011)—Associate Director, Gallery Naga, Boston
Benjamin Evans (BFA Fine Arts, 2011)—Auction Associate, Skinner Auctions, Boston
Janine Byrne (BFA, Interior Design 2006)—Associate, Sasaki Associates
Nico Flannery-Pitcher (MA, Interior Design, 2007)—Associate, Steffian Bradley Architects
John Gonnella (Diploma, Graphic Design 1983)—VP/Group Creative Director, Studiocom
Melanie Pellegrini Hannon (MA, Interior Design 2008)—Associate, CBT Architects
Jen Pompa (MA, Interior Design 2007)—Associate, Sasaki Associates
Bonnie Kalaf (Diploma, Graphic Design 1973)—VP, Grey Worldwide (Los Angeles)
William Kenney (Diploma, Graphic Design 1974)—VP/Creative, BrandEquity International
Michael Moeller (BFA, Interior Design 2001)—Principal, Michael Moeller Design (New York)
Kristine Mortensen (MA, Interior Design 2007)—Manager of Interior Design, Tiffany & Company, NY

NEW HAMPSHIRE INSTITUTE OF ART

148 Concord Street
Manchester, NH 03104

Phone: (866) 241-4918
Website: nhia.edu
Email: admissions@nhia.edu

Tuition: $
Campus student enrollment (undergraduate): 486

Degree(s): BFA
Concentrations: Ceramics, creative writing, design, illustration, fine art, photography as well as a dual degree program with our Master of Arts and Teaching.

Artistic portfolio requirement: Yes
Scholarships available: Yes

NEW YORK SCHOOL OF INTERIOR DESIGN

170 East 70th Street
New York, NY 10021

Phone: (212) 472-1500, toll-free (800) 33-NYSID
Website: nysid.edu
Email: admissions@nysid.edu

Tuition: $
Campus student enrollment (undergraduate): 380

Degree(s): BFA, BA, Certificate
Artistic portfolio requirement: Basic Interior Design (BID) certificate program, Bachelor of Arts (BA): no portfolio is required for admission. Bachelor of Fine Arts (BFA): a portfolio of 10 to 15 pieces is required.
Scholarships available: Yes, multiple scholarships ranging from $500 to $12,000
Number of faculty: 110
Percentage and number of applicants accepted into the department per year: 46% (65 students); for transfers it is 53% (112 students)
Department activities: Student Council, student chapter of the American Society of Interior Designers, Contract Design Club, organized trips to New York City museums, galleries, studios, etc.

Prominent Alumni:
Mariette Himes Gomez
Mica Ertegun
Anne Eisenhower
Osamu Hashimoto
Barbara Ostrom
Sylvia Owen
Alexandra Stoddard
Allan H. France
Kimberly Latham
Pia Ledy
Ted C. C. Odom
David Scott
Rick Saverr
Robert Metzger
Michael de Santis
Ruben de Saavedra
Elizabeth Nebitt Shean

PARSONS SCHOOL OF DESIGN

66 5th Avenue
New York, NY 10011

Phone: (212) 229-5150 or (800) 292-3040
Website: parsons.edu
Email: thinkparsons@newschool.edu

Tuition: $

Degree(s): BFA, BBA, BS
Concentrations:
Fashion Marketing
Fashion Design
Graphic Design
Interior Design
Architectural Design
Communication Design
Strategic Design and Management
Design & Technology
Environmental Studies
Fine Arts
Integrated Design
Illustration
Photography
Product Design
Urban Design
Architecture
Lighting Design
History of Decorative Arts & Design
Transdisciplinary Design
Design Studies
Fashion Studies
Design Business

Artistic portfolio requirement: Depends on the program

Scholarships available: Yes, need- and merit-based

Number of faculty: 158 full-time, 888 part-time. Most faculty are adjunct because they are full-time artists and designers.

Percentage and number of applicants accepted per year: Approximately 63%

Prominent students and alumni:

Edward Hopper
Jasper Johns
Donna Karan
Tom Ford
Marc Jacobs
Ryan McGinley
Steven Meisel
Joel Schumacher
Ai Wei Wei
Sheila Bridges
Albert Hadley
Victoria Hagan
Peter de Seve
Ian Falconer
Paul Rand

PENNSYLVANIA ACADEMY OF THE FINE ARTS

128 North Broad Street
Philadelphia, PA 19102

Phone: (215) 972-7625
Website: pafa.edu
Email: admissions@pafa.edu

Tuition: $

Degree(s): BFA, certificate, postbaccalaureate
Concentrations: Painting, sculpture, drawing, printmaking, illustration
Artistic portfolio requirement: Yes
Scholarships available: Yes
Number of faculty: 21 full-time and 42 part-time

Prominent Alumni:

Bo Bartlett
Cecilia Beaux
Arthur B. Carles
Mary Cassatt
Charles Demuth
Vincent Desiderio
Thomas Eakins
William Glackens
Robert Henri
Louis Kahn
David Lynch
John Marin
Alice Neel
Elizabeth Osborne
Maxfield Parrish
Charles Sheeler
John Sloane
Henry Ossawa Tanner

PRATT INSTITUTE

200 Willoughby Avenue
Brooklyn, NY 11205

Phone: (718) 636-3514, toll-free: (800) 331-0834
Website: pratt.edu
Email: admissions@pratt.edu

Tuition: $$$
Campus student enrollment (undergraduate): 3,226

Degree(s): BFA, BA, five-year B. Arch.
Concentrations: Architecture; art and design education (teacher certification); communications design (advertising art direction, graphic design, illustration); construction management; critical and visual studies; digital arts (3D animation and motion arts, 2D animation, interactive arts); fashion design; film; fine arts (ceramics, drawing, jewelry, painting, printmaking, sculpture); history of art and design; industrial design; interior design; photography, writing.
Artistic portfolio requirement: Yes

Scholarships available: Yes.
Presidential Merit Based Scholarships from $12,000 to $26,000 each academic year. Pratt Restricted and Endowed Awards and Scholarships from $5,000 each academic year. Pratt distributes $36 million in unrestricted scholarship money and $1.5 million restricted scholarship money annually.
Number of faculty: 153 full-time, 960 part-time

Prominent Alumni:

William Boyer—designer, classic Thunderbird
Peter Max—pop artist
Malcolm Holtzman—architect, Rizzoli Bookstores
Betsey Johnson—fashion designer
Robert Mapplethorpe—photographer
Robert Redford—actor and director
Eva Hesse—painter/sculptor
Ellsworth Kelly—painter
Terrence Howard—actor
Jeremy Scott—fashion designer

RHODE ISLAND SCHOOL OF DESIGN

2 College Street
Providence, RI 02903–2784

Phone: (401) 454-6300
Website: risd.edu
Email: admissions@risd.edu

Tuition: $$$
Campus student enrollment (undergraduate): 2,014

Degree(s): BFA; Degrees requiring fifth year: bachelor of architecture (BARC) and Brown/RISD Dual Degree
Concentrations: Apparel design, architecture, ceramics, film/animation/video, furniture design, glass, graphic design, illustration, industrial design, interior architecture, jewelry/metalsmithing, painting, photography, printmaking, sculpture, textiles.
Artistic portfolio requirement: Yes. All undergraduate applicants must submit a portfolio of visual work and additionally submit two solutions to a single prompt chosen from three available options.
Scholarships available: Yes.
Number of faculty: 168 full-time, 302 part-time

Prominent Alumni:

Seth MacFarlane
Nicole Miller
Michael Maltzan
Shahzia Sikander
Gus Van Sant
David Macaulay
Shepard Fairey
Dale Chihuly
Joe Gebbia
Brian Chesky

ROCHESTER INSTITUTE OF TECHNOLOGY

60 Lomb Memorial Drive
Rochester, NY 14623

Phone: (585) 475-6631
Website: rit.edu
Email: admissions@rit.edu

Tuition: $
Campus student enrollment (undergraduate): 15,401

Degree(s): BFA, BS, Certificate, Diploma
Concentrations: Art: fine arts studio, medical illustration, illustration, art education; crafts: clay, glass, metals, wood; design: 3D digital graphics, graphic design, industrial design, interior design, new media design and imaging; film/video/animation: motion picture science, production, animation, stagecraft, live action production, craft foundations; photo: advertising photography, biomedical photographic communications, photojournalism, fine art photography, visual media, imaging and photographic technology; print media: media arts and technology, graphic media.

Artistic portfolio requirement: Yes

Scholarships available: Yes, merit scholarships up to $18,000 per year

SCHOOL OF THE MUSEUM OF FINE ARTS, BOSTON AT TUFTS UNIVERSITY

230 The Fenway
Boston, MA 02115–5596

Phone: (617) 369-3626, toll-free: (800) 643-6078
Website: smfa.edu
Email: admissions@smfa.edu

Tuition: $$

Degree(s): studio diploma, post-baccalaureate certificate and BFA, BFA/BA or BFA/BS with Tufts University; BFA with Northeastern University.

Concentrations: Drawing and painting, liberal arts and sciences, media arts, performance and 3D, print and graphic arts, photography, sculpture, ceramics.

Artistic portfolio requirement: Yes

Scholarships available: Yes; merit scholarships range from $3,000 to full tuition and are renewed annually.

Number of faculty: Approximately 50 full-time and 100 part-time

Prominent Alumni:

David Lynch—filmmaker/director
Nan Goldin—photographer
Ellen Gallagher—mixed media artist
Cy Twombly—painter
Ellsworth Kelly—painter/sculptor/printmaker
Jim Dine—painter/printmaker
Zach Feuer—owner, Zach Feuer Gallery
Torben Giehler—painter
Lalla Essaydi—photographer

SCHOOL OF VISUAL ARTS

209 East 23rd Street
New York, NY 10010–3994

Phone: (212) 592-2100
Website: sva.edu
Email: admissions@sva.edu

Tuition: $
Campus student enrollment (undergraduate): 3,648

Degree(s): BFA

Majors: Advertising; animation; cartooning; computer art, computer animation and visual effects; design; film; fine arts; illustration; interior design; photography and video; visual and critical studies

Artistic portfolio requirement: Yes

Scholarships available: Silas H. Rhodes Scholarship, Chairman's Merit Award, National Scholastic Art Award, SVA Grant (need-based), SVA Matching Outside Scholarship (need-based). Also, a scholarship is awarded each year to one of the finalists selected at the Ohio Governor's Youth Art Exhibition.

Number of faculty: 939

Percentage and number of undergraduate applicants accepted into the university per year: 69%, or 3,673 undergraduates.

Student activities: Community service; student organizations including cultural groups, academic groups, and other interest related groups; discounted tickets to cultural, sporting, and theater events; student center for social events, art exhibitions, and competitions; Visual Arts Student Association, SVA's student government; Student Senator Program; Visual Opinion magazine; outings and trips; WSVA radio station; and yearbook.

Prominent Alumni:

Michael Cuesta—director
Steve Ditko—cocreator, *The Amazing Spider-Man*
Brian (KAWS) Donnelly—artist

Michael Giacchino—Academy Award–winning composer

Pete Hamill—writer

Keith Haring—artist

Julia Hoffmann—creative director, MoMA

Sol Lewitt—artist

Elizabeth Peyton—artist

Bill Plympton—animator

Joe Quesada—chief creative officer, Marvel

Lauren Redniss—illustrator

Carlos Saldanha—director

Stephen Savage—illustrator

Harris Savides—cinematographer

Park Seo-won—CEO and creative director, Big Ant International

Lorna Simpson—artist

Tom Sito—animator

Rebecca Sugar—creator, writer and director of *Steven Universe*

Sarah Sze—artist

Raina Telgemeier—illustrator

Zackary Drucker—artist

SYRACUSE UNIVERSITY

College of Visual and Performing Arts
School of Art, School of Design, and Department of Transmedia
202 Crouse College
Syracuse, NY 13244–1010

Phone: (315) 443-2769
Website: vpa.syr.edu
Email: admissu@syr.edu

Tuition: $$
Campus student enrollment (undergraduate): 14,566

Degree(s): Bachelor of fine arts (BFA), bachelor of science (BS), bachelor of industrial design (BID)
Majors: Art education, art photography, art video, arts in context, communications design, computer art and animation, environmental and interior design, fashion design, film, history of art, illustration, industrial and interaction design, studio arts (with intensives in ceramics, illustration, jewelry and metalsmithing, painting, printmaking, sculpture).

Artistic portfolio requirement: Yes, a portfolio is required for consideration for admission to majors in the School of Art, School of Design, and Department of Transmedia.

Scholarships available: Yes, academic and portfolio based scholarships available.

Activities and opportunities in the School of Art, School of Design, and Department of Transmedia: All three units support interdisciplinary activities across artistic disciplines and with academic areas at Syracuse University. Internationally known visiting artists and designers give lectures, presentations, and critiques of student work. Student organizations afford entrepreneurial and community engagement opportunities. Study abroad opportunities include Florence and Bologna, Italy; London, England; Santiago, Chile; and Prague, Czech Republic.

Prominent Alumni:

Brad Anderson (1951)—creator of syndicated comic panel "Marmaduke"

Robb Armstrong (1985)—creator of "Jump Start" syndicated comic strip, children's author

LaToya Ruby Frazier (2007)—photographer, video, and performance artist

Betsey Johnson (1964)—fashion designer

Warren Kimble (1957)—contemporary folk artist

Bill Viola (1973)—video artist

Gianfranco Zaccai (1970)—cofounder, president, and chief design officer, Continuum

Alan Dye (1997)—vice president of user interface design, Apple Inc.

Thom Filicia (1993)—interior designer and principal, Thom Filicia Inc.

Chris Renaud (1989)—director of *Despicable Me*, *Despicable Me 2*, *The Secret Life of Pets*

THE COLLEGE OF NEW JERSEY

The School of Arts and Communication
P.O. Box 7718
2000 Pennington Road
Ewing, NJ 08628–0718

Phone: (609) 771-2131
Website: artscomm.tcnj.edu
Email: tcnjinfo@tcnj.edu

Tuition: $
Campus student enrollment (undergraduate):
6,758

Degree(s): BA, BFA
Majors: Art Education, Art History, Interactive Media, and Visual Arts (with Specializations in Graphic Design, Fine Arts, and Lens-Based Arts)
Concentrations: Digital Media encompasses digital imaging, animation, virtual reality, motion graphics and video, audio and electronic music, interface and web design.

Interactive Computing explores app development, programming for games, user experience design, interaction design, digital fabrication, and physical computing.

Professional Writing includes proposal writing, technical writing, online journalism, interactive storytelling, and stories and scripts for movies, animations, and video games.

Portfolio requirement: Acceptance to the Visual Arts and Art Education majors requires a successful portfolio review as well as admission by the College. A portfolio review is also required to enter the Dual Visual Arts major, which is offered to students enrolled in one of the following programs: Deaf Education and Art (DEAR), Early Childhood Education and Art (ECAR), Elementary Education and Art (ELAR), or Special Education and Art (SEAR). Please note: A portfolio review is not necessary for students applying for an Art History major. If you do not have a portfolio, you are encouraged to apply as an Open Options student to the School of Arts and Communication. The Open Option Program in the School of Arts and Communication is designed for those students who are not ready to declare a major but are interested in one or more programs within the School. Students in Open Options may enroll in studio art classes as freshmen to build up a portfolio and then can submit an application to apply for a major within the Department of Art and Art History.

Portfolio requirement for Interactive Media program: No portfolio requirement. Apply via the Common Application to The College of New Jersey and select Interactive Multimedia (IMM) as primary choice of major for consideration.

Scholarships available: Off-campus Experience Scholarship Award (students must apply through written proposal). Exceptional Freshmen Merit Scholarship award (based on GPA and creative potential)

Number of faculty (Art programs): 15
Number of majors and minors (Art programs): 185 majors and 42 minors
Number of faculty (Interactive Media): 5 full-time faculty
Number of majors and minors (Interactive Media): 140 majors, 47 minors
Percentage and number of applicants accepted into the department per year (Art programs): 64% students accepted; 132 applicants; 85 accepted
Percentage and number of applicants accepted into the department per year (Interactive Media): Average* Admit Rate for IMM = 67%, Average* Number of Applicants Admitted = 57, Average* Number of Applicants Enrolled = 22 (*five-year average)
Department activities: The Department of Art and Art History hosts guest artists and visiting critics throughout the academic year. Students regularly attend lectures, exhibitions and events in nearby Philadelphia and New York City galleries, museums. and arts organizations. The College of New Jersey Art Gallery presents six exhibitions annually, including curated exhibitions featuring nationally and internationally recognized artists, the annual senior

BFA exhibition, faculty and alumni exhibitions, and a juried statewide K–12 art exhibition.

Since 2010, The Center for the Arts has hosted over 100 guest artists, presenters, lecturers, innovators, and leaders in a vast variety of fields, many of whom are recognized nationally and/or internationally as experts in their field.

Recent Exhibits and Guest Lecturers include "A Palette of Pixels: The Evolving Art of Video Games" (a recent exhibition at the TCNJ Art Gallery; curated by IMM faculty), "Press Play: Inside the Music and Art of Video Games" (a recent guest speaker lecture presented by Gerard Marino and Cecil Kim from Sony PlayStation's *God of War* series of games). Department Annual Special Events: "AIMM After Dark" (an end-of-semester showcase featuring student work), IMM Senior Thesis Showcase (exhibition of IMM senior thesis projects). National competitions: Global Game Jam (48-hour game design competition), Campus Movie Fest (weeklong film competition), TCNJ ACM SIGGRAPH FJORG (48-hour animation competition).

TYLER SCHOOL OF ART AT TEMPLE UNIVERSITY

2001 N. 13th Street
Philadelphia, PA 19122

Phone: (215) 777-9090
Website: temple.edu/tyler
Email: tylerart@temple.edu

Tuition: $$$$
Campus student enrollment (undergraduate): Approximately 1,600

Degree(s): BFA, BA, BS
Concentrations: Division of Architecture and Environmental Design at Tyler: BS Architecture, BS Architectural Preservation, BS Facilities Management, BS Landscape Architecture, BS Horticulture, AS Horticulture, BS Community Development.

Tyler School of Art:
BSED Art Education, BA Art History, Art History Minor, BS Visual Studies, BFA in Ceramics, Glass, Fibers and Material Studies, Metals/Jewelry/CAD-CAM, Graphic and Interactive Design, Photography, Printmaking, Painting and Drawing, or Sculpture.
BFA with teaching certificate
Artistic portfolio requirement: Yes

UNIVERSITY OF THE ARTS

College of Art and Design
320 South Broad Street
Philadelphia, PA 19102

Phone: (215) 717-6030, toll-free (800) 616-2787
Website: uarts.edu
Email: admissions@uarts.edu

Tuition: $$
Campus student enrollment (undergraduate): 1890

Degree(s): BFA, BS
Areas of study:
Animation
Art Education
Ceramics
Crafts
Fibers + Textile Studies
Film + Video
Film + Animation
Film Design + Production
Game Art
Glass
Graphic Design
Illustration
Industrial Design
Interdisciplinary Fine Arts
Jewelry/Metals
Painting + Drawing
Photography
Photo + Film Media

Printmaking + Book Arts
Sculpture
Wood/Furniture
Artistic portfolio requirement: Yes
Scholarships available: Yes, $8,000 to full tuition.
Number of faculty: 105 full-time faculty university-wide; 8-to-1 student faculty ratio
Number of majors and minors: Over 50 undergraduate programs university-wide; theater students may minor in other disciplines including music, fine art, and design
Percentage and number of applicants accepted into the department per year: Approximately 200 new students enroll in the College of Art, Media & Design each year; acceptance rates vary by program.

Prominent Alumni:

Ric Kidney—film producer (*Salt, Legally Blonde, Six Degrees of Separation*)
Joe Dante—film director (*Gremlins*)
Jerry Pinkney—Caldecott Award–winning illustrator
The Quay Brothers—independent filmmakers/animators
Jan and Stan Berenstain—children's book authors
Irving Penn—fashion photographer

UNIVERSITY OF BRIDGEPORT

Shintaro Akatsu School of Design
Department of Art and Design
84 Iranistan Avenue
Bridgeport, CT 06604

Phone: (203) 576-4222
Website: sasd.bridgeport.edu
Email: admit@bridgeport.edu

Tuition: $
Campus student enrollment (undergraduate): 2,897

Degree(s): BS, BFA
Concentrations: Graphic design, industrial design, interior design

Artistic portfolio requirement: Yes
Scholarships available: Yes
Number of faculty: 26

UNIVERSITY OF MASSACHUSETTS DARTMOUTH

College of Visual and Performing Arts
285 Old Westport Road
North Dartmouth, MA 02747

Phone: (508) 999-8605
Website: umassd.edu
Email: admissions@umassd.edu

Tuition: $$$
Campus student enrollment (undergraduate): 7,295

Degree(s): BFA, BA in Music, MFA, MAE, Post-Baccalaureate Certificate and Undergraduate Certificate
Concentrations: Art Education, Art History, Artisanry, Ceramics, Digital Media, Drawing, Fine Arts, Graphic Design, Illustration, Jewelry/Metals, Painting/2D studies, Photography, Printmaking, Sculpture/3D studies, Textile Design/Fiber Arts, Typography, Web & Interaction Design and Wood/Furniture Design.
Artistic portfolio requirement: Yes
Scholarships available: Yes
Number of faculty: 81 in College of Visual and Performing Arts
Number of majors and minors:
511 total enrolled in College of Visual and Performing Arts
447 total enrolled Undergraduates
64 total enrolled Graduates
26 total enrolled in a minor
Percentage and number of applicants accepted into the College of Visual and Performing Arts per year: 81%; 343 applied, 278 accepted

Department activities:
BFA Senior Exhibition; University Art Gallery at the Star Store in New Bedford, MA; Gallery 244 at the Star Store in New Bedford, MA; Boston Young Contemporaries; Emerging Young Artists; Ceramics Club; Digital Media Club; Figure Drawing Club; Paper Making Club.

Prominent Alumni:
Bruce Gray—sculptor based in Los Angeles; created a sculpture for the Zimmer Museum; currently working on a sculpture for the Children's Hospital in Boston, MA

Alex Camlin—creative director for Da Capo Press (nonfiction book publisher); adjunct professor at Emerson College in Boston, MA; work has been featured in the AIGA-Boston Best of New England Book Show

Kevin Foley—owner of KF Design based in Gunma, Japan

Steven Leahy—has been fortunate to win awards with the National Acrylic Painters Association, The Experimental Aircraft Association and the Society of Illustrators; work has been featured in *Airbrush Action* magazine, *Airbrush Art and Action*, and *Naval Aviation News*

Christine Hannon—chairperson of the Wickford Art Association in Rhode Island; her art will be in an upcoming issue of Profiles Magazine.

UNIVERSITY OF PENNSYLVANIA

Department of Undergraduate Fine Art
Charles Addams Fine Arts Hall
200 S. 36th Street
Philadelphia, PA 19104

Phone: (215) 573-5134
Website:
design.upenn.edu/fine-arts/undergraduate/program
Email: info@admissions.upenn.edu

Tuition: $$$$

Campus student enrollment (undergraduate):
11,588

Degree(s): BA
Concentrations: Fine arts
Courses offered: Animation and 3D modeling, ceramics, design, drawing and painting, photography, printmaking, sculpture, and video
Portfolio requirement: Portfolios are not required but may be submitted as supplemental material with admissions application.
Number of faculty: More than 50

WILLIAMS COLLEGE

Department Name: Art History and Studio Art Department
W.L. Spencer Art Building
35 Driscoll Hall Dr.
Williamstown, MA 01267

Phone: (413) 597-3578
Email: admission@williams.edu

Tuition: $$$$
Campus student enrollment (undergraduate):
2,065

Degree: BA
Concentrations: Art history, studio art, history and practice
Courses offered: Art history, architectural design, calligraphy, drawing, film photography, photography, painting, sculpture, video
Artistic portfolio requirement: No
Number of faculty: 29
Department activities: Activities are driven by students majoring in art history or art studio. There is a committee of majors who design and organize outside events including panel discussions, visiting speakers, and other related activities. Students exhibit their work year around in the Wilde Gallery in the Spencer Art Building.

Prominent Alumni:

Meleko Mokgosi (2007)

Laylah Ali (1990)

Wendy W. Jacob (1980)

Liza Johnson (1992)

Inigo Manglano-Ovalle (1983)

Barbara Prey (1979)

Katie Sawyer Rose (1996)

In the graduate art program, we have several alumni who are prominent museum curators and directors.

YALE UNIVERSITY

School of Art

1156 Chapel Street, POB 208339

New Haven, Connecticut, 06520–8339

Phone: (203) 432-2600

Website: art.yale.edu/undergraduate

Email: lisa.kereszi@yale.edu

Tuition: $$$

Campus student enrollment (undergraduate): 5,532

Degree(s): BA

Concentrations: Art

Courses offered: Graphic design, painting, printmaking, photography, sculpture, film, video

Portfolio requirement: Undergraduate applicants wishing to major in art at Yale must apply to Yale College directly. The prerequisites for acceptance into the major are a Sophomore Review, which is an evaluation of work from studio courses taken at Yale School of Art.

Number of faculty: More than 100

Scholarships: Yes

Department activities: Undergraduate art students may apply for funding to help pay for an art exhibition made outside of coursework.

Southeast

EAST CAROLINA UNIVERSITY

School of Art and Design

Jenkins Fine Arts Center

Greenville, NC 27858

Phone: (252) 328-6563

Website: ecu.edu/art/

Email: admis@ecu.edu

Tuition: $

Campus student enrollment (undergraduate): 23,039

Degree(s): BFA, BA

Concentrations: Animation/interactive design, ceramics, film and media production, graphic design, illustration, metal design, painting, photography, printmaking, sculpture, textile design

Artistic portfolio requirement: No

Scholarships available: Yes

Number of faculty: Approximately 50

Number of majors and minors: 700+ in the School of Art

Prominent Alumni:

Many alumni have become art professors and department chairs of art departments at various institutions across the United States. Additional alumni include the following:

Irene Bailey—portrait artist

Ann Brennan—director, Cameron Museum of Art, NC

Todd Coates—chief creative officer, Capstrat

Maggy Costandy—interior designer

Jeff Flemming—director, Des Moines Art Center, IA

Jerry Jackson—deputy director, Penland School of Crafts

Kristi Kloss—metals program director, Columbus Center of Art, OH

Catherine Coulter Lloyd—curator/visual arts specialist, The Imperial Center, Rocky Mount, NC

Amanda Micheletto-Blouin—program and visual arts director, Kinston Community Council for the Arts, NC

Sharon Massey—Martha Gault Art Gallery, Director, Slippery Rock University, PA

Matt Munoz—chief design officer and partner at New Kind

Kymia Nawabi—won season two of Bravo's *A Work of Art: The Next Great Artist*

Ron Probst—clay artist

Teresa Graham Salt—silk tapestry artist

Troy Tyner—partner/creative director at the Mitre Agency

MEMPHIS COLLEGE OF ART

1930 Poplar Avenue
Overton Park
Memphis, TN 38104

Phone: (901) 272-5151, toll-free (800) 727-1088
Website: mca.edu
Email: info@mca.edu

Tuition: $
Campus student enrollment (undergraduate): 358

Degree(s): BFA in Animation; BFA in Graphic Design; BFA in Illustration; BFA in Illustration/Comics; BFA in Painting/Drawing; BFA in Photography
Concentrations: Digital media, drawing/painting, graphic design, metals, photography, printmaking
Artistic portfolio requirement: Yes
Number of faculty: 69

Prominent Alumni:
Amy Carter—painter
Bert Sharpe—chair, American Crafts Council
George Wardlaw—chair, University of Massachusetts Art Department
Larry Thomas—San Francisco artist and twotime Prix de Rome winner
Emily Jacir—film, photography, installation Hugo

Boss Prize award winner; Golden Lion award winner; international exhibitions including Museum of Modern Art in New York and San Francisco and Modern *Art* Oxford

Jina Bolton—interaction designer, Crush & Lovely; former visual interaction designer and front-end web developer, Apple, Inc.

Melissa Ford Hart—partner, Ernest Neuman Studios in New York City; national exhibitions

Jim Ramer—chair and director of graduate studies and photography department, Parsons, the New School for Design

Allison Smith (print/papermaking)—head of exhibitions, Gagosian Gallery in New York

Coleman Coker—principal, buildingstudio; recipient of the Rome Prize; Peabody Fellowship to Harvard; published author

MURRAY STATE UNIVERSITY

Department of Art & Design
604 Fine Arts Building
Murray, KY 42071

Phone: (270) 809-3784
Website: murraystate.edu/art
Email: zsmetana@murraystate.edu

Tuition per semester: $
Campus student enrollment (undergraduate): 10,158

Degree(s): BS, BA, BFA in Studio Art, BA, BS, BFA in Studio Art with Teaching Certification (P-12), BA, BFA in Studio Art with Enhanced Art History
Concentrations: Ceramics, drawing, graphic design, metalsmithing, painting, photography, printmaking, sculpture, woodworking
Artistic portfolio requirement: Yes, for scholarships only
Scholarships available: Yes, numerous available
Number of faculty: 15
Number of majors and minors: 150 majors, 35 minors

Percentage and number of applicants accepted into the department per year: Any student accepted by Murray State University may enter the department. This is approximately 35–40 students per year.

Department activities: Four art galleries, two of them mainly student galleries, 25 to 35 exhibitions per year, 5 to 15 visiting artist lectures/workshops per year.

NEW WORLD SCHOOL OF THE ARTS

300 NE 2nd Avenue
Miami, FL 33132

Phone: (305) 237-7045
Website: nwsa.mdc.edu
Email: nwsainfo@mdc.edu

Tuition: $
Campus student enrollment (undergraduate): 448

Degree(s): BFA, Minor Art History
Concentrations: Art & Technology, graphic design, drawing, painting, photography, sculpture
Artistic portfolio requirement: Yes
Scholarships available: Yes
Number of faculty: 7 full-time, 24 adjunct
Number of majors: 6
Percentage and number of applicants accepted into the department per year: 50 freshmen/transfers selected per year

Prominent Alumni:

Rafael Domenech—painter, Tulsa Arts Fellowship Recipient, CINTAS Recipient
Jen Stark—contemporary artist, sculpture, drawing, animation
Chi Lam
Natalia Benedetti
Hernan Bas
Bert Rodriguez
Adler Guerrier

Naomi Fisher
Jen Stark
Michael Vazquez
Jacin Giordano
Bhakti Baxter
John Espinosa
Joshua Levine
TM Sisters
Martin Oppel

RINGLING COLLEGE OF ART AND DESIGN

2700 N. Tamiami Trail
Sarasota, FL 34234

Phone: (941) 351-5100, toll-free (800) 255-7695
Website: ringling.edu
Email: admissions@ringling.edu or info@ringling.edu

Tuition: $
Campus student enrollment (undergraduate): 1,354

Degree(s): BFA, BA
Majors: Advertising design, Business of art and design, Computer animation, Creative writing, Film, Fine arts, Game art, Graphic design, Illustration, Interior design, Motion design, Photography and imaging, Visual studies
Artistic portfolio requirement: For some majors.
Scholarships available: Yes
Number of faculty: 154

Prominent Alumni:

Patrick Osborne—2015 Academy Award winner for Best Animated Short Film for his debut directorial work on *Feast*
David Bromstad—host of HGTV's *Color Splash*
Brandon Oldenburg—Academy Award winner, Best Animated Short Film, *The Fantastic Flying Books of Morris Lessmore;* co-founder of ReelFx and Moonbot Studios

Jeremy Cox—he and the Imaginary Forces team took home the Creative Arts Emmy for Main Title Design for their work on the critically acclaimed series *Manhattan*

SAVANNAH COLLEGE OF ART AND DESIGN

P.O. Box 77300
Atlanta, GA

Phone: 877.722.3285
Website: scad.edu
Email: scadatl@scad.edu

Tuition: $
Campus student enrollment (undergraduate):
9,611

Degree(s): BA, BFA
Concentrations: Accessory design, animation, advertising, architectural history, architecture, art history, branded entertainment, dramatic writing, equestrian studies, fashion, fashion marketing and management, fibers, film and television, furniture design, graphic design, historic preservation, illustration, industrial design, interactive design and game development, interior design, jewelry, motion media design, painting, performing arts, photography, printmaking, production design, sequential art, sound design, television producing, user experience design, visual effects, writing.
Portfolio requirement: Although portfolios and auditions are not required for undergraduate admission, applicants are strongly encouraged to present performing arts, riding, writing, or visual arts portfolios, or to audition when possible, to enhance the application file and to be considered for scholarships.

WATKINS COLLEGE OF ART AND DESIGN

Admissions Office
2298 Rosa L. Parks Boulevard
Nashville, TN 37228

Phone: (615) 383-4848
Website: watkins.edu
Email: admissions@watkins.edu

Tuition: $
Campus student enrollment (undergraduate):
340

Degree(s): BA, BFA; BFA in film, graphic design, interior design, photography and fine art, BA in art
Concentrations: Illustration, web design
Artistic portfolio requirement: Yes for BFA and MFA, no for BA
Scholarships available: Yes
Number of faculty: 60
Student activities: Student chapters of AAFC, AIGA, ASID, IIDA, Student Filmmakers, Film Student Council, Student Government Association.

Prominent Alumni:
Lee Gilmore (2001, Film)—Sound Effects Editor at Warner Bros. Studios. Credits include: *The Amazing Spider Man, Zero Dark Thirty*, and *The Hunger Games: Catching Fire.*
Kendall Bennett (2006, Film)—Art Director; has worked as a designer and art director on many television series, including *Dexter, Law & Order: Los Angeles*, and *Body of Proof* and as the production designer for *Nashville.*
Gina Edner (2005, Interior Design)—Associate Director for Environmental Sustainability at Starwood Hotels. Gina is currently associate director for Environmental Sustainability at Starwood Hotels (which includes the prestigious brands of Sheraton, Westin, and W hotels). Through her job she is able to make a huge impact on our planet by coming up with plans on how to reduce energy and water usage at more than 1,000 hotels worldwide.

Justin Nolan Key (2005, Photography)—Creative Director, Photographer and Music Video Director at Big Machine Label Group. Justin is creative director, photographer, and video director at Big Machine Label Group, which includes three country music labels with seventeen music acts total, among them superstars Taylor Swift, Reba McEntire, and Rascal Flatts. His job entails photo shoots and television specials (for CMT, ABC, and GAC), directing music videos, and overseeing the creative services department.

UNIVERSITY OF ALABAMA AT BIRMINGHAM

Department of Art and Art History
211 Abroms Engle Institute for the Visual Arts
1221 10th Avenue South
Birmingham, AL 35294–1264

Phone: (205) 934-4941
Website: uab.edu/art
Email: chooseuab.edu

Tuition: $$
Campus student enrollment (undergraduate): 11,511

Degree(s): BA, BFA
Emphasis: Painting, drawing, ceramics, sculpture, photography, printmaking, graphic design, art history, New Media
Minor: Interdisciplinary Film Minor.
Artistic portfolio requirement: For BFA only
Scholarships available: Varies by year. Thirteen scholarship types offered each year; the total number granted per scholarship type varies. Art & Art History Scholarship Website is uab.edu/cas/art/resources/student/scholarships.
Number of faculty: 14 full-time
Number of current undergrad art major students: 240
Department activities: AIGA, Medium: The Art Club at UAB Student Chapter, Juried Student

Annual Exhibition, Pop-Up Studios, Project Space Exhibition, Visiting Artist and Scholar Programs, Friend Lecture Series.

VIRGINIA COMMONWEALTH UNIVERSITY SCHOOL OF THE ARTS (VCUARTS)

325 North Harrison Street
Richmond, VA 23284

Phone: (804) VCU-ARTS / Toll-free (866) 534-3201
Website: arts.vcu.edu
Email: arts@vcu.edu

Tuition: $$$$
Campus student enrollment (undergraduate): 24,051

Degree(s): BA, BFA
Concentrations: Art education, art history, cinema, communication arts, craft (ceramics, wood, metals, glass, fiber), dance and choreography, fashion design and merchandising, filmmaking, graphic design, interior design, kinetic imaging (animation, video, sound), photography, painting, printmaking, sculpture, theater
Artistic portfolio requirement: A portfolio is required for admission into the Art Foundation Program. Students spend two semesters in Art Foundation prior to entering the following majors: Art Education, Communication Arts, Craft/Material Studies, Fashion Design, Graphic Design, Interior Design, Kinetic Imaging, Painting and Printmaking, Photography and Film, and Sculpture + Extended Media.
The portfolio requirements are: Submit 12 to 16 works of art that you have created within the past two years that show your promise in visual art and design. Present your strongest work and demonstrate your potential to develop a diverse set of skills and ideas should you be accepted into VCUarts. We prefer to see a diverse range of 2D and 3D media. Drawing from observation

is recommended, while copying anime, cartoons, graffiti, or tattoos is discouraged.

Scholarships available: Yes

Dean's Scholarship:$6,500 per year, renewable for four years, for an estimated total value of $26,000

Provost's Scholarship: $13,000 per year, renewable for four years, for an estimated total value of $52,000

President's Scholarship: $13,000 per year, plus the cost of room and board, renewable for four years, for an estimated total value of approximately $98,000.

Other scholarships and awards are available. See arts.vcu.edu/scholarships.

Number of faculty: 101

Number of majors and minors: 1666 majors, 81 minors

Department activities:

500+ student organizations offered at VCU.

Recreational Sports

Outdoor Adventure Program

Undergraduate Research Grants

Honors College

Arts Honors

Study abroad

VCUarts CoLaboratory (CoLab) interdisciplinary internship program

Creative Entrepreneurship

VCU da Vinci Center

Art education: student teacher exhibit, various community activities offered through the National Art Education student chapter

Craft/Material Studies: Exhibitions, symposia and visiting artists

Fashion Design + Merchandising: International field trips to Europe in spring and Asia in summer; domestic field trips to NYC and MAGIC Show, Las Vegas, annual fashion show of student work each April, Jeanology program

Midwest

ART ACADEMY OF CINCINNATI

1212 Jackson Street
Cincinnati, OH 45202

Phone: (513) 562-6262, toll-free (800) 323-5692
Website: artacademy.edu
Email: admissions@artacademy.edu

Tuition: $
Campus student enrollment (undergraduate): 210

Degree(s): BFA, associate of science degree in graphic design, art history, audio & video, and MAAE, Master of Arts in Art Education

Majors: design, illustration, drawing & painting, photography, sculpture, print media

Artistic portfolio requirement: Yes

Scholarships available: Yes; entrance scholarships $2,500 to $17,000 per year.

Number of faculty: 7 full-time, 40 part-time

Prominent Alumni:

Malcolm Grear—designer and teacher

Jim Dine—painter and printmaker

Frank Duveneck—painter

Kate Reno Miller—painter

Thom Shaw—painter and printmaker

Tom Wesselman—painter

BOWLING GREEN STATE UNIVERSITY

School of Art
1000 Fine Arts Center
Bowling Green, OH 43403

Phone: BGSU admissions toll-free
(800) CHOOSEBGSU; Fine arts admissions
(419) 372-0107
Website: bgsu.edu/
Email: admissions@bgsu.edu or artschool@bgsu.edu

Tuition: $$

Campus student enrollment (undergraduate): 14,344 (total)

Degree(s): BA, BFA

Concentrations: two-dimensional studies (painting and drawing, photography, printmaking), three-dimensional studies (ceramics, glass, jewelry and metal, sculpture), art education, art history, digital arts, graphic design

Artistic portfolio requirement: No for BA, yes for BFA

Scholarships available: Yes

Number of faculty: 47 full-time, 6 part-time

Percentage and number of applicants accepted into the department per year: Varies

Prominent Alumni:

MaryJo Arnoldi—curator, African Art and Ethnology

Rick Valicenti—designers and owner of design firm Thirst in Chicago

Catherine Zweig and Matt Reynolds—owners of The Drawing Works, a printmaking studio and gallery in San Francisco

Andrea Bowers—installation artist

Bernie Casey—artist, athlete, actor

James Pickens Jr.—artist, actor

COLLEGE FOR CREATIVE STUDIES

Office of Admissions
201 East Kirby Street
Detroit, MI 48202

Phone: (313) 664-7400, toll-free (800) 952-ARTS
Website: collegeforcreativestudies.edu
Email: admissions@collegeforcreativestudies.edu

Tuition: $

Campus student enrollment (undergraduate): 1,420

Degree(s): BFA

Concentrations: BFA: Advertising design, advertising copywriting, art education, crafts (art furniture, ceramics, fiber design, glass, jewelry & metalsmithing), entertainment arts (animation, game design, video), fashion accessory design, fine arts (painting, print media, sculpture), graphic design, illustration, interior design, photography, product design, transportation design.

Artistic portfolio requirement: Yes, 5–8 pieces required

Scholarships available: Yes.

Award of Excellence Walter B. Ford II Scholarship: 10 full-tuition scholarships

CSC Scholarship: $5,000–$10,000 per year

Number of faculty: 260 full-time and part-time

Student activities: 12 student organizations and an active Student Life Office.

Prominent Alumni:

Doug Chiang (industrial design, 1982)—executive vice president, ImageMovers Digital Studio

Ralph Gilles (ID transportation design 1992)—senior vice president, product design, Chrysler; president and CEO, Dodge brand

Kevin Hunter (ID transportation design, 1982)—president, Calty Design Research

Jennifer and Ellery Gave (graphic communication, 2000)—founding partners, CapacityTV

David Hardin (animation/digital media, 2004)—senior character animator, Sony Imageworks

Jason Mayden (industrial design, 2002)—footwear designer, brand Jordan, Nike

Greg Shamus (photography, 1993)—team photographer for New Orleans Hornets; freelance sports photographer

Jay Shuster (industrial design, 1993)—sketch artist, Pixar Animation Studios

Bill Morrison (illustration, 1982)—creative director, Bongo Comics

Gail Taub (graphic communication, 1991)—vice president, creative services, ePrize

Curt Aumiller (ID transportation design, 1995)—senior industrial designer, Microsoft

Matt Canzano (graphic communication, 1981)—executive vice president/executive creative director, McCann-Erickson

Tim Flattery (industrial design 1987)—freelance concept artist/illustrator; worked on more than 30 major motion pictures in the last two decades

Elizabeth Carey Smith (graphic design, 2002)—creative director, Lincoln Center

COLUMBUS COLLEGE OF ART & DESIGN

60 Cleveland Ave.
Columbus, OH 43215

Phone: (614) 224-9101, toll-free (877) 997-CCAD
Website: ccad.edu
Email: admissions@ccad.edu

Tuition: $
Campus student enrollment (undergraduate):
1,087 undergraduate

Degree(s): BFA
Concentrations: Advertising & Graphic Design, Animation, Cinematic Arts, Comics & Narrative Practice, Contemporary Crafts, Fashion Design, Fine Arts (including painting, drawing, ceramics, sculpture, printmaking and glassblowing), Illustration, Industrial Design, Interior Design, Photography, Studio Art with an Emphasis in History of Art & Visual Culture
Artistic portfolio requirement: Yes
Scholarships available: Yes. All admitted students are automatically considered for institutional scholarships. These funds are limited and are awarded to the earliest qualifiers based on materials submitted for review.

Scholastic Art Awards: National Portfolio Gold Medal winners are eligible for half-tuition scholarships, renewable for up to four years. National Gold Medal winners in individual categories are eligible for $2,000 tuition scholarships ($1,000 per year for two years). Scholastic Art Awards-related scholarships are coordinated with other financial aid awards.

Ohio Governor's Youth Art Exhibition: Governor's Award of Excellence winners are eligible for a $10,000 tuition scholarship, renewable for up to four years. Others whose work is in the Ohio Governor's Youth Art Exhibition are eligible for $2,000 tuition scholarships ($1,000 per year for two years). Ohio Governor's Youth Art Exhibition–related scholarships are coordinated with other financial aid awards.

Arts Recognition and Talent Search Scholarship, The National Young Arts Foundation: National winners (Gold, Silver, and Levels I, II and III) are eligible for four-year, half-tuition scholarships. YoungArts-related scholarships are coordinated with other financial aid awards.

National Art Honor Society: Certificate holders are eligible for $4,000 tuition scholarships ($1,000 per year for four years). National Art Honor Society-related scholarships are coordinated with other financial aid awards.

Number of faculty: 188 full-time and part-time
Department activities: Battle Games Alliance, Black Student Leadership Association, CCAD's Got Talent, Chroma: Best of CCAD student exhibition, Comic Book Club, Dodgeball Club, Entrepreneurship Club, Give Back!, International Students Association, Open Figure Drawing, Paranormal Society, Queer Alliance, Semiannual Art Fair, The Big Boo Halloween costume contest, Welcome Fest, Women's Leadership Institute, Yoga, Zumba.

Prominent Alumni:
James Dupree—painter and printmaker
Ming Fay—sculptor
Ron Miller—writer and illustrator
Sally Wern Comport—illustrator
Edward Buchanan—fashion designer and stylist
Amy Butler—home décor and textile designer
Richard Cowdry—*New York Times* best-selling illustrator
Inke Essenhigh—painter
Ming Fay—sculptor and installation artist

Dean Mitchell—painter

Aminah Robinson—artist and MacArthur Foundation fellow

Alice Schille—painter

Jeff Stahler—nationally syndicated cartoonist

Steve Stone—advertising agency principal

Ron Tsang—industrial designer, Emmy Award winner

John Urbano—photographer and filmmaker

GRAND VALLEY STATE UNIVERSITY

Department of Art and Design
1105 CAC Allendale, MI 49401

Phone: (616) 331-3486
Website: gvsu.edu/art
Email: artdept@gvsu.edu

Tuition: $$$
Campus student enrollment (undergraduate): 21,972

Degree(s): BA, BS, BFA
Concentrations: Art education offers the following emphasis areas: ceramics, jewelry/metals, painting, printmaking, sculpture and visual studies. The studio art BFA offers emphasis areas in ceramics, graphic design, illustration, jewelry/metals, painting, printmaking, sculpture and visual studies.
Artistic portfolio requirement: Yes
Scholarships available: $1,000 annually for up to four years plus scholarships for upper classmen
Number of faculty: 28 full-time faculty
Number of majors and minors: 257 majors; 11 art history minors, 103 studio art minors
Percentage and number of applicants accepted into the department per year: 98 applicants, 90% accepted.
Department activities: Multiple exhibitions annually, visiting artist lectures and field trips. Study Abroad
Six-credit faculty-led London Summer Program: A

study abroad program where students take a class at Kingston University and visit cultural centers, museums, and galleries.
Kingston University in London Exchange Program: A study abroad program where students attend full-time for one or two semesters.
Faculty-led international course/experience in the summer: Recent countries have included South Korea and Japan.
Seoul National University of Science and Technology Exchange Program in South Korea.

Prominent Alumni
Jo Hormuth—restorer and designer
David Huang—metalsmith
Chad Pastotnik—printmaker, book artist
Jennifer Schaub—printmaker, board member of the DAAC, marketing chair for the Young Nonprofit Professionals Network of Greater Grand Rapids, MI, secretary for the Heartside Business Association and serves on the Heartside Neighborhood Association
Julie Upmeyer—ceramist, Inititate Caravansarai in Istanbul, Turkey, an independent space and meeting point for an open exploration of the interactive possibilities of food, space, and the Internet

HERRON SCHOOL OF ART AND DESIGN, INDIANA UNIVERSITY–PURDUE UNIVERSITY INDIANAPOLIS (IUPUI)

Eskenazi Hall
735 W. New York Street
Indianapolis, IN 46202

Phone: (317) 278-9400
Website: herron.iupui.edu
Email: herron4u@iupui.edu

Tuition: $
Campus student enrollment (undergraduate): 21,984 at IUPUI, 696 at Herron in Fall 2015

Degree(s): BA, BFA, BAE

Concentrations:

Art education, art history, ceramics, drawing and illustration, furniture design, integrative studio practice, painting, photography, printmaking, sculpture, visual communication design (with a digital design track that senior VCD students can choose to take)

Artistic portfolio requirement: Yes

Scholarships available: Yes

Number of faculty: 50

Number of majors and minors: 696

Study abroad programs:

2 per year; a 1-week spring break trip and 3-week summer trip are typically offered. Destinations vary. Italy, Spain, and other parts of Europe are popular destinations.

Activities:

Herron School of Art and Design's numerous gallery spaces span two buildings and are among the finest university galleries in the United States, and any gallery space public or commercial in Indianapolis. These galleries assure that students gain inspiration from contemporary works by peers, faculty, and regional, national, and international artists and designers. They also facilitate understanding of gallery installation and presentation protocols.

Herrons' Basile Center for Art, Design, and Public Life manages numerous professional practice experiences for students. Since the Basile Center was established in 2006, more than 1,000 students have participated in projects serving approximately 115 community partners.

Herron's innovative Think It Make It Lab was established in 2014–15 and promotes the creative use of new technologies in a collaborative environment. The Lab provides access to digital technologies that help prepare students to become experts in broad applications of design, production, and fabrication for a variety of fields.

Prominent Alumni:

Garo Antreasian

Andrew Blauvelt

Norman Bridwell

Vija Celmins

Rob Day

Daniel Edwards

Don Gummer

Cindy Hinant

Samuel Levi Jones

Bill Justice

Jared Lee

Terrence Main

Stephen Neale

Bill Peet

Francisco Souto

KANSAS CITY ART INSTITUTE

4415 Warwick Boulevard

Kansas City, MO 64111

Phone: Toll-free (800) 522-5224

Website: kcai.edu

Email: admiss@kcai.edu

Tuition: $

Campus student enrollment (undergraduate): 645

Degree(s): BFA

Concentrations: Animation, art history, ceramics, creative writing, digital filmmaking, digital media, fiber, filmmaking, graphic design, illustration, interactive arts, painting, photography, printmaking, sculpture

Artistic portfolio requirement: Yes

Scholarships available: Yes, KCAI Merit Award: $6,000 to $18,000; some competitive awards available.

Number of faculty: 46 full-time, 55 part-time

Percentage of applicants accepted into the department per year: 63%

Prominent Alumni:

Walt Disney

Robert Rauschenberg—multimedia artist

Keith Jacobshagen—painter

Richard Notkin and Akio Takamori—ceramicists

April Greiman—graphic designer

Robert Morris and Kate and Mel Zigler—sculptors

Thomas Barrow—photographer

KENDALL COLLEGE OF ART AND DESIGN OF FERRIS STATE UNIVERSITY

17 Fountain Street NW

Grand Rapids, MI 49503

Phone: (616) 451-2787

Website: kcad.edu

Email: kcadadmissions@ferris.edu

Tuition: $$$$

Campus student enrollment: 1,328

Degrees: BFA: Art Education, Collaborative Design, Digital Media, Drawing, Fashion Studies, Furniture Design, Graphic Design, Illustration, Industrial Design, Interior Design, Medical Illustration, Metals and Jewelry Design, Painting, Photography, Printmaking, Sculpture and Functional Art; BS: Art History.

Artistic portfolio requirement: Yes for all programs except Art History, Collaborative Design, Furniture Design, and Interior Design

Scholarships available: Yes.

Kendall College of Art and Design of Ferris State University Art Day Scholarship Competition: up to $20,000

Kendall Scholarships of Merit: $1,000 to $5,000 per year

Woodbridge N. Ferris Scholarships: up to $11,460 per year

METROPOLITAN STATE UNIVERSITY OF DENVER

Department of Art

Campus Box 59

P.O. Box 173362

Denver, CO 80217–3362

Phone: (303) 556-3090

Website: msudenver.edu/art

Email: msudenver-art@msudenver.edu

Tuition: $

Campus student enrollment (undergraduate): 20,000+

Degree(s): BA in Art, BA in Art History, Theory and Criticism, BFA in Art, BFA in Art Education, BFA in Communication Design. Minors: Art History, Theory and Criticism, Studio Art, Digital Media

Courses: Art education, art history, art theory and criticism, ceramics, communications design, drawing, jewelry and metals, painting, photography, printmaking and sculpture.

Artistic portfolio requirement: Yes for BFA degrees, no for BA degrees

Scholarships available: Not specifically for the Art Department

Number of faculty: 21 full-time, 50 affiliate

Number of majors and minors: 700 majors, 200 minors

Percentage and number of applicants accepted into the department per year: Modified open admission; all students accepted to the university may be accepted to either BA program. Candidates for the three BFA programs must complete art foundations and other studio requirements and meet GPA requirements before applying for portfolio review.

Department activities: Senior thesis exhibits each semester, honors exhibit, annual faculty show, annual student juried exhibition held at the Emmanuel Gallery (on campus), other student exhibitions, varying number of visiting artistsand scholars; events, lectures and panel discussions on campus or at CVA. Off-campus gallery is The Center for Visual Art in the Santa Fe Arts District, msudenver.edu/cva/. Student organizations include The Artists' Guild, Elements Clay Club, Drawing Club, Future Leaders of Design, Metalmorphosis, Vicious Dog Press, Art Education Club, Photography Club.

MINNEAPOLIS COLLEGE OF ART AND DESIGN

2501 Stevens Avenue South
Minneapolis, MN 55404

Phone: (612) 874-3760,
toll-free: (800) 874-6223
Website: mcad.edu
Email: admissions@mcad.edu

Tuition: $
Campus student enrollment (undergraduate): 678

Degree(s): BFA, BS
Concentrations: Advertising, animation, comic art, drawing and painting, entrepreneurial studies, filmmaking, fine arts studio, furniture design, graphic design, illustration, photography, print paper book, sculpture, web and multimedia environments.
Artistic portfolio requirement: Yes, for the BFA
Scholarships available: Yes
Number of faculty: 42 full-time, 69 adjunct/visiting artists
Percentage and number of applicants accepted into the department per year: 60%
Student activities: Off-campus study, visiting artists, student clubs, Radio MCAD, internships, Black + White Ball, gallery openings

Prominent Alumni:
Ta-cumba Aiken—award-winning fine artist; owner/entrepreneur, TBC Studios
Kinji Akagawa—award-winning sculptor; professor of fine arts, MCAD; fine artist
Paul Brown—graphic designer in the music industry

for clients like Blue Note Records, Capital Records, Sony, Warner Bros. Records, October Films, Miramax Films, MGM
Nancy Carlson—children's book illustrator and writer (over 35 published)
Cy DeCosse—former chairman, Cy DeCosse, Inc., which was sold to Cowles Media; entrepreneur and photographer
Dan Lund—animator for Disney including *Beauty and the Beast*, *Aladdin*, *The Lion King*, *Pocahontas*, *Hunchback of Notre Dame*, *Hercules*, *Mulan* and *Tarzan*
Keogh Gleason—four-time Oscar-winning art director
Minda Gralnek—creative director, Target Corporation
Dan Jurgens—illustrator, DC Comics; president, Story Works Inc.
Mike Reed—campaign illustrator, Absolut Vodka
Richard Symkowski—senior designer, Nickelodeon
Mary Grandpre—illustrator, *Harry Potter* books
Ryan Kelly—comic illustrator, Giant Robot Warriors with writer Stuart Moore, received Eisner nomination for work on *Lucifer* for DC Comics
Nancy Rice—worldwide creative director, Miami Ad School; former senior vice president and group creative director, BBDO; founding partner, Fallon, McElligott, Rice; DDB/Needham creative director; faculty member of MCAD's advertising program
Hideki Yamamoto—president, Yamamoto Moss, design firm with clients including 3M, Northwest Airlines, and Procter & Gamble

NORTHERN ILLINOIS UNIVERSITY

School of Art and Design
Jack Arends Building
DeKalb, IL 60115–2883

Phone: (815) 753.1473
Website: niu.edu/art/
Email: jsiblik@niu.edu

Tuition: $$
Campus student enrollment (undergraduate): 14,079

Degrees:
Bachelor of Arts/Science in:
Art
Art History
Bachelor of Fine Arts in:
Emphasis 1: Design
Emphasis 2: Fine Arts—2D Studio
Emphasis 3: Fine Arts—3D Studio
Bachelor of Science in Education in:
Track 1: Teacher Certification
Track 2: Museum & Community Art Education
Admissions requirement: Same as University entrance requirements. Portfolio review may be required for retention in the program.
Number of faculty: 40
Number of majors and minors: 450
Percentage and number of applicants accepted into the department per year: Varies. The School of Art and Design, with a faculty of more than 40 artists, designers, and scholars, and an enrollment of more than 450 undergraduate and 80 graduate students, is one of the best and most comprehensive public university art schools in the United States, with a nationally established reputation in a number of fields. The long-standing quality of the School of Art and Design's programs, its affiliation with a major university, its location near the population centers of northern Illinois, and the competitiveness of its educational costs make Northern's program in the visual arts one of the best education values for art students. The School of Art and Design has been a fully accredited institutional member of the National Association of Schools of Art and Design (NASAD) since 1969. All academic programs at NIU are also accredited by the North Central Association of Colleges and Secondary Schools, while programs in education are accredited by the National Council for Accreditation of Teacher Education.

Prominent Alumni:
Marquis Hill (BM 2009)—winner, 2014 Thelonious Monk Trumpet Competition
Dan Castellaneta (BS Art Ed, 1979)—voice of Homer Simpson
Steve Prina (B.F.A 1977)—Professor of Visual & Environmental Studies, Harvard University
Tom Thayer (MFA 95)—2012 Whitney Biennial
Mike Disa (BFA 85)—known for his work on *Casper* (1995), *Hoodwinked Too!* (2011), *Pocahontas* (1995). Currently at Warner Bros Animation. Formerly a director with RGH Entertainment (Apr 2011–Dec 2013).
Carol Griseto (BFA 1977)—Upshot Design and Marketing (former business); Ruth Consulting LLC (current business)

OHIO NORTHERN UNIVERSITY

Department of Art and Design
525 South Main Street
Ada, OH 45810

Phone: (419) 772-2160
Website: onu.edu/arts_sciences/art_design
Email: art@onu.edu

Tuition: $
Campus student enrollment (undergraduate): 2,401

Degree(s): BFA, BA
Concentrations: Advertising design, graphic design, studio arts, studio arts/2D or 3D, studio arts/pre-art therapy, art education
Artistic portfolio requirement: No, but recommended
Scholarships available: Yes. Art Talent Awards, Shelley C. Petrillo Scholarship and Shelley C. Petrillo Junior Art Award; also Presidential Scholarships, Trustee Scholarships, Deans Scholarships, and Faculty Scholarships at varying amounts.
Number of faculty: 4 full-time, 2 part-time (fall 2015)

Number of majors and minors: 32 majors, 6 minors (fall 2015)

Percentage and number of applicants accepted into the department per year: 58%, acceptance of 15–20 new majors each year

Student activities: Student juried exhibit, senior capstone exhibit, senior work-in-progress exhibit, varying number of visiting artist exhibits and lectures per year, design week, department sponsored trips, AIGA/ONU student group (The Professional Association for Design), Kappa Pi art honorary, Art Student Admissions Committee, Student Art League, summer design camp, internships, Glass Axis glass-blowing workshops, Honors Day, study abroad program, European summer trips.

Prominent Alumni:

Dan Overly (1967)—The Craftmen's Guild of Mississippi

Marilyn Lysohir (1972)—Ceramics

Amy Corle (1988)—Museum of Contemporary Art Detroit

Jennifer Greeson (2000)—Walt Disney Co.

Kyle Hotz (1993)—Illustration

Julie Griffin (1986)—American Greetings Corp.

Karen Sargent (1979)—Hallmark Cards Inc.

THE CLEVELAND INSTITUTE OF ART

11610 Euclid Avenue
Cleveland, OH 44106

Phone: (216) 421-7418
Website: cia.edu
Email: admissions@cia.edu

Tuition: $
Campus student enrollment (undergraduate): 606

Degree(s): BFA
Majors: Animation, Biomedical Art, Ceramics, Drawing, Game Design, Glass, Graphic Design, Illustration, Industrial Design, Interior Architecture, Jewelry and Metals, Painting, Photography and Video, Printmaking, Sculpture and Expanded Media; Master's in Art Education

Artistic portfolio requirement: Yes
Scholarships available: Yes

Prominent Alumni:

Richard Anuszkiewicz—painter

Marc Brown—illustrator

Bruce Claxton—senior director, Motorola

Joseph Dehner—Head of Ram and Mopar Design, FCA—North America

Gerald Hershberg—vice president of design, Nissan

Zac Petroc—model supervisor, Disney

Dana Schutz—painter (hot young painter in NYC, discovered by Saatchi + Saatchi)

Viktor Shreckengost—industrial designer

THE SCHOOL OF THE ART INSTITUTE OF CHICAGO

37 S. Wabash
Chicago, IL 60603

Phone: (312) 899-5219, toll-free (800) 232-7242
Website: saic.edu
Email: admiss@saic.edu

Tuition: $$

Degree(s): BFA (with fashion and interior architecture, designed objects and architecture pathways), BA (with an emphasis in art history, theory and criticism), BFA (with an emphasis in art education), BFAW, BA in visual and critical studies

Concentrations: Architecture, interior architecture and designed objects, art and technology studies, art education, art history, theory and criticism, ceramics, fashion design, fiber and material studies, film, video and new media, painting and drawing, performance, photography, print media, sculpture, sound, visual communication, visual and critical studies.

Artistic portfolio requirement: Yes (alternative portfolio accepted)

Scholarships available: Yes. Multiple scholarships available, including merit scholarships renewed annually from $5,000 to $24,000. Academic incentive scholarships for both high school and transfer students of $2,000 (also annually renewable) are awarded.

Number of faculty: 749 full- and part-time

Number of majors and minors: Students do not declare majors. They are able to design their curriculum across multiple departmental areas or concentrate in a single department.

Student activities: "F" newsmagazine, "Fzine" online arts journal for high school students, ExTV, SAIC Radio, Student Union Galleries, multiple student groups.

Prominent Alumni:

Archibald J. Motley Jr.—painter

Sarah Vowell—writer

Claes Oldenburg—sculptor

Georgia O'Keeffe—painter

Cynthia Rowley—fashion designer

David Sedaris—writer

UNIVERSITY OF AKRON

Fine Arts Division
Mary Schiller Myers School of Art
260 Guzzetta Hall
Akron, OH 44325–1001

Phone: (330) 972-5196
Website: uakron.edu/bcas
Email: admissions@uakron.edu

Tuition: $$
Campus student enrollment (undergraduate): 21,158

Degree(s): BA, BFA
Concentrations: Art, art education, art history, ceramics, graphic design, jewelry and metalsmithing, new media, painting and drawing, photography, printmaking, sculpture, studio art

Artistic portfolio requirement: No

Scholarships available: Yes, a wide array

Number of faculty: 18 full-time faculty

Percentage and number of applicants accepted into the department per year: Varies each year

Student activities: Eight active student organizations: Akron Jewelry and Metals Club, Akron Painting League, Akron Print Enthusiasts, Art History Association, Folk Photo Association, Myers Clay Club, Student Art League, Student Design Society.

WASHBURN UNIVERSITY

Art Department
1700 SW College
Topeka, KS 66621

Phone: (785) 670-1125
Website: washburn.edu/art
Email: art@washburn.edu

Tuition: $
Campus enrollment (undergraduate): 5,800

Degree(s): BA—Art, BA—Art History; BFA—Art Studio, BFA with concentration options: Art History, Ceramics & Sculpture, Graphic Design & Electronic Art, Painting & Drawing, Photography, Printmaking, and the BFA with teacher licensure

Artistic portfolio requirement: Yes for BFA application.

Scholarships available: Yes, varies yearly. Approximately 20–30 per year from Art Department. Other university scholarships and financial aid available including full-tuition awards.

Number of faculty: 9 full-time, 2 half-time, 8–10 adjuncts

Number of majors and minors: Approximately 125 majors, about 1/3 BA and 2/3 BFA, 10–15 minors

Percentage and number of applicants accepted into the department per year: Students apply to the BFA at the sophomore level; approximately 15–20 applicants per year, 90% accepted.

Student activities: 1 annual student show, 5 informal student shows, 2–3 department-sponsored travel opportunities, guest artists, lectures, 10 demonstrations per year.

Prominent Alumni:

Bradbury Thompson—graphic designer, member of Yale faculty

Joan Foth—artist, Santa Fe, New Mexico

John Kuhn—artist, North Carolina

Randy Exon—artist and professor, Swarthmore College, PA

West

ACADEMY OF ART UNIVERSITY

79 New Montgomery Street
San Francisco, CA 94105

Phone toll-free: (800) 544-ARTS
Website: academyart.edu
Email: admissions@academyart.edu

Tuition: $
Campus student enrollment (undergraduate): 9,117

Degree(s): BA, BFA
Majors: Acting, advertising, animation and visual effects, architecture, art education, art history, fashion, fine art, game development, graphic design, illustration, industrial design, interior architecture and design, jewelry and metal arts, landscape architecture, motion pictures and television, multimedia communications, music production and sound design for visual media, photography, visual development, web design and new media, writing for film, television and digital media.
Artistic portfolio requirement: No
Scholarships available: Yes

Prominent Alumni:

Jung-seung Hong—modeler, Industrial Light and Magic

Amy Wheeler—producer, *Living with Soul*

Anuj Anand—visual effects artist, *Constantine*

ART CENTER COLLEGE OF DESIGN

1700 Lida Street
Pasadena, CA 91103

Phone: (626) 396-2373
Website: artcenter.edu
Email: admissions@artcenter.edu

Tuition: $

Campus student enrollment (undergraduate):
1,915

Degree(s): BFA: BS

Concentrations:
Advertising, Entertainment Design, Environmental Design, Film, Fine Art, Graphic Design, Illustration, Interaction Design, Photography and Imaging, Product Design, Transportation Design

Artistic portfolio requirement: Yes

Scholarships available: Yes

Number of faculty: Full-time faculty: 105; part-time faculty: 334

Percentage of applicants accepted into the department per year: 69%

Prominent Alumni:

Advertising: Gary Goldsmith, Harry Cocciolo, Tracy Wong

Entertainment Design: Victoria Ying, Kevin Chan, Patrick Hanenberger

Environmental Design: Tim Kobe, Nolen Niu, Zorine Pooladian

Film: Michael Bay, Tarsem Singh, Miranda Liu

Fine Art: Jorge Pardo, Jennifer Steinkamp, Edgar Arceneaux, Tiffany Trenda, Jeff Soto, Lisa Park

Graphic Design: Michael Osborne, Clement Mok, Dan Goods, Raphael Esquer

Illustration: Mike Shinoda, Phil Hettema, Bruce Heavin, Douglas Aitken, Drew Struzan, Mark Ryden, Martha Rich

Photography and Imaging: Andrew Bernstein, Van Evers, Just Loomis, Jen Rosenstein

Product Design: Yves Behar, Al Van Noy, Willam G. Davidson, Joe Tan, Ian Sands, Mariana Prieto

Transportation Design: Strother MacMinn, Peter Brock, Larry Shinoda, Michelle Christensen, Chris Bangle, Shiro Nakamura, Chip Foose, Tisha Johnson, Frank Saucedo, Miguel Galluzzi, Harald Belker

CALIFORNIA COLLEGE OF THE ARTS

Admissions
1111 Eighth Street
San Francisco CA 94107

Phone: toll-free: (800) 447-1ART

Website: cca.edu

Email: enroll@cca.edu

Tuition: $$

Campus student enrollment (undergraduate):
1,500

Degree(s): BFA, BA, BArch

Concentrations/Majors: Animation, architecture, ceramics, community arts, fashion design, film, furniture, glass, graphic design, illustration, industrial design, interaction design, interior design, jewelry/metal arts, painting/drawing, photography, printmaking, sculpture, textiles, visual studies, writing and literature.

Artistic portfolio requirement: Yes

Scholarships available: Yes, merit- and need-based scholarships. Creative Achievement for first-time freshmen, $10,000–20,000; Faculty Honors for transfer students, $15,000–20,000; CCA Scholarships, $1,000–24,000; Diversity scholarships (in combination with other scholarships and grants) up to full tuition and fees.

Number of faculty: 500

Percentage of applicants accepted into the school per year: 70%

Department activities: Internships, community service, study abroad, sponsored studios, lectures and symposia by guest artists.

Prominent Alumni:

Robert Arneson, Viola Frey, and Peter Voulkos—ceramicists

Jules de Balincourt, Raymond Saunders, and Nathan Oliveria—painters

Harrell Fletcher and David Ireland—conceptual artists

Wayne Wang—film director

Michael Vanderbyl, Gary Hutton, and Lucille Tenazas—designers

CALIFORNIA INSTITUTE OF THE ARTS

School of Art
24700 McBean Parkway
Valencia, CA 91355

Phone: (661) 255-1050
Website: calarts.edu
Email: admiss@calarts.edu

Tuition: $$$
Campus student enrollment (undergraduate): 946 (64.3%)

Degree(s): BFA
Concentrations: Art, Graphic Design, Photography /Media, Art and Technology (MFA only)
Artistic portfolio requirement: Yes
Scholarships available: Yes, need- and merit-based
Number of faculty: 45+. We also invite to our campus each year some 75 visiting artists, designers and theorists from around the world to broaden the debate on contemporary art.
Percentage of applicants accepted into the department per year: 24% for fall 2016
Student Activities: CalArts has seven on-campus galleries for student work. Students in the School of Art participate in a number of group and solo shows. Every Thursday evening during the academic year, CalArts gallery opening receptions for the School of Art that are open to the greater CalArts community and general public. Other events include weekly Visiting Artist and Designer Lecture Series, T-Shirt Design Show, Print Fair, Open Studios, Motion Graphics Showcase, Digital Arts Expo, and more.

Prominent Alumni:
Catherine Opie (Photo, MFA 1988)—photographer
Mark Bradford (Art, MFA 1997, BFA 1995)—mixed-media painter, MacArthur Fellow
Laura Owens (Art, MFA 1994)—painter
Sam Durant (Art, MFA 1991)—sculptor
Barbara Glauber (Graphic Design, MFA 1990)—designer
Mike Kelley (Art, MFA 1978)—artist
Tony Oursler (Art, BFA)

CORNISH COLLEGE OF THE ARTS

Art Department
1000 Lenora Street
Seattle, WA 98121

Phone: toll-free: (800) 726-ARTS
Website: cornish.edu
Email: admission@cornish.edu or art@cornish.edu

Tuition: $
Campus student enrollment (undergraduate): 720

Degree(s): BFA
Concentrations: Painting, sculpture, photography, digital media, and more.
Courses offered: All visual arts students at Cornish share a Foundations year in which studio work is integrated with the Humanities and Sciences, and Critical and Contextual Studies. During this time, students are encouraged to explore all visual arts disciplines taught. Those who select a BFA in art then progress in studio, with self-selected practice, inquiry-led research, and development of critical skills. Collaboration with other departments in visual and performing arts is encouraged through Creative Corridor classes (multidisciplinary practice with a view toward life after college).
Portfolio review requirement: Yes
Scholarships available: Yes, based on both merit and need
Number of faculty: 20 Foundations and Art faculty
Number of majors/students in department: 76 students in Art (2015–16), 81 in Foundations (2015–16)
Number of applicants accepted into the department per year: Approximately 80 slots are open annually for incoming freshmen (Foundations) and 20 for transfers.

Department activities: Student participate in exhibitions and site-specific installations in the community through all four years at Cornish. The senior EXPO includes exhibitions of all the visual arts and occupies up to four galleries on campus. This is a widely attended event, drawing gallery owners and artists from the greater Seattle community.

Prominent Alumni:

Aleah Chapin, first American to win the BP Portrait Award at the National Portrait Gallery in London.
Heather Hart
Mark Tobey, American painter and Cornish's first Chair of Art

CORNISH COLLEGE OF THE ARTS

Design Department
1000 Lenora Street
Seattle, WA 98121

Phone toll-free: (800) 726-ARTS
Website: cornish.edu
Email: admission@cornish.edu or design@cornish.edu

Tuition: $
Campus student enrollment (undergraduate): 720

Degree(s): BFA
Concentrations: Narrative, type/image design, or user experience
Courses offered: All visual arts students at Cornish share a Foundations year in which studio work is integrated with the Humanities and Sciences, and Critical and Contextual Studies. During this time, students are encouraged to explore all visual arts disciplines taught. Those who select a BFA in design can specialize in narrative (animation, motion graphics, or game art); type/image design (advertising, graphic design, illustration, branding, graphic novels, or publishing); or user experience (information architecture, interactive design, wearables, or web).

Portfolio review requirement: Yes
Scholarships available: Yes, based on both merit and need
Number of faculty: 28 Foundations and Design faculty
Number of majors/students in department: 123 students in Design (2015–16), 81 in Foundations (2015–16)
Number of applicants accepted into the department per year: Approximately 80 slots are open annually for incoming freshmen (Foundations) and 25 to 30 for transfers.
Department activities: Students participate in exhibitions and work with local companies. Projects done in the 2015–16 academic year included the installation of a Star Trek universe timeline for a museum exhibition at the Seattle Center and the creation of mixed-reality works for Microsoft's prototype HoloLens. Design seniors participate in the year-end EXPO, which includes an "industry night" for Seattle design firm owners to meet students and review their work.

Prominent Alumni:

Victor Melendez—senior designer at Starbucks
Justin Kane Elder—founder of Electric Coffin

CORNISH COLLEGE OF THE ARTS

Film+Media Department
1000 Lenora Street
Seattle, WA 98121

Phone: toll-free: (800) 726-ARTS
Website: cornish.edu
Email: admission@cornish.edu or film@cornish.edu

Tuition: $
Campus student enrollment (undergraduate): 720

Degree(s): BFA established in 2015
Concentrations: Narrative or non-narrative film or digital media

Courses offered: All visual arts students at Cornish share a Foundations year in which studio work is integrated with the Humanities and Sciences, and Critical and Contextual Studies. Those who select a BFA in Film+Media can specialize in narrative or nonnarrative film and are encouraged to integrate nontraditional media into their work.

Portfolio review requirement: Yes

Scholarships available: Yes, based on both merit and need

Number of faculty: 12 in Foundations and Film

Number of majors/students in department: 8 students in Film (2015–16), 81 in Foundations (2015–16)

Percentage and number of applicants accepted into the department per year: Approximately 80 slots are open annually for incoming freshmen (Foundations) and 5 to 10 for transfers.

Department activities: Student participate in exhibitions and work with local film festivals like NFFTY and Seattle International Film Festival (one of the largest in the United States). Film seniors participate in the year-end EXPO, which includes screenings of their work. Students are encouraged to submit work to local and national festivals throughout their four years.

Prominent Alumni:

This is one of the newest degrees offered at Cornish, but the college has a century-long history of students from other departments working in the film industry, from silent-era film actors to blockbuster movie star Brendan Fraser to Academy Award winner Colleen Atwood.

CORNISH COLLEGE OF THE ARTS

Interior Architecture Department
1000 Lenora Street
Seattle, WA 98121

Phone toll-free: (800) 726-ARTS
Website: cornish.edu

Email: admission@cornish.edu or interiorarchitecture@cornish.edu

---

Tuition: $

Campus student enrollment (undergraduate): 720

Degree(s): BFA established in 2016

Concentrations: Interior architecture

Courses offered: All visual arts students at Cornish share a Foundations year in which studio work is integrated with the Humanities and Sciences, and Critical and Contextual Studies. Those who select a BFA in interior architecture, previously a concentration in design, specialize in the analytic creation and transformation of space. Areas of study include environments, interior design, lighting, construction, biotechnology, transportation design, object design, and sustainability.

Portfolio review requirement: Yes

Scholarships available: Yes, based on both merit and need

Number of faculty: 12 in Foundations and Interior Architecture

Number of majors/students in department: 81 in Foundations (2015–16)

Number of applicants accepted into the department per year: Approximately 80 slots are open annually for incoming freshmen (Foundations) and 5 to 10 for transfers into interior architecture.

Department activities: Students participate in exhibitions and work with local architecture firms. Interior architecture seniors participate in the year-end EXPO, which includes an "industry night" with local architecture and design firms.

Prominent Alumni:

This is the newest degree offered at Cornish, but this course of study was previously offered as a concentration in design. In 2015 and 2016, Cornish College of the Arts seniors won the prestigious Donguia Scholarship for interior architecture.

LAGUNA COLLEGE OF ART AND DESIGN

2222 Laguna Canyon Road
Laguna Beach, CA 92651

Phone: toll-free: (800) 255-0762
Website: lcad.edu
Email: admissions@lcad.edu

Tuition: $
Campus student enrollment (undergraduate):
571

Degree(s): BFA, postbaccalaureate
Majors: Drawing and painting, drawing and painting with sculpture emphasis, graphic design, graphic design, graphic design with action sports design emphasis, graphic design with illustration emphasis, animation, game art, illustration, illustration with drawing and painting emphasis, illustration with entertainment emphasis
Artistic portfolio requirement: Yes
Scholarships available: Yes
Number of faculty: 128 full-time and part-time
Percentage of applicants accepted into the department per year: 45%

Prominent Alumni:
Bruce Kuei (2004)—animator, Pixar Animation
Lisa Waggoner (2002)—animator, *The Simpsons*
Marcus Harris (1998)—storyboarded for McDonald's Corporation, Sears, *The Felicity Show* and the *X-Men* TV special
Erin Kant (2002)—illustrator for Kagan Publishing and Professional Development, a publisher and distributor of cooperative learning and multiple-intelligences books and resources

OREGON COLLEGE OF ART AND CRAFT

College of Art
8245 SW Barnes Road
Portland, OR 97225

Phone: (503) 297-5544,
toll-free: (800) 390-0632
Website: ocac.edu
Email: admissions@ocac.edu

Tuition: $
Campus student enrollment (undergraduate):
111

Degree(s): BFA and two certificate programs
Concentrations: Applied craft and design, book arts, ceramics, craft, cross media, digital strategies, drawing and painting, fibers, general studies, image and narrative, metals, sculptural practice, photography, wood
Artistic portfolio requirement: Yes
Scholarships available: Yes; OCAC offers a comprehensive merit scholarship and need-based financial aid program. OCAC scholarships and grants range from $2,000 to up to full tuition for four years of study for undergraduates. Special scholarships are available annually in fibers, metals, and wood.
Number of faculty: 15 full-time, 20 part-time
Department activities: Hoffman Gallery Juried Student Exhibition, Hoffman Gallery Thesis Exhibitions, Off-Campus Thesis Gallery Show, Centrum Gallery Department Exhibitions, Annual Student Holiday Art Sale, Ceramic Guild's Student Cup Sale, Annual Spring Student Art Sale, Student Commonwealth (Government).

Prominent Alumni:
Laura Domela—represented by Laura Russo Gallery, Portland, OR
Hilary Pfeifer—represented by Velvet Da Vinci, San Francisco, CA
Sarah Turner—received Fulbright Grant to study in Amsterdam

Cindy Vargas—custom furniture designer and maker, Glendale, CA

Ryan Pierce—represented by Elizabeth Leach Gallery

Nicole Gibbs—visiting professor, Evergreen State College, Olympia, WA

Blue Mitchell—exhibitions coordinator, Plates to Pixels gallery; editor and publisher, *Diffusion* magazine

Kristin Shiga—metalsmith, teacher, arts administrator

OTIS COLLEGE OF ART AND DESIGN

9045 Lincoln Boulevard
Los Angeles, CA 90045

Phone: (310) 665-6800 or (310) 665-6820, toll-free (800) 527-6847
Website: otis.edu
Email: admissions@otis.edu

Tuition: $$
Campus student enrollment (undergraduate): 1,102

Degree(s): BFA
Concentrations: Fine arts (painting, sculpture/new genre, photography), communication arts (graphic design, illustration, advertising), digital Media (Animation, Game & Entertainment Design), fashion design (Costume Design), toy design, interactive product design, architecture/landscape/interiors
Artistic portfolio requirement: Yes
Number of faculty: 55 full-time and 382 part-time
Percentage of applicants accepted into the department per year: 54%
Activities:
Otis College of Art and Design has college-to-career initiative called Your Creative Future. This professional preparation program highlights and augments the College's studio and liberal arts and sciences curricula to ensure that all students develop the full set of professional, business, and entrepreneurial skills needed to launch and sustain successful careers. This initiative includes five key elements: (1) Business practices course for every student, (2) Discipline-specific professional preparation, (3) Real-world engagement, (4) Career Services and individual mentoring and (5) a new entrepreneurial studies minor.

Your Creative Future begins when students arrive on campus. Students will benefit from new course offerings that teach business skills tailored for artists and designers in addition to their industry-standard practice courses focusing on portfolio development, presentation delivery, and client relations.

Opportunity for engagement with outside partners and organizations is ever expanding through the College's renowned Creative Action program (which offers project-based courses that match multidisciplinary teams of students with local and international community partners), internships, and travel study opportunities.

PACIFIC NORTHWEST COLLEGE OF ART

1241 NW Johnson Street
Portland, OR 97209

Phone: (503) 226-4391
Website: pnca.edu
Email: admissions@pnca.edu

Tuition: $
Campus student enrollment (undergraduate): 407

Degree(s): BFA
Concentrations: Animated arts, communication design, illustration, illustration, intermedia, painting, photography, printmaking, sculpture, video and sound, writing
Artistic portfolio requirement: Yes
Scholarships available: Yes, from $3,000 to more than $31,500

Number of faculty: 120
Percentage and number of applicants accepted per year: 666 applicants, 87% accepted

SAN FRANCISCO ART INSTITUTE

800 Chestnut Street
San Francisco, CA 94133

Phone toll-free: (800) 345-7324
Website: sfai.edu

Tuition: $$
Campus student enrollment (undergraduate): 400

Degree(s): BFA, BA
Concentrations: Art and technology, filmmaking (narrative, documentary, and experimental cinema), history and theory of contemporary art, new genres (performance art, video, and installation), painting, photography, printmaking and sculpture, urban studies
Artistic portfolio requirement: Yes
Scholarships available: Yes
Freshman scholarships: Trustee Scholarship ($14,000); Presidential Scholarship ($13,000); Dean's Scholarship ($10,000); Visionary Scholarship ($9,000) Transfer Scholarships: Trustee Scholarship ($12,000); Presidential Scholarship ($11,000); Dean's Scholarship ($8,000); Visionary Scholarship ($5,000)
Number of faculty: Approximately 120 full-time and visiting faculty

Prominent Alumni:
Gutzon Borglum—sculptor, Mt. Rushmore
Henry Kiyama—graphic novelist
Sargeant Claude Johnson—wood artist
Louise Dahl Wolf—fashion photographer
John Collier—photographer, Security Farm Administration
Jerry Garcia—musician, The Grateful Dead
Annie Leibovitz—photographer, *Rolling Stone*, *Vogue, Vanity Fair*
Christopher Coppola—filmmaker
Kathryn Bigelow—Oscar-winning filmmaker
Barry McGee—painter, printmaker, installation artist
Kehinde Wiley—painter
Karen Finley—performance artist
Catherine Opie—photographer

SOUTHERN METHODIST UNIVERSITY

Meadows School of the Arts
Division of Art
P.O. Box 750356
Dallas, TX 75275–0356

Phone: (214) 768-3217
Website: meadows.smu.edu
Email: meadowsrecruitment@smu.edu

Tuition and fees: $$$$
Campus student enrollment (undergraduate): 6,391

Degree(s): BA, BFA, minor
Concentrations: Art, art/digital game development. Minors in fashion media (with communications department), graphic design, and studio art.
Courses: Art (general studio), art history, ceramics, digital and hybrid media, drawing, graphic design, painting, printmaking, sculpture, photography
Artistic portfolio requirement: Yes
Scholarships available: Yes. Academic merit scholarships available through SMU admissions process. Artistic merit scholarships available based on audition or portfolio evaluation. Scholarship amounts vary.
Number of faculty: 11
Number of majors and minors: 73
Percentage and number of applicants accepted into the School of Art per year: 150 portfolios submitted; approximately 43% accepted

Department activities: Student Art Association, New York Colloquium, SMU-in-Taos summer school and retreat, Visiting Artist and Speakers Series, MAYA summer school for high school students wishing to study art at a university, engaged learning projects throughout Dallas, Pollock Gallery events and exhibitions throughout the academic year.

Prominent Alumni:

John Alexander (MFA, 1971)

Deborah Ballard (MFA, 1990)

Shawnee Barton (BFA, 2002)

David Bates (MFA, 1978)

Michael Collins (MFA, 1998)

Matt Cusick (MFA 2003)

David Dreyer (MFA, 1992)

Lionel Maunz (MFA, 2004)

Sherry Owens (MFA, 1972)

Kanishka Raja (MFA, 1995)

Dan Rizzie (MFA, 1976)

Ludwig Schwarz (BFA, 1986)

Aqsa Shakil (MFA, 2007)

Bret Slater (MFA, 2011)

Theo Stanley (MFA, 2004)

Gina Williams (MFA, 1989)

Jeff Zilm (MFA, 2011)

UNIVERSITY OF CALIFORNIA LOS ANGELES

UCLA Department of Art

Broad Art Center, Suite 2275

240 Charles E. Young Drive North

Box 951615

Los Angeles, CA 90095–1615

Phone: (310) 825-3281

Website: art.ucla.edu/undergraduate/index.html

Email: artinfo@arts.ucla.edu

Tuition: $$$

Campus student enrollment (undergraduate): 29,505

Degree(s): BA

Concentrations: Art

Courses offered: Painting and drawing, photography, sculpture, ceramics, art theory, and new genres (including performance art, video, installation, and nonstudio work).

Portfolio requirement: Yes, portfolio required

Number of faculty: 14

Department activities: Visiting Artist Lecture Series.

UNIVERSITY OF OREGON

Department of Art

5232 University of Oregon

Eugene, OR 97403–5232

Phone: (541) 346-3610

Website: art.uoregon.edu

Email: artuo@uoregon.edu

Tuition: $$

Campus student enrollment (undergraduate): 22,820

Degree(s): BA, BS, BFA

Concentrations: Art, ceramics, art + technology, ceramics, fibers, metalsmithing and jewelry, painting, printmaking, photography, sculpture

Artistic portfolio requirement: Yes

Scholarships available: Returning students only

Number of faculty: 30 full-time, 15 part-time

Number of majors and minors: 561 majors, 312 minors

Percentage and number of applicants accepted into the department per year:

Undergraduate art majors: 146 accepted each year/100%

Undergraduate digital arts majors: 94 accepted each year/89%

Student activities: Student art gallery, 30 shows each year.

Art and Design Programs by State

Note: Programs with an asterisk (*) are accredited by the National Association of Schools of Art and Design.

ALABAMA

Alabama A&M University
Alabama State University*
Athens State University
Auburn University*
Auburn University at Montgomery*
Birmingham–Southern College
Faulkner University
Huntingdon College
Jacksonville State University*
Judson College
Samford University
Spring Hill College
Stillman College
Troy University
University of Alabama*
University of Alabama at Birmingham*
University of Alabama in Huntsville*University of Mobile
University of Montevallo
University of North Alabama*
University of South Alabama

ALASKA

University of Alaska Anchorage*
University of Alaska Fairbanks
University of Alaska Southeast

ARIZONA

Arizona State University*
Arizona State University West campus Art Center Design College-Tucson
Art Institute of Phoenix

Grand Canyon University
Northern Arizona University
Prescott College
University of Arizona*

ARKANSAS

Arkansas State University*
Arkansas Tech University
Harding University
Henderson State University
Hendrix College
John Brown University
Lyon College
Ouachita Baptist University
Southern Arkansas University
University of Arkansas
University of Arkansas at Little Rock*
University of Arkansas at Monticello
University of Arkansas at Pine Bluff*
University of Central Arkansas*
University of the Ozarks
Williams Baptist College

CALIFORNIA

Academy of Art University*
ArtCenter College of Design*
Art Institute of California—Los Angeles
Art Institute of California—Orange County
Art Institute of California—San Diego
The Art Institute of California—San Francisco
Azusa Pacific University*
Biola University*
California Baptist University
California College of the Arts*
California Design College
California Institute of the Arts*
California Lutheran University
California Polytechnic State

University, San Luis Obispo*
California State Polytechnic University, Pomona*
California State University, Bakersfield
California State University, Chico*
California State University, Dominguez Hills
California State University, Fresno
California State University, Fullerton*
California State University, Hayward
California State University, Long Beach*
California State University, Los Angeles*
California State University, Monterey Bay
California State University, Northridge*
California State University, Sacramento*
California State University, San Bernardino*
California State University, San Marcos
California State University, Stanislaus*
Chapman University
Claremont McKenna College
Cogswell Polytechnical College
Coleman College
Columbia College Hollywood*
Concordia University
Design Institute of San Diego
Dominican University of California*
Fashion Institute of Design & Merchandising*
Fresno Pacific University
Holy Names University
Humboldt State University*
Laguna College of Art and Design*

La Sierra UniversityLoyola
    Marymount University*
Mills College
Mount St. Mary's University
New York Film Academy—Los
    Angeles*
Notre Dame de Namur University
Occidental College
Otis College of Art and Design*
Pacific Union College
Pepperdine University
Pitzer College
Point Loma Nazarene University
Pomona College
Saint Mary's College of California
San Diego State University*
San Francisco Art Institute*
San Francisco State University*
San Jose State University*
Santa Clara University
Scripps College
Silicon Valley College
Sonoma State University*
Stanford University
University of California, Berkeley
University of California, Davis
University of California, Irvine
University of California, Los
    Angeles
University of California, Riverside
University of California, San Diego
University of California, Santa
    Barbara
University of California, Santa
    Cruz
University of La Verne
University of Redlands
University of San Diego
University of San Francisco
University of Southern California
University of the Pacific*
Westmont College
Whittier College
Woodbury University*

COLORADO

Adams State College
Art Institute of Colorado
Colorado Christian University
Colorado College
Colorado State University
Colorado State University–Pueblo
Fort Lewis College
Mesa State College
Metropolitan State University of
    Denver*
Naropa University
Platt College
Rocky Mountain College of Art
    and Design*
University of Colorado at Boulder
University of Colorado Colorado
    Springs
University of Colorado at Denver
University of Denver*
University of Northern Colorado*
Western State Colorado University

CONNECTICUT

Albertus Magnus College
Central Connecticut State
    University
Connecticut College
Eastern Connecticut State
    University
Fairfield University
Hartford Art School*
Lyme Academy College of Fine
    Arts*
Quinnipiac University
Sacred Heart University
Southern Connecticut State
    University
Trinity College
University of Bridgeport*
University of Connecticut*
University of Hartford
University of New Haven
University of Saint Joseph

Wesleyan University
Western Connecticut State
    University
Yale University

DISTRICT OF COLUMBIA

American University
Catholic University of America
Corcoran College of Art and
    Design*
Gallaudet University
George Washington University
Georgetown University
Howard University*
Trinity University
University of the District of
    Columbia Delaware
Delaware State University
University of Delaware

FLORIDA

Art Institute of Fort Lauderdale
Barry University
Eckerd College
Edward Waters College
Flagler College
Florida A&M University
Florida Atlantic University
Florida International University*
Florida Southern College
Florida State University*
International Academy of Design
    and Technology
Jacksonville University
Lynn University
New World School of the Arts*
Palm Beach Atlantic University
Ringling College of Art and
    Design*
Rollins College
Stetson University
University of Central Florida
University of Florida*
University of Miami

University of North Florida
University of South Florida*
University of Tampa
University of West Florida

GEORGIA
Agnes Scott College
Albany State University
Armstrong State University
Art Institute of Atlanta
Atlanta College of Art
Augusta State University*
Berry College
Brenau University
Brewton–Parker College
Clark Atlanta University
Clayton State University
Columbus State University*
Covenant College
Emory University
Fort Valley State University
Georgia College & State
   University
Georgia Institute of Technology*
Georgia Southern University*
Georgia Southwestern State
   University
Georgia State University*
Kennesaw State University*
LaGrange College
Mercer University
Morehouse College
Oglethorpe University
Georgia Piedmont Technical
   College
Reinhardt University
Savannah College of Art and
   Design
Savannah State University
Shorter University
Spelman College
University of Georgia*
University of North Georgia*
University of West Georgia*

Valdosta State University*
Wesleyan College

HAWAII
Brigham Young University–Hawaii
Chaminade University of Honolulu
University of Hawaii at Hilo
University of Hawaii at Manoa

IDAHO
Albertson College of Idaho
Boise State University*
Brigham Young University–Idaho
Idaho State University
Northwest Nazarene University
University of Idaho*

ILLINOIS
American Academy of Art
Augustana College
Benedictine University
Blackburn College
Bradley University*
Chicago State University*
College of DuPage*
Columbia College Chicago
Concordia University
DePaul University
Dominican University
Eastern Illinois University*
Elmhurst College
Eureka College
Governors State University
Greenville College
Illinois College
Illinois Institute of Art
Illinois Institute of Art—Schaumburg
Illinois Institute of Technology
Illinois State University*
Illinois Wesleyan University
International Academy of Design
   and Technology
Judson College
Knox College

Lake Forest College
Lewis University
Loyola University Chicago
McKendree College
MacMurray College
Millikin University
Monmouth College
National-Louis University
North Central College
North Park University
Northeastern Illinois University*
Northern Illinois University*
Northwestern University
Olivet Nazarene University
Principia College
Quincy University
Robert Morris University
Roosevelt University
Saint Xavier University
School of the Art Institute of
   Chicago*
Southern Illinois University,
   Carbondale*
Southern Illinois University,
   Edwardsville
Trinity Christian College
University of Chicago
University of Illinois at Chicago
University of Illinois at Springfield
University of Illinois-Urbana
   Champaign*
University of St. Francis
Western Illinois University*
Wheaton College

INDIANA
Anderson University
Ball State University*
Bethel College
Butler University
Calumet College of St. Joseph
DePauw University
Earlham College
Goshen College

Grace College and Theological
   Seminary
Hanover College
Herron School of Art and Design*
Huntington University
Indiana State University*
Indiana University, Bloomington*
Indiana University, East
Indiana University, Northwest
Indiana University–Purdue
   University Fort Wayne*
Indiana University–Purdue
   University Indianapolis*
Indiana University South Bend
Indiana University Southeast
Indiana Wesleyan University
Manchester University
Marian University
Oakland City University
Purdue University*
Saint Joseph's College
Saint Mary-of-the-Woods College
Saint Mary's College*
Taylor University
University of Evansville
University of Indianapolis
University of Notre Dame*
University of Saint Francis*
University of Southern Indiana*
Valparaiso University
Vincennes University*
Wabash College

IOWA

Ashford University
Briar Cliff University
Buena Vista University
Central College
Clarke College
Coe College
Cornell College
Dordt College
Drake University*
Graceland University

Grand View University
Grinnell College
Iowa State University
Iowa Wesleyan University
Loras College
Luther College
Maharishi University of
   Management
Morningside College
Mount Mercy University
Northwestern College
St. Ambrose University
Simpson College
University of Iowa
University of Northern Iowa
Upper Iowa University
Waldorf College
Wartburg College

KANSAS

Baker University
Benedictine College
Bethany College
Bethel College
Emporia State University*
Fort Hays State University
Friends University
Kansas State University*
Kansas Wesleyan University
McPherson College
MidAmerica Nazarene University
Ottawa University
Pittsburg State University
Sterling College
Tabor College
University of Kansas*
University of Saint Mary
Washburn University*
Wichita State University*

KENTUCKY

Asbury University
Bellarmine University
Berea College
Brescia University
Campbellsville University
Centre College
Eastern Kentucky University
Georgetown College
Kentucky State University
Kentucky Wesleyan College
Lindsey Wilson College
Morehead State University
Murray State University*
Northern Kentucky University
Spalding University
Thomas More College
Transylvania University
University of the Cumberlands
University of Kentucky*
University of Louisville
University of Pikeville
Western Kentucky University*

LOUISIANA

Centenary College of Louisiana
Dillard University
Grambling State University
Louisiana College
Louisiana State University*
Louisiana State University in
   Shreveport
Louisiana Tech University*
Loyola University New Orleans
McNeese State University*
Nicholls State University*
Northwestern State University of
   Louisiana*
Southeastern Louisiana University*
Southern University and A&M
   College*
Tulane University
University of Louisiana at
   Lafayette*

University of Louisiana at Monroe

University of New Orleans*

Xavier University of Louisiana

MAINE

Bates College

Bowdoin College

Colby College

Maine College of Art*

University of Maine*

University of Maine at Augusta

University of Maine at Farmington

University of Maine at Machias

University of Maine at Presque Isle

University of Southern Maine*

MARYLAND

Bowie State University

Frostburg State University

Goucher College

Hood College

Johns Hopkins University

Loyola University Maryland

Maryland Institute College of Art*

McDaniel College

Morgan State University

Mount St. Mary's University

Notre Dame of Maryland
University

Salisbury University

St. Mary's College of Maryland

Towson University

University of Maryland, Baltimore
County

University of Maryland, College
Park

University of Maryland Eastern
Shore

Washington College

MASSACHUSETTS

Amherst College

Anna Maria College

Art Institute of Boston*

Assumption College

Atlantic Union College

Bard College at Simon's Rock

Bay Path University

Becker College

Boston College

Boston University*

Brandeis University

Bridgewater State University*

Clark University

College of the Holy Cross

Curry College

Dean College

Eastern Nazarene College

Elms College (College of Our Lady
of the Elms)

Emerson College

Emmanuel College

Endicott College

Fitchburg State University

Framingham State University

Gordon College

Hampshire College

Harvard University

Lasell College

Lesley University*

Massachusetts College of Art and
Design*

Merrimack College

Montserrat College of Art*

Mount Holyoke College

Mount Ida College*

New England Institute of Art

New England School of Art and
Design at Suffolk University*

Newbury College

Northeastern University

Pine Manor College

Regis University

Salem State University*

Simmons College

Smith College

Springfield College

Stonehill College

Suffolk University

Tufts University

Tufts School of the Museum of Fine
Arts*

University of Massachusetts,
Amherst*

University of Massachusetts,
Boston

University of Massachusetts,
Dartmouth*

University of Massachusetts,
Lowell*

Wellesley College

Wentworth Institute of Technology*

Westfield State College

Wheaton College

Wheelock College

Williams College

MICHIGAN

Adrian College

Albion College

Alma College

Andrews University

Aquinas College

Calvin College

Central Michigan University*

College for Creative Studies*

Concordia University

Cornerstone University

Cranbrook Academy of Art*

Eastern Michigan University

Ferris State University

Grand Valley State University*

Hope College*

Kalamazoo College

Kendall College of Art and Design
of Ferris State University*

Lake Superior State University

Lawrence Technological
University*

Madonna University

Marygrove College

Michigan State University

Northern Michigan University

Oakland University

Olivet College

Saginaw Valley State University

Siena Heights University*

Spring Arbor University

University of Michigan*

University of Michigan–Dearborn

University of Michigan-lint

Wayne State University

Western Michigan University*

MINNESOTA

The Art Institutes International
    Minnesota

Augsburg College

Bemidji State University

Bethany Lutheran College

Bethel University

Carleton College

College of Saint Benedict

College of Visual Arts*

Concordia College, Moorhead

Concordia University, St Paul

Gustavus Adolphus College

Hamline University

Macalester College

Minneapolis College of Art and
    Design*

Minnesota School of Business

Minnesota State University,
    Mankato*

Minnesota State University
    Moorhead*

Northwestern College

Saint Cloud State University*

Saint John's University

Saint Mary's University of
    Minnesota

St. Catherine University

St. Olaf College*

Southwest Minnesota State
    University

University of Minnesota Duluth

University of Minnesota, Morris

University of Minnesota Twin Cities

University of St. Thomas

Winona State University

MISSISSIPPI

Belhaven University*

Delta State University*

Jackson State University*

Millsaps College

Mississippi College

Mississippi State University*

Mississippi University for Women*

Mississippi Valley State University*

Tougaloo College

University of Mississippi*

University of Southern Mississippi*

William Carey University

MISSOURI

Avila University

Central Missouri State University*

College of the Ozarks

Columbia College

Culver-Stockton College

Drury University

Evangel University

Fontbonne University

Hannibal-LaGrange University

Kansas City Art Institute*

Lincoln University

Lindenwood University

Maryville University of Saint Louis*

Missouri Southern State University

Missouri Valley College

Missouri Western State College

Northwest Missouri State
    University

Park University

Saint Louis University*

Southeast Missouri State University

Southwest Baptist University

Southwest Missouri State University

Stephens College

Truman State University

University of Central Missouri*

University of Missouri

University of Missouri–Kansas City

University of Missouri–St Louis

Washington University in St.
    Louis*

Webster University

Westminster College

William Jewell College

William Woods University

MONTANA

Montana State University*

Montana State University Billings*

Montana State University–
    Northern

Rocky Mountain College

University of Great Falls

University of Montana*

NEBRASKA

Bellevue University

Chadron State College

College of Saint Mary

Concordia University

Creighton University

Doane University

Hastings College

Midland Lutheran College

Nebraska Wesleyan University

Union College

University of Nebraska at Kearney

University of Nebraska–Lincoln*

University of Nebraska Omaha*

Wayne State College*

York College

NEVADA

The Art Institute of Las Vegas

Sierra Nevada College

University of Nevada, Las Vegas*

University of Nevada, Reno

NEW HAMPSHIRE

Colby-Sawyer College
Dartmouth College
Franklin Pierce University
Keene State College
New England College
New Hampshire Institute of Art*
Plymouth State University*
Rivier University
Saint Anselm College
University of New Hampshire

NEW JERSEY

Bloomfield College
Caldwell College
Centenary University
The College of New Jersey
College of Saint Elizabeth
Drew University
Fairleigh Dickinson University
Felician University
Georgian Court University
Kean University*
Monmouth University
Montclair State University*
New Jersey City University*
New Jersey Institute of
    Technology*
Princeton University
Ramapo College
Rider University
Rowan University*
Rutgers University–Camden
Rutgers University–New Brunswick
Rutgers University–Newark
Saint Peter's University
Seton Hall University
William Paterson University of
    New Jersey*

NEW MEXICO

College of Santa Fe
Eastern New Mexico University
Institute of American Indian Arts*

New Mexico Highlands University
New Mexico State University
Southwest University of Visual
    Arts–Albuquerque
University of New Mexico
Western New Mexico University

NEW YORK

Adelphi University
Alfred University*
Bard College
Barnard College
Canisius College
Cazenovia College
Colgate University
College of New Rochelle
College of Saint Rose*
Columbia University
Cooper Union*
Cornell University
CUNY, Baruch College
CUNY, Brooklyn College
CUNY, City College
CUNY, College of Staten Island
CUNY, Hunter College
CUNY, Lehman College
CUNY, New York City College of
    Technology
CUNY, Queens College
CUNY, York College
Daemen College
Dowling College
Elmira College
Fashion Institute of Technology*
Five Towns College
Fordham University
Hamilton College
Hartwick College*
Hobart and William Smith
    Colleges
Hofstra University
Houghton College
Ithaca College
Long Island University, Brooklyn

Long Island University, CW Post
    Campus
Manhattanville College
Marist College
Marymount Manhattan College
Mercy College*
Molloy College
Nazareth College
New School University
New York Academy of Art*
New York Institute of Technology
New York School of Interior
    Design*
New York University
Pace University
Parsons School of Design*
Pratt Institute*
PrattMWP*
Purchase College, SUNY *
Rensselaer Polytechnic Institute
Roberts Wesleyan College*
Rochester Institute of Technology*
Rochester Institute of Technology,
    National Technical Institute for
    the Deaf*
Sage College of Albany*
The Sage Colleges
St. Bonaventure University
Saint John's University*
Saint Thomas Aquinas College
Sarah Lawrence College
School of Visual Arts*
Siena College
Skidmore College*
Sotheby's Institute of Art*
Southampton College of Long
    Island University
St. John's University
St. Lawrence University
State University of New York
    College at Buffalo*
SUNY at Albany
SUNY at Binghamton
SUNY at Buffalo

SUNY at Stony Brook
SUNY College at Brockport
SUNY College at Cobleskill
SUNY at Cortland
SUNY at Fredonia*
SUNY at Geneseo
SUNY at New Paltz*
SUNY at Old Westbury
SUNY at Oneonta
SUNY at Oswego*
SUNY at Plattsburgh
SUNY Potsdam
SUNY College of Technology at
    Alfred State College
Syracuse University*
Union College
University at Buffalo, SUNY*
University of Rochester
Vassar College
Wagner College
Wells College

NORTH CAROLINA

Appalachian State University*
Barton College
Bennett College
Brevard College
Chowan University
Davidson College
Duke University
East Carolina University*
Elizabeth City State University
Elon University
Fayetteville State University
Greensboro College
Guilford College
High Point University
Johnson C. Smith University
Lenoir-Rhyne University
Mars Hill University
Meredith College
Methodist College
North Carolina A&T State
    University

North Carolina Central University
North Carolina State University*
Pfeiffer University
Queens University of Charlotte
Saint Augustine's University
Salem College
Shaw University
St. Andrews University
University of Mount Olive
University of North Carolina at
    Asheville
University of North Carolina at
    Chapel Hill
University of North Carolina at
    Charlotte
University of North Carolina at
    Greensboro
University of North Carolina at
    Pembroke*
University of North Carolina at
    Wilmington
University of North Carolina
    School for the Arts
Wake Forest University
Warren Wilson College
Western Carolina University*
William Peace University
Wingate University
Winston-Salem State University

NORTH DAKOTA

Dickinson State University
Minot State University
North Dakota State University*
University of Jamestown
University of Mary
University of North Dakota*
Valley City State University

OHIO

Antioch College
Art Academy of Cincinnati*
Ashland University
Baldwin Wallace University

Bluffton University
Bowling Green State University*
Capital University
Case Western Reserve University
Cedarville University
Central State University*
Cleveland Institute of Art*
Cleveland State University
College of Wooster
Columbus College of Art and
    Design*
Defiance College
Denison University
Hiram College
John Carroll University
Kent State University*
Kenyon College
Lake Erie College
Lourdes University
Malone College
Marietta College
Miami University*
Mount St. Joseph University
Mount Vernon Nazarene
    University
Muskingum College
Notre Dame College
Oberlin College
Ohio Dominican University
Ohio Northern University
Ohio State University*
Ohio University*
Ohio Wesleyan University
Otterbein University
Shawnee State University
UC Blue Ash College, University of
    Cincinnati
The University of Findlay
University of Akron*
University of Cincinnati*
University of Dayton*
University of Mount Union
University of Rio Grande
University of Toledo*

Ursuline College
Wilberforce University
Wittenberg University
Wright State University
Xavier University
Youngstown State University*

OKLAHOMA

Cameron University
East Central University
Northeastern State University
Northwestern Oklahoma State
    University
Oklahoma Baptist University
Oklahoma Christian University
Oklahoma City University
Oklahoma Panhandle State
    University
Oklahoma State University
Oral Roberts University
St. Gregory's University
Southeastern Oklahoma State
    University
Southwestern Oklahoma State
    University
University of Central Oklahoma*
University of Oklahoma
University of Science and Arts of
    Oklahoma
University of Tulsa

OREGON

Art Institute of Portland
Eastern Oregon University
George Fox University
Lewis & Clark College
Linfield College
Marylhurst University
Oregon College of Art and Craft*
Oregon State University
Pacific Northwest College of Art*
Pacific University
Portland State University*
Reed College

Southern Oregon University
University of Oregon*
University of Portland
Western Oregon University
Willamette University

PENNSYLVANIA

Albright College
Allegheny College
Arcadia University*
Art Institute of Philadelphia
Art Institute Pittsburgh
Bloomsburg University of
    Pennsylvania*
Bryn Mawr College
Bucknell University
Cabrini University
California University of
    Pennsylvania*
Carlow University
Carnegie Mellon University*
Cedar Crest College
Chatham College
Chestnut Hill College
Cheyney University of
    Pennsylvania
Clarion University of
    Pennsylvania*
Dickinson College
Drexel University*
Duquesne University
East Stroudsburg University of
    Pennsylvania
Eastern University
Edinboro University of
    Pennsylvania*
Elizabethtown College
Franklin & Marshall College
Gannon University
Geneva College
Gettysburg College
Grove City College
Haverford College
Holy Family University

Indiana University of
    Pennsylvania*
Juniata College
Kutztown University of
    Pennsylvania*
La Roche College*
La Salle University
Lafayette College
Lebanon Valley College
Lehigh University
Lock Haven University of
    Pennsylvania
Lycoming College
Mansfield University of
    Pennsylvania
Marywood University*
Mercyhurst College
Messiah College*
Millersville University of
    Pennsylvania*
Moore College of Art and Design*
Moravian College
Muhlenberg College
Pennsylvania Academy of the Fine
    Arts*
Pennsylvania College of Art and
    Design*
Pennsylvania College of
    Technology
Pennsylvania State University*
Philadelphia University*
Point Park University
Rosemont College
Saint Joseph's University
Saint Vincent College
Seton Hill University
Slippery Rock University of
    Pennsylvania*
Susquehanna University
Swarthmore College
Thiel College
Tyler School of Art, Temple
    University*
University of Pennsylvania

University of Pittsburgh

University of the Arts*

Ursinus College

Villanova University

Washington & Jefferson College

Waynesburg College

West Chester University of
    Pennsylvania*

Westminster College

Wilson College

York College Pennsylvania

RHODE ISLAND

Brown University

New England Institute of
    Technology

Providence College

Rhode Island College*

Rhode Island School of Design*

Roger Williams University

Salve Regina University*

University of Rhode Island

SOUTH CAROLINA

Anderson College*

Benedict College*

Bob Jones University

Charleston Southern University

Claflin University

Clemson University*

Coastal Carolina University*

Coker College

College of Charleston

Columbia College*

Converse College*

Erskine College

Francis Marion University*

Furman University

Lander University*

Limestone College

Newberry College

Presbyterian College

South Carolina State University*

University of South Carolina*

University of South Carolina Aiken

University of South Carolina
    Upstate*

Winthrop University*

Wofford College

SOUTH DAKOTA

Augustana College

Black Hills State University

Dakota Wesleyan University

Northern State University

Sinte Gleska University

South Dakota State University

University of Sioux Falls

University of South Dakota*

TENNESSEE

Austin Peay State University*

Belmont University*

Carson–Newman University*

Cumberland University

East Tennessee State University*

Fisk University

Freed–Hardeman University

King University

Lambuth University

Lincoln Memorial University

Maryville College

Memphis College of Art*

Middle Tennessee State University*

Milligan College

Nossi College of Art

O'More College of Design

Rhodes College

Sewanee: The University of the South

Southern Adventist University

Tennessee State University*

Tennessee Technological
    University*

Tennessee Temple University

Union University*

University of Memphis*

University of Tennessee at
    Chattanooga*

University of Tennessee, Knoxville*

University of Tennessee at Martin

Vanderbilt University

Watkins College of Art, Design &
    Film*

TEXAS

Abilene Christian University

Angelo State University

Art Institute of Dallas

Art Institute of Houston

Austin College

Baylor University

Dallas Baptist University

Hardin–Simmons University

Houston Baptist University

Howard Payne University

Lamar University*

Lubbock Christian University

McMurry University

Midwestern State University*

Our Lady of the Lake University

Rice University

St. Edward's University

Sam Houston State University*

Schreiner University

Southern Methodist University*

Southwestern Adventist University

Southwestern University

St. Mary's University

Stephen F. Austin State University*

Sul Ross State University

Tarleton State University

Texas A&M International University

Texas A&M University

Texas A&M University–Commerce*

Texas A&M University–Corpus
    Christi

Texas A&M University–Kingsville

Texas Christian University*

Texas College

Texas Lutheran University

Texas Southern University

Texas State University, San Marcos

Texas Tech University*

Texas Wesleyan University

Texas Woman's University

Trinity University

University of Dallas

University of Houston

University of Houston–Clear Lake

University of Mary Hardin–Baylor*

University of North Texas*

University of St. Thomas

University of Texas at Arlington*

University of Texas at Austin*

University of Texas at Brownsville

University of Texas at Dallas

University of Texas at El Paso

University of Texas at San
   Antonio*

University of Texas at Tyler

University of Texas of the Permian
   Basin*

University of Texas–Pan American

University of the Incarnate Word

Wayland Baptist University

West Texas A&M University

UTAH

Brigham Young University*

Dixie State University

Southern Utah University*

University of Utah

Utah State University

Utah Valley State College

Weber State University*

Westminster College

VERMONT

Bennington College

Castleton University

Champlain College

Green Mountain College

Johnson State College

Lyndon State College

Marlboro College

Middlebury College

Norwich University

Saint Michael's College

University of Vermont

VIRGINIA

Art Institute of Washington

Averett University

Bluefield College

Bridgewater College

Christopher Newport University

College of William & Mary

Eastern Mennonite University

Emory and Henry College

Ferrum College

George Mason University*

Hampden–Sydney College

Hampton University

Hollins University

James Madison University*

Liberty University

Longwood University

Lynchburg College

Mary Baldwin College

Marymount University

Norfolk State University

Old Dominion University*

Radford University*

Randolph–Macon College

Roanoke College

Shenandoah University

Southern Virginia University

Sweet Briar College

University of Mary Washington

University of Richmond

University of Virginia

Virginia Commonwealth
   University*

Virginia State University*

Virginia Tech*

Virginia Union University

Virginia Wesleyan College

Washington and Lee University

WASHINGTON

The Art Institute of Seattle

Central Washington University

Cornish College of the Arts*

Eastern Washington University

Gonzaga University

Northwest College of Art

Pacific Lutheran University

Photographic Center Northwest*

Seattle Pacific University

Seattle University

University of Puget Sound

University of Washington

Walla Walla University

Washington State University

Western Washington University*

Whitman College

Whitworth College

WEST VIRGINIA

Alderson Broaddus College

Bethany College

Concord University

Davis & Elkins College

Fairmont State University

Marshall University

Shepherd University

University of Charleston

West Liberty State College

West Virginia State University

West Virginia University *

West Virginia Wesleyan College

WISCONSIN

Beloit College

Cardinal Stritch University

Carroll College

Carthage College

Concordia University Wisconsin

Edgewood College

Lakeland College

Lawrence University

Marian University

Milwaukee Institute of Art & Design*

Mount Mary College

Northland College

Ripon College

St. Norbert College

Silver Lake College

University of Wisconsin–Eau Claire

University of Wisconsin–Green
　　Bay*

University of Wisconsin–La Crosse

University of Wisconsin–Madison*

University of Wisconsin–
　　Milwaukee

University of Wisconsin–Oshkosh

University of Wisconsin–Parkside

University of Wisconsin–Platteville

University of Wisconsin–River Falls

University of Wisconsin–Stevens
　　Point*

University of Wisconsin–Stout*

University of Wisconsin–Superior

University of Wisconsin–
　　Whitewater*

Viterbo University

Wisconsin Lutheran College

WYOMING

University of Wyoming

CHAPTER

5

Colleges for Dancers

Dance is unlike any other field when it comes to higher education. High school students often go to college undecided as freshmen and then take their time choosing a major. If you are a dancer who has spent many childhood years training, choosing a college may seem even more complicated than it is for other students. Your body is your instrument, so you already know you have a limited number of years that it will be in peak condition.

Logic tells you not everyone who studies dance throughout childhood and high school will become a professional dancer. But graduation doesn't mean your dancing days are over, so don't hang up your shoes just yet!

You may have already seriously considered whether you want to pursue life as a professional dancer or life as a college student after high school. The good news is that you can do both. Dancing in college can be a great way to keep the hope of professional dance alive while also discovering your other talents. Thousands of highly trained dancers attend programs at colleges across the country each year. Soon, you may be one of them! You could end up having more choices in your future than you ever imagined.

Types of Dance Programs

Not all dance programs are created equal, and certainly most aren't the same. It all depends on what kind of dance you want to study in college and at what level of intensity you want to study it.

There are two main types of degree plans for dance at the undergraduate level: a bachelor of arts (BA) and bachelor of fine arts (BFA). It's important to understand the differences between the types of dance programs. Although many offer excellent training and ample performance opportunities, some are geared more for students who intend to become professional dancers and others for students who may seek another career in dance but not necessarily as a performer.

The BFA degree offers the most dance technique classes and is often conservatory-based. If you hope to audition for professional dance companies after college, the BFA program is probably the best type of program to consider. You should know that BFA programs are often very rigorous and leave little room for electives or a double major. But if dancing is your life, then you'll love it!

LIBBY
BUTLER UNIVERSITY

"I was conflicted during my senior year of high school," says Libby. "I wasn't sure whether or not I wanted to pursue dance professionally."

Libby considered elementary education, but ultimately her instinct led her back to dance. She is now a junior at Butler pursuing a BS in dance with an emphasis on arts administration.

It was during an intensive summer dance program at the Boston Ballet that Libby learned about Butler University's dance program.

"I didn't really make my decision until I came to Butler for the audition," remarks Libby. "They have a unique process." For sure, Butler auditions are a bit different from the traditional one or two large audition days that many colleges host. Butler University chooses to have ten to twelve small auditions with only ten to twelve students each, and there is no solo performance requirement.

Libby is quick to note the advantages of this approach. She says it is less intimidating than a traditional audition and compares it to taking a master class. Students take two ballet classes at two different levels within regular ballet classes with dance majors already at Butler. "This allows the faculty to see how you would work with the dancers already in the program, and you get a feel for the classes you would take as a Butler student," she explains.

Like the majority of dance students at Butler, Libby came to the program as a freshman intending to be a dance performance major. However, she came to realize that she could increase her options after college by declaring the arts administration emphasis instead.

"After talking with dancers here, I realized that I could continue challenging myself artistically and also have a second option of working on the administrative side of dance as well as performing," says Libby. "I thought it was a good idea to have more possibilities in the future than I already have."

Dancers at Butler have the opportunity to perform with the Butler Ballet, the program's dance company, all four years of their education. Butler Ballet mounts three major productions per year, including the *Nutcracker* and a full-length classical ballet. In 2004, the school expanded its dance performance opportunities by founding Butler Chamber Dance, a contemporary performance group.

Hot Tips from Libby

→ Remember that college is a time to grow. Jump in, take risks, and challenge yourself.

→ Understand that college is a good option for professionally minded dancers; dance companies want intelligent dancers.

→ Find a place where you feel comfortable so you can push yourself.

→ Take advantage of every opportunity the dance program offers.

Last summer, Libby traveled with other Butler dancers to St. Petersburg, Russia, to train for two months with teachers from the Rimsky-Korsakov Conservatory. They took classes, performed, attended multiple ballet performances and toured the city. On this inaugural trip, every dancer who expressed interest was able to attend.

"The dance department here is intense, but it is challenging, yet supportive," concludes Libby about her experience at Butler. "And every day, I am inspired by my teachers and fellow dancers."

A few schools, such as Skidmore College in Saratoga Springs, New York, and Indiana University in Bloomington, Indiana, offer a bachelor of science (BS) degree in dance. However, there is a great difference between these two schools: Skidmore College is a small, private, liberal arts college, while Indiana University is a large public university with a more conservatory-based approach to dance training. If you want to pursue quality dance training but also have other academic interests, a college such as Skidmore might be a good choice. On the other hand, if you are a student mainly interested in preprofessional dance training at the college level, then a school like Indiana University might be perfect for you.

Students should also be aware that several dance forms emphasize one technique over another. To decide where you'd like to attend college, consider your long-term goals. Do you want to become a professional ballet dancer or a professional modern dancer? Do you want to dance on Broadway or become a dance teacher? The answers to these questions should help you narrow down the number of dance programs you are considering in order to help you find the right college fit.

The majority of dance programs emphasize modern technique. If a college's dance program doesn't specify that there are ballet-performing opportunities, it is safe to assume that most, if not all, performances are modern dance and that the department specializes in modern dance.

A fewer number of higher education institutions offer programs that are predominantly ballet-oriented. Examples of dance programs with ballet emphasis are Butler University in Indianapolis, Indiana; Mercyhurst College in Erie, Pennsylvania; Indiana University; and the ballet department at the University of Utah in Salt Lake City (this university has a separate department for modern dance).

Some programs have an equal emphasis on either ballet and modern or ballet, modern, and jazz. Point Park College in Pittsburgh, Pennsylvania, allows students to focus on any one of these techniques exclusively. The University of the Arts in Philadelphia also has a program that offers students the opportunity to specialize in one of three dance techniques.

But suppose you want to study all forms of dance! What then? Research programs that purposefully advertise that they offer all types of dance technique courses and that do not concentrate on one dance form over another. The University of Arizona in Tucson is one of these few unique dance programs that emphasizes ballet, modern, and jazz dance equally.

Maybe your dream has always been to own your own dance studio. If you are certain you want to be dance teacher, consider a college program that includes a concentration in dance education. Several colleges have programs that focus on dance education, and a little research will help you find them.

In some states, dance education majors can become certified to teach dance in public schools. Not every dance program grants teacher certification, so it is important to find out which states offer this. This is particularly important if you think you might want to teach dance in schools as well as privately. The National Dance Education Organization's publication *Dance Teacher Licensure: State by State Requirements* contains information about becoming a certified dance teacher for public schools.

College Options: Dancing without a Dance Major

Some high school dancers know they want to keep dancing in college but don't want to pursue dance as a major. Does this mean you have to give up dancing at a high technical level to pursue your college education? Maybe not! Believe it or not, some colleges allow nonmajors to participate fully in a college dance program. As you are looking at programs, find out if the dance department allows nonmajors to perform and participate in dance classes, including master classes by visiting artists (most of these programs are offered by dance departments at liberal arts colleges). If you are not sure about majoring in dance, minoring in dance is also an option.

In 1999, highly trained ballet dancers at Harvard were so dedicated to their passion that despite not having a campus dance department, they created their own dance company, the Harvard Ballet Company. Although there is no formal dance major, ballet dancers at Harvard have ample opportunity to take classes and perform. If an Ivy League education is what you desire, but you want to continue dancing, Harvard might be another possibility to explore.

There are other options for studying dance after high school besides programs in colleges and universities. Consider colleges and universities in major metropolitan areas that have excellent dance schools and companies. You could attend a college in New York City, the dance capital of the world, and study any academic subject while taking myriad professional dance classes from a wealth of world-renowned studios. Just imagine the possibilities! You could take classes in the American Ballet Theatre (ABT) Open Classes program, at Alvin Ailey American Dance Theater, or at STEPS on Broadway while studying at a local higher education institution. Living in a large metropolitan area with a bustling dance community could even land you professional auditions that could keep you performing, even if you are in college obtaining a degree in a field other than dance.

Dance Auditions

Many college dance programs require an audition for acceptance into the program. This is most common at colleges that have very rigorous training with plenty of performing opportunities and most likely offer the BFA in dance. Auditions for programs usually take place in early spring at the college's campus, but some schools have audition tours.

JORY HANCOCK
HEAD OF THE DANCE DIVISION, UNIVERSITY OF ARIZONA

Expert Tips from Professor Hancock

→ Students need to start thinking about entrance requirements early. Don't wait until your senior year. Start thinking about college in your sophomore or junior year in high school.

→ Research a college dance program to find out if faculty members create a positive environment focused on individual students making progress rather than competitiveness among students.

→ Look for a college that offers many performance opportunities. (There are twenty-five to thirty performances per year at the University of Arizona.) It's not enough to be on stage only once or twice a semester.

→ If you are a male dancer, find a program that has other male dancers. The more, the better.

→ For female dancers, finding a program that has enough male dancers is important too. Women need to be partnered, so if the student population in the dance department isn't balanced in terms of gender, it can diminish your college dance experience.

Audition Spotlight

At the University of Arizona, students may pursue a bachelor of fine arts (BFA). From as early as the audition, the philosophy of the department is clear. Three dance techniques—ballet, modern, and jazz—are all equally emphasized in the dance program rather than one of the disciplines taking precedent.

"The students have to be technically proficient in enough disciplines so they can survive the program," remarks Jory Hancock, head of the dance division.

The department auditions four hundred students for approximately thirty-five spots for the undergraduate dance program on campus each year.

"We look for a combination of... the quality of the students' dance technique already in addition to their potential," explains Hancock. "We try to imagine what the student could accomplish at the end of a few years of study in our program."

The University of Arizona audition lasts four hours, and students take classes in ballet, modern, and jazz, not just in one dance form.

"A lot of people think even though dancers excel in one primary technique, they can't excel in others," says Hancock. "Our programs prove that theory wrong. The students we accept have the potential to become advanced dancers in more than one technique, and many we accept are already well on their way."

→ Look for a low faculty-student ratio for more one-on-one attention from professors.

→ Consider a college that also has an MFA (master of fine arts) program, because the presence of graduate students can improve the experience of undergraduates.

→ Find out if the dance program is appreciated by the campus community. It is good to be at place that appreciates dance, because students can feel more valued in the campus community and have a better experience as a result.

EILEEN
COLUMBIA UNIVERSITY: A FOOT ON EITHER SIDE OF BROADWAY

A native of Lincoln, Nebraska, Eileen traveled to the East Coast to find the right college for her studies. Not only did she combine two majors, but she also stretched her college experience between two institutions! With an interest in art history and dance, Eileen wanted to attend an Ivy League institution and pursue dance as well. She discovered Columbia University's unique partnership with nearby Barnard College: As a Columbia University student, she can obtain a degree in dance by taking classes at the Barnard College dance department. She found the best of both worlds as a double major in art history and dance. This means that Eileen studies art history at Columbia and dance at Barnard College, and will graduate with a dual degree from Columbia.

Eileen was familiar with Columbia University long before high school. A family friend a few years her senior had attended the school and written letters to her about what college life was like.

"I had this vision of Columbia," she recalls. "It was the image of what college was supposed to be."

Attending college in New York City was appealing to Eileen because of the abundance of performance and internship opportunities.

On finding the Columbia-Barnard partnership to obtain her dance major, Eileen says, "I lucked out. Columbia is one of the only Ivies to offer the opportunity to obtain a dance degree."

As a double major, Eileen studies both art history and dance to investigate the collaborative relationships between artists and choreographers. Eileen enjoys nineteenth- and twentieth-century art history most, and according to her, "That is the ideal time to be studying dance history."

Eileen's personal interest in dance is academically rooted. "I'm interested in the history of dance, in how it develops in the art historian's eye," she says. "I study art history as a lens to better understand dance."

Eileen describes the Barnard College dance department as something she "happily fell upon" and spends half her day there and the other half at Columbia.

"The Barnard College dance department approaches dance from a very academic perspective," Eileen reveals. "And students are definitely capable of being professionals just like students in conservatory programs."

Renowned dance scholar Lynn Garafola is Eileen's adviser. Eileen has taken several academic dance classes that aren't offered at many undergraduate college dance programs and says one of the most popular classes is Dance in New York City. Because it satisfies a general education arts requirement, there are quite a few non-dancers in the class.

Eileen sums up her college choice like this: "I've had a good experience in participating in both schools," she says. "I have an Ivy League university environment and also enjoy the closeness of a liberal arts college while studying dance at Barnard. I have what I've always wanted—a foot on either side of Broadway."

Often, auditions consist of a ballet class, a modern dance class, and a solo. Preparing the solo can be the most nerve-wracking part of the audition. Not only do you have to choose the right piece of choreography, but you must also practice it as if you were performing it on stage. But don't worry—you can choose what you do best! A solo can range from a piece of standard choreo-graphic repertoire, like a solo from a classical ballet, or it can be original. If you choose to do original choreography, you may ask a dance teacher to borrow choreography or to help you create your own choreography. Judges for auditions that are strictly for modern dance programs might prefer to see a choreo-graphed piece by Martha Graham or another well-known modern choreogra-pher, so you might want to keep this in mind. Improvisation may also be part of

Day in the Life of a Dance Major	
8:30–9:50 a.m.	Ballet class
11 a.m.–12:30 p.m	Learning theories and Practicum (required for education minor)
12:30 p.m.	Lunch
1:30–2:50 p.m.	Laban studies
3–4:20 p.m.	Teaching of dance (lecture/workshop)
4:30–6 p.m.	Rehearsals/work at Peer Academic Advising
6–11 p.m.	Rehearsals, club duties/meetings, homework, dinner and once a month if I am lucky, some free time

an audition for a modern-based dance program, because it is a key element in the genre.

Of course, a professional *appearance* counts at college dance auditions. A standard dance uniform (black leotard and pink tights, or perhaps black tights for a modern audition) is almost always expected. Hair should be pulled back, and you shouldn't wear jewelry. At many auditions, students will be asked to wear numbers on their leotards. While "being numbered" can be intimidating, just remember that it is customary in an audition and shouldn't make you feel self-conscious. Put yourself in the shoes of the college department hosting the audition: They can focus on your dancing rather than on how to pronounce your name.

You may wonder if dancing *en pointe* is part of the audition. It's good to see you are on your toes—and it's likely you will be at your audition as well if the dance program empha-sizes ballet. In most cases, dancing *en pointe* will be required at an audition. However, dance programs that have equal concentrations in ballet and another dance discipline like modern or jazz may or may not require this.

To be on the safe side, be prepared to dance *en pointe* at your audition. Some high school students decide to stop taking pointe classes once they decide they want to concen-trate on modern or jazz instead of ballet in college. But because the dance audition for your college program might require dancing *en pointe*, it is best to continue pointe classes to have the best chances of acceptance into the dance program of your choice. Also, make sure that on the day of the audition, you have chosen pointe shoes that fit and are comfort-able for dancing—ones that are already broken in.

"Audition?" you may be saying. "Me?" Don't panic. You may be a student who doesn't want to deal with the stress of auditioning for a college dance program. Or you may want to continue studying dance in college, but just aren't sure that a professional performing career is in your future. Good news: many high-quality programs don't require auditions for acceptance. However, you should remember that these programs are usually not the most rigorous, and if you want to pursue professional dance after college, consider a dance program that *does* require an audition.

CAROL K. WALKER
FORMER DEAN OF THE SCHOOL OF THE ARTS AND DIRECTOR OF THE CONSERVATORY OF DANCE, PURCHASE COLLEGE, SUNY

Expert Tips from Dean Walker
Preparing Your Solo

→ Choose a solo in a genre you are comfortable with. Don't choose a ballet solo if you are a modern dancer or vice versa.

→ Get coaching from a dance teacher.

→ Don't try to learn the choreography for your solo from a video.

→ Don't perform a prima ballerina divertissement unless you are able to do it well, technically and emotionally. There are plenty of other solos to choose from without doing one that the most experienced prima ballerinas perform.

→ Rehearse your solo in different spaces and in different directions. You never know what size studio your audition will be held in. You want to make sure you can perform your solo in all types of spaces and from different directions.

→ A solo should show your best performance ability; by the time you do a solo, we will

Audition Spotlight

Like other competitive dance programs, the audition at Purchase College determines whether a student will be accepted to the college. Admission to the Conservatory of Dance means admission to the college.

The program has five auditions on campus each spring and four to eight off-campus regional auditions in California, Chicago, Florida, and Texas at the end of January each year. Regional auditions usually have between fifteen and forty students; on-campus auditions usually have approximately seventy students in attendance.

Purchase College dance auditions consist of a ballet and modern class. Selected students are then invited to present a solo in the afternoon.

"Students who audition for our department must have had training," says Walker. "We are looking to see what they have already done with the training they have."

Because "the entire world of dance relies on the eyes outside the dancer," Walker says that the dance faculty looks for many attributes in evaluating dancers during the audition:

★ *Kinesthetic connection*
★ *Musicality*
★ *Ability to present*
★ *A dancer who has something to say through dance*

After the audition, the dance department makes one of three decisions for each dancer: admitted, denied, or callback. The names of students who are admitted to the program are forwarded to the Purchase College admissions office.

"Callbacks are very rare," says Walker. "It happens only when a student is inconsistent during the audition or if faculty members disagree on a student—which hardly ever happens."

The average size of the incoming freshman dance program class at Purchase is forty-five students, but it varies. The class has been as small as thirty-two and as large as sixty-seven. "There were a lot of talented students auditioning that year," explains Walker. Seventy-five percent of freshmen are female and 25 percent are male.

have seen you in class. Now we want to see you perform. Know how to reference yourself as a dancer in any space.

→ Make every second of your solo count. From the first second we want to see you dance, so make sure there is not ten to fifteen seconds of waiting time at the beginning of your music.

→ Never be over time in your solo. If your solo is supposed to be a minute and 30 seconds, don't go beyond that time limit.

WHEN YOU ARRIVE ON CAMPUS

→ Try not to come to campus thinking this will be like what you have done before.

→ Be willing to listen, adapt, and move in new directions.

→ Be disciplined, on time, and 100 percent present in class.

→ If you are not cast to perform right away first semester, don't be discouraged—there will be another chance to perform.

→ Find a mentor in an older student and try to learn from their experiences.

→ Talk to your teachers and don't be afraid to ask questions.

Colleges that do not require auditions often have ample performing opportunities and offer classes with world-renowned guest artists. Many of these schools do not have auditions for acceptance into the dance program but may have auditions for dance scholarships. The audition format for dance scholarships is similar to a normal audition for acceptance into the dance program. These almost always require a dance solo.

Regardless of which type of college dance program you ultimately attend—one that requires a dance audition or one that doesn't—almost every program will have an informal audition upon arrival to the campus. This informal audition simply determines your dance technique level for classes. There is usually an audition in the dance styles that correspond to the classes you want to take. An audition helps instructors place students in the appropriate class level. If you have ever studied at a summer dance program, the audition on the first day is virtually the same as the audition upon arrival to a college dance department. It'll be a breeze!

AMY
GOUCHER COLLEGE

A native of Long Island, Amy was an experienced ballet dancer by the time she was in high school. But she had another academic interest—science. For dancers, finding the right college dance program is difficult enough without adding a specialized academic interest into the equation!

"I knew I really wanted to find a place where I could focus on my dance training to have a professional career but also be prepared academically for another career," explains Amy. "I couldn't have it one way or the other."

Luckily, Amy found a place where she could nurture her interest in science while pursuing dance as well. Goucher College in Baltimore, Maryland, is one of the few colleges that Amy found that is notable in both its dance and biology programs. While in college, Amy had the opportunity to do a summer internship with

Tip from Amy

Go and take dance classes from the teachers on a regular class day—not just the audition day. This way, you can see if you like the environment of the dance department on a normal day without the anxiety of an audition. Putting yourself in the ordinary campus environment can make a big difference when making the choice about which college to attend.

the Harkness Center for Dance Injuries. Here, she worked with certified athletic trainers and physical therapists who exposed her to dance medicine research and physical screening practices. She also shadowed a podiatrist whose work includes the specialized foot problems of dancers.

Amy plans on auditioning for professional companies after graduation and is also considering pursuing physical therapy or podiatry in the future. Naturally, with either choice, she'd like to specialize in working with dancers.

"Here I am seeing all of the possibilities," she says. "I feel lucky I found Goucher."

KAYLEN
UNIVERSITY OF CALIFORNIA AT IRVINE

Raised in Southern California, Kaylen started dancing at age three. By the time she was a high school student, she was surrounded by dancers who were going on to professional careers immediately after graduation. Kaylen recognized that she would have to figure out what her future in dance would be.

"It was clear to me that I would not reach the professional level right out of high school," explains Kaylen.

So college became the natural choice. Kaylen is now a senior at University of California at Irvine pursuing a BA in dance with a minor in educational studies.

Kaylen describes the school as "quite competitive." She says there were 300 students at her audition, and eighty were accepted. At first, Kaylen wasn't sure which school she would attend, but when she visited UCI she knew it was the right choice. Not only is the school competitive in taking the best applicants, but the dance program is also rigorous.

"The caliber of dancers here is pretty high," asserts Kaylen.

Dance majors at UCI typically enroll in two dance technique courses per quarter. Kaylen takes ballet every day and has modern about four times a week. In total, she dances about thirty hours a week between dance classes and rehearsals.

Although Kaylen did not perform during her freshman year, she has had a great deal of performance experience since then. She has enjoyed various opportunities, including the performance of George Balanchine ballets and works by modern dance

Hot Tips from Kaylen

→ Apply to college as a dance major even if you are not sure of declaring that major. This way, you can be sure you can be a dance major at the college if you decide that is really what you want.

→ Find out if non-dance majors can perform. If you decide the dance major is not for you, there might be a chance to still participate in the dance program.

→ Look into other majors the school has to offer in case you want to double major.

→ Be aware of opportunities the university has to offer outside of the dance department.

→ Observe dance classes before enrolling in the school to ascertain the spirit of the dance department.

→ Live on campus at least for your freshman year to become part of the campus community.

legend Martha Graham. As a sophomore, Kaylen participated in an international exchange program with the Paris Conservatory. She is also part of the UCI Etude Ensemble led by Donald McKayle, an internationally recognized Tony- and Emmy-nominated choreographer who once danced with Alvin Ailey. Kaylen also participated in the North American premiere of *The Questioning of Robert Scott*, choreographed by William Forsythe.

"More than anything, the performing opportunities have exceeded my wildest expectations," Kaylen states. "Being a dance major is extremely intellectually stimulating as well as physically demanding."

For prospective college dancers, Kaylen says that college is a great option. But she also believes that if a student has the ability and opportunity to join a dance company immediately after high school graduation, he or she might want to consider doing that first.

"If a dancer is technically ready to join a dance company right away after high school, I'd say join a company and postpone college," advises Kaylen. "Jobs in professional dance are scarce, and it would be difficult to maintain that level of technical ability once a dancer is in college."

How They Stack Up: Comparing College Dance Programs

Having trouble deciding which college dance program is right for you? Answering these questions will help narrow your search.

1. Does the Program Have a Dance Major or Minor?

The first step in narrowing your college search is to decide whether or not you want to major in dance. Request information from colleges that interest you to find out if they offer a dance major or minor and if you can participate in the dance department if you decide not to major in dance. You'll want as much flexibility as possible.

2. Does the Program Offer the Degree You Want?

Not all dance programs are the same. Each degree (BFA, BA, or BS) has a different number of dance credits required for graduation. A BFA requires the most dance credits for graduation and is often focused on performance. A BA is usually offered at liberal arts colleges and requires roughly the same amount of credits as other disciplines, so it makes it easier to double major. A BS degree is the least common dance degree and varies considerably depending on the program—some are designed more like a BFA, and others like a BA. You'll have to contact the department to learn exactly how the program is structured. Figure out how much time you want to spend dancing to find out which degree is your best option.

3. What Type of Dance Technique Does the Program Emphasize?

Do you want to be a ballerina, dance on Broadway, or join a modern dance company? Each college dance program is different—some focus on modern dance, ballet, or jazz. Make sure the programs you are interested in specialize in the technique you want to study.

4. Does the Program Require Auditions?

Some dance programs require auditions for admission to the program, and others don't. If auditions are required, ask if you need to prepare a solo. Many schools that don't have auditions for acceptance to the program often have auditions once you are on campus to determine your dance technique level to place you in classes appropriately. Other schools may not have auditions at all and are open to both dance majors and nonmajors taking the same classes.

5. Are Performance Opportunities Available?

Many programs have performances in the fall and spring. However, some programs provide more opportunities to perform, such as attending the American College Dance Festival.

6. Does the Program Have a Dance Education Concentration?

If you want to become a dance teacher, find out which programs have concentrations in dance education. In some states, dance education majors can become certified to teach dance in public schools. Ask the department if this option is available and how long it takes—dance certification can usually be completed within four years, but it can take an extra semester in some cases.

7. Can You Double Major?

Some dance programs allow students to major in dance and another field, while some may not. Find out if double majoring is an option before choosing a college if you want to study another subject in conjunction with dance.

8. Do Guest Artists Visit the Department?

Studying with renowned dancers and choreographers can be a fulfilling part of the college dance experience. Find out if artists you'd like to study with have visited dance departments that you're researching.

9. What Are the Career Paths of Dance Alumni?

The success of dance alumni can you help you decide if a program is right for you. Graduates who pursue careers similar to your aspirations can help you decide if a program might be a good match. Many schools list successful dance alumni on their websites and their department brochures.

10. Is the Program Affiliated with a Dance Organization?

Dance departments can be accredited by the National Association of Schools of Dance (NASD) or be members of Dance/USA. NASD sets standards for dance departments to ensure that students have a varied dance faculty and different concentrations within their programs, which enables for a quality dance education. Dance/USA members receive information on nationwide developments in dance, including federal funding opportunities; develop relationships with dance companies; and receive professional dance periodicals so they can stay informed about the dance profession and share information with students. Professional accreditation or membership shows that the professional dance community recognizes these programs as being reputable to the dance community.

Sample Dance Essay

By Cristina S.

The sound of laughter vibrates off the walls, the intense vibe penetrates the air, an aura of liveliness emanates backstage; the music begins, I hear my cue, and through the tremendous energy, I focus on my final dance number. At this precise moment, I am a dancer! As I step into the spotlight, I appear to have an animated personality with hyperbolic facial expressions and exaggerated gestures. When I look inside myself, I realize that my behavior is not innate, but has evolved from the stage exposure that I have embraced. To prepare for a performance, I have learned to harness my entire being and analyze every minute detail of my dance routine. Whereas I used to agonize over the conscious process of analysis and self-examination, now I intuitively function this way, naturally criticizing the smallest facets of my performance, including my gestures, facial expressions, movements, placement, relationship to other dancers both emotionally and physically, and emotive communication with the audience. Spending three hours on a "count of eight" is often the norm as I work to bring each movement to life.

I know that the innumerable hours spent rehearsing and dancing with my gifted friends have played a significant role in my personal development. By bonding socially and emotionally with these multi-talented personalities, my essence, the real me, has been challenged to grow and mature not only in dance, but also in my entire being. My ensemble friends do not allow me to be a normal, dreary, everyday type of person; our shared exuberance and life-embracing antics when we practice and perform are contagious, actually infectious. I am thoroughly elated to catch this "bug" of freedom, to be spontaneous, outgoing, random, and tolerant. Although emulation is a tool used to teach awareness and perfection in dance, even when I emulate another dancer's style or movements, I still have the power to reveal my individuality.

My daily life is a balance of expected, conventional, routine events: I go to school, do homework, study, go to dance, teach dance, volunteer for community service, and spend time with my family and friends. No matter where I am or what I am doing, my true passion—the creative, disciplined world of dance—is never far from my thoughts or heart. I accomplish what is expected of me, but I do it all because I choose to, because I love to.

Many of my relatives, classmates, and teachers occasionally refer to me as being "overly conscientious and cautious," which I admit I sometimes am. However, when I am with my closest friends, my artsy, dancing "soul mates," I am more uninhibited than at any other moment. At such times, the essence of who I am is revealed. I am a dancer. The arts are essential, enriching components of our lives, and I know that when I dance, I fulfill a purpose for expression in myself and, hopefully, inspire passion in others. The music begins, I hear my cue. I am ready to step into the next spotlight.

SAMPLE APPLICATION QUESTIONS

Imagine that you have been asked to present a statement to your local school board in favor of retaining the high schools' performing arts programs, all threatened by budget cuts. What would you tell them?

Can you imagine a world without music? Music is heard everywhere: the radio, TV, the car, the movies, even in elevators. Can you imagine going to the movies and hearing no music with the film? Can you imagine no symphonies to play modern composed music expressing the beat of our times? Can you imagine actors and actresses working only because of physical characteristics and not because of their well-practiced acting craft expertise? Can you imagine having to deliver a speech to a large group of people and never having had any experience with public speaking? Can you imagine Christmas without the *Nutcracker* Ballet? What would New York, Chicago, Los Angeles, or Miami be without the performing arts?

My questions should compel you to examine carefully the void and the waste of talent that would occur should performing arts vanish from high school students' lives. Performing arts allow students to express themselves in a way not possible with conventional academic subjects. Students need to know how to communicate effectively, and the performing arts train students to feel confident speaking in front of other people, which is essential for job interviews and delivering presentations. Students who participate in the performing arts experience working cooperatively and collaboratively, skills that are mandatory for success in the workplace and society. For students in the population who cannot afford private lessons in any of the areas of performing arts, a viable high school performing arts program is the only way they can experience music, dance, drama, and debate. Without funding for school programs, thousands and thousands of young people will never find their passion and talent through performing arts subjects. Students will not have any exposure to the performing arts if schools don't maintain programs, and many adults would not have had any introduction to the fine arts without the high school programs from the past and the ones that are current. Although the cutting of performing arts only pertains to a local school board, cutting performing arts programs and opportunities will have a domino effect throughout society. We cannot afford to cease funding for performing arts in the schools!

What led you to choose the area(s) of academic interest that you have listed in your application to the University of Michigan? If you are undecided, what areas are you most interested in, and why?

Having spent most of my free time involved with dance either practicing, performing, or teaching, it would have been logical for me to apply to a dance conservatory. But a conservatory would have been limiting to me because I also have an intense interest in academics, specifically history, and I want to combine the dance and academic disciplines. Having spent most of my time outside of school participating in dance as a student, teacher, and choreographer, I can't imagine not being able to dance to express myself. Yet, history as a subject area interests me too, because there are multiple ways to view what has happened historically. I find it interesting how society and cultures have evolved. History teaches lessons from the events of the past, and the study of history explains that many answers are a possibility; thus history is not limiting as a subject. Not knowing where my passion for dance and history will lead me, only through an in-depth academic program in both disciplines will I be able to ultimately decide what steps I will take on my career path. The University of Michigan provides the selective, perfectly balanced program where I can explore dance and history simultaneously. By living and studying in the diverse, eclectic and tolerant atmosphere of Ann Arbor, I will be able to pursue my dance and academic passions completely.

Sample Dance Résumé

Krystal A.

WEIGHT: 120 LBS   **HEIGHT 5'5"**

TRAINING

University of California, Irvine	Irvine, CA	2016–present
Jimmie DeFore Dance Center Costa Mesa	Costa Mesa, CA	2015–present
The EDGE Performing Arts Center Los Angeles	Los Angeles, CA	2015–present
The Dance Factory	Los Alamitos, CA	2012–2016
Los Alamitos High School	Los Alamitos, CA	CA 2008–2012
Orange County Dance Center	Huntington Beach, CA	2001–2011

BALLET

University of California, Irvine	David Allan, Eloy Barragan, El Gabriel, Leslie Peck
Orange County Dance Center	Terri Sellars, Anthony Sellars, Carrie Yamate Los Alamitos High School Rikki Jones

JAZZ

Jimmie Defore Dance Center	Leann Alduenda, Mike Esperanza The EDGE Performing Arts Center Doug Caldwell
The Dance Factory	Laura Schierhorn
Los Alamitos High School	Rikki Jones, Tianna Avalos
Orange County Dance Center	Laura Atkinson, Tiffany Billings, Briana Haft, Shelly Macy, Cindy Pecca, Coby Vincent, Carrie Yamate

MODERN

University of California, Irvine	Lisa Naugle, Loretta Livingston

HIP HOP

Jimmie DeFore Dance Center	Cruz, Tim Stevenson
The Dance Factory	Cruz

TAP

Orange County Dance Center	Carrie Yamate

MUSICAL THEATER

Orange County Dance Center	Shelly Macy, Carrie Yamate

MASTER CLASSES & WORKSHOPS

University of California, Irvine	Mike Esperanza	October 2016
Dance In Action Convention	Monie Adamson, Jon Bond, Rashida Kahn, Lorilee Silvaggio	summer 2016
Southland Ballet Academy	Charles Maple	winter 2015
Orange County Dance Center	Sophie Monat, Cindy Dolin (Pecca), Dan Wong, Keith Diorio, Heather Ahern, Tiffany Billings, Spencer Gavin	summer 2015
Jimmie DeFore Dance Center	Malaya	summer 2015
Orange County Dance Center	Cindy Dolin (Pecca)	2014

EXPERIENCE

Ballet Repertory Theatre	dir. Terri & Anthony Sellars	2012–2016

PERFORMANCE

Bare Bones "Body Art"	"Mandarin Tango"	University of California, Irvine
Ballet Repertory Theatre	*The Nutcracker, Les Corsaires, Giselle, Coppelia, Hansel & Gretel, La Bayadere, Paquita, Bolero, Les Sylphides, The Seasons, Violin Concerto, Sleeping Beauty—Act III, Rachmaninoff, Expressions, Carnival,* Ballet Studio	
Los Alamitos High School	*Dreamscape, Dreamscape II: The Dream Dimension, Avant Garde, Joy & Pain, Once Upon a Time…, Xanadu, A Time to Dance*	

CHOREOGRAPHY

"Fighter" by Christina Aguilera	Jazz solo for Katy Felsenthal	summer 2015
"Have You Ever Been in Love?" by Celine Dion	Lyrical duet	spring 2015

TEACHING

Orange County Dance Center	substitute teaching	2012–2015

AWARDS

Scholarship Winner	Dance In Action Convention 2016
Talent Competition Winner	National American Miss Beauty Pageant 2015
1st place Senior duet (platinum)	Showstoppers Regional Competition 2014

OUTSIDE OF SCHOOL

Orange Country Dance Center	15 years	Student/Substitute Teacher
Ballet Repertory Theatre	4 years	Principal Dancer

INSIDE OF SCHOOL		
Advanced Dance Program	4 years	Student/Choreographer
Safe Rides	2 years	Member, Commissioner (give free and safe rides to drunk people)
Bottles for the Bay	1 year	Co-President (started it at school, collect bottles and cans and recycle them)
Christian Club	3 years	Member, Leader
Resonance	1 year	Executive Board (school literary magazine)
D.A.N.C.E.	2 years	Secretary, Vice President (Drug Alternative Nights & Community Events—host dances to keep students out of drugs and alcohol)
Japanese Club	2 years	Member

HONORS & AWARDS		
Principal's Honor Roll	4 years	3.5 GPA or higher
Japanese National Honors Society	3 years	

WORK EXPERIENCE		
Choreographed a dance routine for student at Los Alamitos High School	($15/hr)	

SUMMER PROGRAMS/TRAVEL EXPERIENCE		
Associate Student Body conference	summer 2015	UCSB
Summer Dance Intensive	summer 2015	Orange County Dance Center
Cancun, Mexico	summer 2014	
Grand Canyon	summer 2013	
Niagara Falls	summer 2015	
San Francisco	2014–2015	

OTHER SPECIAL EXPERIENCES/UNUSUAL HOBBIES		
Lifeguard Training	summer 2016	Belmont Plaza Pool (Long Beach)
National American Miss Pageant	August 2016	Hyatt Regency (Anaheim)
Master class with Malaya	summer 2016	Jimmie DeFore Dance Center

Sample Résumé

Cristina S.
EXTRACURRICULAR AND LEADERSHIP ACTIVITIES

Literary Magazine, grades 10–12

Editor, grade 12

Editorial Staff, grade 11

Contributing Writer, grades 10–12

Spanish National Honor Society, grades 10–12

President, grade 12

Secretary, grade 11

Kids for 9/11, grades 10–12

President, grade 12

Vice President, grade 11

Student Government, grades 9–12

Junior Class Secretary, grade 11

Homecoming Activities Co-Chair, grades 9–11

Annual Fundraising Dinner Chair, grades 11–12

Key Club, grades 9–12

Class Representative, grades 9–12

Adopt-a-Grandparent Chair, grades 11–12

Tourette's Syndrome Annual Auction, grades 10–12

Communications Director, grade 11

Fundraising Coordinator, grade 10

Love Jen Family Festival Volunteer, grades 9–12

Fundraiser benefiting the Joe DiMaggio Children's Hospital

Festival for the Heart Annual Dance Fundraiser, grades 10–12

Coral Gables Junior Women's Club, grades 10–12

Juniorette, grades 10–11

Fundraiser benefiting May Van Sickle Dental Clinic for low-income families, grades 10–11

Lower School Kindergarten Student Aide, grade 12

Volunteer Mathematics Tutor, grades 11–12

HONORS AND AWARDS

Washington University Book Award for Outstanding Leadership and Scholarship, grade 11

Outstanding Citizen-Scholar of the Year Award, grade 10

Outstanding Math Student Award, grade 10

Mu Alpha Theta Math Honor Society, grades 11–12

English Honor Society, grades 11–12

Quill and Scroll, grades 10–12

National Honor Society, grades 10–12

Spanish National Honor Society, grades 10–12

Junior National Honor Society, grade 9

Headmaster's Honor Roll, grades 9–11

WORK EXPERIENCE

Dance Teacher/Choreographer

Choreographer, grades 11–12

Dance Unlimited, grades 9–12

Student Fundraising and Artistic Director

Dance Teacher/Choreographer

Ballet, Tap, Jazz, and Modern Dance Instructor

DANCE TRAINING AND WORKSHOPS

Jazz: Scott Benson, Ricardo Pena, Mindy Hall, Amanda Alvarez, Judy Rodriguez

Ballet: Vivian Tobio, Deborah Buttner, Gerri Caruncho, Dana Susanj, German Dragers, Magda Aunon, Ingrid Houvenaeghel

Tap: Judy Ann Bassing, Danie Beck, Ron Daniels

Modern: Kiki Lucas, Kim Wolfe

Hip Hop: Lena Blake, Natalya Hall

Voice: Patricia Castellon

Schools: Danie Beck's Dance Unlimited, International Ballet Academy, Ballet Elite, Magda Aunon's Ballet Academy

Years Studied: Ballet 14 years, Modern 4 years, Jazz/Lyrical 14 years, Tap 14 years, Hip Hop 4 years, Pointe 8 years, Voice 1 year

Hours Weekly: Ballet/Pointe 7 hours, Jazz/Lyrical 5 hours, Modern 4 hours,

Tap 2 hours, Hip Hop 2 hours

Point Park University International Summer Dance Intensive

NYC Dance Alliance Summer Intensive

Summer Intensive with Pamela Bolling and Karen Herbert

International Ballet Academy Summer Intensive

Broadway Dance Center

West Coast Dance Explosion

Dance Power Express

Florida Dance Masters

STEPS, Peridance, JUMP, Shock Dance Workshop

STAGE EXPERIENCE

Magic Music Days Featured Dancer, Walt Disney Entertainment

Sweet Dreams Ensemble, Dade County Auditorium

Numbers and Nonsense Ensemble, Dade County Auditorium

Main Attraction Featured Dancer, Lakeland Civic Center

NYCDA Summer Gala Featured Dancer, La Guardia High School

The Nutcracker Ensemble, Bailey Concert Hall

Viscaya Holiday Show Ensemble, Viscaya Gardens

NYCDA World Finals Featured Dancer, Waldorf Astoria

Florida Dance Celebration Featured Dancer, University of South Florida

Good News Gazette Ensemble, Ransom Everglades Aud.

Point Park Summer Show Featured Dancer, Pittsburgh Playhouse

TELEVISION EXPERIENCE

2013 Orange Bowl Parade, Ensemble, WSVN Network

2014 Macy's Thanksgiving Day Parade, Ensemble, ABC Network

2013–14 Miami Dolphins, Featured Dancer, ABC Network

2014 Showstoppers, Featured Dancer, ESPN

2015–16 Disney Holiday Show, Ensemble, ABC Network

2015 Showstoppers, Featured Dancer, ESPN

2016 *Raise the Roof*, Featured Dancer, Channel 51—Telemundo

DANCE AWARDS

Ballet Student of the Year (Received Twice)—Danie Beck's Dance Unlimited

Performer of the Year—Danie Beck's Dance Unlimited

Senior Miss ADA Dancer of the Year—Ft. Lauderdale

Outstanding Teen Dancer—New York City Dance Alliance, Ft. Myers

Outstanding Senior Dancer—New York City Dance Alliance, Orlando

Miss Teen StarQuest—Ft. Lauderdale, Panama City

Miss Senior StarQuest—Ft. Lauderdale

Miss Senior StarQuest National—First Runner-Up

Senior Miss West Coast Dance Explosion—Ft. Myers

Miss Dance Explosion—Ft. Lauderdale

Miss Dance Rave—Ft. Lauderdale

Junior Miss Dance Runner-Up—Florida Dance Masters

Miss Dance First Runner-Up—Florida Dance Masters

SCHOLARSHIPS

Broadway Dance Center, STEPS, Peridance, Dance Power Express, West Coast Dance Explosion,

Point Park University Summer Dance Intensive, International Ballet Academy, Florida Dance Masters

SAMPLE DANCE CURRICULUM*

University of Arizona Dance Division

Four-Year Suggested Plan of Study

This is only a suggested program for the BFA in dance. The order in which degree requirements are completed depends on course availability, transfer units, deficiencies at the time of admission, summer/winter coursework, and other factors. Students should consult with their Dance Major advisor, if possible, to determine the program of study that will work best for their specific situation. Make sure to keep track of your upper division units (300/400 level classes) in order to meet the 42 upper-division credit requirement for the BFA in Dance.

FRESHMAN–FALL SEMESTER	CREDITS	FRESHMAN–SPRING SEMESTER	CREDITS
ENGL 101	3	ENGL 102	3
*MATH 110 (College Algebra) Or PHIL 110	4 (3)	Tier 1: NATS	3
Tier 1: TRAD	3	Tier 1: INDV	3
DNC 145 Improvisation	1	DNC 343 Ensemble	1
DNC 201A, 301 Pilates or 302 DNC Inj. Prevention	1	DNC 243 Creating w/Mvt. & Rh.	2
DNC Technique I (200 level or above, Ballet, Modern, or Jazz)	2	DNC Tech I (200 level or above Ballet, Modern, or Jazz)	2
DNC Tech II (300 level or above Ballet, Modern, or Jazz)	2	DNC Tech II (300 level or above Ballet, Modern, or Jazz)	2
	TOTAL: 15/16		TOTAL: 16
SOPHOMORE–FALL SEMESTER	CREDITS	SOPHOMORE–SPRING SEMESTER	CREDITS
Tier 1: NATS	3	Tier II: INDIVIDUALS AND SOCIETIES	3
Tier 1: TRAD	3	Tier II: Humanities	3
Tier 1: INDV	3	DNC 343 Ensemble	2
DNC 343 Ensemble	1	DNC Technique I (200 level or above, Ballet, Modern, or Jazz)	2
DNC 245B Basic Choreography	2	DNC Technique II (300 level or above, Ballet, Modern, or Jazz)	2
DNC Technique 1 (200 level or above, Ballet, Modern, or Jazz)	2	DNC 200 Dance History	3

DNC Technique II (300 level or above, Ballet, Modern, or Jazz)	2	DNC 245A Basic Choreography	2
	TOTAL: 16		**TOTAL: 17**
JUNIOR—FALL SEMESTER	**CREDITS**	**JUNIOR—SPRING SEMESTER**	**CREDITS**
Tier II: Natural Science	3	General Academic Elective	3
Dept. Spec. MUS	3	Dept. Spec. MUS	3
General Acad. Elective	3	DNC 343 Ensemble	1
DNC 343 Ensemble	1	DNC 455 Biomechanics	3
DNC Elective	2	DNC 445B Advance Chor.	2
DNC Tech II: (300 level or above Ballet, Modern, or Jazz)	2	DNC Tech II (300 level or above Ballet, Modern, or Jazz)	2
DNC 445 A Advanced Chor.	2	DNC 394B Production Project	1
	TOTAL: 16		**TOTAL: 15**
SENIOR—FALL SEMESTER	**CREDITS**	**SENIOR—SPRING SEMESTER**	**CREDITS**
General Academic Elective	3	General Academic Elective	2
General Academic Elective	4	Dept. Spec. TAR	3
DNC 343 Ensemble	2	DNC 343 Ensemble	1
DNC Tech III (400 level or above Ballet, Modern, or Jazz)	2	DNC Tech III (400 level or above Ballet, Modern, or Jazz)	2
DNC 498 Senior Capstone	1	DNC 446 Careers in Dance	3
DNC Elective	2	DNC Elective	2
		DNC 400 Dance & Culture	3
	TOTAL: 14		**TOTAL: 16**

(15 units if PHIL 110 used for math credit)

**This sample curriculum is reprinted with permission. The course schedule shown here is representative of courses for a dance major. Of course, each institution has slightly different emphases and requirements, and students are advised to investigate the curriculum at each program they apply to.

DANCE PROGRAMS

Profiles of Selected Programs

Northeast / 220

Southeast / 233

Midwest / 237

West / 244

Comprehensive List of Colleges with Dance Programs

By State / 252

Northeast

BARNARD COLLEGE/ COLUMBIA UNIVERSITY

Department of Dance
3009 Broadway Street
New York, NY 10027

Phone: (212) 854-2995
Website: barnard.edu/dance
Email: dance@barnard.edu

Tuition: $$
Campus student enrollment (undergraduate):
2,573

Degree(s): BA
Courses offered: Anatomy, African, Afro-Cuban, ballet, biomechanics, classical Indian dance, composition, contact improvisation, dance criticism, dance history, Feldenkrais, flamenco, hip hop, jazz, modern, movement and analysis, Pilates, tap. Also, the opportunity to work with established and emerging choreographers, performing both new and restaged works in concert settings.
Audition requirement: No
Scholarships available: Yes
Number of faculty: 35
Number of majors and minors: 30
Department activities: Many performance opportunities, master classes, and public events.

Prominent Alumni:

Twyla Tharp—choreographer
Suzanne Vega—singer
Cynthia Nixon—actress
Laurie Anderson—musician and performance artist
Greta Gerwig—film actress

BOSTON CONSERVATORY AT BERKLEE

8 Fenway
Boston, MA 02215

Phone: (617) 912-9137
Website: bostonconservatory.berklee.edu
Email: admissions@bostonconservatory.edu

Tuition: $$
Campus student enrollment (undergraduate):
563

Degree(s): BFA
Concentration: Major: Contemporary Dance Performance; Area of Emphasis: Ballet, Modern, Jazz, Pedagogy, Creating Performance
Courses offered: Ballet, modern, Horton technique, Limon technique, release technique, jazz, hip hop, improvisation, contact skills, African dance, salsa, partnering, Pilates, gyrokinesis, floor barre, yoga, composition, collaborative process, Alexander technique, repertory, pedagogy, experiential anatomy, Laban movement analysis, music literature, dance history, dance and popular culture, history of hip hop, dance on film and video, European dance theater trends, voice for dancers, dance production, acting for dancers, senior seminar, senior performance project
Audition requirement: Yes
Scholarships available: Yes
Number of faculty: 30
Department activities: Students perform three mainstage concerts per year plus numerous studio and off-campus concerts featuring reconstructed masterpieces, premieres by major living artists and original student works.

Prominent Alumni:

Dance division alumni have joined the companies of Alvin Ailey, Complexions Contemporary Ballet, Cedar Lake Ballet, Merce Cunningham, Martha Graham, Jose Limón, Paul Taylor, Elisa Monte, Buglisi Dance Theatre, Stephen Petronio, Sean

Curran, London's Richard Alston, Bill T. Jones/Arnie Zane, Hubbard Street, Anna Sokolow's Players Project, Pilobolus, and MOMIX. In addition, dance alumni have joined ballet companies including Boston Ballet, Metropolitan Opera, Ballet Hispanico, Atlanta Ballet, Les Grands Ballet Canadiens, Alberta Ballet, Eliot Feld, Oakland, Indianapolis, Dayton, Louisville, Arizona, Baryshnikov's White Oak, National Ballet of Portugal. and Hamburg Ballet. They have danced in Broadway productions including *Cats*, *Movin' Out*, *Chicago*, *Ragtime*, *A Chorus Line*, *The Wiz*, Jerome Robbins's *Broadway*, *The King and I*, and *Carousel*.

FORDHAM UNIVERSITY/ THE AILEY SCHOOL

Lincoln Center Campus
New York, NY 10458

Phone: (212) 405-9124
Website: theaileyschool.edu/BFA
Email: bfa@alvinailey.org

Tuition: $$$
Campus student enrollment (undergraduate): 8,855 total, 1,775 at Fordham Lincoln Center campus

Degree(s): BFA
Courses offered: Daily classes in classical ballet, Horton, and Graham-based modern. Other courses include pointe, men's technique, partnering, modern partnering, anatomy and kinesiology, West African dance, improvisation, dance composition (I–III), dance history (III), repertory workshop, performance and art, yoga, jazz, tap, senior project, senior seminar, independent study in choreography, Cunningham technique, Limon technique, Taylor technique, release technique, music.
Student activities: Students perform both at the Ailey Citigroup Theater and at Fordham University's Pope Auditorium. In their senior year, students also perform in venues in the greater New York

City area. The Ailey/Fordham program offers its most advanced students the unique opportunity to dance professionally while earning credit toward their BFA degree. Seniors and occasionally juniors with outstanding dance and academic records may dance with professional companies as apprentices or members with the approval of the BFA director.

FIVE COLLEGE DANCE DEPARTMENT

A collaboration of the dance departments and programs from Amherst, Hampshire, Mount Holyoke, and Smith Colleges and the University of Massachusetts Amherst, which functions as a unique intercampus department.

Five College Dance Department
Hampshire College
Dance Building
893 West Street
Amherst, MA 01002

Phone: (413) 559-6622
Website: fivecolleges.edu/dance
Email: fcdd@hampshire.edu

Tuition:
Amherst College: $$$$
Hampshire College: $$$
Mount Holyoke College: $$$
Smith College: $$$
University of Massachusetts, Amherst: $$$$

Campus student enrollment (undergraduate):
Amherst College: 1,796
Hampshire College: 1,396
Mount Holyoke College: 2,189
Smith College: 2,500
University of Massachusetts, Amherst: 21,640

Degrees: BA (all campuses), BFA (UMass Amherst)
Courses offered: Technique classes in ballet, pointe, contact improvisation, jazz, modern/ contemporary, tango, and West African dance are

offered every semester. Other technique classes, including group improvisation, hip hop, musical theater, salsa, and tap, are offered some semesters. Theory courses include dance history, dance and culture, research in dance, three levels of composition, dance education, dance in the community, scientific foundations of dance, rhythmic analysis, lighting design, costume design, and others.

Audition requirement: Only the UMass BFA and Smith College MFA programs require an entrance audition. The FCDD offers appropriate training and resources for everyone from beginning to advanced dancers. For the undergraduate dance programs at Amherst, Hampshire, Smith, and Mount Holyoke Colleges, it is possible to begin your dance studies as a first -ear student and complete a dance major/concentration. For entering students with significant previous dance experience, there is a department-wide advanced placement audition for upper-level ballet and modern/contemporary technique classes during the first week of classes.

Scholarships available: Each member campus offers scholarships, but the FCDD does not award scholarships of our own.

Number of faculty: 18 permanent faculty members, and 12–15 adjunct faculty members each year.

Department activities: There are about 35 performance events under the umbrella of the FCDD over the course of an academic year. This includes faculty concerts, student concerts, and thesis projects. The FCDD organizes a major repertory project each year for which all FCDD dancers may audition. Recent rep projects include Pilobolus's *Megawatt*, Delfos Danza's *Full and Empty*, Gallim Dance's *Wonderland*, and Ohad Naharin's *Echad Mi Yodea*. There are additional guest artists each year who come to choreograph or restage work on Five College dancers. Recent examples include Ephrat Asherie, Idan Cohen, John Heginbotham, Sidra Bell, and Kathleen Hermesdorf. And, of course, our accomplished faculty members create work on FCDD students every year as well. If you want to perform, you will·find no shortage of opportunities. Additional opportunities include American College Dance Association festivals; opportunities for students to artistic direct student dance concerts; senior seminars in special topics; student-designed study abroad experiences; New York Professional Outreach Program (NYPOP) at UMass; and master classes with prominent dance artists. The FCDD has an agreement with the UMass Fine Arts Center that every dance company that performs as part of their Center Series teach at least one master class open to FCDD students. Recent master classes include Doug Varone and Dancers, Bridgman|Packer Dance, Cloud Gate Dance Theatre of Taiwan, Stephen Petronio Company, Grupo Corpo, Martha Graham Dance Company, Alonzo King LINES Ballet, Parsons Dance, and Kyle Abraham/Abraham.in.Motion. The FCDD's member dance programs often host additional master classes of their own, which FCDD dancers are welcome to join.

Prominent Alumni:

FCDD graduates have won Bessie and Fulbright awards, started their own companies (e.g., Stephen Petronio, HC '74), and danced with artists and companies such as Bebe Miller, David Parsons, Lucinda Childs, Trisha Brown, Doug Elkins, Winnipeg Contemporary Dancers, Ballet Nacional de Caracas, Metropolitan Opera Ballet, Louisville Ballet, Faye Driscoll, Ailey II, and Pilobolus.

GOUCHER COLLEGE

1021 Dulaney Valley Road
Baltimore, MD 21204

Phone: (410) 337-6100, toll-free (800) GOUCHER ext. 6100
Website: goucher.edu/dance
Email: admissions@goucher.edu

Tuition: $$
Campus student enrollment (undergraduate): 1,478

Degree(s): BA

Courses offered: Studio courses in ballet, modern augmented by courses in African dance and drumming, partnering, improvisation, repertory/variations, men's technique, hip hop, musical theater, Pilates, and jazz. Theory courses in dance history, criticism, dance therapy, composition, dance education, lighting design, music for dance, Labanotation, and anatomy. Ability to double major or concentrate in arts administration and science with a dance concentration. Students may also choose to take specific courses in preparation for successful entry into graduate or professional programs for identified careers in dance such as dance therapy and dance science.

Audition requirement: Yes. for students interested in scholarship consideration.

Scholarships available: Yes

Number of faculty: 14

Department activities: Numerous opportunities to perform throughout the academic year; five artists-in-residence per academic year; Pilates Center; opportunities to study abroad; internship opportunities; ability to double major; dance courses, including performing and choreographic opportunities, are open to all students registered for dance courses or with the appropriate prerequisites.

Prominent Alumni:

Alums direct their own companies or schools, attend graduate school, perform with ballet and modern dance companies, are professors at various colleges and universities, teach in public and private schools, are writers and editors of dance publications, attend medical and physical therapy school, among other career choices.

THE JUILLIARD SCHOOL

Dance Division
60 Lincoln Center Plaza
New York, NY 10023–6588

Phone: (212) 799-5000
Website: juilliard.edu
Email: danceadmissions@juilliard.edu

Tuition: $$
Campus student enrollment: 530 undergraduate; 894 total

Degree(s): BFA

Courses offered: The core curriculum requires intensive study and performance in classical ballet and modern dance and includes courses in repertory, partnering, pointe or men's class, dance composition, anatomy, acting, stagecraft, production, and music theory.

Audition requirement: Yes

Scholarships available: Yes

Number of faculty: 30

Students admitted each year: 24
(12 women/12 men)

Department activities: Juilliard dancers perform in approximately 15 performances annually, including fully staged concerts and workshops.

Prominent Alumni:

Robert Battle
Pina Bausch
Martha Clarke
Mercedes Ellington
Robert Garland
Charlotte Griffin
Kazuko Hirabayashi
Adam Hougland
Saeko Ichinohe
Loni Landon
Jessica Lang
Lar Lubovitch
Bruce Marks
Susan Marshall

Austin McCormick
Andrea Miller
Ohad Naharin
Paul Taylor
Alumni have performed with nearly every major ballet and modern dance company in the United States and abroad.

THE HARTT SCHOOL/ UNIVERSITY OF HARTFORD

The Hartt School/University of Hartford
200 Bloomfield Avenue
West Hartford, CT 06117–1599

Phone: (860) 768-4465
Website: hartford.edu/hartt
Email: harttadm@hartford.edu

Tuition: $
Campus student enrollment (undergraduate): 5,246

Degree(s): BFA
Concentrations: Ballet performance, pedagogy
Courses offered: Dance technique classes include ballet, pointe, pas de deux, men's work, character dance, Martha Graham technique and contemporary dance. The curriculum also includes course work in music, dance composition, pedagogy, kinesiology, repertory, and dance history.
Audition requirement: Yes
Scholarships available: Yes
Number of faculty: 20
Department activities: Two mainstage repertory programs each year and two black box theater performances each year.

MERCYHURST COLLEGE

Dance Department
501 E. 38th Street
Erie, PA 16546

Phone: toll-free: (800) 825-1926 x2202
Website: dance.mercyhurst.edu
Email: admissions@mercyhurst.edu

Tuition: $
Campus student enrollment (undergraduate): 2,762

Degree(s): BA
Concentrations: Choreography, pedagogy, performance, arts administration (minor)
Audition requirement: Yes
Scholarships available: Yes
Number of faculty: 5
Department activities: The department offers a curriculum that focuses on classical ballet supported by modern, jazz, and tap; four main stage performances with The Mercyhurst Dancers and Liturgical Dance Ensemble, and Mercyhurst Ballet Theatre and SoMarDance Works (by audition only); internationally recognized guest artists; returning professional program; accreditation by the National Association of Schools of Dance.

Prominent Alumni:
Alumni have performed with Alvin Ailey American Dance Theater, Ballet Arizona, BalletMet, Bodiography Contemporary Ballet, Boston Ballet, Chicago Ballet, Cincinnati Ballet, Dance Theatre of Harlem, Dayton Ballet, Disney World, Louisville Ballet, Missouri Contemporary Ballet, Nashville Ballet, Charlotte Ballet, Pittsburgh Ballet Theatre, Radio City Rockettes, Royal Caribbean Cruise Lines, St. Louis Ballet, and European companies.

MIDDLEBURY COLLEGE

Middlebury College Dance Program
Mahaney Center for the Arts
72 Porter Field Road
Middlebury, VT 05753

Phone (department): (802) 443-3136
Email: Dance@middlebury.edu

Tuition: $$$
Campus student enrollment (undergraduate): 2,450

Degree(s): BA
Concentrations: Dance majors at Middlebury College choose to concentrate in one of our three academic tracks: Choreography and Performance, Production and Technology, or Theory and Aesthetics.
Courses offered: Ballet technique, anatomy and kinesiology, dance history courses, dance production, Gaga dance technique, modern dance technique, West African dance technique, yoga
Audition required: No
Number of faculty: 4–7
Department activities: Fall concerts, faculty concerts, and class showings take place each semester in addition to our Performing Arts Series, masterclasses, lectures, and workshops that bring world-renowned artists and scholars to campus to interact and collaborate with our students through commissions and the touring of The Dance Company of Middlebury.

Prominent Alumni:

Cameron McKinney
Paul Matteson
Sophie Levine
Davis Anderson

MONTCLAIR STATE UNIVERSITY

Department of Theatre and Dance
1 Normal Avenue
Upper Montclair, NJ 07043

Phone: (973) 655-7000
Website: montclair.edu/arts/theatre-and-dance/

Tuition: $
Campus student enrollment (undergraduate): 16,336

Degree(s): BA and BFA and minor in dance
Concentrations: Dance and dance education
Audition requirement: Yes
Scholarships available: Yes:
Cento Amici Award (Theatre & Dance)
Choreographic Excellence Award
Danceaturgy Award
Department of Theatre & Dance Service Award
Doris Bianchi Senior Award
Jeanne Wade Heningburg Award
Joseph F. Bella Production/Design Award
Linda Roberts Outstanding Senior Dance Award
Marc Mattaliano Theatre Award
Mary Ann Peins Dance Scholarship
MSU Dance Education Award
MSU Dance Spirit Award
Outstanding Performer Award
Senior BFA Acting Award
Wycoff Award
Number of faculty: 6 full-time, 31 part-time
Number of Majors: 149 majors, 35 minors
Percentage and number of applicants accepted into the department per year:
Undergraduate: Approximately 14%; 395 applied, 56 accepted
Student Activities: Department of Theatre and Dance students learn acting, dance, theater studies, and theater production with imminent faculty and visiting professionals. The Dance programs combine a conservatory-based approach to training with a liberal arts curriculum to prepare students for extraordinary lives and careers as professional

dancers and dance educators. Our intensive course of study is based on anatomically sound, sequential technique to train dancers in modern dance, ballet, jazz, African dance, and hip hop. Our location just 14 miles west of Manhattan puts students just minutes away from Broadway productions, world-class dance performances, and career-building internships. There are many study abroad programs as well as opportunities to work and perform in our exceptional performance and teaching facilities—from the state-of-the-art Alexander Kasser Theater to fully equipped dance studios, a 2,000-seat amphitheater, and the intimate L. Howard Fox Theatre.

Prominent Alumni:

Mark Willis (BFA 2014)—dancer in the Jose Limón Dance Company

Sharrod Williams (BFA Dance 2012)—joined the cast of *Tuck Everlasting* on Broadway

Jay Selesky (BA Dance 2014)—dancer with Asha Dance Company and recently played the lead in *Viva Africa* produced by the Truth Group

Colleen Lynch (BFA)—teaching artist for the Paul Taylor Dance Company, dancer with Impetus Dance Collaborative

MUHLENBERG COLLEGE

Department of Theatre and Dance
Trexler Pavilion for Theatre and Dance
Muhlenberg College
Allentown, PA 18104

Phone: (484) 664-3330
Website: muhlenberg.edu
Email: richter@muhlenberg.edu

Tuition: $$$
Campus student enrollment: 2,200

Degree(s): BA
Concentrations: Full dance major and complete musical theater training

Audition/portfolio requirement: No, recommended but not required

Scholarships available: Yes; Baker Talent Grants and Muhlenberg Talent Scholarships range from $1,000 to $4,000

Number of faculty: 23 full-time, 12 part-time

Number of majors and minors: 100 dance majors and minors; there is no theater minor

Percentage and number of applicants accepted into the department per year: Accepts about 40% of applicants, about 70 new students in the theater major each year and 20 students in the dance major

Department activities: Three major dance concerts, two informal dance concerts

NEW YORK UNIVERSITY, TISCH SCHOOL OF THE ARTS

Department of Dance
111 Second Avenue
3rd Floor
New York, NY 10003

Phone: (212) 998-1980
Website: tisch.nyu.edu/dance
Email: tisch.dance@nyu.edu

Tuition: $$$$
Campus student enrollment (undergraduate): 3,283 (Tisch)

Degree(s): BFA
Courses offered: All students take two technique classes daily, one each in ballet and contemporary dance. Other courses include dance composition, pointe, partnering, Pilates, yoga, kinesthetics of anatomy, music theory, dance history, acting, improvisation and music literature.

Audition requirement: Yes
Scholarships available: Yes
Number of faculty: 23
Department activities: The dance department focus is on technical training, choreography, and

performance. Thirty-five performances a year offer students frequent opportunities to perform and choreograph. Additional workshops and master classes are offered throughout the year.

Prominent Alumni:

Nicole Currie and Jillian Harris (2003)—performed with the Metropolitan Opera Ballet

Deeann Nelson (2003)—dancer with Streb Dance Company

Neal Beasley (2003)—dancer with the Trisha Brown Dance Company

Kimberly Petros and Karen Anne Lavelle (2000)—dancers with the Rockettes

Timothy Bish (2000)—dancer in the Broadway musical *Movin' Out*

Jennifer Conley (2000)—member of the Martha Graham Dance Company

Lauren Grant (1996)—member of the Mark Morris Dance Group

Kate Mattingly (1996)—writer for the *New York Times* and *Dance* Magazine

POINT PARK UNIVERSITY

Department of Dance
201 Wood Street
Pittsburgh, Pennsylvania 15222

Phone: (800) 321-0129
Website: pointpark.edu
Email: enroll@pointpark.edu

Tuition: $
Campus student enrollment (undergraduate): 3,827

Degree(s): BA, BFA
Concentrations: Ballet, modern, jazz, pedagogy
Audition requirement: Yes
Scholarships available: Yes
Number of full-time faculty: 10
Number of adjunct/other faculty members: 26

PURCHASE COLLEGE, STATE UNIVERSITY OF NEW YORK (SUNY)

School of the Arts
Conservatory of Dance
735 Anderson Hill Road
Purchase, NY 10577

Phone: (914) 251-6800
Website: purchase.edu/dance
Email: dance@purchase.edu

Tuition: $
Campus student enrollment (undergraduate): 4,077

Degree(s): BFA
Courses offered: Ballet performance, composition, dance production
Audition requirement: Yes, solo must be prepared as well
Scholarships available: Yes
Number of faculty: More than 20
Number of majors and minors: 150
Percentage and number of applicants accepted into the department per year: 20% acceptance rate; 45–55 accepted into program
Department activities: Purchase Dance Corps, tours, lecture demonstrations

Prominent Alumni:

Alumni have performed with the following companies:

George Thompson—American Ballet Theatre (NYC)

Peng-yu Chen—American Repertory Ballet (NJ)

Kyle Abraham—Bill T. Jones/Arnie Zane (NYC)

Chris Anderson—Boston Ballet (MA)

Devon Bailey—Buglisi/Foreman Dance

Andrew Carter—Carolyn Dorfman Dance Company (NJ)

Gregory Livingston—City Contemporary Dance Co. (Hong Kong)

Tamarah Tossey—Clemantuz Danstheater (Holland)

Corey Colfer—Cleveland/San Jose Ballet (Ohio)

Marsha Carter—Cloud Nine (Holland)

Caitlin Cook—Dance by Neil Greenberg (NYC)

Elizabeth Koeppen—David Parsons Dance Company (NYC)

Angela Reid—Dayton Contemporary Dance Co. (Ohio)

Nancy Coenen—Doug Varone and Dancers (NYC)

Alexander Escalante—Doug Varone at the Metropolitan Opera

Kathryn Warakomski—Houston Ballet (TX)

Jason Ohlberg—Hubbard Street Dance Company (IL)

Kathryn Alter—Limón Dance Company (NYC)

Doug Varone—Lar Lubovitch Dance Company (NYC)

Ruth Davidson—Mark Morris Dance Group (NYC)

Hellen Barron—Merce Cunningham Dance Company (NYC)

Ja'hain Clark—MOMIX (NYC)

Nicolo Fonte—Nacho Duato (Spain)

William Brown—RIOULT Dance (NYC)

Maureen Domaso—Peter Pucci Plus Dancers (NYC)

Alexa Kershner—Shen Wei Dance Arts (NYC)

Ashleigh Leite—Stephen Petronio (NYC)

Graham Smith—Theater Ulm (Germany)

Marc Mann—Toronto Dance Theater, ZviDance (NYC)

Lance Gries—Trisha Brown Dance Company (NYC)

Mauri Cramer—Twyla Tharp and Dancers (NYC)

Hernando Cortez—White Oak Dance Project (NYC)

Alvin Ailey American Dance Theater

Frankfurt Ballet (Germany)

Martha Graham Dance Company (NYC)

Paul Taylor Dance Company (NYC) Taylor 2

Shapiro & Smith (MN)

Alumni have performed on Broadway in *Aida*, *The King and I*, *The Lion King*, *Movin' Out*, and *The Phantom of the Opera* and with the Rockettes. Graduates have become professors at CalArts; Shenandoah University; New World School of the Arts; University of California, Los Angeles; George Mason University; Purchase College; Goucher College; North Carolina School of the Arts; Juilliard; and others.

SKIDMORE COLLEGE

Dance Department
815 North Broadway
Saratoga Springs, NY 12866

Phone: (518) 580-5360
Website: skidmoredance.org/, skidmore.edu/admissions/academics/dance/
Email: mdisant1@skidmore.edu

Tuition: $$$$
Campus student enrollment (undergraduate): 2,634

Degree(s): BS
Concentrations: Dance
Courses offered: Dance technique, dance history/criticism, theoretical, improvisation and composition
Audition requirement: No
Number of faculty: 15
Department activities: Guest artists are regularly invited to choreograph original works for our concerts, offer workshops, master classes, performances and lectures for the campus community and general public.

SLIPPERY ROCK UNIVERSITY

Dance Department
114 West Gym/Pearl K. Stoner Instructional Complex
Slippery Rock, PA 16057

Phone: (724) 738-2036
Website: sru.edu/dance
Email: ursula.payne@sru.edu

Tuition: $$
Campus student enrollment (undergraduate): 7,583

Degrees: Bachelor of Arts in Dance; Bachelor of Fine Arts in Dance; Minor in Dance; Dual Degree with Adapted Physical Activity (4+1)

Courses: Performance, choreography and teaching with additional components of dance technology and wellness

Audition requirements: Yes

Scholarships available: Yes, for current dance majors; ranges from $500 to $1,000

Number of faculty: 6 full-time, 1 part-time; 1 full-time musician

Undergraduate majors: 71

Undergraduate minors: 27

Percentage and number of applicants accepted into the department per year: 60 applicants, 60% accepted

Department activities: SRU Dance Theatre, 4–6 performances each year; SRU Jazz and Tap Ensemble, 1–2 performances each year; SRU Touring Group, 2–4 performances each year.

International opportunities: The department of dance at SRU provides opportunities for a variety of international dance studies. For students who desire an in-depth and cultural immersion experience, the Dance in India Initiative allows students who have completed the "World Dance" course to travel and study classical Indian dance for one month in southern India. Students are also able to participate in various pre-session and spring break travel seminars accompanied by dance faculty. Dance students and faculty recently participated in dance seminars in France, Italy, and Colombia.

Slippery Rock University is an accredited member of the National Association of Schools of Dance. The SRU Department of Dance offers the only Bachelor of Arts (BA) and Bachelor of Fine Arts (BFA) in dance degree programs in Pennsylvania's State System of Higher Education. The BA in dance major focuses equally on performing, choreography and teaching, thereby providing students with a well-rounded dance education. The BFA is a professional baccalaureate degree that deepens and expands artistic training at the advanced level and includes entrepreneurial skills development in Business Administration.

SMITH COLLEGE

Dance Department
Northampton, MA 01063

Phone: (413) 584-2700
Website: smith.edu/dance/
Email: admission@smith.edu

Tuition: $$$
Campus student enrollment (undergraduate): 2,478

Degree(s): BA
Concentrations:
Courses offered: Contemporary modern, ballet, jazz, West African, dance history, dance composition, cultural studies, anatomy-kinesiology, and advanced seminars in special topics
Audition requirement: No. Students with strong backgrounds in music, visual art, or dance are welcome to submit supplementary materials to support their freshman application.
Number of faculty: 4
Department activities: The Five College Dance Department combines the programs of Amherst College, Hampshire College, Mount Holyoke College, Smith College, and the University of Massachusetts at Amherst. The faculty operates as a consortium, coordinating curricula, performances and services.

STATE UNIVERSITY OF NEW YORK COLLEGE AT BROCKPORT

Department of Dance
350 New Campus Drive
Brockport, NY 14420

Phone: (585) 395-2153
Website: brockport.edu/dance
Email: dance@brockport.edu

Tuition: $
Campus student enrollment (undergraduate): 7,069

Degree(s): BFA, BA, BS, Pre K-12 Dance Education

Courses offered: Modern dance, ballet, improvisation, music for dance, composition, anatomy and physiology, kinesiology, Laban-based theory, dance history, and production. Courses in dance repertory, performance techniques, aesthetics and criticism, body therapies, children's dance, and teaching methods round out the dance major.

Audition requirement: Yes

Scholarships available: Yes

Number of faculty: 11

Number of majors and minors: 98 majors, 10 minors

Department activities: Six to eight concert performances, per semester, two to four Sankofa African Dance and Drum Ensemble touring performances per year.

Prominent Alumni:

Alumni are working as professional dancers and choreographers as well as in higher education, musical theater programming dance production, dance management, medicine, in private studies, community arts centers, and in regional ballet and modern institutions. A few prominent alumni are:

Barbara Wagner Bashaw, chair of the Dance Education Program at New York University

Janice Dulak, chair of the Dance Department at Stephens College, Columbia, Missouri

Theresa Maldonado, part-time instructor at Stanford University and physical therapist with Pilates Certification

Jill Matriciano, arts administrator working as assistant director at the Yard on Martha's Vineyard

Edward Murphy, founder and director of the award-winning Drumcliffe Irish Dance Company and teaches Irish Dance at SUNY Brockport

Elizabeth Streb, is the founder and director of Elizabeth Streb Ringside in NYC and a Guggenheim Fellowship and MacArthur Fellowship recipient

Sabatino Verlezza, former soloist with the May O'Donnell Dance Company and founder of Verlezza Dancers in New York City

TEMPLE UNIVERSITY

Dance Department
1700 N. Broad Street Ste. 309
Philadelphia, PA 19122

Phone: (215) 204-0533
Website: temple.edu/boyer/dance
Email: dance@temple.edu

Tuition: $$$$
Campus student enrollment (undergraduate): 28,754

Degree(s): BFA

Concentrations: Focus in modern dance technique with a strong emphasis in Ballet and choreography. Ballet classes follow the American Ballet Theatre National Training Curriculum.

Audition requirement: Yes

Scholarships available: Yes; limited scholarships are offered based on artistic merit as determined by the audition and interview

Number of faculty: 9 full-time, 37 part-time

Number of majors and minors: 90

Percentage of applicants accepted into the department per year: 40–55%

Department activities: Master classes, annual guest artist residencies, American College Dance Festivals, field experience in dance education, annual Summer Dance Intensive Program in Rome, Reflection: Response Choreographic Commission, Dance Studies Colloquium and constant opportunities for student dance performance, choreography, and production in the Conwell Dance Theater.

Prominent Alumni:

Graduates from Boyer's dance programs have danced in companies such as Streb, Philadanco!, Urban Bush Women, Ballet X, Rennie Harris Puremovement, and Dance Theatre X and have performed on Broadway, but also have gone on to become leading choreographers, artistic directors, dance therapists, studio owners, dance administrators, dance writers, dance researchers, and dance advocates.

TOWSON UNIVERSITY

Department of Dance
Center for the Arts
8000 York Road
Towson, MD 21252–0001

Phone: (410) 704-2760
Website: towson.edu/dance
Email: spink@towson.edu

Tuition: $$
Campus student enrollment (undergraduate):
19,049

Degree(s): BFA
Concentrations: Dance performance and chore-ography, dance performance with education certification
Courses offered: Additional optional education coursework for K–12 teacher certification in dance education is nationally accredited by NCATE.
Audition requirement: Yes
Scholarships available: Yes; Talent scholar-ships are $3,000–5,000 per year, and Dean schol-arships are $2,000 per year. Additional academic scholarships are available.
Number of faculty: 12 full-time, 16 part-time
Department activities: 11 performance opportunities for students annually, including Fall Choreographer's Showcase (three weekends of three different concerts); Fall Winter's Rejoicing (TU Dance Company and invited repertory groups); Faculty/Alumni Dance Concert; Senior Class Dance Concert (draft concert in fall and final concert in spring); Dance Composition IV Concert; TU Children's Dance Division Company Concert; tour to adjudicated concerts in the spring American College Dance Festival (ACDFA); Dance Majors Performance Project (DMPP) combined with the Sigma Rho Delta Invitational Dance Concert; Spring Traditions and Legacies Concert (TU Dance Company and invited repertory groups) and June TU Children's Dance Division End of the Year Concert.

Prominent Alumni:
Alumni have performed with:
Suzanne Farrell Ballet
New York Theatre Ballet
Joffrey Concert Group
Eliot Feld Ballet Company
Pennsylvania Ballet
Ballet Theatre of Maryland
Alvin Ailey Dance Company
Martha Graham Dance Company
Pilobolus Dance Theatre
Lar Lubovitch Dance Company
Complexions Contemporary Ballet
Peter Pucci Plus Dancers
Dance Alloy
Gus Giordano Dance Company
Hubbard Street Dance Company
The Rockettes (NYC, Vegas)
The Oscars
The Tonys
The Emmys
GAP "West Side Story" Commercials
Madonna On Tour
Ultra Nate On Tour
Smokey Robinson On Tour
The Lion King
Aida
Chicago
The Hunchback of Notre Dame
The King and I
Fame
42nd Street
Will Rogers Follies
Alumni have taught in K–12 private/public educa-tional systems in 35 states and at the following higher education institutions:
New York University, Illinois State University, George Washington University, George Mason University, James Madison University, Texas Women's University, Hunter College, Bowling Green State University
Over the past 15 years, 84 percent of dance alumni have remained working in the field.

UNIVERSITY OF THE ARTS

College of Performing Arts
320 South Broad Street
Philadelphia, PA 19102

Phone: (215) 717-6049
Website: uarts.edu
Email: admissions@uarts.edu

Tuition: $$
Campus student enrollment (undergraduate):
1,890

Degree(s): BFA in Dance
Audition requirement: Yes
Scholarships available: Yes, from $8,000 up to full tuition.
Number of faculty: 10 full-time, 45 part-time
Number of majors and minors: 300
Department activities:

The School of Dance's major course of study takes the depth and rigor of a discipline-based dance conservatory while engaging students in open discussions within their own practice, valuing their voices as capable of developing new and critical perspectives in dance. These strategies give way to student-driven pathways and expand the ways students can access and think about the practices and techniques of making and performing dance. This curriculum is divided into two parts: Foundation Series (freshman and sophomore years) and Portfolio & Research Series (junior and senior). Students also have the opportunity to create alongside faculty members, and other world-renown guest artists in Pedagogies of Performance in Dance (PODS). PODS offer students the opportunity to make connections through multiple access points, especially in areas of performance. These performances are typically shared during the Spring and Winter Dance Series in the 1,800-seat Merriam Theater. Students also have the opportunity to perform in works created by senior students during the Festival of Senior Dance Works, which are performed in the newly renovated "gray box"

Y-Gym Dance Theater. Along with PODS and senior pieces, students are also encouraged to create their own works within our Thinking, Making, Doing curriculum, which encompasses our improvisation, composition, and choreography courses.

Study abroad and international opportunities:
The first American school selected to participate in the Centre National de la Danse's prestigious "Camping 2016" held in Paris, France; Montpellier Danse Festival, Montpellier, France.

Study abroad programs/partnerships:
Jerusalem Academy of Music and Dance, Israel; Venice Biennale, Italy; Seoul, South Korea; Brussels, Belgium; Frankfurt, Germany; Antwerp, Belgium; Luxembourg; Paris, France; Lyon, France.

Prominent Alumni:
Alumni have performed with Trisha Brown, David Parsons Dance, Alvin Ailey American Dance Theater, Limón Dance Company, Pilobolus, MOMIX, Complexions Contemporary Ballet, Cirque du Soleil, Hubbard Street Dance Chicago, Paul Taylor Dance Company 2, Bill T. Jones/Arnie Zane Dance Company (NY), Suzanne Farrell Ballet (Washington, D.C.), Urban Bush Women (NY), Koresh Dance Company, Group Motion Dance Company, Dance New Amsterdam, Chicago Tap Theatre, Sarasota Ballet, Philadanco!, Nai-Ni Chen Dance Company (NY), The Rockettes, Disney (Tokyo), Princeton Ballet Company, River North Dance Chicago, Rennie Harris Puremovement, Ballet X

FLORIDA STATE UNIVERSITY

Department of Dance
201 Montgomery Gym
Tallahassee, FL 32301–2120

Phone: (850) 644-1023
Website: dance.fsu.edu
Email: info@admin.dance.fsu.edu

Tuition: $
Campus student enrollment (undergraduate):
32,948

Degree(s): BFA, BFA, BA/MFA
Concentrations: Performance, choreography, dance history
Courses offered: Courses offered in ballet, choreography, conditioning, kinesiology, injury prevention, modern, dance technology, production, dance history, Labanotation, music and repertory.
Special opportunities: Study abroad programs to Valencia, Spain, and Paris, France.

Southeast

GEORGE MASON UNIVERSITY

School of Dance
MS 3D4
Fairfax, VA 22030–4444

Phone: (703) 993-1114
Website: dance.gmu.edu
Email: dance@gmu.edu

Tuition: $$$
Campus student enrollment (undergraduate):
22,627

Degree(s): BA, BFA
Concentrations: Modern dance performance and choreography
Courses offered: Daily technique classes in modern and ballet. Additional course work includes improvisation, choreography, repertory, performance, production, anatomy and kinesiology for dancers, somatic techniques, music theory, dance history, teaching methods and Senior Seminar.
Audition requirement: Yes
Scholarships available: Yes
Number of faculty: 9 full-time, 10–12 part-time
Department activities: Five fully produced performances per year, two to four showcase performances per year. Other performance opportunities include the Kennedy Center Millennium Stage and other Washington, D.C. metropolitan area venues. The department has an active artist residency program bringing guest artists to campus frequently for residencies and master classes. Most recently, students have performed the work of Mark Morris, Lar Lubovitch, Ulysses Dove, Alejandro Cerrudo, Robert Battle, David Parsons, Paul Taylor, Nick Pupillo, Andrea Miller, Twyla Tharp, and Doug Varone.

Prominent Alumni:
George Mason alumni are professional performers,

choreographers, university faculty members, dance educators, health practitioners and arts managers. Recent alumni are members of the Mark Morris Dance Group, Broadway cast of *Hamilton*, Streb, Parsons Dance Company, Limón Dance Company, Jane Comfort, Battleworks, Elisa Monte, Amanda Selwyn Dance Theater, City Dance 2, danceTactics, and others. They have also performed with Mark Morris, Patrick Corbin, Jane Comfort, Metropolitan Opera Ballet Company, Washington Opera, and Chicago Lyric Opera.

NEW WORLD SCHOOL OF THE ARTS

Dance Division
300 NE 2nd Avenue
Miami, FL 33132

Phone: (305) 237-3341
Website: nwsa.mdc.edu
Email: nwsainfo@mdc.edu

Tuition: $
Campus student enrollment (undergraduate): 448

Degree(s): BFA
Concentrations: Ballet, modern dance
Courses offered: Choreography, music, dance history, anatomy and kinesiology, movement analysis and dance production
Audition requirement: Yes
Scholarships available: Yes
Number of faculty: 6 full-time, 10 part-time

Prominent Alumni:
Gaby Diaz—2015 winner, *So You Think You Can Dance*
Robert Battle—Artistic Director, Alvin Ailey American Dance Theater
Johan Rivera—Ballet Hispanico
Jacqueline Bulnes (2006)—Martha Graham Dance Company
David Martinez (2003)—Parsons Dance, NYC

Lloyd Night (2005)—Martha Graham Dance Company
Melissa Toogood
Merce Cunningham

UNIVERSITY OF NORTH CAROLINA SCHOOL OF THE ARTS

School of Dance
Office of Admissions
1533 South Main Street
Winston-Salem, NC 27127

Phone: (336) 770-3290
Website: uncsa.edu
Email: admissions@uncsa.edu

Tuition: $
Campus student enrollment (undergraduate): 856 (includes all five conservatories)

Audition requirement: Yes
Scholarships available: Yes
Degree(s): BFA, Undergraduate Arts Certificate
Concentrations: Classical ballet, contemporary dance
Courses offered: Ballet technique, contemporary technique, composition, pointe/variations/repertory, men's class, ballet partnering, contemporary partnering, dance composition and improvisation, theater dance, contemporary repertory, dance perspectives, etc.
Number of faculty: 14-plus guest artists
Department activities: 50-plus performances each year, including Fall Dance, Winter Dance, Spring Dance, *The Nutcracker*, and Emerging Choreographers Concert.

Prominent Alumni:
Olivia Bowman—Alvin Ailey Dance Theater
Mark Dendy—founder, Mark Dendy Dance
Gillian Murphy—principal dancer, American Ballet Theatre
Katita Waldo—principal dancer, San Francisco Ballet

Maria Riccetto—Sodre in Uruguay (formerly with ABT)

Blaine Hoven—soloist, American Ballet Theatre

Manelich Minnifee—Pilobolus

Claire Kretzschmar—corps de ballet, New York City Ballet

Trey McIntyre—Trey McIntrye Project

Matt Del Rosario—Pilobolus

Camille A. Brown—Camille A. Brown and Dancers

UNIVERSITY OF NORTH CAROLINA AT GREENSBORO

School of Dance
323 Coleman Building, Box 26170
Greensboro, NC 27402–6170

Phone: (336) 334-5570
Website: performingarts.uncg.edu/dance
Email: dance@uncg.edu

Tuition: $
Campus student enrollment (undergraduate): 16,000 (approx.)

Degree(s): BA, BFA
Concentrations: BA in dance studies, BFA in choreography and performance; both offer a K–12 licensure option.
Courses offered: Four levels of modern dance, four levels of ballet, three levels of jazz, three of African, and two of tap dance are offered. In addition, there are classes in capoeira, performance/repertory, choreography, dance history, dance production, body science for dance, yoga for dance, dance for film, and dance education.
Audition requirement: Yes
Number of faculty: 8
Department activities: The department produces 10–15 in-house concert programs each year with 2–4 performances each; most of these offer a chance for undergraduates to perform.

VIRGINIA COMMONWEALTH UNIVERSITY

Department of Dance and Choreography
P.O. Box 843007
1315 Floyd Avenue
Richmond, VA 23284–3007

Phone: (804) 828-1711;
University: (800) 828-0100; School of the Arts (central number): toll-free (866) 534-3201 or (804) 828-ARTS
Website: arts.vcu.edu/dance
Email: dance@vcu.edu

Tuition: $$
Campus student enrollment (undergraduate): 23,000

Degree(s): BFA
Concentrations: Dance and choreography; joint BFA in performance, with Richmond Ballet Trainee Program
Audition requirement: Yes
Scholarships available: Yes. The VCU Arts Scholarship in Dance ranges from $4,000 to $8,000 and is renewable for four years based on sustained excellence in the dance curriculum.
Number of faculty: 11
Number of majors and minors: 99 majors, 3 minors
Percentage of applicants accepted into the department per year: 35%
Department activities: VCU dance students have multiple opportunities to perform and present choreography throughout the four year program. The department produces six to eight concerts per year, four of which include three or more performances. The department sends students to the American College Dance Festival. Study abroad opportunities include Italy and Serbia and have included Costa Rica. Groups are also supported in travel and accommodations when opportunities arise for outside performances of faculty work performed by students. Such opportunities have

taken students to New York, Washington, D.C., and across Virginia. BFA/Richmond Ballet Trainee Program: VCU Dance offers a joint BFA dance major with the Richmond Ballet Trainee Program. This program is a four-year degree track within the BFA that is specifically designed for Richmond Ballet trainees. The two-year trainee program of the Richmond Ballet provides intensive study and opportunities to perform in concert with the Richmond Ballet Company. Students must pass auditions for both programs and meet VCU academic requirements for admission. Upon completion of the two-year trainee program, students may become full-time dance majors at VCU, on track to finish a BFA in dance and choreography in two more years.

Prominent Alumni:

Courtney Cook (2011)—performs and tours with Urban Bush Women

Kimara Wood (2013)—dances with Dallas Black Dance Theatre

Ryan Smith (2013)—apprentice with New York–based Kate Weare Company

Aaron Burr Johnson (2009)—performing with the New York–based dance company John Jasperse Company, as well as presenting his own work

Alyssa Gregory (2010)—continues to perform with The Moving Architects in Chicago, IL

Bravitta Threat (2007)—Miss Black Los Angeles, performed with Dallas Black Dance Theatre Company, and was a dancer in the feature film *Avatar*

Donna Vaughn (2006)—performed with Hubbard Street 2 and is now in the cast of Disney's *The Lion King* on Broadway in New York City

Gerri Houlihan (2006)—former soloist and company member of Lar Lubovitch Dance Company, tenured faculty at Florida State University, and co-dean and faculty member of the American Dance Festival

Sarah Ferguson (2005)—education and outreach coordinator for Richmond Ballet's Minds in Motion; tour representative and photographer for the Richmond Ballet; Ferguson's photographs of the company have been featured in the *New York Times, Dance* Magazine and *The Richmond Times*

Dispatch, among others

Samantha Speis (2005)—continues to perform with Urban Bush Women and was a 2012 recipient of the Alvin Ailey New Directions Choreography Lab

Nicolle Wasserman Greenhood (2005)—director of school administration for the American Dance Festival

Jason Somma (2003)—2009 recipient of the Rolex Mentor and Protégé Arts Initiative, continues his work with Jiri Kylian, screening films at the Rotterdam Dansacademie on "performance and new technology"

Leslie Kraus (2003)—*Dance* Magazine's "25 Artists to Watch" 2009, featured dancer in Kate Weare Company, and performs as Lady Macbeth in Punchdrunk's long-running dance theater work, *Sleep No More*

Alexandra Holmes (2002)—tours internationally with Sara Pearson/Patrik Widrig Dance Company

Prosenjit Guy Kundu (1998)—has continued to perform and choreograph internationally since his graduation from VCU

Christina Briggs (1996)—founding member and choreographer for the New York–based dance company, Incidents Physical Theatre

Paule Turner (1994)—has a tenured teaching position at Rowan University and has his own dance company

Ray Eliot Schwartz (1992)—continues to direct the Dance program at the Universidad de las Americas in Puebla, Mexico

Stephanie George (1993)—toured internationally with the Mimi Garrard Dance Company, danced with Mark Jarecke Dance Company, and is currently dancing with Jeanine Durning, a New York choreographer who danced with David Dorfman

Adrienne Clancy (1991)—founding and artistic director of ClancyWorks Dance Company based out of Maryland; in addition to creating, performing in, and directing the company, she recently received her MFA from Texas Woman's University and is a PhD candidate

Richard Move (BFA 1988)—set a new work, *Achilles Heal*, on the White Oak Project featuring Mikhail Baryshnikov

Midwest

BUTLER UNIVERSITY

Jordan College of Fine Arts
Department of Dance
4600 Sunset Avenue
Indianapolis, IN 46208

Phone: (800) 368-6852 ext. 9656
Website: butler.edu/dance/
Email: info@butler.edu

Tuition: $
Campus student enrollment (undergraduate):
4,798

Degrees: BFA in Dance—Performance, BA in Dance—Pedagogy, BS in Dance—Arts Administration
Concentrations: Performance, pedagogy, and dance—arts administration
Courses offered: Ballet, modern, jazz, pointe, pas de deux, contemporary partnering, body placement, character dance, world dance, choreography, acting for dancers, Laban movement analysis, dance history, theory and philosophy of dance, teaching analysis of classical ballet, teaching analysis of modern, teaching analysis of jazz, music for dance, Butler Ballet, and Butler Chamber Dance.
Audition requirement: Yes
Scholarships available: Yes
Number of faculty: 8 full-time, 6 part-time
Department activities: The Butler Ballet performs three to four major productions each year, including full-length classical ballets—such as *Nutcracker*, *Swan Lake*, *Sleeping Beauty*, *Coppélia*, *Cinderella*, *Giselle*—as well as original contemporary works, licensed and commissioned work by master choreographers such as Antony Tudor, George Balanchine, Nacho Duato, James Kudelka, Gustavo Ramírez Sansano, Lesley Telford, and Paul Taylor. The department has a central but non-exclusive focus on classical ballet, integrated with a liberal arts education.

Prominent Alumni:
Alumni have performed with the following companies, among others:
Boston Ballet
Grand Rapids Ballet
Wonderbound
Dance Theatre of Harlem
Sarasota Ballet
Milwaukee Ballet
Ballet Austin
Richmond Ballet
Louisville Ballet
Colorado Ballet
Charlotte Ballet
Dayton Ballet
Paul Taylor Dance Company
Dance Kaleidoscope
Nevada Ballet Theatre
Peridance

THE DANCE CENTER OF COLUMBIA COLLEGE CHICAGO

1306 South Michigan Avenue
Chicago, IL 60605

Phone: (312) 369-8353
Website: dancecenter.org
Email: danceinfo@colum.edu

Tuition: $
Campus student enrollment (undergraduate):
9,671

Degree(s): BA, BFA
Concentrations: Teaching, dance studies, performance, choreography
Audition requirement: No, but students will participate in a placement activity
Scholarships available: Yes
Number of faculty: 10 full-time, 42 part-time

Number of majors and minors: 150 majors, 30 minors

Percentage and number of applicants accepted into the department per year: Any student accepted by Columbia College Chicago may enter the department. Level placement audition required.

Department activities: Includes Student Performance Night; Repertory and Performance Workshop; the Presenting Season, which includes international and national companies; and a Faculty Concert.

Prominent Alumni:

Hettie Barnhill—*Fela!* Broadway Cast

Margi Cole—Collective Dance Company

Krenly Guzman—Lucky Plush Productions

Keesha Johnson—Gus Giordano Dance Company

Atalee Judy—BONEdanse

Cara Sabin—The Seldoms

Vershawn Sanders—Red Clay Dance Studio

Noah Vinson—Mark Morris Dance Company

HOPE COLLEGE

Department of Dance
Dow Center
168 East 13th Street
Holland, MI 49423

Phone: (616) 395-7700
Website: hope.edu/academic/dance
Email: farmer@hope.edu

Tuition: $
Campus student enrollment: 3,200

Degree(s): BA, BM, BS, BSN
Concentrations: Dance performance/choreography, dance/education, dance/engineering, dance/therapy (psychology), dance/medicine (biology or chemistry), dance/foreign language, dance/history, musical theater composite
Audition requirement: No

Scholarships available: Yes, Distinguished Artist Award (12 per year) for $2,500 renewable (4 years)

Number of faculty: 3 full-time, 4 part-time, 3 guest faculty/artist in residence

Number of majors and minors: 27 majors, 37 minors

Number of applicants accepted into the department per year: 40 students

Department activities: Faculty choreographed concert, four student-choreographed concerts, two pre-professional dance companies (StrikeTime and H2 Dance Co.), sacred dancer ministry, national and international internships. Participation in the American College Dance Association, National Dance Education Association, National Association of Schools of Dance, International Association for Dance Medicine and Science, and Dance Movement Therapy Association.

Prominent Alumni:

Dr. Kathleen Davenport (MD)—Company Physician, Miami City Ballet, Miami

Lydia Dawson—musical theater performer, New York City

Matthew Farmer—Department Chair, Hope College, Holland

Lindsey Ferguson—professional dancer and performer (*The Illusionist*), New York

Timothy Heck—professional performer (Blue Man Group, *Sleep No More*) New York

Emily Henry—novelist (*The Love That Split the World*), Cincinnati

Alexandria LeGare—engineer, Tesla Motors, Palo Alto

Linelly Olmeda-Santos (MA)—Dance Movement Therapist

Emily Poel—professional performer, Germany

Nathan Rommel—professional dancer, Giordano Dance Chicago II, Chicago

Lola G. Sanchez—professional tap dancer, New York

Tara Snyder—rehearsal and production assistant Thodos Dance Chicago, Chicago

Molly Vass—professional tap dancer (jorsTAP Chicago), Chicago

INDIANA UNIVERSITY

Ballet Department in the Jacobs School of Music
Merrill Hall 101
1201 East Third Street
Bloomington, IN 47405–7006

Phone: (812) 855-7998
Website:
music.indiana.edu/departments/academicballet/
Email: musicadm@indiana.edu

Tuition: $$
Campus student enrollment (undergraduate):
39,184

Degree(s): BS, BS with outside field
Concentrations: Ballet
Courses offered: Five technique classes a week plus pointe, variations, adagio, men's class, choreography, jazz, and pedagogy.
Audition requirement: Yes
Number of faculty: 4 plus guest faculty
Department activities: The IU Ballet Theater offers four sets of performances (fall ballet, *Nutcracker*, spring ballet and a choreography presentation) per year, which include classical and contemporary works from the international repertoire. Guest teachers, choreographers, repetiteurs, and artists include many major figures in the field of ballet, such as Merrill Ashley, Phillip Broomhead, Stacey Calvert, Bart Cook, Daniel Duell, Cynthia Gregory, Dana Hanson, Sandra Jennings, Roy Kaiser, Zippora Karz, Victoria Simon, Bruce Simpson, and Daniel Ulbricht.

Prominent Alumni:
These include dancers who have joined the following companies in the past five years:
Ballet Arizona, Ballet Memphis, Ballet Nouveau, Ballet West, Boston Ballet, Cincinnati Ballet, Festival Ballet of Rhode Island, Kansas City Ballet, Nevada Ballet Theatre, North Carolina Dance Theatre, Pennsylvania Ballet, Sarasota Ballet, St. Louis Ballet, amongst others

INDIANA UNIVERSITY

Department of Theatre, Drama and Contemporary Dance
275 North Jordan Ave, A300
Bloomington, IN 47405–1101

Phone: (812) 855-7020
Website: indiana.edu/~condance/
Email: eshea@indiana.edu

Tuition: $$
Campus student enrollment (undergraduate):
39,184

Degree(s): BFA in dance; minor in dance
Concentrations: Contemporary dance
Courses offered: Dance techniques (modern, ballet, cultural choreographies, jazz, tap, musical theater), repertory, improvisation, composition, choreography, acting, pedagogy, history, music, production, movement analysis, kinesiology and Pilates, yoga and personal training certifications. Service-learning opportunities are available through Dance for Parkinson's and children's programs.
Audition requirement: Yes
Number of faculty: 3 full-time; 8 adjuncts; staff musicians
Department activities: Internationally recognized guest artists visit each year—most recently, dance majors have performed in the works of Andrea Miller (Gallim Dance), Kyle Abraham, Angie Hauser, Ihsan Rustem, Roger Jeffrey, Paul Taylor, David Parsons, Bella Lewitzky and Martha Graham (both funded by the National Endowment for the Arts), Larry Keigwin, Ben Munisteri, William Evans, and Laurie Eisenhower. Daily training in modern dance and ballet is required, and majors also study jazz and urban dance forms, as well as world dance. Elective offerings include musical theater and tap. Students participate in repertory rehearsals daily for guest artist, faculty and student choreography. The Indiana University Contemporary Dance Theatre (IUCDT) performs in the state-of-the-art Ruth N. Halls Theatre, as well as

in other university and community venues. Many productions are held each year, and there are ample performance and choreographic opportunities locally, nationally, and internationally. Attending the American College Dance Festival, where IUCDT has regularly been selected for gala performance, and most recently the National Festival, is a spring tradition. Students can also participate in Dance Jerusalem, an overseas program offered by the Jerusalem Academy of Music and Dance/Hebrew University, as well as pursue other study abroad opportunities and summer programs, like Dance Italia. The performing arts and technology environment at IU provide for two particularly strong areas of specialization. The world renowned Jacobs School of Music offers dance majors an opportunity to collaborate with composers and perform with world-class musicians, and dance majors can audition for musical theater and dramatic works. With regard to dance and technology, faculty and students work in the areas of real-time video projection, motion capture, and video analysis. Graduates of the dance major are working as professional dancers, choreographers, arts administrators, company managers, dance journalists, teachers, and fitness specialists, and pursue graduate studies in dance, physical therapy, and related fields.

Prominent Alumni:

Dr. Sheila Ward—Executive Director, Eleone Dance Theatre

Liz Monnier—Artistic Director (retired), Fort Wayne Dance Collective

Suzanne Lappas—former dancer for ODC/San Francisco and Joe Goode Performance Group

Ricardo Alvarez—former dancer with Dana Tai Soon Burgess Dance Company

Ryan Galloway—dancer with Giordano Dance Chicago

Lalah Hazelwood—former dancer with Philadanco!

Jordan Mazur—dancer with Missouri Contemporary Ballet

Noah Trulock—dancer with Dance Kaleidoscope

Missy Trulock—dancer with Dance Kaleidoscope

Kelly McCormick Bangs—former dancer with Amy Marshall Dance Company

Krissy Jones—owner, Sky Ting Yoga, NY, NY

Selena Watkins—Visiting Assistant Professor of Dance, Valparaiso University

Molly O'Reilley—Performances and Community Programs Coordinator, American Dance Festival

Maureen Maryanski—dance librarian, Dance Notation Bureau

Debra Knapp—dancer with Bill Evans Dance Company, and Professor of Dance, New Mexico State University

OHIO UNIVERSITY

Dance Division, School of Dance, Film, and Theater
Putnam Hall
Athens, OH 45701

Phone: (740) 593-1826
Website: finearts.ohio.edu/dance/
Email: dance@ohiou.edu

Tuition: $$
Campus student enrollment (undergraduate): 23,701

Degree(s): BFA, BA, minor
Concentrations: Choreography, performance
Audition requirement: Yes
Scholarships available: Yes
Number of faculty: 6
Number of majors and minors: 50
Percentage of applicants accepted into the department per year: 60%
Department activities: Eight to twelve performance productions per year. Two productions are mainstage concerts of dances created by faculty and visiting artists and performed by student dancers. Two to four productions are touring productions of student works. Two productions are created by a student dance performance organization.

Prominent Alumni:

Vanessa Bell Calloway—dancer/actress

Sarah Gamblin—Bebe Miller Dance Company

Kristen Daley—Doug Elkins Dance Company

Sinead Kimbrell—Spugmotion Dance Company

Christopher Whitney—Pilobolus

Jesse Keller—Stefanie Batten Bland's Birdlegs Dance

Sarah Gamblin—Bebe Miller Dance Company, Texas Woman's University

Lesley Kennedy—Aszure Barton Dance Co.

Kathleen Turner—Deeply Rooted Dance Theater

UNIVERSITY OF AKRON

Dance Program

Guzzetta Hall, Room 394

Akron, OH 44325–1005

Phone: (330) 972-7948
Website: uakron.edu/dtaa/
Email: dance@uakron.edu

Tuition: $$
Campus student enrollment (undergraduate): 19,465

Degree(s): BA, BFA
Concentrations: The BA degree (in dance studies with a business cognate) is for students who wish to pursue teaching in private and public schools or own and manage a private dance studio. The dance curriculum includes ballet, modern, jazz and tap dance, world dance, somatic techniques and ballroom with additional coursework in dance education, dance history, philosophy and criticism, kinesiology, choreography, and business. The BFA professional training emphasizes ballet and modern techniques, performance, and choreography with additional coursework in dance education, dance history, philosophy and criticism, kinesiology, world dance, and somatic techniques.
Audition requirement: Yes (for placement)

Scholarships available: Yes
Number of faculty: 15
Department activities: UA Dance Company, Terpsichore Dance Club, Touring Ensemble, Choreographers' Workshop.

Prominent Alumni:

Karen Ziemba—Tony Award winner (best actress in musical for role in *Contact*)

Curt King—director of prime-time publicity for NBC-TV

THE UNIVERSITY OF IOWA

Department of Dance

E114 Halsey Hall

Iowa City, IA 52242–1000

Phone: (319) 335-2228 or toll-free (800) 553-IOWA
Website: dance.uiowa.edu
Email: dance@uiowa.edu

Tuition: $
Campus student enrollment (undergraduate): 23,357

Degree(s): BA, BFA
Concentrations: Performance and choreography, performing arts entrepreneurship
Courses offered: Ballet and modern dance technique, choreography, dance history and theory, dance pedagogy, dance kinesiology, dance production, improvisation, music essentials in dance, digital performing arts, global dance techniques and cultures.
Audition requirement: Yes
Scholarships available: Yes, Iowa Center for the Arts (incoming freshmen only): $7,000 nonrenewable; Dance Department Scholarships (sophomore status and above): amount varies.
Number of faculty: 9
Number of majors and minors: 107 majors; 14 minors

Percentage of applicants accepted into the department per year: 46%

Department activities: Dance students have many opportunities to perform and choreograph during the year, including the University of Iowa touring company Dancers In Company, the annual Dance Gala, faculty and student concerts, MFA thesis concerts, the School of Music Opera Theatre, musical theater in conjunction with the theater arts department, community performances and participation in Gala Festival Concerts of the American College Dance Festival Association.

Prominent Alumni:

Alumni have danced with Bill T. Jones/Arnie Zane Company, Cleo Parker Robinson Dance Ensemble, Dayton Contemporary Dance Ensemble, David Dorfman Dance, Doug Varone and Dancers, Hubbard Street Dance Chicago, James Sewell Ballet, Kim Robards Dance, Martha Graham Dance Company, Minnesota Dance Theatre, Pacific Northwest Ballet, Rennie Harris Puremovement, Shen Wei Dance, Lucky Plush, Thodos Dance Chicago, Trisha Brown Dance Company, among others.

UNIVERSITY OF OKLAHOMA

School of Dance
560 Parrington
Oval Room 1000
Norman, OK 73019

Phone: (405) 325-4051
Website: ou.edu/finearts/dance/
Email: dance@ou.edu

Tuition: $$
Campus student enrollment (undergraduate): 22,152

Degree(s): BFA, dance history minor
Concentrations: Ballet performance, ballet pedagogy, modern dance performance.

Audition requirement: Yes
Scholarships available: Yes
Number of faculty: 14 full-time, 3 part-time
Number of majors: 72
Department activities: Oklahoma Festival Ballet and Contemporary Dance Oklahoma

Prominent Alumni:

Former students have established professional careers in dance with the Boston, Cincinnati, Dallas, Frankfurt, Houston, Joffrey, Louisville, Miami City, Pacific Northwest, and Pittsburgh ballet companies, as well as in Broadway musicals, national touring companies, and modern dance companies such as Jennifer Muller, the Ailey Repertory Ensemble (Ailey II), and the Graham Ensemble. Many teach in professional schools and colleges. Others serve as choreographers, managers, and technicians.

UNIVERSITY OF MICHIGAN

Department of Dance
3501 Dance Building
1310 N University Court
Ann Arbor, MI 48109–2217

Phone (department): 734.763.5460
Website: music.umich.edu/departments/dance/
Email: smtd.dance@umich.edu or smtd.admissions@umich.edu

Tuition: $$$$
Campus student enrollment (undergraduate): 28,312

Degree(s): BFA
Courses offered: Modern dance, ballet, composition, anatomy and kinesiology, introduction to Afro-Caribbean dance, production, choreography, performance, production and design lab, teaching methods.
Audition requirement: Yes. All dance applicants must upload a set of five video recordings

as outlined below in addition to be considered for in-person audition.

Number of faculty: More than 20

WESTERN MICHIGAN UNIVERSITY

Department of Dance
3107 Dalton Center
1903 West Michigan Avenue
Kalamazoo, MI 49008–5417

Phone: (269) 387-5830
Website: wmich.edu/dance
Email: dance-info@wmich.edu

Tuition: $$$
Campus student enrollment (undergraduate): 18,567

Degree(s): BA, BFA
Courses offered: Ballet, jazz, and modern technique to advanced levels; choreography; dance theory.
Number of majors and minors: 120 majors, 50 minors
Audition requirement: Yes
Scholarships available: Yes; several from $1,000 to $3,000. The university offers the Medallion Scholarship (up to $12,500 per year) and other university scholarships up to $9,000 annually.
Number of faculty: 7 full-time, 7 part-time
Number of majors and minors: 114 majors, 55 minors
Percentage and number of applicants accepted into the department per year: 30–35 new students each year, percentage varies depending on number of applicants
Department activities: Seven to ten dance performances per year; Great Works Dance Project, which brings works of professional choreographers such as Anthony Tudor, Paul Taylor, Donald McKayle, Robert Battle, Doug Varone, Rennie Harris, and others to students and audiences; National Choreography Competition in which today's contemporary choreographers compete for the opportunity to create new works on WMU students; Western Dance Project (touring company with 12–15 performances each year); senior class trip to major metropolitan city such as New York, Los Angeles, San Francisco, Montreal, and Philadelphia; participation in the American College Dance Association; funding and grants available for summer study and collaboration projects with other artists; active student organizations involved in local and international community outreach.

Prominent Alumni:
Matthew Baker—dancer, Abraham.In.Motion
Derrick Evans—freelance choreographer and teacher
Kathleen Hermesdorf—artistic director of Motion-Lab, a perpetual experiment of dance training, choreography, improvisation, performance and music production; member of companies of Sara Shelton Mann/Contraband and Bebe Miller Company
Erin Lamont—freelance choreographer, dancer and teacher, Los Angeles
Trent McEntire—creator and owner of the McEntire Workout Method: Expanding Pilates with Integrity; President, Pilates Method Alliance
Diane Makas-Weber—educator, artistic director and dance department chair at the Academy for the Performing Arts, Huntington Beach, California
Edgar Page—dancer, Cleo Parker Robinson Dance
Morella Petrozzi—codirector of Danza Viva, Lima, Peru
Lonnie Poupard—dancer, *Einstein on the Beach* international tour
Cathy Roe—owner and president of Cathy Roe Video Productions Inc., which has produced over 100 instructional dance videotapes that sell internationally
Terk Waters—dancer, Complexions Contemporary Ballet

West

CALIFORNIA INSTITUTE OF THE ARTS

The Sharon Disney Lund School of Dance
24700 McBean Parkway
Valencia, CA 91355

Phone: (800) 545-ARTS
Website: calarts.edu
Email: admissions.calarts.edu

Tuition: $$$
Campus student enrollment (undergraduate):
946

Degree(s): BFA in Dance and MFA Choreography
Concentrations: Dance performance, Choreography
Courses offered: Contemporary and ballet techniques, composition/choreography, improvisation, jazz technique, pointe, partnering, production, music for dancers, video, dance for camera, anatomy, Pilates, dance history, lighting design, costume design. Balinese, Javanese, and African dance are available through the School of Music.
Audition requirement: Yes
Scholarships available: Yes
Number of faculty: 15
Percentage of applicants accepted into the department per year: 50%
Department activities: Open House Dance Concert, Noon(ish) Dance Concert, Winter Dance Concert, Dance Concert, Spring Dance Concert.

Prominent Alumni:
Bryn Cohn—Artistic Director, Bryn Cohn + Artists
Jonathan Fredrickson—dancer, Pina Bausch/ Tanztheater Wuppertal; former dancer, Hubbard Street Dance Chicago; former dancer, Limón Dance Company
Laura Gorenstein—Artistic Director, Helios Dance Theater, Lester Horton Award winner
Jacques Heim—Artistic Director, Diavolo/ Architecture in Motion
Alonzo King—Artistic Director, LINES Ballet
Ryan Mason—former dancer/Rehearsal Director, Staatstheater Kassel; former dancer, Limon Dance Company
Dallas McMurray—dancer, Mark Morris Dance Group
Nycole Ray—Artistic Director, Dallas Black Dance Theatre II, former dancer, Dallas Black Dance Theatre
Dawn Stoppiello—Artistic Director of Troika Ranch Dance Company, Bessie Award Winner
Wang Yuanyuan—Artistic Director, Beijing Dance Theater
Kate Weare—Artistic Director, Kate Weare Company

CORNISH COLLEGE OF THE ARTS

Dance Department
1000 Lenora Street
Seattle, WA 98121

Phone toll-free: (800) 726-ARTS
Website: cornish.edu
Email: admission@cornish.edu or dance@cornish.edu

Tuition: $
Campus student enrollment (undergraduate):
720

Degree(s): BFA
Courses offered: Daily technique classes in both ballet and modern dance. Choreography and improvisation courses form the core of the dance curriculum, which is supplemented by general education courses. Additional dance courses include jazz, pointe, partnering (modern and ballet), men's technique, hip hop, world dance, somatic and conditioning techniques, history, anatomy, Laban Movement Analysis, music, lighting design, teaching methods, dance film and dance business practices. Students can complete a Pilates

matwork teaching certificate. Study abroad is available. Dance studios are located in historic Kerry Hall, which is shared with the music department. Collaboration between dance and other departments in visual and performing arts encouraged.

Audition requirement: Yes

Scholarships available: Yes, based on both merit and need

Number of faculty: 21 dance faculty

Number of majors/students in department: 99 students (2015–16)

Number of applicants accepted into the department per year: Approximately 20 slots are open annually for incoming freshmen and transfers. Early audition is highly recommended.

Department activities: Cornish Dance Theater, the department's performing ensemble, presents biannual concerts with choreography by faculty and professional guest choreographers. Annual student choreography concerts and Senior Project concerts provide additional performance and choreographic opportunities.

Prominent Alumni:

Merce Cunningham—dancer/choreographer
Bonnie Bird—educator
Syvilla Fort—dancer/teacher
Robert Joffrey—dancer/Joffrey Ballet founder
Amy O'Neal—dancer/choreographer
Ezra Dickinson—dancer/TEDx Talk/activist
Kate Wallich—dancer/choreographer

MILLS COLLEGE

Dance Department
5000 MacArthur Boulevard
Oakland, CA 94613

Phone: (510) 430-2135
Website: mills.edu/undergrad
Email: admission@mills.edu

Tuition: $$
Campus student enrollment: 1,345

Degree(s): BA

Concentrations: Dance majors can choose to focus on choreography or performance. Dance minors can choose from concentrations in choreography or dance theory.

Courses offered: The curriculum at Mills is designed to help dance students discover the creative potential of thinking bodies and moving minds. Students here explore the power of dance as a social, cultural, and spiritual force. Rigorous training in various dance techniques provides students with the foundation for an individualized program that integrates their physical and intellectual practice. Mills dance students develop expertise in three areas of study: technique, choreography, and history/theory.

Sample courses include:

African Haitian and Dunham Technique, Dance Forms from Here, There, and Everywhere (including hula, hip hop, butoh, tango, ballroom, and spiritual dance), Dance Improvisation, Introduction to Dance Studies: Theory and Practice, Early Modern Women: Western Dance Pioneers, Group Choreography, Jazz, Intermediate Ballet, Laboratory of Teaching Dance, Movement Research, Music and Dance, Screendance, Somatic Arts

Audition requirement: No

Scholarships available: Merit and need-based scholarships from Mills can total up to $26,000 for first-year students and up to $17,000 for transfer students. More than 80% of our incoming students receive some form of financial aid. Visit mills.edu/cost-and-aid for more information.

Number of faculty: 5

Number of majors and minors: 5 dance majors, 4 dance minors

Department activities: Mills students benefit from department activities that tap into the culture of innovation on campus and the energy of the San Francisco Bay Area. The Mills Repertory Dance Company prides itself on its broad array of choreographers, and in recent years has commissioned work from Robert Battle, Yvonne Rainer, Risa Jaroslow, Seán Curran, Trisha Brown,

Amy Raymond, and Mari Osanai. Students enjoy additional performance opportunities through the BA and MFA thesis concerts, as well as collaborations with our MFA and MA dance students and artists in other disciplines, including music, studio art, art and technology, and theater studies. The Mills Dance Department also fosters creative partnerships with external arts and education organizations such as Alonzo King LINES Ballet, Luna Dance Institute, Dancers Group, and Integrated Movement Studies.

Prominent alumnae:

Trisha Brown, Nora Chipaumire, and Molissa Fenley—pioneering dancer/choreographers

Lori Belilove—Isadora Duncan Dance Company Artistic Director

Professor Linda Goodrich—Dunham expert

Patricia Reedy—Luna Dance Institute founder

Janice Garrett—choreographer

Penny Hutchinson—former Mark Morris dancer

SOUTHERN METHODIST UNIVERSITY

Division of Dance
Meadows School of the Arts
P.O. Box 750356
Dallas, TX 75275–0356

Phone: (214) 768-2718
Website: smu.edu/meadows
Email: smudance@smu.edu

Tuition: $$$$
Campus student enrollment (undergraduate):
6,391

Degree(s): BFA and minor
Concentrations: Dance performance
Courses offered: The program includes a comprehensive sequence of technique courses in ballet, modern and jazz and courses in choreography, dance history, stage production, repertory, dance theory, kinesiology and music analysis.

Audition requirement: Yes
Scholarships available: Yes. Academic merit scholarships available through SMU admissions process. Artistic merit scholarships available based on audition or portfolio evaluation. Scholarship amounts vary.
Number of faculty: 11
Number of majors and minors: 77
Percentage and number of applicants accepted into the department per year: 199 auditions; 22% accepted
Department activities: The Dance Division has two full mainstage concerts per year as well as additional performance opportunities. Through documentation and preservation projects, students have danced in pieces by Martha Graham, José Limón, and Agnes de Mille. The division was the first university dance department to receive a grant from the National Endowment for the Arts for a dance documentation and preservation project.

Prominent Alumni:

Alumni have performed with companies including:
Alvin Ailey American Dance Theater
Ballethnic
Ballet Hispanico
Ballet Memphis
Bruce Wood Dance Company
Charleston Ballet Theatre
Cirque du Soleil
Colorado Ballet
Cortez and Company
Dance Theatre of Harlem
Dark Circles Contemporary Dance
David Parsons Company
Dayton Contemporary Dance Company
Spectrum (Donald Byrd's dance company)
El Teatro de Danza Contemporanea de El Salvador
Hubbard Street 2
Momix
Paul Taylor Dance Company
Philadanco!
Amy Marshall Dance Company

TEXAS CHRISTIAN UNIVERSITY

The School for Classical and Contemporary Dance
TCU Box 297910
Fort Worth, TX 76129

Phone: (817) 257-7615
Website: dance.tcu.edu
Email: dance@tcu.edu

Tuition: $$
Campus student enrollment (undergraduate):
8,800

Degree(s): BFA
Concentrations: Ballet, modern dance, ballet and modern dance
Audition requirement: Yes
Scholarships available: Yes, in the areas of dance and/or academic merit, minority and/or international status, need-based and middle-income scholarships, in addition to work-study programs.
Number of faculty: 8 full-time, 6 part-time
Number of majors and minors: 65 majors (no minors)
Department activities: Numerous guest artists annually, five produced concerts annually, informal concerts, lecture demonstrations, special event performances, travel to conferences and festivals, study abroad at University of Roehampton.

Prominent Alumni:
Jenny Mendez—Pilobolus
Clayton Cross—River North DanceChicago
Domingo Estrada Jr.—Mark Morris Dance Group
Bethany Farmer—Orlando Ballet
Andrew Parkhurst—*Mamma Mia!* touring company
Leah Cox—Dean, American Dance Festival (formerly Bill T. Jones/Arnie Zane Company)
Caryn Heilman—formerly with Paul Taylor (ten years), artistic director of Liquid Body Dance
TCU graduates' former or current company affiliations:
Garth Fagen
Eugene Ballet Company

River North Dance Company,
Texas Ballet Theater
Pilobolus
Bill T. Jones/Arnie Zane Company.
Mark Morris Dance Group
Orlando Ballet
Paul Taylor Dance Company
Atlanta Ballet
Charleston Ballet
Boston Ballet
Kentucky Ballet Theatre
Chattanooga Ballet
Others are performing on Broadway and in touring companies, have established schools and companies and are teaching in universities around the U.S. and abroad.

UNIVERSITY OF ARIZONA

School of Dance
1713 E University Blvd
P.O. Box 210093
Ina Gittings Building, Room 121
Tucson, AZ 85721–0093

Phone: (520) 621-4698
Website: dance.arizona.edu/
Email: dance@cfa.arizona.edu

Tuition: $$$
Campus student enrollment (undergraduate):
32,987

Degree(s): BFA
Concentrations: Ballet, jazz, modern or "triple track" (specializing in all three)
Courses offered: The BFA degree emphasizes both the studio and performance experience. The core curriculum for dance majors includes history, biomechanics, kinesiology, choreography, technique, music forms and literature, production, and career planning.
Audition requirement: Yes
Scholarships available: Yes

Number of faculty: 11

Number of undergraduate majors and minors: 142 (101 women, 41 men)

Percentage and number of applicants accepted into the department per year: 9% (450 students audition, 41 accepted)

Department activities: The senior project may be in performance, choreography, teaching, production, or scholarly research. Each year faculty and students produce six to eight full evening dance performances. Undergraduates also have the opportunity to travel out of state to perform. The UA Dance Ensemble has been invited to perform around the world including China, Japan, Germany, the Netherlands, Scotland, Ecuador, and Mexico, as well as in twelve states throughout the U.S.—including the Kennedy Center in DC and the Joyce Theater in NYC.

Prominent Alumni:

Alumni include many dancers and choreographers who have gone on to careers with national and regional dance companies such as:

Pacific Northwest Ballet, WA

Houston Ballet, TX

Ballet West, UT

City Ballet of San Diego, CA

Rochester City Ballet, NY

Ballet Hispanico II, NYC

10 Hairy Legs, NYC

Hubbard Street Dance Company, IL

Taylor 2, NYC

BODYTRAFFIC, CA

Giordano Dance Chicago, IL

Keigwin & Company, NYC

Broadway/Las Vegas/Touring Shows

Chicago

Wicked

Billy Elliot

Radio City Rockettes (NYC cast)

Steve Wynn's Show Stoppers

Cirque du Soleil, numerous productions

UNIVERSITY OF CALIFORNIA, IRVINE

Department of Dance

Claire Trevor School of the Arts

300 MAB

Irvine, CA 92697–2275

Phone: (949) 824-7283

Website: dance.arts.uci.edu

Email: dance@uci.edu

Tuition: $$$$

Campus student enrollment (undergraduate): 25,256

Degree(s): BA, BFA

Concentrations: Dance performance, choreography

Courses offered: The program focuses on the dance techniques of ballet, modern, jazz, tap, Pilates for dancers (including Pilates mat and reformer), world dance, and dance and technology. Theoretical studies include history; philosophy, aesthetics, and criticism; Laban studies; dance pedagogy; dance ethnography; dance science; and aesthetics of digital media.

Audition requirement: Yes for ballet, modern, jazz

Scholarships available: Yes

Number of faculty: 14 full-time, 4 part-time

Number of majors and minors: 151 majors

Percentage and number of applicants accepted into the department per year: 16%

Department activities: Many opportunities for students to perform in graduate and faculty choreography concerts as well as to choreograph and perform in the undergraduate concert. Students can audition for Donald McKayle's Etude Ensemble, Chad Michael Hall's INTERFACE Ensemble, and Sheron Wray's Jazz Ensemble; participate in faculty-directed projects with experimental media; perform in community-based work; and participate in national and international travel and performance.

Prominent Alumni:

Alumni have become professional dancers in ballet companies (including the Metropolitan Opera Ballet, San Francisco Ballet, Nashville Ballet, Boston Ballet, and Joffrey Ballet); in modern dance companies (including Hubbard Street Dance Company, MOMIX, and Martha Graham Dance Company); in touring companies (including *The Lion King, Fame: The Musical, Carousel,* and Cirque du Soleil) and in films, television, and theater.

UNIVERSITY OF CALIFORNIA, RIVERSIDE

Department of Dance
Riverside, CA 92521

Phone: (951) 827-3343
Website: dance.ucr.edu
Email: paadvising@ucr.edu

Tuition: $$$$
Campus student enrollment (undergraduate): 18,607

Degree(s): BA
Courses offered: Dance history and theory, choreography, pedagogy, digital and screen studies and dance history, theory and cultural studies, dance practice.
Audition requirement: No
Scholarships available: Yes, Chancellor's Performance Award up to $2,250
Number of faculty: More than 10
Number of majors and minors: 30 majors, 10 minors
Department activities: Performances, conferences, guest scholar and guest artist residencies, cultural shows.

Prominent Alumni:

Alumni from graduate programs are placed in dance departments across the country.

CALIFORNIA STATE UNIVERSITY AT LONG BEACH

Dance Department
1250 Bellflower Boulevard
Long Beach, CA 90840–7201

Phone: (562) 985-4747
Website: csulb.edu/dance
Email: dance@csulb.edu

Tuition: $
Campus student enrollment (undergraduate): 32,195

Degree(s): BA, BFA
Concentrations: Performance/choreography, dance science
Courses offered: Curriculum emphasizes modern dance performance and composition with supporting course work in ballet, jazz, tap, world dance, and dance theory.
Audition requirement: Yes
Number of faculty: 8 full-time, several part-time
Number of majors and minors: 140
Department activities: Five formal and two informal productions scheduled throughout the academic year. Guest choreographers restage or create new works for students each semester. Recent choreographers have included David Dorfman, Andrea Woods, Laurence Blake, Holly Williams, David Parsons, Robert Moses, Bill Young, Della Davidson, Janis Brenner, Lar Lubovitch, Dan Wagoner, José Limón, Martha Graham, Laura Dean, and Bella Lewitzky. The department also participates annually in the regional festivals of the American College Dance Festival.

Prominent Alumni:

Alumni have danced with the following companies and choreographers:
Cirque du Soleil, Davalos Dance, Butoh Company (Japan), Bella Lewitzky, Pilobolus, David Dorfman, Doug Elkins

UNIVERSITY OF COLORADO AT BOULDER

Department of Theatre and Dance
Dance Division
261 UCB
Boulder, CO 80309–0261

Phone: (303) 492-7355
Website: colorado.edu/theatredance/
Email: thtrdnce@colorado.edu

Tuition: $$$$
Campus student enrollment (undergraduate):
25,484

Degree(s): BA, BFA
Courses offered: Technique (African, ballet, modern, jazz, hip hop, Alexander technique, Transnational Fusion), composition, production, music theory and practice, pedagogy, history and philosophy, professional orientation, somatic awareness.
Audition requirement: No, for BA application; yes, for dance BFA
Scholarships available: Yes
Number of faculty: 24
Number of majors and minors: 61 majors, 65 minors
Percentage of applicants accepted into the department per year: 100%
Department activities: There are seven dance concerts per academic year. BFA students are expected to show their own choreography each semester in a formal or informal concert. BFA students will present choreography in a shared concert with other BFA students during their senior year. BA students are encouraged to choreograph for the annual Student Dance Concert and to audition for student and faculty choreography as well as for the annual departmental musical.

UNIVERSITY OF OREGON

Department of Dance
161 Gerlinger Annex
1214 University of Oregon
Eugene, OR 97403–1214

Phone: (541) 346-3386
Website: dance.uoregon.edu
Email: audition@uoregon.edu

Tuition: $$
Campus student enrollment (undergraduate):
20,797

Degree(s): BA, BS
Courses offered: The department emphasizes modern dance with a strong supporting area in ballet.
Audition requirement: No
Scholarships available: Yes, from $500 to $5,000
Number of faculty: 7 full-time, 6 part-time
Number of majors and minors: 65 majors, 30 minors
Percentage and number of applicants accepted into the department per year: 80%; 15–17 students. Students admitted to the university may declare a dance major and must fulfill all the requirements in order to obtain the degree.
Department activities: Dance Oregon, Dema: African music and dance ensemble, dance department productions, theatrical collaborations with the school of music or theater arts department, University of Oregon Repertory Dance Company.

Prominent Alumni:

Karen Bradley—associate professor and director of graduate studies in dance, University of Maryland
Teri Carter—contact improvisation artist, New York City
Barry McNabb—New York choreographer and director
Tiffany Mills—Tiffany Mills Dance Company, New York City

UNIVERSITY OF UTAH

School of Dance
330 South 1500 East
Room 106
Salt Lake City, UT 84112–0280

Phone: (801) 581-7327
Website: dance.utah.edu
Email: info@dance.utah.edu

Tuition: $
Campus student enrollment (undergraduate):
21,675

Degree(s): BFA in Ballet (Character Dance, Performance, Teaching), BFA in Modern Dance, minor in modern dance, graduate certificate in screen dance, secondary teaching licensure in dance
Concentrations: Modern dance: performance, choreography, pedagogy, screen dance. Ballet: performance, choreography, pedagogy.
Courses offered: Daily technique classes in modern and ballet including pointe/variations, men's class, partnering and character dance, as well as other dance forms such as jazz, composition, improvisation, dance kinesiology, dance history, cultural dance studies, conditioning, philosophy and aesthetics, internships, criticism, lighting and video production, music theory and practice, media, dance administration, pedagogy, and dance repertory.
Audition requirement: Yes
Number of faculty: 19 full-time as well as adjunct faculty (non–full time)
Number of majors and minors: 226 majors, 24 minors
Department activities: The School of Dance has ten fully produced performances per year as well as multiple informal and alternative venue performances. The Performing Dance Company and Utah Ballet present new works by faculty members plus new and repertory works by distinguished guest artists. The School has exchanges programs in Panama and with the Berlin State Ballet School. Seniors have internships with local arts organizations.

Prominent Alumni:
Tamara Tiewe
Bene Arnold
Linda Smith
Phyllis Haskell Tims
Julia Gleich
Derryl Yeager
Sandra Allen
Jiang Qi
Bart Cook
Douglas Sontaag
Victoria Morgan
Ann Carlson
Bill Evans
Della Davidson
Steve Koplowitz
Carolyn Carlson
Keith Johnson
Many alumni are working with international, national and regional dance companies as dancers, choreographers, and artistic directors. Others are teachers and administrators in high schools, universities, and professional studios.

Dance Programs by State

Note: Programs with an asterisk (*) are accredited by the National Association of Schools of Dance.

ALABAMA
Birmingham–Southern College
University of Alabama*

ARIZONA
Arizona State University
University of Arizona*

CALIFORNIA
California Institute of the Arts*
California State University, Fullerton*
California State University, Long Beach*
Chapman University*
Loyola Marymount University*
Mills College
Pitzer College
Pomona College
San Diego State University
San Francisco State University
San Jose State University*
Santa Clara University
Scripps College
St. Mary's College of California
University of California, Berkeley
University of California, Irvine
University of California, Los Angeles
University of California, Riverside
University of California, Santa Barbara*

COLORADO
Colorado College
University of Colorado at Boulder

CONNECTICUT
Connecticut College
Trinity College
The Hartt School/University of Hartford*
Wesleyan University

DISTRICT OF COLUMBIA
George Washington University

FLORIDA
Florida International University
Florida State University*
Jacksonville University*
New World School of the Arts*
Palm Beach Atlantic University
University of Florida*
University of South Florida*

GEORGIA
Brenau University*
Emory University
University of Georgia*

HAWAII
University of Hawaii at Hilo
University of Hawaii at Manoa

IDAHO
Brigham Young University–Idaho

ILLINOIS
Columbia College Chicago
Northwestern University
Southern Illinois University, Edwardsville
University of Illinois-Urbana Champaign*

INDIANA
Ball State University*
Butler University*
Indiana University, Bloomington

IOWA
University of Iowa*

KANSAS
Friends University
University of Kansas
Wichita State University*

KENTUCKY
Western Kentucky University*

LOUISIANA
Centenary College of Louisiana
Tulane University

MAINE
Bates College

MARYLAND
Frostburg State University
Goucher College
Towson University*
University of Maryland, Baltimore County*
University of Maryland, College Park

MASSACHUSETTS
Amherst College
Boston Conservatory at Berklee
Dean College
Hampshire College
Mount Holyoke College
Smith College
Springfield College
University of Massachusetts, Amherst

MICHIGAN
Alma College
Eastern Michigan University
Hope College*
Marygrove College
Oakland University*
University of Michigan *

Wayne State University*
Western Michigan University*

MINNESOTA
Gustavus Adolphus College
St. Olaf College*
University of Minnesota Twin
    Cities*

MISSISSIPPI
Belhaven College*
University of Southern Mississippi*

MISSOURI
Lindenwood University
Southwest Missouri State University
Stephens College
University of Missouri–Kansas City*
Washington University in St. Louis
Webster University

MONTANA
University of Montana

NEBRASKA
Creighton University
University of Nebraska–Lincoln*

NEVADA
University of Nevada, Las Vegas

NEW JERSEY
Montclair State University*
New Jersey City University
Rutgers, The State University of
    New Jersey*
Stockton University

NEW MEXICO
New Mexico State University
University of New Mexico*

NEW YORK
Adelphi University

Barnard College*
Columbia University
Cornell University
CUNY, Hunter College
Fordham University/The Ailey
    School*
Hamilton College
Hobart and William Smith
    Colleges
Hofstra University
Juilliard School
Long Island University, Brooklyn
Long Island University CW Post
    Campus
Manhattanville College
Marymount Manhattan College
New School University
New York University
Purchase College, SUNY
Skidmore College
SUNY College at Brockport*
SUNY at Potsdam
University at Buffalo, SUNY

NORTH CAROLINA
Appalachian State University*
East Carolina University
Elon University
Meredith CollegeUniversity of
    North Carolina, Charlotte*
University of North Carolina,
    Greensboro*
University North Carolina School
    of the Arts

OHIO
Antioch College
Denison University
Kent State University*
Kenyon College
Oberlin College
Ohio State University*
Ohio University*
University of Akron*

University of Cincinnati*
Wright State University

OKLAHOMA
Oklahoma City University
St. Gregory's University
University of Central Oklahoma
University of Oklahoma

OREGON
University of Oregon
Western Oregon University

PENNSYLVANIA
Cedar Crest College
DeSales University
La Roche College
Marywood University
Mercyhurst College*
Muhlenberg College
Point Park University*
Slippery Rock University of
    Pennsylvania*
dSwarthmore College
Temple University*
University of the Arts
Ursinus College

RHODE ISLAND
Rhode Island College
Roger Williams University

SOUTH CAROLINA
Coker College
Columbia College*
Winthrop University*
University of South Carolina*

TEXAS
Lamar University
Sam Houston State University
Southern Methodist University*
Stephen F. Austin State University
Texas Christian University*

Texas State University
Texas Tech University*
Texas Woman's University*
University of North Texas
University of Texas at Austin*
University of Texas at El Paso
West Texas A&M University

UTAH

Brigham Young University*
Southern Utah University*
University of Utah*
Utah State University
Weber State University

VERMONT

Bennington College
Middlebury College

VIRGINIA

George Mason University
Hollins University
James Madison University*
Radford University
Randolph–Macon College
Shenandoah University
Sweet Briar College
Virginia Commonwealth University*

WASHINGTON

Cornish College of the Arts
University of Washington

WEST VIRGINIA

West Virginia University

WISCONSIN

Beloit College
University of Wisconsin–Madison*
University of Wisconsin–
    Milwaukee*
University of Wisconsin–Stevens
    Point*

WYOMING

Casper College
University of Wyoming

Colleges for Musicians

usic is a passion that normally hits at an early age, grabs your soul, and encompasses your life from then on. If you are considering studying music after high school or even becoming a professional musician, certainly you have already spent a majority of your time during childhood mastering your talent. You already know the amount of dedication, patience, and time it takes to nurture your talent to reach its potential. There is no doubt that you've already spent countless hours practicing and performing. And you are probably very talented—or you wouldn't be considering furthering your study of music into adulthood, now, would you?

As you approach the end of your high school career, you have a decision to make—one that can change your life! The question is this: Do you want to become a professional musician? Many of your peers don't have the same pressure that you do now. Because you already consider yourself a musician and have devoted a substantial part of your life to music thus far, you are at a crossroads. Other students have the luxury of waiting until they get to college to declare a major. But for musicians, the study of music at the college level requires 100 percent commitment right away. Only you can decide if music is a part of you that is so vital to a fulfilling life that you want to earn your living using your talent. Answering this question is the first step in deciding what type of college experience is right for you.

Types of College Music Programs

No matter what kind of musician you are, you have several choices available to further your study beyond high school. You may decide to prepare for a future career as a professional musician or a music teacher. Maybe you want to continue studying music for your own personal interest and enjoyment. Either way, there are two settings in which to pursue music studies after high school. The first is the professional music conservatory.

Professional music conservatories offer intense music training with the sole purpose of preparing students for professional careers in music. For the most part, the goal of these programs is to produce performers. At a professional music conservatory, you'll be surrounded by professional musicians. You'll live and breathe music every day, all the time. If you have decided that your ultimate goal is to be a performer, a conservatory might suit your needs. When considering conservatories, remember that some universities have a conservatory-like atmosphere. Examples include Indiana University or the Eastman School of Music at the University of Rochester. These offer the combination of the music-focused intensity of a conservatory within a university setting.

MEAGAN
UNIVERSITY OF MINNESOTA TWIN CITIES

Helping People with Music

As a singer, Meagan knew she wanted to pursue music in college. When the teacher of her high school course in human behavior assigned topics for a research paper, Meagan began investigating music therapy. The end result was that she wrote a great paper and found the program at the University of Minnesota Twin Cities on a listing from the American Music Therapy Association.

Meagan decided to pursue acceptance to the University of Minnesota Twin Cities. Although she was not applying to the program as a music performance major, much of the audition process for the program was similar to the process for music performance majors.

"I had to prepare two contrasting pieces of music—one in French and one in Italian," Meagan explains. "I also had to do some sight-reading and have an interview with music faculty members, in addition to filling out a substantial survey about why I was interested in the department."

Like many specialized artistic programs, music therapy students must take their fair share of foundation coursework before getting to the music therapy curriculum.

Meagan's program is four years plus a six-month internship. The first two years are devoted to core music requirements plus one introduction-to-music-therapy course. In the third year of the program, students may enroll in courses specific to becoming music therapists.

Even in the field of music therapy, a student is expected to be proficient in one major instrument—in Meagan's case, voice—and have functional skills in both keyboard and guitar. "I was attracted to the field because it combines a lot of different elements with music such as psychology, anatomy, and education," she says.

A key component of Meagan's music therapy program is the fieldwork portion of her studies. This element of the program includes observation and participation in music therapy sessions outside the university in real-life settings.

"I really appreciate the hands-on opportunity," Meagan states. "It really helps you narrow down which special populations you want to work with, like with adults or in a classroom setting with children."

Meagan's first off-campus field experience in music therapy was at the University Good Samaritan Center, a long-term care facility.

Hot Tips from Meagan

→ Do your research on a lot of different programs. Websites at each school usually have a great deal of information that is useful.

→ Engage the faculty who are auditioning you—ask them questions and get to know their personalities.

→ Make sure you inform yourself about all the institution has to offer. Many factors come into play during your college experience. Consider location (urban versus rural) and recreational outlets.

→ Check out the community arts scene where the campus is located and see what opportunities it might offer you.

→ Consider that it may be easier to apply to internships and jobs after college in the geographic area where you graduated from college. Location should be a factor in your college decision, since the local connections you make as a student may help start your career.

"I was fortunate that during my first practicum, the clients were familiar with music therapy. They even had three full-time music therapists," Meagan recalls.

Meagan says that in music therapy, each client has identified goals for achievement. An example of a goal is to improve fine motor skills. Objectives are established that represent individual tasks that will aid the client in reaching his or her goal. For example, the goal could be to improve fine motor skills. The objective would be to grasp a mallet and beat a drum five times to the beat of music that is played for the exercise.

"A lot of clients have physical or emotional disabilities," Meagan explains. "A music therapist needs to tailor the session to suit the needs of the clients, whether it is one on one or in a group setting."

The second setting for studying music at the postsecondary level is the traditional college campus. It could be a small liberal arts college or a medium-to-large state university. Both of these environments can be good options for studying music if you are not sure whether you want to pursue a professional career or are interested in music education or another subset of music besides performance. Such schools offer students the opportunity to explore other options in education or possibly double major.

Of course, the setting you choose for advanced music training also affects the type of degree you will earn. Your goals in music will play a large part in determining what type of degree is best for you.

Types of Music Degrees

The bachelor of music (BM) is a performance-oriented degree for those who seek to become professional musicians after college. Most of the coursework for this degree is within the music department. Approximately 80 percent of your studies will be in music, while the rest of your coursework will fulfill the institution's general education requirements.

The bachelor of music education (BME) is geared toward training talented musicians who want to become certified elementary and secondary school teachers. In most cases, the music courses required for a music performance major are part of the degree plan, as well as courses in education. Students will also want to learn other instruments besides their primary instrument.

The bachelor of fine arts (BFA) is similar to the BM degree. It is usually performance-oriented and requires about the same number of credits within the music department as the bachelor of music. Most college music programs and conservatories offer the BM degree, but some institutions offer the BFA instead, which is comparable.

The bachelor of art (BA) or bachelor of science (BS) in music is offered by many colleges and universities. Both of these are typically less intensive than a BM or BFA program and allow room for exploration of other interests outside of music. These may be best for students who are interested in a particular focus in music rather than on performance.

Music Specialties

Many large music departments are divided into different departments to focus on specific instruments and subjects within music. A typical breakdown within a competitive college music program might look like this:

- ★ Accompanying
- ★ Chamber music
- ★ Composition
- ★ Conducting and ensembles
- ★ Jazz studies
- ★ Music education
- ★ Musicology
- ★ Organ
- ★ Piano and keyboard skills
- ★ Voice
- ★ Winds, brass, percussion

Music Auditions

The audition is a major component in the admissions process for prospective college music majors. This is even more important for students considering studying at a conservatory or applying to a professional degree program at a college or university. Often the audition counts more—or is even the deciding factor—in determining whether students are admitted to a program for institutions granting the BM degree. At these schools, auditions are competitive. A high grade point average, SAT scores, or great teacher recommendations usually won't help improve your odds in being accepted if you don't audition well. Because the goal is to prepare you to become a professional musician, your performance is what matters the most to many music departments.

ROBIN

INDIANA UNIVERSITY SCHOOL OF MUSIC

As a recent graduate in viola performance, Robin is studying for a postbaccalaureate artist's diploma. She has some perspective to offer about her experience at the Indiana University School of Music.

Hot Tips from Robin

→ Consider whether the school is a large university or a small conservatory.

→ Visit the music department before your audition.

→ Talk to students on campus.

→ Try to get a private lesson with a faculty member before your audition to see if you like their teaching style.

Robin believes that it is important for music students to realize that at many schools there is substantial academic coursework in addition to music technique classes. The requirements for many degree programs include courses in music history and music theory as well as general education classes.

Robin says that some places are "pretty competitive... But it's nice to be someplace where people understand your passion for music."

Studying music at a conservatory is pretty serious business. Before taking the leap to become a professional musician, Robin advises students to "know that this is what you really want."

"Once you are in a conservatory, it is very intense. It is a big commitment. Also, take advantage of what the university has to offer outside of music to expand your college experience."

Robin's goal, like a lot of music conservatory graduates, is to play in a professional symphony one day. She has been auditioning in the United States and in Europe, where there can be more opportunities for young musicians.

Auditions are less intense for students hoping to major in music in a BA or BS program. Sometimes they aren't even required for admission. While college and university music departments offer quality music education, the sole purpose of the student's education in these programs is not necessarily preparation for a professional music career. Other factors in the application matter equally. If there is an audition require-ment, you want to do well, but you will also need to have the other standard application components like good grades and SAT/ACT scores for acceptance into the program. At many of the colleges and universities that grant the BA or BS degree, auditions are optional, or they are required for music scholarship consideration. Even if you don't have to audition at one of these schools, it still may be advisable to do so, because you can get an up-close-and-personal feel for the music department and the faculty members.

KATHRYN
VOCAL PERFORMANCE MAJOR, EASTMAN SCHOOL OF MUSIC AT THE UNIVERSITY OF ROCHESTER

When Kathryn saw *Phantom of the Opera* at age eight, something inside her made her want to perform. By age twelve, she was bugging her parents for voice lessons. But when it came time to research colleges, Kathryn faced a common dilemma among music students—she wasn't sure if she wanted to attend a music conservatory or a liberal arts college.

Kathryn discovered the Eastman School of Music through her church. Two of the parishioners are the parents of a music professor at Eastman. Because of the local connection, she decided to visit the school. "I immediately fell in love with the atmosphere," Kathryn confides.

To calm her nerves, Kathryn asked her voice teacher to accompany her at the Eastman audition. Her voice teacher also helped her choose the three songs she needed to prepare for the audition. Kathryn describes the day of the audition as intense. She arrived at nine a.m. and took a music theory test. "I was really nervous and started feeling like 'I don't belong here,'" she recalls. After lunch, Kathryn had an audition at one p.m. and a group interview with an admissions officer at two p.m.

For the audition, Kathryn sang two of her three prepared songs before three vocal performance faculty members. She selected one, and the faculty chose the other. Kathryn remembers hoping they would not choose the French piece, but they did. "And then it turned out that the piece I sang in French was the best I ever sang!" she shares.

Later, one of the Eastman voice teachers pulled her aside and said, "We look forward to seeing you next year."

"I was told that if they don't want you, they try to inform you as soon as possible so you can explore other options," Kathryn remarks.

A week after the audition, Eastman sent her an email informing her that she had been accepted into the voice performance program.

"I still had some difficulty making the decision," Kathryn explains. "But then my friend from school helped me. She told me, 'Eastman is all you talk about. You know you want to go,' and then I realized she was right."

Four years into her studies, Kathryn believes she made the right decision. Now she is looking at life after she finishes her BM in vocal performance.

"I'm about eight to ten years away from a professional singing career," Kathryn explains. "A singer's voice doesn't reach its prime until around age thirty, so I have to think about what's next in the meantime."

Kathryn has decided to attend the University of North Carolina at Greensboro for a master's degree in either vocal performance or vocal pedagogy.

For other music students, Kathryn wants them to know: "Attending graduate school after a college music program is the two most important years of vocal training because the voice is undergoing changes right before it reaches its maturity."

Kathryn wants to sing on stage for a live audience, and she is open to both opera and musical theater. "When I perform for people in a recital, there is something about it that makes me so happy."

Audition requirements vary widely by school. Typically, the audition will be five or ten minutes. You may be asked to prepare two or three musical pieces. The number of adjudicators present varies among programs—some schools have a panel of several faculty members sit in on each audition, and other schools may only have two faculty members present.

One thing that is fairly standard for any audition is the need for at least two *contrasting* pieces of music prepared for audition. Faculty members want to see the level of your technical ability, and they also want to determine if you have a wide range of repertoire that you can perform well. Being able to play or sing a breadth of musical pieces is essential for professional auditions. Competition for full-time performance jobs is fierce, so the better you are at performing different styles, the better prepared you'll be at auditions for college programs. And that will be good practice for all professional opportunities that are going to be waiting for you!

Evaluating College Music Programs

Just because a specific music school has a great reputation doesn't mean it's the right place for you. Programs vary in their focus on various instruments. You must find the school that offers intensive study in *your* instrument. For example, most conservatories and colleges and universities offer intensive study in voice and piano. However, not every music program is going to have the best faculty in other less common instruments like the bassoon or the oboe. Figuring out which schools offer a high-quality curriculum in your particular instrument is one of the most important steps in narrowing down the schools on your list. The best source for obtaining this information is usually the school itself. With the Internet, it's easy to find out details about instruments and programs that are offered by the various colleges by going to their music department websites.

ATAR ARAD
PROFESSOR OF MUSIC (VIOLA), INDIANA UNIVERSITY

Audition Spotlight

To students who want to pursue a professional music career, Atar Arad says, "My first thought is 'you must be crazy.'"

At first blush, such a comment may seem a bit over the top, but Arad goes on to explain that the competition in the field of music is very fierce. As a professor at Indiana University, he understands firsthand the commitment that it takes to be a music student. "Ideally, we like to admit students who know they can't live without music as a vocation…people who feel music is in their blood and soul," Arad says.

> ### Expert Tips from Professor Arad
> → Adjudicators look for potential for musical growth and understanding, not just technical ability.

Professor Arad considers many things when he hears students in auditions, but his main focus is on the student's potential as a performer. "Most of the time, I can determine whether or not the student has the potential to become a professional musician," he explains.

Students are generally required to prepare two or three contrasting pieces for auditions, and he suggests that the pieces reveal different musical and technical styles.

Choosing a college music program is unique compared to other fields of study because students in music programs usually have a strong connection with faculty members. More than in any other artistic discipline, the close one-on-one connection between a student and faculty can make all the difference in a musician's success. A great deal of instruction will involve private lessons from faculty members in your instrument.

If possible, try to schedule a private lesson during your visit to each institution that you are seriously considering—this way, you can get a good idea of what studying with a particular faculty member would be like if you were to enroll as a student there.

Day in the Life of a Voice Major	
8:35 a.m.	Music theory
10:35 a.m.	German (or Italian or French)
11:35 a.m.	German diction (or Italian, French, English)
12:35 p.m.	Lunch
1:35 p.m.	Lesson or rehearsal with pianist
2:35 p.m.	Ensemble or choir rehearsal
3:35 p.m.	Practice/stagings/musical coaching/opera workshop
5 p.m.	Dinner
6 p.m.	Homework, practicing, free time
11 p.m.	Bed

There are several other factors you'll want to consider when you evaluate the music programs of different colleges. The best source of information can be the music departments themselves. You can contact representatives of the department and ask them your questions directly. Also, don't overlook talking to current students, because they will often give you an unbiased account of what it's really like to be a student in that particular music department.

Here are some questions that you might want to ask:

- *Faculty.* What are the credentials of the faculty in your instrument? Where have they trained? Where have they performed? Do they still perform? Students can only be as good as their teachers. To reach your potential, you'll need to have the best teachers in your discipline.

- *Performance opportunities.* How many performance opportunities are available per semester? Can you perform during your freshman year? Are you permitted to perform outside the program in the local community? Does the program have the kind of performing ensemble you want, such as a jazz band, marching band, opera company, or chamber orchestra?

- *Guest artists*. Do guest artists visit the campus? How frequently? What is the caliber of their careers? Can students take private lessons with them?

- *Facilities*. What are the facilities like? How many practice rooms are available? What is the accessibility of practice rooms? Can students rehearse any time during the day, or are practice rooms limited?

- *Alumni*. Where are they now? Did they go on to professional performing careers? Did they attend graduate school in music (specifically, master in music performance programs [MM or MMus])? Do they teach at the high school or college level? Have alumni from liberal arts colleges or universities gone on to be successful in other careers such as commercial music, arts administration, teaching, or even other fields like journalism or law?

ROBERT MCIVER
FORMER CHAIRMAN, DEPARTMENT OF VOICE AND OPERA AND PROFESSOR OF VOICE, EASTMAN SCHOOL OF MUSIC

Audition Spotlight

The faculty members of the Eastman School of Music try to simplify the audition process as much as possible. They know how nerve-wracking it can be for some students! Three pieces are to be prepared—all equally honed and fine-tuned. Then, at the audition, students perform one piece of their choice. They may be asked by the faculty panel to perform one or both of the other pieces as well.

According to Robert McIver, Chairman of the Department of Voice and Opera, preparing an age-appropriate repertoire is key to a successful audition.

"Some students think it is better to perform an advanced piece, but it is more impressive for a student to perform a piece within their range *well*," says McIver. "The danger of preparing a piece that is beyond the student's capabilities is that it doesn't show their best performing ability because he or she may not perform it well."

There's a lesson to be learned: Prepare your music for auditions carefully and seek assistance from music teachers to choose a repertoire of pieces that best demonstrate your abilities and talents.

Expert Tips from Professor McIver

"Every music student knows that where you attend college is very important to your career," explains McIver. "Students need to do their research. They cannot be too informed."

➜ Conduct extensive research and narrow down school choices.

➜ Visit the schools, sit in on classes and get into the atmosphere.

➜ Talk to students—they have the most information about what it is like to be a student.

At the audition, McIver advises students to think of it as an opportunity rather than a challenge.

"At Eastman, prospective students audition in Kilbourne Hall, which is one of the great recital halls in the world," McIver shares. "Just the chance to perform there is an honor."

McIver's advice to students is to focus on communicating during the audition. "If students concentrate on how they should communicate their performance to the audience [in this case, adjudicators], it will allow them to focus; and this way, they won't have the energy to be nervous."

MARK
WEST VIRGINIA UNIVERSITY

Mark started studying music in elementary school as a third grader but became serious about it in high school. Now a senior at West Virginia University, he is a music education major and is the saxophone section leader in WVU's Pride of West Virginia, the renowned marching band.

"I thought I had my college all picked out," says Mark. "My first high school band director went to Indiana University of Pennsylvania, and because of that, I thought that [was] where I wanted to go."

But his experience performing in the honor band on the WVU campus and seeing its marching band at Bands of America changed his mind.

The audition experience is what ultimately allowed Mark to make the best choice for himself. Mark describes his audition experience at WVU and IUP as drastically different. "At IUP, there were two people auditioning, and at WVU five or six people were in the audition room," he says.

The music department at WVU offered a private lesson with a professor so that potential enrollees could see what studying there would be like. IUP didn't offer this option. Mark points to the one-on-one time with the professor as a turning point in his decision-making process. "It was really helpful to find out what my actual interaction with faculty would be like. From the first day, I realized that WVU was a family," he explains.

The Pride of West Virginia has 350 members. Each summer, band members come to campus a week early for band camp, which runs Monday through Saturday from eight a.m. to ten p.m. During the academic year, practice is held Tuesday through Friday from four to six p.m. On game days, the band rehearses for two hours prior to its start.

As a music education major, Mark has to learn a variety of instruments. In addition to his mastery of the saxophone, he is now proficient in clarinet, oboe, trumpet, and trombone.

"It was a little intimidating at first to learn all of the instruments,"

Hot Tips from Mark

→ If you are studying music education, make sure the music education curriculum in particular is top-notch. For example, the University of Michigan, West Virginia University, Indiana University, and Ohio State University are excellent, so look at their curriculum and compare it to others that you are considering.

→ Find out where the professors at the school studied, especially the professors who teach your primary instrument.

→ Remember you are only as good as the professors with whom you study.

→ Always be musical!

comments Mark. "But once you get used to it, it is not as hard as you thought." This is because, according to Mark, "The learning structure is based on the instrument you have already mastered, so teachers describe it in terms you already understand."

Mark has gained experience using his music education studies by spending the summers helping his high school band director back home. After graduation, he wants to become a music educator himself.

Mark is pleased that he found WVU. He is particularly proud to be part of the community, which in a large part has been due to his participation in the marching band.

"One of the weirdest things is that in high school, being in the band wasn't respected," recalls Mark. "But here, fans go nuts for this band. It is really indescribable."

The Pride of West Virginia has had pregame shows for thirty years. The Circle Song, which is Aaron Copland's "Simple Gifts," is a favorite among the fans.

"It sends chills up your back," says Mark.

Mark says that his experience in the marching band at WVU is something he will cherish forever. "As a senior, the last time we performed, I had tears in my eyes."

After considering all your options and asking questions, you should be in an excellent position to make your final college decision. Soon you'll be on your way to your collegiate music career!

Preparing for Your Audition: Suggestions for Prospective Music Majors
COURTESY OF THE NORTHWESTERN UNIVERSITY SCHOOL OF MUSIC

The titles suggested in this section illustrate the kind and quality of music appropriate for an audition. Applicants are free to choose a program that will best show their ability, using music from this list or music of comparable quality. Whenever possible, music should be selected from a variety of stylistic periods. The audition program should consist of four different compositions, or in some cases three compositions and orchestral excerpts. Instrumentalists should be prepared to play scales in all keys.

The Northwestern University School of Music has specific audition requirements for certain instruments, which are noted below. This list is meant to serve as a guide for prospective students on what pieces of music they want to prepare for an audition (remember that each school has different requirements, and this list is an example from only one institution).

Bassoon
Sonatas by Telemann, Etler, Hindemith; concertos by Vivaldi, Mozart, Weber; Weber's *Hungarian Fantasie*. orchestral excerpts.

Cello
Etudes by Duport, Popper; two contrasting movements from a Bach suite; a movement from concertos by Haydn, Tchaikovsky, Schumann, Elgar, Shostakovich; other pieces from the standard repertoire.

Clarinet

Northwestern's School of Music has more specific requirements for the clarinet. Required repertoire includes choice of one selection from each of these categories:

* An allegro movement from a concerto by Carl or Johann Stamitz, Mozart, Spohr, or Weber
* *Solo de Concours* by Messager, *Premiere Rhapsodie* by Debussy, *Three Pieces* by Stravinsky, *Rhapsody for Solo Clarinet* by Osborne, or the *Sonata for Clarinet and Piano* by either Poulenc or Martinu
* One of the following Rose Études from the 32 Études (No. 3, 5, 17, 19, or 21) or from the 40 Studies (No. 13 or 18)
* One of the following Rose Études from the 32 Études (No. 4, 10, 14, or 20) or from the 40 Studies (No. 11, 17, or 19)

Double Bass

A movement from concertos by Dragonetti, Dittersdorf, Koussevitzky; sonatas by Eccles, Vivaldi, Telemann; movements from the Bach Suites for Cello; *Valse Miniature*, "Chanson Triste" by Koussevitzky; *Reverie, Elegy, Tarantella* by Bottesini. Orchestral excerpts from Beethoven's Symphonies Nos. 5 and 9, Mozart's Symphony No. 40.

Euphonium

Fantasia, by Gordon Jacob, *Introduction and Dance* by Barat; choice of Nos. 1 through 14 of the characteristic études in the Arban Complete Conservatory Method. Orchestral excerpts: Strauss's *Ein Heldenleben, Don Quixote*; Holst's *The Planets* (tenor tuba part in orchestra version, euphonium part in band version); Schoenberg's *Theme and Variations*, William Schuman's *When Jesus Wept*. Major scales and sight-reading required.

Flute

Bach Sonatas in E-flat Major or E Major; sonatas by Handel, Poulenc, Hindemith; the Mozart concertos, *Poem* by Griffes, *Concertino* by Chaminade, *Fantasie* by Fauré, *Syrinx* by Debussy; orchestral excerpts from Brahms's Symphony No. 4, Beethoven's "Leonore" Overture No. 3, Debussy's *Prelude to the Afternoon of a Faun*. Sight-reading required.

Guitar

A program of varied solo literature and études, including one or two movements from a suite by Bach; preludes, sonatas, or theme and variations by Sor, Giuliani, Ponce, Torroba, Turina, Villa-Lobos, or Brouwer, or equivalent repertoire; *Études* by Carcassi, Sor, Brouwer, or Villa-Lobos.

Harp

First movements of Mozart's *Concerto for Flute and Harp* and Handel's *Concerto*; *Introduction et Allegro* by Ravel; *Danse sacrée et Danse profane* by Debussy. Orchestral excerpts: *Death and Transfiguration* by Strauss, *Young Person's Guide to the Orchestra* by Britten, *Prelude to the Afternoon of a Faun* by Debussy, *Firebird Suite* by Stravinsky, *España* by Chabrier, Overture to *Romeo and Juliet* by Tchaikovsky. Cadenzas: *Nutcracker Suite, Swan Lake, Sleeping Beauty* by Tchaikovsky; *La Bohème* (Act 3), *Madama Butterfly* (Act 1) by Puccini; "Prelude and Liebestod" from *Tristan und Isolde* by Wagner.

Horn

Northwestern's School of Music has more specific requirements for the horn. Required repertoire includes choice of one from each of the following two solo categories: concertos by Mozart, Franz Strauss, or Concerto No. 1 by Richard Strauss; and sonatas by Beethoven, Heiden, or Hindemith. Études from Kopprasch Book #1 and *Maxim-Alphonse* Book #3. Orchestral excerpts: Beethoven's *Symphony No. 6*, Brahms's *Symphony No. 3*, Strauss's *Till Eulenspiegel.*

Oboe

Concertos by Cimarosa, Marcello, Handel, Mozart; sonatas by Telemann, Handel, Hindemith; *Three Romances, Six Metamorphoses.*

Percussion

Audition should include snare drum, timpani, and keyboard percussion. Snare drum: Cirone's *Portraits in Rhythm*; Peters's Intermediate or Advanced Studies. Timpani: Beck's *Sonata for Timpani*; Carter's *Eight Pieces for Solo Timpani*; Firth's *The Solo Timpanist.* Keyboard percussion: Creston's *Concertino for Marimba*; Musser's Études and Preludes;

Stout's Mexican Dances and Nocturnes; G. H. Green's Xylophone Solos. Audition may also include drum set and orchestral excerpts. Sight-reading required.

Piano

A required program which must be all memorized. A contrapuntal baroque composition equivalent in difficulty to a three-voice fugue from *The Well-Tempered Clavier* by Bach; a sonata-allegro movement from a classical sonata preferably by Haydn, Mozart, Beethoven, or Schubert; a romantic work; and a work from the impressionist or contemporary period. Applicants must also submit a list of significant repertoire studied during the previous four years.

Saxophone

Sonatas by Creston, Heiden, Hindemith; concertos by Glazunov, Husa, Ibert, Tomasi; *Tableaux de Provence* by Paule Maurice; Improvisation I, II, or III by Ryo Noda; *Scaramouche* by Darius Muilhaud; *Cadenza* by Lucie Robert; *Fantasia* by Heitor Villa-Lobos.

Trombone (Tenor)

Must prepare all of the following: *Cavatina* by Saint-Saëns. Orchestral excerpts: *Hungarian March* by Berlioz; Tuba Mirum from Mozart's *Requiem*; *Bolero* by Ravel; *Symphony No. 3 in C Minor* by Saint-Saëns; *Ride of the Valkyries* by Wagner. Substitutions are not permitted.

Trombone (Bass)

Must prepare all of the following: *Concerto* by Lebedec. Orchestral excerpts: *Hungarian March* by Berlioz; *Creation, No. 26* by Haydn; *Symphony No.7*, first movement, by Mahler; *Symphony No.3*, fourth movement, by Schumann; *Ride of the Valkyries* by Wagner. Substitutions are not permitted.

Trumpet

Required repertoire (no substitutions allowed):

* ★   Required solo: Enesco's *Legend*
* ★   Required etude: Charlier's *Etudes Transcendantes #2*

* ★   Other contrasting solos and/or études of your choice
* ★   Required orchestral excerpts: Stravinsky's *Petrouchka* 1947 ballerina's dance and waltz
* ★   Optional: other contrasting orchestral excerpts.

Tuba

Solo literature and etudes demonstrating tone, intonation, range, technique. *Concerto* by Vaughan Williams; sonatas by Hindemith, Marcello; *Introduction and Dance* by Barat. Orchestral excerpts: Prelude to *Die Meistersinger*, *Ride of the Valkyries* by Wagner; *Symphonie Fantastique* by Berlioz; Mahler's *Symphony No. 1*, third movement; Prokofiev's *Symphony No. 5*, first movement; Bruckner's *Symphony No. 7*, fourth movement. Major scales and sight-reading required.

Viola

Program should include two contrasting movements of unaccompanied Bach; a Kreutzer Étude or a Campagnoli caprice; and a movement from concertos by Stamitz, Hoffmeister, Bartok, or Walton.

Violin

Memorization required (except for études). Program should include two contrasting movements of unaccompanied Bach; the first movement of a major concerto such as Mozart, Bruch, Saint-Saëns, Wieniawski, Lalo, Barber, etc.; any standard étude.

Voice

The program should be performed from memory and with accompaniment. Four art songs or arias, at least one selection in Italian, one in English, and one in either French or German. Suggested titles: "Per la gloria"; "Se tu m'ami"; "Sebben, crudele"; "Voi che sapete"; *Heidenroslein*; *Les Berceaux*; *Le Violette*; *The Daisies*; *The Black Swan*; *The Vagabond*.

JAZZ STUDIES

Jazz auditions are performed in a combo setting. The combos will be organized as follows:

* ★   Trumpets, saxophones, and trombones auditioning will perform with a rhythm section consisting of piano (or guitar), bass, and drums.

* Guitarists auditioning will perform with piano, bass, and drums.
* Pianists auditioning will perform with bass and drums.
* Bassists auditioning perform with piano (or guitar) and drums.
* Drummers auditioning will perform selections with piano (or guitar) and bass.

For your audition, choose one tune from each of the following four categories and be prepared to perform the tune's melody. Rhythm section instruments should demonstrate the ability to accompany a soloist.

1. Rhythm Changes

* "Oleo"—Sonny Rollins—Bb major
* "Moose the Mooche"—Charlie Parker—Bb major
* "Dexterity"—Charlie Parker—Bb major

2. Blues

* "Au Privave"—Charlie Parker—F major
* "Tenor Madness"—Sonny Rollins—Bb major
* "Blue Monk"—Thelonious Monk—Bb major
* "Bessie's Blues"—John Coltrane—Eb major

3. Ballads

* "In a Sentimental Mood"—Duke Ellington—F major
* "I Can't Get Started"—Vernon Duke—C major
* "Embraceable You"—George Gershwin—Eb major
* "You Don't Know What Love Is"—Gene DePaul—F minor

4. Waltz

* "Jitterbug Waltz"—Fats Waller—Eb major
* "Someday My Prince Will Come"—Frank Churchill—Bb major

* "Emily"—Johnny Mandel—Bb

NOTE TO DRUMMERS: In addition to the selections listed above drummers should prepare the following grooves:

* Swing grove with sticks (slow, medium, and fast)
* Swing groove with brushes (slow, medium, and fast)
* New Orleans groove
* Afro-Cuban 6/8 groove
* Shuffle groove with backbeat

REQUIREMENTS FOR MUSIC CONCENTRATIONS

Concentration in Music Cognition or Music Theory

Applicants, in addition to the performance audition, should submit an essay discussing a piece of music of their choice addressing formal, stylistic, or performance-related aspects of the work. Applicants must also complete a performance audition. Applicants who are applying for the Bachelor of Arts in Music should refer to the audition requirements for that degree program.

Concentration in Composition

Applicants, in addition to the performance audition, should prepare a portfolio including three well-produced scores for a variety of performance media, preferably with corresponding digital recordings of performances. At least one score must be intended for performance by acoustic instrumentation. Scores produced with notation software will be expected to demonstrate the applicant's skill both in using the software and in compositional sophistication; handwritten scores are not required, but well-executed handwritten musical notation will be considered as a positive attribute in admissions decisions. In addition, a complete portfolio should include: one (1) research paper written while in high school (music subject preferred); related documents (programs of performances, awards, name(s) of composition teacher(s), etc.); and a recording demonstrating performance ability.

Concentration in Music Education

Applicants, in addition to the performance audition, must interview with a music education faculty member and also submit one-paragraph answers (using complete sentences) to the following essay questions:

1. Describe any of your teaching and/or leadership experiences.
2. Why are you interested in teaching music?
3. What are some of your personal qualities that will allow you to be an effective music teacher?
4. What person or experience has inspired you to pursue music education?
5. What do you hope to learn as a result of your music education experience at Northwestern University?

Your essay answers should be sent to the School of Music, and an interview will then be scheduled with a music education faculty member. The answers you provide will be used for the basis of the interview.

Concentration in Musicology

Applicants, in addition to the performance audition, should submit one high school research paper (preferably on a musical subject) and a brief essay describing their musical background, interests, and goals, and should address the following where appropriate: performing experience (lessons, ensembles); training in music theory; repertoires with which the applicant is familiar (orchestral, vocal, or piano literature, popular or non-Western music); studies in related areas (foreign languages, literature, history). Applicants who are applying for music should refer to the audition requirements for that degree program.

Concentration in Music Technology

Applicants, in addition to the performance audition, should submit examples of projects they have created, such as tapes of compositions or examples of computer programs. Applicants should also submit a brief essay describing their goals, their background in both music and technology, and the reasons they have chosen music technology as an area of concentration. Applicants must also complete a performance audition. Applicants who are applying for music should refer to the audition requirements for that degree program.

ATAR ARAD
PROFESSOR OF MUSIC (VIOLA) AT INDIANA UNIVERSITY

Inside the Indiana University School of Music

Professor Atar Arad describes the School of Music as "extremely friendly" and qualifies that statement by adding that for such a large school of music there still is a "sense of community."

One of many unique features of Indiana University's School of Music is that students have the opportunity to perform as soloists with ad hoc orchestras that they form. This can give students a sense of ownership in the end result.

Professor Arad instructs his students in ways to be prepared for life after college. He says that in the professional world of music, "It's not enough just to be good... Students must also service their talent by knowing how to promote themselves."

Arad admits that whenever one of his students gets a job, he feels greatly relieved. "What I try to do is to prepare my students so that when they graduate they do not have to ask, 'Now what do I do with my degree?' Fortunately, most of my students find a future in music."

SAMPLE MUSICIAN ARTIST STATEMENT

Music has been an integral part of my life since I was a very young child. My parents used to play showtunes in the car, so that I knew every word to *Guys and Dolls* and *Les Miserables* before I was eight. However, it was not until seventh grade that I singled out singing as my greatest passion, and it was even longer before I discovered what being a singer would mean to me.

I believe that I have always been a singer to my core, despite years of viewing singing only as a hobby. In fifth grade, Mrs. Silverstein, my substitute teacher, asked me if I was a singer. After a moment of reflection, I said yes, and she told me she could hear the music in my speaking voice. It surprises me that this particular memory should still stand out so vividly in my mind. Looking back, I can pinpoint that moment as the moment when I unconsciously signed my identity over to my singing. Throughout middle school, I sang at every opportunity: in choirs, in voice classes, and in musical revues.

Nevertheless, it did not occur to me to label myself a "singer" until high school. During freshman year, a time when most fourteen-year-olds struggle to find their identities and their passions, I was able to bypass most of this angst by aligning myself solidly with my singing. To tell the truth, I thought of singing as a sort of social leg up; because I had, I believed, a certain amount of vocal talent, more of my classmates took an interest in me, including some upper-classmen. My voice gave me confidence; while singing in Chorale, I neither worried nor cared about my physical imperfections or the stresses of my course load.

I was faced with a predicament about this view of singing when my family moved to Arizona. There, no one knew that I could sing, and I was inclined to keep it quiet for a while. The last thing I wanted was to be set apart from the masses during my first months at a new school. I soon discovered, however, that singing alto in choir and humming to myself in the shower could not satisfy my singer's soul. By November, I had begun working once more with a voice teacher, and after Thanksgiving, I auditioned for and won the role of Marian Paroo in *The Music Man*. During those three exhilarating months spent rehearsing, I found that I stood taller and prouder when I sang my solos. When we performed the show for an audience, I felt a shiver of joy up my spine as I opened my mouth to sing into the darkness. It was this experience that helped me to once again find my identity as a singer.

Of course, singing has never been all play and no work for me. Being a singer in high school has meant constant sacrifice, usually in my social activities. I have declined invitations to go bowling and have avoided school dances as a rule in order to preserve my vocal health. I know that when my voice is hoarse and exhausted, I slip into an unhappy funk because I can't express myself properly. Although maintaining my developing voice is a challenge, singing itself presents an even greater one. I practice singing every day, sometimes trying desperately to reach notes that seem to be placed in the stratosphere. For a long time, these tasks proved so difficult that I nearly denounced singing classically altogether. However, my acceptance into Oberlin Conservatory's Vocal Academy for High School students changed everything. There, I met thirty-seven other high school singers like me, all of whom were facing similar challenges. I was inspired during that week by my friends' commitment to their music; they sang for themselves and strove daily to improve to satisfy their own goals.

I know now that my voice is the single most important defining factor of my identity. I will always sing, wherever I am and whatever I choose to do with my life. I hope very much to be able to continue to discover new facets of my vocal ability throughout my undergrad-uate experience.

Sample Music Application Essay

(Double Major Prospect)

As a prospective dual-degree student at Oberlin, I plan to further my study of classical voice while also continuing my education in the liberal arts, specifically in literature and foreign language. I hope to be able to incorporate aspects of my liberal arts education into my study of music and vice versa.

Over the course of my education, I have become fascinated with words. I think that one thing that attracts me to classical music is the sincere poetry of its lyrics, in contrast to many other styles of music. I believe that learning how to analyze both prose and poetry has helped and will continue to help with my interpretation of the lyrics of my repertoire. I also enjoy singing music with lyrics by favorite poets such as Emily Dickinson because that allows me to connect even more with what I am singing. I hope that taking classes in the superb English department at Oberlin College will continue to affect my development as a vocalist. I also hope to continue my study of foreign languages at Oberlin. I am currently fluent in French and would like to achieve the same level of fluency in both Italian and German. I believe that this quest for fluency will improve my interpretation of repertoire in these languages because I will be familiar with the words I am singing and truly understand their meaning. Also, because I hope to study music in Europe, either during or after my undergraduate years, the study of foreign languages will be enormously useful to me in the future. I am certain that continuing to study the liberal arts will be invaluable to my study of classical voice.

I view my voice and my music education as something of an adventure. I came to classical singing only two years ago and am just beginning to explore the many facets of my complicated instrument. I marvel at the sheer number of performance opportunities available to students at Oberlin, and I am anxious to take part in them in order to help me hone my performance skills. I am curious about the mechanics of music, having not had access to a music theory course in high school, and I look forward to learning the complex language of music as well as to taking classes in music history. Most exciting to me about Oberlin is the prospect of working with such accomplished professors and teachers.

At the Vocal Academy this past summer, I worked with both Ms. Mahy and Mr. Crawford and was astounded by how much technique I took away from just a half hour with each. They taught me how to practice, how to preserve my voice, and how best to learn a piece of music.

I am anxious to begin studying with any one of Oberlin's voice teachers, who will be able to help me achieve my goals in technique and performance. After completing my undergraduate education, I would like to attend graduate school or an apprentice program at an opera company; however, I understand that it is impossible for me to know today exactly where my voice will take me in the future. Ideally, after graduate school, I would like to begin auditioning and working towards a career in classical vocal performance. Whether in fully staged productions or as a concert vocalist, I believe that Oberlin is the perfect place for me to begin my journey to reach my dream of singing professionally.

Sample Musician Repertoire List

"Se tu m'ami, se sospiri"—Pergolesi

"Sebben, crudele"—Caldara

"Per la gloria d'adorarvi"—Bononcini

"Tu lo sai"—Torelli

"Vedrai, carino" (*Don Giovanni*)—Mozart

"Batti, batti o bel Masetto" (*Don Giovanni*)—Mozart

"Deh vieni, non tardar" (*Le Nozze Di Figaro*)—Mozart

"Un moto di gioia" (*Le Nozze Di Figaro*)

"Lachen und Weinen"—Schubert

"Du Ring an Meinem Finger"—Schumann (*studied*)

"Widmung"—Schumann (*studied*)

"En Prière"—Fauré

"Après un Rêve"—Fauré

"The Jewel Song" (*Faust*)—Gounod (*studied*)

"Les papillons"—Chausson

"Plum Pudding"—Bernstein (*studied*)

"O Had I Jubal's Lyre"—Handel

"Nymphs and Shepherds"—Purcell

"Steal Me, Sweet Thief" (*The Old Maid and the Thief*)—Menotti

"Poor Wand'ring One" (*The Pirates of Penzance*)—Gilbert and Sullivan

"The Lass With the Delicate Air"—Arne

"When I Bring to You Colored Toys"—Carpenter

"Will There Really Be a Morning?"—Gordon

"The Lass from the Low Countree"—Niles

"On the Steps of the Palace" (*Into the Woods*)—Sondheim

"The Girls of Summer" (*Marry Me a Little*)—Sondheim

"Green Finch and Linnet Bird" (*Sweeney Todd*)—Sondheim

"Goodnight, My Someone" (*The Music Man*)—Willson

"My White Knight" (*The Music Man*)

"Till There Was You" (*The Music Man*)

"And This Is My Beloved" (*Kismet*)—Forrest and Wright

"Will He Like Me?" (*She Loves Me*)—Bock and Harnick

Sample Musician Résumé

Awards Received

SENIOR YEAR (2016-2017)

National Honor Society

Tri-M Music Honor Society

Morris Hills Excelsior Award

Morris Hills Fine Arts Student of the Month (Band)

Homecoming Princess

High Honor Roll

JUNIOR YEAR (2015-2016)

National Honor Society

Honor Guard

Morris Hills Excelsior Award

High Honor Roll

SOPHOMORE YEAR (2014-2015)

Morris Hills Fine Arts Student of the Month

Chorus

Morris Hills Excelsior Award

High Honor Roll

FRESHMAN YEAR (2013-2014)

Morris Hills Excelsior Award

High Honor Roll

Extracurricular Activities

SENIOR YEAR (2016-2017)

National Honor Society

Morris Hills Regional District Wind Ensemble *+

Marching Band

Advanced Band +

Concert Band +

Pit Band +

Jazz Band +

Madrigals Choir *

Knights Templars Chorus *

Concert Chorus

Homecoming Court

Mr. Morris Hills Pageant GT Talent Showcase *

JUNIOR YEAR (2015-2016)

National Honor Society

Honor Guard

Morris Hills Regional District Wind Ensemble *+

Morris Hill Wind Ensemble *+

Marching Band

Advanced Band *+

Concert Band +

Pit Band, *Bye Bye Birdie* +

Jazz Band +

Madrigals Choir *

Knights Templars Chorus *

Concert Chorus

New Jersey Math League

Physics Club

GT Talent Showcase *

SOPHOMORE YEAR (2014-2015)

Marching Band

Advanced Band +

Concert Band +

Pit Band, *Annie* +

Jazz Band +

Madrigals Choir *

Knights Templar Chorus *

Concert Chorus

Project L.E.A.D.

FRESHMAN YEAR (2013-2014)

Advanced Band +

Concert Band +

Pit Band, *Oliver* +

Jazz Band +

Knights Templar Chorus *

Concert Chorus

Soccer

New Jersey Math League

Key Club

* denotes audition-only activity

+ denotes first-chair ranking

Leadership Positions

SENIOR YEAR (2016-2017)

Drum Major—Marching Band

Soprano Section Leader—Concert Chorus

JUNIOR YEAR (2015-2016)

Alto Sax/Mellophone Section Leader—Band

Soprano Section Leader—Concert Chorus

Additional Music Activities

SENIOR YEAR (2016-2017)

Independent Study—Band Director

Private Alto Saxophone Lessons

Private Piano Lessons

JUNIOR YEAR (2015-2016)

MENC All-Eastern Chorus*

NJMEA All-State Chorus (ranked 6th in S2 voice)

NJSMA Region 1 Chorus*

Teen Arts Festival—piano accompanist

Private Alto Saxophone Lessons

Private Piano Lessons

SOPHOMORE YEAR (2014-2015)

NJSMA Region 1 Chorus*

Rockaway Township Community Band

Private Alto Saxophone Lessons

Private Piano Lessons

FRESHMAN YEAR (2014-2015)

Carnegie Hall Easter Choral Production

Private Alto Saxophone Lessons

Private Piano Lessons

*denotes audition-only activity

Community Activities

SUMMER 2016

Wharton School Summer Band Program, Assistant Instructor

Work Experience

2015-PRESENT

Private music teacher (alto saxophone, piano)

SUMMER 2015

TM Construction—construction/electrical assistant

Sample Music Curriculum*

Duquesne University

The Mary Pappert School of Music

BM Music Performance (Voice)

Freshman Year	Fall	Spring
Musicianship I & II	4	4
Computers for Musicians	2	—
Voice	3	3
Piano	1	1
Eurhythmics I & II	2	2
Choral Ensemble	1	1
Italian for Singers	2	—
Italian Diction and Repertory	—	2
Core	3	3
	18	16
Sophomore Year	**Fall**	**Spring**
Musicianship III & IV	4	4
Seminar	0	0
Voice	3	3
Core	3	3
Piano	1	1
Choral Ensemble	1	1
Opera Workshop	1	1
French for Musicians	2	—
French Diction and Repertory	—	2
Electives	2	2
	17	17
Junior Year	**Fall**	**Spring**
Musicianship V & VI	4	4
Seminar	0	0
Voice	3	3
Pedagogy	2	—

Choral Ensemble or Opera Workshop	1	1
Conducting I & II	2	2
German for Singers	2	—
German Diction and Repertory	—	2
Vocal Coaching	1	1
Junior Recital	—	0
Core	3	3
Electives	—	2
	18	18
Senior Year	**Fall**	**Spring**
Musicianship VII	4	—
Seminar	0	0
Voice	3	3
Choral Ensemble or Opera Workshop	1	1
English Diction and Repertory	2	—
Vocal Coaching	1	1
Career Prospectives in Music	2	—
Senior Recital	—	1
Core	3	3
Electives	—	3
BM Performance	—	0
	16	12
TOTAL CREDITS	**132**	

Music Education

Performance/Music Ed Major

A five-year program combining both programs is available for music education majors with a performance emphasis. Please see your adviser for more information.

Freshman Year	Fall	Spring
Musicianship I & II	4	4
Seminar	0	0
Piano for Music Ed I & II	2	2
Computers for Musicians	2	—
Voice for Music Ed I & II	1	1
Intro to Music Ed	1	—
Music Ed Methods I	—	2
Applied Music	2	2
Ensemble	1	1
Eurhythmics I & II	2	2
Guitar Class for Music Ed	—	1
Core	3	3
Total Credits	18	18
Sophomore Year	**Fall**	**Spring**
Musicianship III & IV	4	4
Seminar	0	0
Applied Music	2	2
Ensemble	1	1
Conducting I & II	2	2
Brass Techniques I & II	1	1
String Methods	1	1
Percussion Techniques	1	1
Music Ed Methods II & III	2	3
Classroom Music Techniques	1	—
Core	3	3
Total Credits	18	18
Junior Year	**Fall**	**Spring**
Musicianship V & VI	4	4

Seminar	0	0
Applied Music	2	2
Ensemble	1	1
Music Ed Methods IV & V	3	3
Woodwind Techniques I & II	1	1
Educational Psychology I & II	4	3
Instrumental Materials Lab	—	1
Marching Band Techniques	1	—
Choral Materials Lab	1	—
Children's Choir Lab	1	—
Core	—	3
Total Credits	18	18
Senior Year	**Fall**	**Spring**
Musicianship VII	4	—
Optional Applied Music	(2)	—
Ensemble	1	—
Core	9	—
Student Teaching—Vocal	—	6
Student Teaching—Instrumental	—	6
Senior Seminar	—	0
B.S. Music Education	—	0
Total Credits	14	12
	(16)	
	134 (136)	

*These sample curriculums are reprinted with permission. The course schedule shown here is representative of courses for a music/music education major. Of course, each institution has slightly different emphases and requirements, and students are advised to investigate the curriculum at each program they apply to.

MUSIC PROGRAMS

Profiles of Selected Programs

Northeast / 289

Southeast / 300

Midwest / 310

West / 319

Comprehensive List of Colleges with Music Programs

By State / 327

Northeast

BERKLEE COLLEGE OF MUSIC

1140 Boylston Street
Boston, MA 02214

Phone: (800) BERKLEE (237-5533) or
(617) 747-2221
Website: berklee.edu
Email: admissions@berklee.edu

Tuition: $$
Campus student enrollment (undergraduate):
5112

Degree(s): BM, BFA, BPS, professional diploma;
dual major options available
Concentrations: Emphasis is on contemporary
music studies with majors in the following fields:
performance, composition, jazz composition,
contemporary writing and production, film scoring,
song writing, music production and engineering,
music synthesis, music business/management, music
therapy, music education, and professional music.
Audition requirement: Yes
Scholarships available: Yes, over $15 million
available annually. Scholarships are merit-based only.
Number of faculty: Approximately 530
**Percentage and number of applicants
accepted into the department per year:**
19%; accepted 1,061 of 5,538 students
Department activities: Over 700 student
performances throughout the year, from student
band performances in the cafeteria to solo recitals
to ensemble class performances. Numerous large
shows, including Singer Showcase twice per year,
Nothing Conservatory About It Concert Series,
Convocation concert. Over 350 ensembles are
available for students to choose from.

Prominent Alumni:
John Abercrombie (1967)—jazz guitarist
Cindy Blackman (1980)—former drummer for
Lenny Kravitz, solo drummer/recording artist
John Blackwell (1988)—drummer for Prince
Gary Burton (1962)—Grammy Award–winning
jazz vibist
Terri Lyne Carrington (1983)
Cyrus Chestnut (1985)—studio drummer/ record-
ing artist
Alf Clausen (1966)—former Wynton Marsalis and
Betty Carter pianist, touring and recording artist;
composer for television show *The Simpsons*
Bruce Cockburn (1965)—platinum-selling
songwriter and performer
Paula Cole (1990)—Grammy Award–winning
singer/songwriter
Al DiMeola (1974)—jazz fusion guitarist
Melissa Etheridge (1980)—Grammy Award–
winning singer-songwriter
Kevin Eubanks (1979)—guitarist/bandleader for
Tonight Show band, jazz recording artist
Jan Hammer (1969)—keyboardist, composer of
platinum-selling *Miami Vice* theme
Roy Hargrove (1989)—Grammy Award–winning
jazz trumpeter
Juliana Hatfield (1990)—singer-songwriter, former
member of Blake Babies
Ingrid Jensen (1989)—Grammy nominated and
Juno-winning jazz trumpeter
Quincy Jones (1951)—Grammy Award–winning
composer, arranger, record and concert producer
Diana Krall (1983)—Grammy Award–winning
jazz vocalist, pianist and composer
Joey Kramer (1971)—drummer for Aerosmith, Rock
and Roll Hall of Fame inductee
Abraham Laboriel, Sr. (1972)—studio bassist and
recording artist
Abe Laboriel, Jr. (1993)—drummer for Paul
McCartney, former drummer for SEAL, studio
drummer
Patty Larkin (1974)—singer-songwriter, guitarist
Joe Lovano (1972)—Grammy Award–winning
jazz saxophonist

Aimee Mann (1980)—Grammy Award–winning and Oscar Award–nominated singer/songwriter

Arif Mardin (1961)—Vice President Atlantic Records, Grammy Award–winning producer

Branford Marsalis (1980)—Grammy Award–winning saxophonist

John Mayer (1998)—Grammy Award–winning singer/songwriter

Makoto Ozone (1983)—jazz pianist, Verve recording artist

Danilo Perez (1988)—Grammy Award–nominated Latin-jazz pianist

John Scofield (1973)—jazz guitarist

Howard Shore (1969)—Grammy Award–winning and Oscar Award–winning film score composer

Alan Silvestri (1970)—Grammy Award–winning and Oscar Award–nominated film score composer

Mike Stern (1976)—Grammy-nominated jazz guitarist

Susan Tedeschi (1991)—Grammy Award nominee, W.C. Handy winning blues singer/guitarist

Steve Vai (1979)—Grammy Award–winning rock guitarist, former Frank Zappa sideman

Gillian Welch (1992)—Grammy Award–winning bluegrass singer-songwriter

Brad Whitford (1971)—Guitarist for Aerosmith, Rock and Roll Hall of Fame inductee

BOSTON CONSERVATORY AT BERKLEE

8 Fenway
Boston, MA 02215

Phone: (617) 912-9137
Website: bostonconservatory.berklee.edu
Email: admissions@bostonconservatory.edu

Tuition: $$
Campus student enrollment (undergraduate): 563

Degree(s): B.M., M.M., G.P.D. (Graduate Performance Diploma), P.S.C. (Performance Studies Certificate), A.D. (Artist Diploma).

Areas of Study: Brass, Choral Conducting, Orchestral Conducting, Classical Contemporary Music, Composition, Harp, Music Education, Percussion/Marimba, Piano, Collaborative Piano, Strings, Voice/Opera, Vocal Pedagogy, and Woodwinds.

Audition requirement: Yes
Scholarships available: Yes
Number of faculty: 112
Number of majors and minors: 401
Department activities: Students perform regularly throughout the year in Boston Conservatory's many music ensembles, including Orchestra, Wind Ensemble, Brass Ensemble, Chorale, Women's Chorus, Percussion Ensemble, Sinfonietta, Contemporary Music Ensemble, and pit orchestras for dance, opera, and theater productions, as well in various chamber music groups. Singers may also perform in the conservatory's fully produced opera productions, which are presented three times per year on the school's mainstage, accompanied with a full pit orchestra. In addition, music students perform regularly in master classes with renowned guest artists, recitals, and studio concerts.

Prominent Alumni:

Kelly Corcoran (Voice)—director of Nashville Symphony Chorus

James Orleans (Bass)—former Tanglewood Fellow; Boston Symphony Orchestra member

Wendy Bryn Harmer (Soprano)—Metropolitan Opera Company

Mike Renzi (Piano)—musical director and pianist in the quartet for Tony Bennett and Lady Gaga's *Cheek to Cheek* album and tour

Kristhyan Benitez (Piano)—Artist in Residence, Piano and Chamber Music Specialist at Fundamusical Simon Bolivar, *El Sistema*

Vladimir Kulenovic—Award-winning Music Director of the Lake Forest Symphony

Victoria Livengood (Mezzo-soprano)—Metropolitan Opera Company

Sandra Piques Eddy—Metropolitan Opera, Boston

Lyric Opera, Lyric Opera of Kansas, Portland Opera, Opera North UK, Austin Lyric Opera, New York City Opera, Florentine Opera, Hawaii Opera Theatre, Chicago Opera Theatre, among others
Konstantinos Protopapas—Artistic Director of Opera Santa Barbara since August 2015, Director of Tulsa Opera
Mihail Jojatu—cellist with Boston Symphony, Boston Cello Quartet
Lily Afshar—classical guitarist, recording artist
Jonathan Heyward—Assistant Conductor of the Hallé Orchestra, International Competition for Young Conductors in Besançon winner
Christina Bouey—Fischoff Competition Grand Prize winner as a member of the Ulysses Quartet

BOSTON UNIVERSITY

School of Music
College of Fine Arts
855 Commonwealth Avenue
Boston, MA 02215

Phone: (617) 353-3341
Website: bu.edu/cfa
Email: cfamusic@bu.edu

Tuition: $$$$
Campus student enrollment (undergraduate): 16,496; 155 in School of Music

Degree(s): BM, Opera Institute certificate, performance diploma
Concentrations: Performance, theory and composition, musicology, music education
Audition requirement: Yes
Scholarships available: Yes
Number of applicants accepted into the department per year:
Approximately 750 applicants, 245 admitted
Department activities: Symphony orchestra, chamber orchestra, baroque orchestra, wind ensemble, brass ensemble, chamber ensemble, symphonic chorus, chamber choir, Time's Arrow,

Muir String Quartet in residence, the Center for New Music, the Center for Early Music.
For the Boston University community: marching band, pep band, winter percussion, winter guard, concert band, all-campus orchestra, symphonic chorus, alumni concert band, big band, jazz workshop.

Prominent Alumni:
Karin Bliznik—principal trumpet, St. Louis Symphony
Fred Bronstein—Dean of Peabody Institute
Velvet Brown—tuba soloist, music educator
Marcus Haddock—tenor
Eugene Izotov—principal oboist, San Francisco Symphony
Georgia Jarman—soprano
Kelly Kaduce—soprano
Dominique LaBelle—soprano
Alexandre LeCarme—cellist, Boston Symphony Orchestra
Missy Mazzoli—composer, faculty Mannes College of Music
Beth Morrison—opera producer, Beth Morrison Projects
Ikuko Mizuno—violinist, Boston Symphony Orchestra
Ryan Murphy—conductor, associate Music Director, Mormon Tabernacle Choir
Joseph Pereira—principle percussionist, Los Angeles Philharmonic
Anthony Tommasini—chief music critic, the *New York Times*
Morris Robinson—bass
Rita Shapiro—executive director, National Symphony Orchestra
Albert Sherman—stage director
Julian Wachner—conductor, Director of Music Trinity Wall Street

THE COLLEGE OF NEW JERSEY

Department of Music
P.O. Box 7718
2000 Pennington Road
Ewing, NJ 08628–0718

Phone: (609) 771-2551/2552
Website: tcnj.edu/~music
Email: music@tcnj.edu

Tuition: $$$$
Campus student enrollment (undergraduate): 6,758

Degree(s): BA, BM
Concentrations: Music performance, music education, general music
Audition requirement: Yes
Scholarships available: Yes, talent-based scholarships from $1,000–10,000, renewable for four years; additional merit-based academic scholarships offered by the College between $1,000–$5,000, renewable for four years.
Number of faculty: 9 full-time, 34 adjuncts
Number of majors and minors: 100 majors, 11 minors
Number of applicants accepted into the department per year: 85 freshman applicants for 2015, 61 accepted, 20 enrolled.
Department activities: 25–30 concerts and recitals per academic year, Tuesday Afternoon Recital and Lecture Series that is free and open to the public.

THE CURTIS INSTITUTE OF MUSIC

1726 Locust Street
Philadelphia, PA 19103

Phone: (215) 893-5252
Website: curtis.edu
Email: admissions@curtis.edu

Tuition: $
*All students at Curtis receive merit-based full-tuition scholarships. There is no tuition fee. Students pay a comprehensive fee of $1,350, a $125 Internet fee, a health insurance fee of $1,000, and $3,360 for health insurance annually. Students may request exemption from Curtis's plan if they have a parental or private health insurance plan that provides adequate protection while they are attending Curtis.
Campus student enrollment: 177 total— this includes students in the Diploma, Bachelor of Music, Post-Baccalaureate Diploma, Master of Music in opera, and Professional Studies Certificate in opera programs

Degree(s): Diploma, BM, Post-Baccalaureate Diploma; vocal students only—Master of Music, Professional Studies Certificate
Courses offered: Performance courses (lessons and coachings, instrumental repertoire studies, vocal studies, supplementary performance); musical studies (techniques of music, harmony, solfège, keyboard, music history); liberal arts; career studies. Students who have completed Curtis's liberal arts requirements may enroll at no cost at the University of Pennsylvania for additional courses not available at Curtis.
Concentrations: Composition, conducting, guitar, keyboard instruments (piano and organ), orchestral instruments (strings, harp, woodwinds, brass, timpani and percussion), vocal studies (voice and opera)
Audition requirement: Yes
Scholarships available: Yes, all students accepted at Curtis receive merit-based full-tuition scholarships.
Number of faculty: 113
Number of majors and minors: 19
Majors: Bassoon, clarinet, composition, conducting, double bass, flute, harp, horn, oboe, organ, piano, timpani and percussion, trombone, trumpet, tuba, viola, violin, violoncello, vocal studies; no minors.
Percentage and number of applicants accepted into the department per year:

Although hundreds of musicians apply each year, the school admits only enough students to fill the places of the previous graduating class. Enrollment is limited to the number of musicians needed for a symphony orchestra, opera department, and select programs in piano, organ, guitar, and composition; and conducting and string quartet fellowship programs. With an average acceptance rate around 4%, Curtis is among the most selective schools in the United States.

Department activities: In keeping with its philosophy that students "learn by doing," Curtis presents more than 200 public performances each year, including orchestra concerts, opera productions and solo and chamber music recitals.

Student Recital Series: Curtis offers more than 100 free public performances each season through the Student Recital Series. Students perform solo and chamber works almost every Monday, Wednesday, and Friday night throughout the school year with additional recitals in the spring.

Curtis Symphony Orchestra: The orchestra performs a three-concert season in Philadelphia's Verizon Hall at the Kimmel Center for the Performing Arts as well as programs elsewhere in the region.

Curtis Opera Theatre: Each season, the Curtis Opera Theatre presents several fully staged performances and concert productions at venues around the city. All of the department's twenty-five voice and opera students are cast repeatedly each season, providing them a rare level of performance experience.

Curtis on Tour: Curtis on Tour brings the extraordinary artistry of the Curtis Institute of Music to national and international audiences, with students performing alongside celebrated Curtis alumni and faculty. Curtis on Tour has performed in more than fifty destinations in Europe, Asia, and North and South America, with new venues added each year.

Family Concerts: Family Concerts are presented twice a year. Through performance and audience interaction, Curtis students illustrate the basic elements of music and share their experiences as musicians. The Family Concerts are part of the Curtis Community Engagement Program, which aims to bring classical music to young people and others in the community who may not otherwise have access to music.

Prominent Alumni:
Samuel Barber
Leonard Bernstein
Jonathan Biss
Jorge Bolet
Yefim Bronfman
Ray Chen
Vinson Cole
John de Lancie
Roberto Díaz
Juan Diego Flòrez
Lukas Foss
Pamela Frank
Alan Gilbert
Richard Goode
Gary Graffman
Daron Hagen
Hilary Hahn
Lynn Harrell
Miguel Harth-Bedoya
Shuler Hensley
Eugene Istomin
Jennifer Higdon
Paul Jacobs
Paavo Järvi
Leila Josefowicz
Lang Lang
Jaime Laredo
Leon McCawley
Anthony McGill
Gian Carlo Menotti
Anna Moffo
Vincent Persichetti
John Relyea
George Rochberg
Ned Rorem
Aaron Rosand
Nino Rota
Peter Serkin

Rinat Shaham
Ignat Solzhenitsyn
Nadja Salerno-Sonnenberg
Robert Spano
Michael Stern
Time for Three
Benita Valente
George Walker
Yuja Wang

DUQUESNE UNIVERSITY

Mary Pappert School of Music
600 Forbes Avenue
Pittsburgh, PA 15282

Phone: (412) 396-6080 main office
Website: duq.edu/music
Email: musicadmissions@duq.edu

Tuition: $$
Campus student enrollment (undergraduate):
6,052

Degree(s): BM Performance, BM Music
Technology (Sound Recording, Electronic
Performance, Electronic Composition tracks),
BM with Elective Studies in Business, BS Music
Education, BS Music Therapy, BA Music, Minor in
Music
Audition requirement: Yes
Scholarships available: Yes
Department activities: Voices of Spirit, Pappert
Chorales, University Singers, Opera Workshop,
Symphony Orchestra, Wind Symphony, Symphony
Band, Jazz Ensemble I & II, Jazz Guitar Ensemble,
Classic Guitar Ensemble, Percussion Ensemble,
Electronic Ensemble, Brass Ensemble, Saxophone
Quartets, Chamber Music.

Prominent Alumni:
Marianne Cornetti, mezzo-soprano

THE HARTT SCHOOL/ UNIVERSITY OF HARTFORD

200 Bloomfield Avenue
West Hartford, CT 06117–1599

Phone: (860) 768-4465
Website: hartford.edu/hartt
Email: harttadm@hartford.edu

Tuition: $
Campus student enrollment (undergraduate):
5,246

Degree(s): BM, BA, BSE
Concentrations: Instrumental studies (instrumental performance, guitar performance, piano performance), vocal studies (choral singing, opera singing, recital singing), music education (instrumental or vocal), composition, music theory, music history (research or performance practices), jazz studies, music production and technology, music management, performing arts management (BA), music (BA), acoustics and music (BSE)
Audition requirement: Yes
Scholarships available: Yes

Prominent Alumni:
Janet Arms—flutist
Leo Brouwer—Cuban composer, guitarist, and conductor
Peter Boyer—Grammy-nominated composer
Steve Davis—trombonist
Peter Niedmann—musical composer
Matthew Plenk and Marie Plette—Metropolitan Opera
Shane Shanahan—percussionist

THE JUILLIARD SCHOOL

Music Division
60 Lincoln Center Plaza
New York, NY 10023–6588

Phone: (212) 799-5000 ext. 223

Website: juilliard.edu/apply-audition
Email: musicadmissions@juilliard.edu

Tuition: $$
Campus student enrollment: 530 undergraduate, 894 total

Degree(s): BM, graduate diploma
Audition requirement: Yes
Scholarships available: Yes
Number of faculty: 255
Percentage of applicants accepted per year: 7.2%
Department activities: Juilliard Orchestra, Juilliard Chamber Orchestra, New Juilliard Ensemble, AXIOM, recitals and concerts, master classes, undergraduate opera, Juilliard Opera, Juilliard415, Juilliard Jazz Ensembles, Juilliard Jazz Orchestra, Juilliard Jazz Artist Diploma Ensemble, concerts in clubs around the city (for jazz).

Prominent Alumni:

Itzhak Perlman

Yo-Yo Ma

Renée Fleming

Wynton Marsalis

Alan Gilbert

Christian McBride

Philip Glass

Steve Reich

Audra McDonald

Marin Alsop

James Conlon

Isabel Leonard

Midori

Jeremy Denk

Gil Shaham

James Levine

MANHATTAN SCHOOL OF MUSIC

120 Claremont Avenue
New York, NY 10027

Phone: (212) 749-2802
Website: msmnyc.edu
Email: admission@msmnyc.edu

Tuition: $44,100
Campus student enrollment: 412 undergraduate, 537 graduate (949 total)

Degree(s): BM
Certificates: Professional Studies Certificate (one year), Artist Diploma (one year)
Classical Majors: Bass, bassoon, cello, clarinet, composition, flute, horn, guitar, harp, oboe, percussion, piano, saxophone, trombone (and bass trombone), trumpet, tuba, viola, violin, voice, accompanying, orchestral performance program, contemporary performance, contemporary composition. Pinchas Zukerman Performance Program: viola, violin.
Jazz Majors: Bass (acoustic and electric), drumset, guitar, jazz voice, piano, saxophone, trombone, trumpet, vibraphone, violin.
Audition requirement: Yes
Scholarships available: Yes
Number of faculty: 275
Department activities: Over 400 concerts, recitals, and master classes per year

---

Prominent Alumni:
John Musto (BM 1976 and MM 1980, piano)—Pulitzer Prize finalist, two-time Emmy Award winner, Academy of Arts and Letters Award
Shuler Hensley (BM 1990)—Tony Award winner
Larry Hochman (BM 1975, Theory)—Tony Award–winning orchestrator for *Book of Mormon*
Jose Llana (1995)—*Flower Drum Song; Spelling Bee; The King & I*
Joseph Joubert (BM 1979, MM 1981)—former pianist/conductor for Oprah Winfrey's *The Color Purple* on Broadway; orchestrator for *Caroline or Change; Motown,* the Musical

Guy Braunstein (1995)—Concertmaster, Berlin Philharmonic (Zukerman Program)

Laura Hamilton (BM 1981, MM 1982, DMA 1984)—Principal Associate Concertmaster, Metropolitan Opera Orchestra

Alondra de la Parra (BM 2006, MM 2008)—Music Director, Queensland Symphony Orchestra

George Manahan (BM 1973, MM 1976)—Music Director of the American Composers Orchestra and the Portland Opera, former Music Director of the New York City Opera and Richmond Symphony; Grammy for Best Engineered Album, Classical

Simon O'Neill (MM 2000)—Heldentenor: Metropolitan Opera, Royal Opera House, Covent Garden, La Scala

Judith Blazer (BM 1977)—Broadway

Kirill Gerstein (BM 1999, MM 2000)—concert pianist

Alexandre Moutouzkine (MM 2003, PS 2005, AD 2006)—concert pianist

NEW ENGLAND CONSERVATORY

290 Huntington Avenue
Boston, MA 02115

Phone: (617) 585-1100
Website: necmusic.edu
Email: admission@necmusic.edu

Tuition: $$
Campus student enrollment: 750

Degree(s): BM, Undergraduate Diploma, MM, Graduate Diploma, DMA, and Artist Diploma
Concentrations: Strings: violin, viola, violoncello, double bass, guitar, harp; woodwinds: flute, oboe, clarinet, bassoon, saxophone; brass and percussion: horn, trumpet, trombone, tuba, percussion; keyboard instruments: piano, collaborative piano; jazz studies and improvisation: jazz performance/composition, contemporary improvisation; voice: vocal performance; historical performance; composition; music history; theoretical studies.

Audition requirement: Yes
Scholarships available: Yes, merit-based
Percentage of applicants accepted into the department per year: 30%
Number of faculty: 225
Department activities: Three full orchestras and chamber orchestra, two wind ensembles, full concert choir, chamber choir, jazz orchestra, jazz composers' orchestra, percussion ensemble, contemporary music ensembles, two fully staged opera productions plus numerous scene programs, small jazz ensembles, guitar ensembles, contemporary improv ensembles, Bach and historical ensembles.

Prominent Alumni:

Denyce Graves—opera singer

Regina Carter, violinist

Cecil Taylor—jazz pianist

Fred Hersch—jazz pianist

Vic Firth—percussionist

Richard Danielpour—composer

Sarah Jarosz—singer/songwriter

Lake Street Dive—multigenre band

Bernie Worrell—funk/rock musician

Coretta Scott King—singer and civil rights leader

THE NEW SCHOOL COLLEGE OF PERFORMING ARTS

Mannes School of Music
55 W. 13th Street
New York, NY 10011

Phone: (212) 229-5150
Website: newschool.edu/mannes
Email: performingarts@newschool.edu

Tuition: $$
Campus student enrollment: 150 students

Degree(s): Bachelor of Music
Majors: Orchestral instruments, piano, harpsichord, guitar, voice, orchestral conducting, composition, and theory

Audition requirement: Yes. Pre-screening required for select majors only.

Scholarships available: Yes

Number of faculty: 309

Percentage and number of applicants accepted into the department per year: Approximately 53%; 190 admitted annually

Department activities: Mannes Orchestra, Mannes Opera, Mannes Chorus, NewMusicMannes, Guitar Ensemble, Percussion Ensemble, Mannes Chamber Music Series, Chamber Music Concerts, Baroque Chamber Players, MACE—Mannes American Composers Ensemble, Mannes Theater Orchestra, iOrchestra, and Improvisation Ensemble.

Prominent Alumni:

Richard Goode

Murray Perahia

Mary Hammann

Nardo Poy

Bruce Revesz

David Ceratti

Yael Weiss

THE NEW SCHOOL COLLEGE OF PERFORMING ARTS

School of Jazz

55 W. 13th Street

New York, NY 10011

Phone: (212) 229-5150

Website: newschool.edu/jazz

Email: performingarts@newschool.edu

Tuition: $$

Campus student enrollment: 270 students

Degree(s): BFA in jazz and contemporary music; BA/BFA dual degree with Eugene Lang College of Liberal Arts

Concentrations: Instrumental performance, vocal performance

Audition requirement: Yes. Pre-screening required for all applicants.

Scholarships available: Yes

Number of faculty: 5 full-time, 63 part-time, 300 private lesson faculty

Percentage and number of applicants accepted into the department per year: Approximately 60%; 330 admitted annually

Department activities: 150+ concerts per year, annual participation in the Bern Jazz Festival, Winter Jazzfest, Jazz in the Square.

Prominent Alumni:

Peter Bernstein

Brad Mehldau

John Popper

Larry Goldings

Walter Blanding Jr.

Avishai Cohen

Jesse Davis

Rebecca Coupe Franks

Robert Glasper

Roy Hargrove

Susie Ibarra

Ali M. Jackson

Virginia Mayhew

Carlos McKinney

Shedrick Mitchell

Vickie Natale

Bilal Oliver

Jaz Sawyer

Alex Skolnick

E. J. and Marcus Strickland

PEABODY CONSERVATORY OF THE JOHNS HOPKINS UNIVERSITY

1 East Mount Vernon Place

Baltimore, MD 21202

Phone: (667) 208-6600

Website: www.peabody.jhu.edu

Email: admissions@peabody.jhu.edu

Tuition: $$
Campus student enrollment (undergraduate):
267

Degree(s): BM, MM, DMA, PC, AD, GPD, MA in in Audio Sciences
Concentrations: Brass (Trumpet, French Horn, Trombone, Tuba, Euphonium), Chamber Music, Composition, Computer Music, Conducting, Early Music, Guitar, Harp, Jazz, Music Education, Opera, Organ, Pedagogy, Percussion, Piano, Recording Arts and Sciences, Strings (Violin, Viola, Cello, Double Bass), Voice, Woodwinds (Flute, Piccolo, Clarinet, Saxophone, Oboe, Bassoon)
Audition requirement: Audition required
Number of faculty: 175
Department activities: Peabody Symphony Orchestra, Peabody Concert Orchestra, Peabody Modern Orchestra, Peabody Wind Ensemble, Peabody Singers, Peabody-Hopkins Chorus, Peabody Jazz Ensemble, Peabody Improvisation & Multimedia Ensemble, Peabody Renaissance Ensemble, Baltimore Baroque Band. Joint-degree program where students earn a bachelor's degree from both Peabody, Johns Hopkins University and Yong Siew Toh Conservatory of Music, National University of Singapore.

Prominent Alumni:
Andre Watts—pianist
James Morris and Richard Cassilly—vocalists of the Metropolitan Opera
Joe Byrd—jazz bassist
Dominick Argento—Pulitzer Prize–winning composer

UNIVERSITY OF CONNECTICUT

Department of Music
1295 Storrs Road
Unit 1012
Storrs, CT 06269–1012

Phone: (860) 486-3728
Website: music.uconn.edu
Email: music@uconn.edu

Tuition: $$$
Campus student enrollment (undergraduate):
18,826

Degree(s): BA, BM
Majors: Music, music history, jazz studies, music theory, performance (instrumental and vocal), composition
Audition requirement: Yes
Scholarships available: Yes, total of $240,310 available
Number of faculty: More than 40
Number of majors and minors: 157 majors, 47 minors
Percentage and number of applicants accepted into the department per year: 68%; 144 auditioned, 98 accepted
Department activities: Student, faculty and guest artist performances, Raymond and Beverly Sackler Music Composition Prize, partnership with the Metropolitan Opera and Alice Murray Heilig Memorial Concert.

UNIVERSITY OF MARYLAND

School of Music
2110 Clarice Smith Performing Arts Center
College Park, MD 20742

Phone: (301) 405-1313
Website: music.umd.edu
Email: musicadmissions@umd.edu

Tuition: $$
Campus student enrollment (undergraduate):
27,443

Degree(s): BA, BM, BM Education
Concentrations: Composition, jazz, music education, music theory, piano, strings, voice, winds and percussion
Audition requirement: Yes
Scholarships available: Yes; Director's Awards from $1,000 to $15,000 per year

Number of faculty: 100, including Guarneri String Quartet (artists in residence) and 16 members of the National Symphony Orchestra

Number of majors and minors: 225 undergraduates

Percentage and number of applicants accepted into the department per year: 35%, 125 undergraduates

Department activities: Ensembles, faculty and student recitalists present over 300 public performances each year with over 30 performance ensembles. Two main orchestras, three main jazz bands, three bands, marching band, six choirs, chamber music, etc.

Prominent Alumni:

Yoon Soo Shin (MM 2004)—New York City Opera performer

Dale Balthrop (BM 2002)—Principal Second Violin in the Street Paul Chamber Orchestra and member of Verklarte Quartet

Jay White (BM 1991)—soloist and member of Grammy-nominated Chanticleer vocal ensemble

Gordon Hawkins (BM 1982)—baritone opera singer

Chris Gekker (MM 1980)—trumpet player and UMD faculty member

Cristina Nassif (BM 1999)—Washington National Symphony Orchestra

UNIVERSITY OF ROCHESTER, EASTMAN SCHOOL OF MUSIC

26 Gibbs Street
Rochester, NY 14604

Phone: (585) 274-1000
Website: rochester.edu/Eastman/
Email: admissions@esm.rochester.edu

Tuition: $$$$
Campus student enrollment (undergraduate): 500

Degree(s): Certificate, BM, dual degrees with BA and BS offered through the University of Rochester

Concentrations: BM applied music (performance) composition, jazz studies and contemporary media, music education, musical arts, theory

Audition requirement: Yes

Scholarships available: Yes, all admitted undergraduates are offered scholarships

Number of faculty: 130

Department activities: Orchestras: Eastman Philharmonia and Philharmonia Chamber Orchestra, Eastman School Symphony Orchestra (freshman/sophomore), Eastman Studio Orchestra. Wind ensembles: Eastman Wind Ensemble, Eastman Wind Orchestra (freshman/sophomore). Choral emsembles: Eastman Chorale, Eastman Repertory Singers, Eastman-Rochester Chorus, Eastman Women's Chorus. Opera: Eastman Opera Theatre. Jazz: Eastman Jazz Ensemble, Eastman New Jazz Ensemble, Jazz Lab Band; Eastman Studio Orchestra. New music: Musica Nova, Ossia, World Music, Gamelan, Mbira Ensemble. Studio ensembles: Eastman Horn Choir, Eastman Marimba Ensemble, Eastman Percussion Ensemble, Eastman Trombone Choir, Tuba Mirum; Early Music Ensemble.

Prominent Alumni:

Renée Fleming—opera singer

Joyce Castle—opera singer

Pamela Coburn—opera singer

William Warfield—opera singer

Ron Carter—conductor

Chuck Mangione—conductor

Steve Gadd—conductor

Maria Schneider—conductor

John Fiore—conductor

Paul Freeman—conductor

Mitch Miller—conductor, oboist and record producer

Peter Mennin—composer

Dominick Argento—composer

Michael Torke—composer

Gardner Read—composer

Robert Ward—composer

Charles Strouse—composer (*Bye Bye Birdie; Annie*)
Alexander Courage—composer (*Star Trek; The Waltons*)
Alarm Will Sound
Break of Reality
Raymond Gniewek—former concertmaster of the Metropolitan Opera Orchestra
Richard Woitach—Met conductor and pianist
Mark Volpe—managing director of the Boston Symphony Orchestra
Doriot Anthony Dwyer—former principal flute of the Boston Symphony and one of the first women to be named a principal in a major American orchestra

Southeast

BRENAU UNIVERSITY

Department of Music
500 Washington Street SE
Gainesville, GA 30501

Phone: (770) 534-6234
Website: brenau.edu/fineartshumanities/music/
Email: admissions@brenau.edu

Tuition: $
Campus student enrollment: 3,500+

Degree(s): BA in music (which is achieved through music secondary track, pre-OT secondary track, pre-nursing secondary track, psychology secondary track, business secondary track, or mass communications); BA in music education
Concentrations: Vocal performance, collaborative piano, wind instruments, music education
Audition requirement: Yes
Scholarships available: Yes
Number of faculty: 9
Number of majors and minors: 22 majors

Prominent Alumni:
Kristin Clayton Knezevic—actress and soprano
Wong Xi—voice faculty, Macao Polytechnic Institute
Jie Pan—San Francisco Conservatory of Music
Portia Burns—Gainesville Middle School
Gabriel Lopez—founder and faculty of Passion Institute, Georgia

EAST CAROLINA UNIVERSITY

School of Music
Greenville, NC 27858

Phone: (252) 328-6851
Website: www.ecu.edu/cs-cfac/music
Email: Music@ecu.edu

Tuition: $
Campus student enrollment (undergraduate): 23,039

Degree(s): BM: Music Education; BM: Music (Performance, Therapy, Theory/Composition)
Concentrations: Performance, Choral or Instrumental Conducting, Sacred Music (organ), Suzuki Pedagogy, Vocal Pedagogy
Audition requirement: Yes
Number of faculty: 42 full-time
Department activities:
University Orchestra, Wind Ensemble, Symphonic Band, Concert Band (non-majors), Marching Band, Basketball Pep Band, Chamber Singers (mixed), Women's Choir, Men's Choir, Opera Theatre, Four Seasons Chamber Music Festival, NC New Music Initiative.

Prominent Alumni:
Loonis McGlohon—songwriter and pianist
Michael Haithcock—director of bands, University of Michigan
Mark Ford—director of percussion studies, University of North Texas
Velton Ray Bunch—Hollywood film/TV composer
Jeanne Smith Piland—mezzo–soprano

EMORY UNIVERSITY
Music Department
1804 North Decatur Road
Atlanta, GA 30322

Phone: (404) 727-6445
Website: .music.emory.edu
Email: music@emory.edu

Tuition: $$
Campus student enrollment (undergraduate): 7,803

Degree(s): BA in music
Concentrations: Performance, research (history and culture), composition

Audition requirement: Yes
Scholarships available: Yes, half-tuition music merit scholarships
Number of faculty: 18 full-time, 60 artist affiliates
Number of majors and minors: 120
Number of applicants accepted into the department per year: 40 new majors annually
Department activities: Wind ensemble, orchestra, concert choir, university chorus, chamber music, jazz ensembles, percussion ensemble, guitar ensemble, gamelan ensemble

FLORIDA ATLANTIC UNIVERSITY
Department of Music
777 Glades Road
Boca Raton, FL 33431

Phone: (561) 297-3820
Website: fau.edu/music/
Email: music@fau.edu

Tuition: $
Campus student enrollment (undergraduate): 25,471

Degree(s): BM, BA
Concentrations: Performance, music education, commercial music, jazz studies
Audition requirement: Yes
Scholarships available: Yes, over $100,000 awarded annually
Number of faculty: 18 full-time, 21 part-time
Number of majors and minors: Approximately 274
Department activities: There are many student performance ensembles, including university bands (Wind Ensemble, Symphony Band, FAU Marching Owls, Jazz Band, Concert Percussion Ensemble, Chamber Winds), instrumental ensembles (Symphony Orchestra, chamber music groups, chamber jazz groups, Brazilian Percussion Ensemble, Classical Guitar Ensemble, and Electric

Guitar Ensemble), as well as vocal ensemble performance opportunities.

GEORGIA STATE UNIVERSITY

School of Music
P.O. Box 4097
Atlanta, GA 30302–4097

Phone: (404) 413-5900
Website: music.gsu.edu
Email: music@gsu.edu

Tuition: $$
Campus student enrollment (undergraduate): 54,000

Degree(s): BM, BS
Concentrations: Composition, jazz studies, performance, music education, music recording technology, music management
Audition requirement: Yes
Scholarships available: Yes, University Scholar Award, $2,500 per year renewable up to four years. Additional scholarships available.
Number of faculty: 70
Number of majors and minors: 460 majors, 100 minors
Department activities: University Symphony Orchestra, Symphonic Wind Ensemble, Wind Orchestra, University Chamber Winds, four Chorus Ensembles, brass ensemble, Jazz Ensembles, New Music Ensemble, University Opera Theater Workshop, Harrower Summer Opera Workshop, University Brass Ensemble, Percussion Ensemble, Marching Band, Summer Jazz Program

Prominent Alumni:

Michael Anderson, BMu 1978, MM 1983, Music Education—Chair, Music Department, University of Illinois-Chicago

J. Lynn Thompson, BMu 1983, MM 1997, Instrumental Conducting—Music Director/Conductor, Atlanta Lyric Theatre

Peggy Benkeser, MM 1988, Percussion—cofounder of Thamyris (contemporary chamber ensemble); percussionist with Macon and Columbus Symphony Orchestras

Richard Clement, BMu 1989, Voice—tenor, soloist with major American orchestras and European opera houses

Peter Bond, BMu 1991, Trumpet—Assistant Principal Trumpet, Metropolitan Opera Orchestra

Nanette Soles, MM 1992, Voice—alto, soloist in concert and on recordings with Robert Shaw and the Atlanta Symphony Orchestra

Hee-Churl Kim, MM 1997, Choral Conducting—Conductor of World Vision Korea Children's Chorus, Korea Music Institute, Seoul, Korea

Karl Egsieker, BMu 1998, Music Technology—recording engineer, Southern Tracks Recording

Atlanta Kyong Mee Choi, MM 1998, Composition—internationally awarded composer; winner of the Luigi Russolo competition

Terrance McKnight, MM 1998, Piano—music programming for NPR's Performance Today, Washington, D.C.

Predrag Gosta, MM 2000, Voice/Choral Conducting—founder of New Trinity Baroque, an international ensemble specializing in music of the seventeenth and eighteenth centuries

Alisa McCance, BMu 2001, Music Technology—founder of RiverSage, a country/bluegrass band

Jim Stallings, MMu 2003, Composition—composer, commissioned by the Atlanta Symphony Orchestra for Symphony Street concerts

Magdalena Wor, BMu 2003, Voice—national finalist in the 2002 Metropolitan Opera Auditions; participant in San Francisco Opera Merola Program and the Placido Domingo Young Artists' program

John Samuel Roper, BMu 2004, Flute—Flute Faculty, Gustavus Adolphus College, St. Peter, Minnesota

Tanner Smith, BMu 2004, Recording Technology—Operations Manager, Atlanta Symphony Orchestra's Chastain and Pops Series

Coy Bowles, BMu 2004, Jazz Studies—member of

the Zac Brown Band (guitar, piano, organ), 2010 Grammy award winner, Best New Artist

JACKSONVILLE UNIVERSITY

Department of Music
Phillips College of Fine Arts
2800 University Blvd. N.
Jacksonville, FL 32211

Phone: (904) 256-8000
Website: ju.edu
Email: admissions@ju.edu

Tuition: $
Campus student enrollment (undergraduate):
2,949 on-campus; 4,048 including online students

Degree(s): BM, BME, BA, BS, BFA
Concentrations: Applied music, music business, commercial music, music performance, music theater, composition, jazz.
Audition requirement: Yes
Scholarships available: Yes, generous talent scholarships available based on audition
Number of faculty: 15 full-time, 14 part-time
Department activities: Chorale, University Singers, Men's and Women's Choirs, Opera/Music Theatre Workshop, University Orchestra, Wind Ensemble, Jazz Ensemble, Percussion Ensemble, Chamber Ensembles.

Prominent Alumni:
Frank Pace
Jay Thomas
William Forsythe
Bill Boston
Bob Moore
Jennifer Pascual

JAMES MADISON UNIVERSITY

School of Music
MSC# 7301
Harrisonburg, VA 22807

Phone: (540) 568-6197
Website: jmu.edu/music
Email: music_admit@jmu.edu

Tuition: $$
Campus student enrollment (undergraduate):
19,396

Degree(s): BM
Concentrations: Music education, performance, jazz, composition, music industry, music theater.
Audition requirement: Yes
Scholarships available: Yes, to outstanding music majors based on performing ability and availability of funds
Number of faculty: 47 full-time, 28 part-time
Number of majors and minors: 360 majors, 300 minors
Department activities: 140 concerts/performances, 140 student recitals, 21 guest artists/clinicians. Performance opportunities: Bach aria group, brass band, brass chamber ensembles, chamber orchestra, chorale, collaborative piano, Collegium Musicum, concert band, flute choir, guitar ensemble, horn choir, jazz chamber ensembles, jazz ensemble, KOR (men's choral ensemble), Madison Modern Music Ensemble, Madison Singers, Marching Royal Dukes, marimba orchestra, men's choir, Monticello Strings, musical theater, opera theater, opera/theater orchestra, percussion ensemble, steel drum bands, symphonic band, symphony orchestra, trombone choir, trumpet ensemble, tuba-euphonium ensemble, university chorus, wind symphony, women's choir, woodwind ensembles.

NEW WORLD SCHOOL OF THE ARTS

Music Division
300 NE 2nd Avenue
Miami, FL 33132

Phone: (305) 237-3622
Website: nwsa.mdc.edu
Email: nwsainfo@mdc.edu

Tuition: $
Campus student enrollment (undergraduate):
448

Degree(s): BM
Concentrations: Instrumental, Piano, Vocal, Composition
Audition requirement: Yes
Scholarships available: Yes
Number of faculty: 5 full-time, 21 part-time

UNIVERSITY OF NORTH CAROLINA SCHOOL OF THE ARTS

School of Music
Office of Admissions
1533 South Main Street
Winston-Salem, NC 27127

Phone: (336) 770-3290
Website: uncsa.edu
Email: admissions@uncsa.edu

Tuition: $
Campus student enrollment (undergraduate):
856 (includes all five conservatories)

Degree(s): BFA, BM, Undergraduate Arts Certificate
Concentrations: Brass (horn, trombone, trumpet, tuba/euphonium), composition, harp, guitar, organ, percussion, piano, strings (cello, double bass, viola, violin), voice, woodwinds (bassoon, saxophone, clarinet, flute, oboe)
Audition/portfolio requirement: Yes
Scholarships available: Yes

Number of faculty: 46 plus guest artists
Department activities: The symphony orchestra, cantata singers, jazz ensemble, wind ensemble, percussion ensemble, contemporary ensemble, opera workshop and chamber groups in every medium.

Prominent Alumni:

Lisa Kim—violin, New York Philharmonic
Ru-Pei Yeh—cello, New York Philharmonic
Stefan Jezierski—horn, Berlin Philharmonic
Rene Barbera—tenor, first prize, Placido Domingo's Operalia, Paris Opera, Lyric Opera of Chicago, Santa Fe Opera
Robert Oppelt—principal double bass, National Symphony
Stefan Jezierski—horn, Berlin Philharmonic
Ulla Jorgensen—principal flute, Danish Radio Symphony
Karl Mailand—trumpet, Army Band

UNIVERSITY OF MIAMI

Frost School of Music
PO Box 248165
Coral Gables, FL 33128–7610

Phone: (305) 284-2241 general;
(305) 284-6168 admission
Email: admission.music@miami.edu

Tuition: $$$
Campus student enrollment (undergraduate):
10,615

Degree(s): Bachelor of Music, Bachelor of Science, Bachelor of Arts, Master of Music, Master of Science, Master of Arts, Artist Diploma, DMA, PhD
Concentrations: Majors: classical performance (instrumental/vocal/keyboard); Studio Music & Jazz (instrument, keyboard, vocal); Composition; Media Writing & Production; Music Education; Music Therapy; Music Engineering Technology; Music Business & Entertainment

Industries, Musicianship, Artistry Development & Entrepreneurship.

Grad: Choral/Instrumental Conducting; Art Presenting; Studio Jazz Writing; Sound Recording Arts; Jazz Pedagogy; Keyboard Pedagogy; Musicology; Digital Arts & Sound Design; Vocal Pedagogy

Courses offered: Courses in all the above areas

Audition requirement: Yes

Number of faculty: Approximately 60 full-time

Department activities: The University of Miami has more than 50 performance ensembles, including Frost Symphony Orchestra, Henry Mancini Orchestra, Frost Symphonic Winds, Frost Wind Ensemble, University Band, Frost Chamber Orchestra, String Chamber Music, Stamps Quartet and Quintet, Brass Chamber Music, Woodwind Ensemble, Frost Concert Jazz Band, Front Salsa Orchestra, among others.

UNIVERSITY OF WEST GEORGIA

Music Department
1601 Maple Street
Carrollton, GA 30118

Phone: (678) 839-6516
Website: westga.edu/music
Email: musicdpt@westga.edu

Tuition: $
Campus student enrollment (undergraduate): 11,155

Degree(s): BM in music education, composition, performance, performance with emphasis in piano pedagogy, performance with emphasis in jazz studies, with elective studies in business

Audition requirement: Yes

Scholarships available: Yes

Number of faculty: 10 full-time, 10 part-time

Number of majors and minors: 97 majors, 41 minors

Prominent Alumni:
Jamie Lipscomb—Georgia Teacher of the Year
John LaForge—Fulton County Music Supervisor
Benjamin Pruett—Vocal/Choral Faculty at Emmanuel College

TOWSON UNIVERSITY

Department of Music
8000 York Road
Towson, MD 21252–0001

Phone: (410) 704-2839
Website: towson.edu/music
Email: mcriss@towson.edu

Tuition: $$
Campus student enrollment: 19,049

Degree(s): BM in composition or performance, BS in music education or music, minor

Concentrations: MUED vocal-general and instrumental; BM composition, guitar performance, jazz/commercial composition, keyboard, voice, winds/strings/percussion

Audition requirement: Yes

Scholarships available: Yes; some cover four years of tuition, and there are other competitive creative competitions for performance majors held each semester

Number of faculty: 31 full-time, 50 part-time

Number of majors and minors: 278 majors, 50 minors

Department activities: Symphonic orchestra, symphonic bands, marching band; commercial music ensemble, brass band, chamber music groups of various size and composition, jazz combos, big band, improvisation ensemble, vocal jazz ensemble, choral union, choral union society, men's and women's chamber choirs, opera and musical theater; more than 50 performing opportunities per year.

Prominent Alumni:

Eleanor Allen—orchestra director, Newburgh Enlarged City School District, Newburgh, NY

Steve Ashcraft—drummer, Peabody Ragtime Ensemble; performed at the Copenhagen Jazz Festival and recorded with Don Junker Big Band

James Bailey—Chorus Member, Baltimore Opera Company and the Washington National Opera Company

Sheldon Bair—founder and Music Director of the Susquehanna Symphony Orchestra

Antonio Barata—Associate Professor, Cal Poly State University

Elizabeth Borowsky—pianist; has performed as a soloist with orchestras in the U.S., Germany, Poland, China, and Israel

Art Bouton—Associate Professor of Saxophone and Woodwind Department Chair at the University of Denver's Lamont School of Music

Todd Butler—trumpet player; has performed with Little Feat, Bela Fleck, Lenny Pickett, Jackson Browne, Billy Bob Thornton, Ron Holloway, Sam Bush, Warren Haynes, Dana Carvey, David Spade, Robert Townsend, Jim Snidero, and the Drifters

Robert Carnochan—Director of Bands, University of Texas at Austin.

Gary Carr—instrumental music teacher, former Supervisor of Music, Baltimore Company

Glenn Cashman—assistant professor of Music, Colgate University, N.Y

Joe Corral—performed with Tony Bennett, Steve Allen, Liberace, Sammy Davis Jr., Gladys Knight, the Temptations, Joan Rivers, Diana Ross, Al Martino, Red Skelton, Ethel Ennis, Milton Berle, Bob Hope, Frankie Valli, and Stan Kenton

Ray Disney—founded the Baltimore Philharmonic Orchestra; toured the U.S. and Canada with the Admirals; currently owner and president of Sonority Records

David Donovan—U.S. Army Band and former music critic for the Baltimore *Sun*

Barbara Duke—instructor of Bassoon, Radford College, Roanoke, VA

Ellery Eskelin—tenor saxophonist. Tours regularly and has performed hundreds of concerts in the U.S., Canada, and throughout Europe

Tammy (Avery) Gibson—E-Flat clarinet player, Longwood Symphony Orchestra and New England Philharmonic, Boston, MA

Nicholas Karousatos—baritone; leading opera singer in New York

Pamela Kinney—mezzo-soprano; opera director and manager, southwest, Mexico and Washington DC

Jamie Lantz.—trumpeter, U.S. Air Force Band of the Golden West

Al Maniscalco—jazz saxophonist; has performed with Branford Marsalis, Chuck Mangione, the Temptations, Hal Linden, the Guy Lombardo Orchestra, the Shirelles, Little Anthony and the Imperials, and the Count Basie Orchestra

Dave Marowitz—formerly recorded arranger for Buddy Rich and his Big Band, played trombone for Lionel Hampton Big Band and many others; instrumental music teacher/band director in N.J. public schools for the past 27 years

Carol McDavit—soprano; international singing career in the U.S., South America, and Europe

Ed Nagel—Former Principal Horn, Air Force Band of Flight; founding member of Conversation Jazz Brass; United Musical Interments Performing Artist; currently Director of Bands at Fairborn High School in Ohio

Helen Nathan—full-time Director of Music and Liturgy at Street James Catholic Church in Mukwonago, WI

Phillips Peters—conductor, National High School Music Institute Orchestra, Northwestern University

Tommy Pitta—performs in the U.S. Navy Band and Jazz Ensemble in Annapolis

Kathy Quinlan—soprano, Broadway musical theater performer

Gil Rathel—lead trumpet for Don Ellis, Woody Herman, Frankie Valli, and Barry White; recorded "Oh What a Night"

Paul Roberts—principal bassoon in the U.S. Navy Band in Honolulu

Eddie Sanders—bassoon, U.S. Air Force Band in Washington, D.C.

Kathryn (McDougall) Scarbrough—active performer and on the Flute Faculty of David G. Hochstein Memorial School of Music and Dance Rochester, NY

William Terwilliger—violin teacher at the University of South Carolina

Louise Thompson—violin professor at Red Deer College, Red Deer, Canada

Tim Topper—baritone; television star, *Seven Wives for Seven Brothers*

Robert Tracy—Sudbrook Middle Magnet School, Baltimore County. Vocal Music

Mark Trautman—music director of Christ Church in New Brunswick, NJ

Steve Uibel—member of the Philly Pops.

Chris Walker—lead trumpet with the Commodores

Erin Wegner—soprano on Broadway and in regional musical theater

Sandy (Edmondson) Wieprecht—soprano; Director, Social Security Administration Chorus

UNIVERSITY OF ARKANSAS AT LITTLE ROCK

Department of Music
2801 South University Avenue
Fine Arts Building 164
Little Rock, AR 72204

Phone: (501) 569-3294
Website: ualr.edu/music
Email: jslane@ualr.edu

Tuition: $
Campus student enrollment (undergraduate): 10,900

Degree(s): BA; BM in Performance; BME
Concentrations:
BA: applied music, music history, music theory
BM in performance: winds, percussion, strings, piano, voice
BME: instrumental; vocal/choral
Audition requirement: Yes

Scholarships available: Yes
Number of faculty: 14 full-time, 10 part-time
Number of majors and minors: 55 majors; 20 minors
Department activities: Opera workshop, concert choir, gospel chorale, community orchestra, pep band, wind ensemble, percussion ensemble, guitar ensemble, jazz combo, community chorus, women's chorus, South India drum ensemble, chamber music for strings, jazz ensemble

UNIVERSITY OF CENTRAL ARKANSAS

Department of Music
201 Donaghey Avenue
Conway, AR 72035

Phone: (501) 450-3163
Website: uca.edu/cfac/music/
Email: music@uca.edu

Tuition: $
Campus student enrollment (undergraduate): 9,887

Degree(s): BA, BM
Concentrations: Brass, music education, percussion, piano, strings, theory/composition, voice, woodwinds
Audition requirement: Yes
Scholarships available: Yes, from $400 to $3,000
Number of faculty: More than 40
Number of majors and minors: Approximately 220
Department activities: Concert choir/chamber, university chorus, marching band, symphonic band, wind ensemble, opera, jazz band, symphony orchestra.

VIRGINIA COMMONWEALTH UNIVERSITY

Department of Music
922 Park Avenue
P.O. Box 842004
Richmond, VA 23284–2004

Phone: (804) 828-1166
Website: arts.vcu.edu
Email: music@vcu.edu

Tuition: $$$
Campus student enrollment (undergraduate):
31,242, School of the Arts 3,200

Degree(s): BM, BA, music minor
Concentrations: Classical, performance, jazz studies, music education
Audition requirement: Yes
Scholarships available: Yes, Dean's Scholarship of half in-state tuition; Provost's Scholarship of in-state tuition and most fees; President's Scholarship of in-state tuition, room, board, and most fees; audition scholarships and other one-time scholarships of various amounts through each department and the VCU Honors Program.
Number of faculty: 35 full-time, 44 part-time
Number of majors and minors: 246 majors, 22 minors
Percentage and number of applicants accepted into the department per year: 60%; 90 applicants accepted
Department activities: Mary Anne Rennolds Chamber Concerts (six concerts per year by world-class artists; with master classes), two wind ensembles, two jazz orchestras, symphony orchestra, two choral groups, small jazz and chamber ensembles, Opera Theatre, guitar ensemble, and pep band.

Prominent Alumni:
Julianna Evans Arnold—U.S. Air Force Band, Washington, D.C.
Dr. James Worman—Director of Bands, Trinity University in San Antonio, Texas

Dr. Daryl Kinney—assistant professor of music education, Kent State University
Katherine Strand—assistant professor of music education, Indiana University
Jennifer Gabrysh—oboist, U.S. Army Field Band
Pamela Armstrong—Metropolitan Opera
Steve Wilson—sax, Chick Corea's Origin
James Genus—bass, *Saturday Night Live* Band; recordings with Dave Douglas, Michael Brecker, Mike Stern, and John Abercrombie
Victor Goines—sax/clarinet, Lincoln Center Jazz Orchestra; Director, Juilliard Jazz Studies
Alvester Garnett—drums, recordings with Abbey Lincoln, Cyrus Chestnut, James Carter, Regina Carter
Mark Shim—sax, Blue Note recording artist, member of Terence Blanchard sextet
Al Waters—sax, featured with Ray Charles
Alvin Walker—trombone, Count Basie Orchestra
Clarence Penn—drums, Maria Schneider Orchestra, NY recording artist

WEST VIRGINIA UNIVERSITY

School of Music
College of Creative Arts
P.O. Box 6111
Morgantown, WV 26506–6111

Phone: (304) 293-5511
Website: music.wvu.edu/
Email: music@mail.wvu.edu

Tuition: $
Campus student enrollment (undergraduate):
22,827

Degree(s): BM, BA
Majors: 225
Minors: 120
Concentrations: Performance (piano pedagogy and jazz emphasis), music education, music BA, music therapy, music industry, composition, music history, music composition
Audition requirement: Yes

Scholarships available: Yes
Number of faculty: 44
Department activities: Trombone/Euphonium Club, Horn Club, Jazz Club, Kappa Kappa Psi, Music Teachers National Association, Music Educators National Conference, WVU Marching Band, Sigma Alpha Iota, Phi Mu Alpha Sinfonia.

Prominent Alumni:

Michael Albaugh—Director of Education for Jazz at Lincoln Center

Margaret (Peggy) Baer—flutist, principal flute, United States Navy Band

Michael Bays—member of the Navy Concert Band in Washington, D.C.

Kevin Beavers—Pris de Rome composition finalist; published composer; winner of ASCAP Awards, BMI Award and Ives Award from American Academy of Arts and Letters; Doctoral Fellow, University of Michigan; residencies at MacDowell Colony and Tanglewood

Stephen Beall—principal second violin in the South Carolina Philharmonic

Charles Burke—Music Director and Conductor of the Detroit Symphony Civic Orchestra and Director of Education for the Detroit Symphony Orchestra

Jay Chattaway—composer of music for *Star Trek Deep Space Nine*

Dan Cloutier—Principal Trombone Oregon Symphony

Mike Dawson—Managing Editor, *Modern Drummer* magazine

Matt Dubbs—public school band director and President of the Maryland Bandmasters Association

Brian Eldridge—principal clarinet, United States Field Band

Diana Foster—Director of Choral Activities at Andrew College

Ken Gale—singer with the Seattle Opera Company

Leslie Filben Garrett—public school music educator, Choral Director, Wheeling Park High School, Wheeling, West Virginia

Patrick Garrett—Music Education Faculty West Liberty University, Wheeling, West Virginia

Daniel Goff—saxophonist, member United States Field Band

Robert Hamrick—retired member of the Pittsburgh Symphony

Marcie Ley—European opera performer

John Locke—Director of Bands at University of North Carolina (Greensboro)

Heung Wing Lung—Artistic Director, Hong Kong Percussion Centre

Paul MacDowell—member of the Boston Pops

Alison Miller—NYC-based jazz drummer

John Neurohr—Associate Professor. Central Washington University

Ken Ozello—Director of Bands at University of Alabama

Jackie Picket—member of the Detroit Symphony Orchestra

Tean-Hwa P'ng—member of the faculty at Sedaya College in Malaysia

Jen Presar—instructor of horn and theory at Southern Illinois University

Jeff Price—saxophonist with the U.S. Army Field Band

Curtis Scheib—Chair of the music department at Seton Hill College (PA)

David Schmalenberger—Associate Professor of Music at University of Minnesota (Duluth)

Kurry Seymour—Director of Percussion and Assistant Director of Bands at Coastal Carolina University

Scott Simons—singer-songwriter

George Edward Stelluto—Associate Professor of Orchestras at Juilliard and winner of the Bruno Walter Memorial Prize

Christopher Tanner—Associate Professor of Music at Miami University of Ohio

David Torns—Music Director/Conductor of the Louisiana Youth Orchestra and violinist with the Baton Rouge Symphony Orchestra

James Valenti—winner of the Metropolitan Opera Auditions and internationally known opera tenor

Chad Winkler—trumpet, member of the Pittsburgh Symphony Orchestra

William Winstead—bassoonist and composer; principal bassoon, Cincinnati Symphony

Orchestra, and professor, Cincinnati College Conservatory of Music

Brian Wolfe—drummer/percussionist for Sharon Jones and the Dap-Kings

Midwest

CLEVELAND INSTITUTE OF MUSIC

11021 East Boulevard
Cleveland, OH 44106

Phone: (216) 791-5000
Website: cim.edu
Email: admission@cim.edu

Tuition: $$$
Campus student enrollment: 432

Degree(s): BM, undergraduate diploma
Concentrations: Audio recording, bass trombone, bassoon, cello, clarinet, composition, double bass, eurhythmics, flute, french horn, guitar (classical), harp, harpsichord, oboe, organ, percussion, piano, trombone, trumpet, tuba, viola, violin, voice (soprano/mezzo/tenor/baritone/bass)
Audition requirement: Yes
Scholarships available: Yes
Number of faculty: 182
Percentage and number of applicants accepted into the department per year: 32% admitted
Department activities: Concert series with over 125 concerts each year featuring CIM Orchestra, opera theater, faculty and visiting artists

Prominent Alumni:
More than 4,000 conservatory graduates represent all 50 states and 46 foreign countries. Thirty-five are members of the Cleveland Orchestra. CIM alumni perform with many of the world's most acclaimed organizations, including the New York Philharmonic, Boston Symphony Orchestra,

Chicago Symphony Orchestra, Philadelphia Orchestra and both the Metropolitan Opera and the Metropolitan Opera Orchestra. Our graduates also hold prominent teaching positions worldwide and serve as concertmasters for major symphonies.

DEPAUW UNIVERSITY

School of Music
605 S. College Avenue
Greencastle, IN 46135
Greencastle, IN 46135–0037

Phone: (800) 447-2495 or (765) 658-4118
Website: music.depauw.edu
Email: admission@depauw.edu or schoolofmusic@depauw.edu

Tuition: $$$
Campus student enrollment (undergraduate): 2,265

Degree(s): BM, BMA, BME, BA (through College of Liberal Arts), five-year BM/BA
Concentrations: Music performance, vocal performance, piano performance, organ performance, string, wind, brass, and percussion performance. BM: performance with a music/business emphasis; vocal performance, piano performance, organ performance, string, wind, brass and percussion performance. BMA: general music emphasis, double major, music/business emphasis. BME: choral/general music education emphasis, instrumental/general music education emphasis.
Audition requirement: Yes
Department activities: University bands, orchestras, choirs, opera theater, jazz ensembles, chamber music

GUSTAVUS ADOLPHUS COLLEGE

Department of Music
Admission Office
800 West College Avenue
Saint Peter, MN 56082

Phone: (800) 487-8288
Website: gustavus.edu
Email: admission@gustavus.edu

Tuition: $$$
Campus student enrollment (undergraduate):
2,353

Degree(s): BA
Concentrations: Music, music education
Audition requirement: Yes
Scholarships available: Yes
Number of faculty: 12 full-time, 23 part-time
Number of majors and minors: 51 majors,
17 minors
Department activities: 35 percent of student
body is involved in music at some point during four
years of study.

Prominent Alumni:

Diane Loomer—recipient of Order of Canada for
choral conducting and composition
Kurt Elling—Grammy winner in jazz performance
Steve Heitzeg—composer
Paula Lammers—jazz vocalist
Mark Thomsen—opera singer
Adam Rupp—founder of Home Free

ILLINOIS STATE UNIVERSITY

School of Music
Campus Box 5660—Music
Normal, IL 61790–5660

Phone: (309) 438-7631
Website: finearts.illinoisstate.edu/music
Email: music@illinoisstate.edu

Tuition: $$$$
Campus student enrollment (undergraduate):
18,427

Degree(s): BME, BM, BA, BS, minor, music jazz
minor
Concentrations: Music (liberal arts), music educa-
tion, music therapy, band and orchestral instru-
ment performance, classical guitar performance,
keyboard pedagogy and performance, voice
performance, music composition, music business.
Audition requirement: Yes
Scholarships available: Yes, tuition waiver,
variable grant amounts
Number of faculty: 56
Number of majors and minors: 400
**Percentage of applicants accepted into the
department per year:** 50%
Department activities: 300 performances
per school year; student organizations include:
Crescendo Music Therapy organization, Illinois
Music Educators Association, Delta Omicron, Phi
Mu Alpha, Sigma Alpha Iota, Tau Beta Sigma,
Music Business Student Association.

INDIANA UNIVERSITY

Jacobs School of Music
Office of Music Admissions
Merrill Hall 101
1201 East Third Street
Bloomington, Indiana 47405–7006

Phone: (812) 855-7998
Website: music.indiana.edu
Email: musicadm@indiana.edu

Tuition: $$
Campus student enrollment: 39,184

Degree(s): AS, BM, BM Education, BS. BM:
Composition, Early Music (instrumental empha-
sis), Early Music (vocal emphasis), Jazz Studies,
Performance (guitar, harp, orchestral instrument,

organ, piano, voice, woodwind instruments); BM Education: choral emphasis, general emphasis, instrumental—band, instrumental—string; BS: Music and an Outside Field (composition emphasis, jazz emphasis), Recording Arts; AS: Audio Engineering, String Instrument Technology

Number of faculty: 170 full-time

Audition requirement: Yes

Scholarships available: Yes

Department activities: 12 choral ensembles; 7 bands; 4 jazz ensembles; 6 orchestras; 3 other ensembles including new music ensemble, Baroque and classical orchestra and Latin American Music Ensemble.

Prominent Alumni:

More than 13,000 living alumni who perform in major orchestras and opera houses throughout the world:

Kenny Aronoff

Steve Fissel

Joshua Bell

Daniel Gaede

Chris Botti

Elizabeth Hainen

Ralph Bowen

Robert Hurst

Michael Brecker

Joan Jeanrenaud

Randy Brecker

Sylvia McNair

Angela Brown

Edgar Meyer

Andrés Cárdenes

Heidi Grant Murphy

Frederic Chiu

William Preucil

Hank Dutt

Michael Weiss

LAWRENCE UNIVERSITY

Conservatory of Music

711 E. Boldt Way

Appleton, WI 54911

Phone: (800) 227-0982

Website: lawrence.edu

Email: admissions@lawrence.edu

Tuition: $$

Campus student enrollment (undergraduate): Roughly 1,500

Degree(s): BA, BM, double-degree BA and BM (five-year program)

Concentrations: Majors within the BM are performance, music education (choral, general, and instrumental), theory, and composition. Theatre Department offers the BA with focuses in performance, design and technical theater, and dramatic theory, history, and literature.

Audition requirement: Students must audition for the BM or double degree.

Number of applicants accepted into the department per year: Approximately 420 applicants, roughly 240 admitted

Scholarships available: Yes; music scholarships available to BM and double-degree applicants from $15,000 to $23,000 based on audition; academic merit scholarships from $15,000 to $23,000.

Number of faculty: Approximately 63 faculty members

Number of majors and minors: 340 students

Department activities: Conservatory of Music: More than 20 ensembles with numerous performance opportunities. Most ensembles perform once or twice in each of the three terms. The Voice Department and Theatre Department collaborate on fully staged opera and musical theater productions each year.

Music-specific study abroad programs:

Milan: This program offers an opportunity to combine highly customized musical instruction with beginning and intermediate language study and area-studies courses.

Amsterdam: Music students may apply to the prestigious Amsterdam School of Music, which offers a highly individualized course of study both in classical and contemporary music.

Paris: Music students may pursue performance and/or content study at the École Normale de Musique de Paris/Alfred Cortot.

Vienna: Music students may choose to enroll in the Music Performance Workshop, combining individual music instruction with a German language course and three other courses selected from area studies, music history and music theory offerings.

London: Lawrence University flagship program (established in 1970). London Centre courses cover a range of areas including theater, music history, anthropology, history, government, and art history. Music students are able to arrange music lessons for credit.

Prominent Alumni:

Dale Duesing (1967)—Grammy award winner, operatic baritone

Campbell Scott (1983)—American actor, director, producer, and voice artist

Heidi Stober (2000)—opera: soprano

Garth Neustadter (2010)—film composer

NORTHERN ILLINOIS UNIVERSITY

School of Music
1425 Lincoln Highway
DeKalb, IL 60115–2528

Phone: (815) 753-1551
Website: niu.edu/music
Email: music@niu.edu

Tuition: $$$
Campus student enrollment (undergraduate): 16,552

Degree(s): BM, BA
Concentrations: Music education, performance, jazz studies
Audition requirement: Yes
Number of faculty: 60
Number of majors and minors: 350
Percentage and number of applicants accepted into the department per year: Varies
Department activities: Over 300 concerts and recitals per year; three choirs, three concert bands, marching and pep bands, three jazz bands, many small ensembles in all genres, steelband, world music. NIU students participate in a diverse array of award-winning instrumental and vocal ensembles, and many also take part in a number of world music performance activities. The school's ensembles include choirs, orchestra, concert and marching bands, large and small jazz ensembles, steelbands, early music ensemble, percussion ensemble, new music ensemble, Javanese and Balinese gamelans, tabla, Chinese, Middle Eastern, and Afro-Caribbean ensembles, various chamber music ensembles, and others. Each spring we stage a full opera in Boutell Memorial Concert Hall, and every year we host a world music festival and a new music festival. Throughout the year, we invite guest artists from the United States and beyond to perform and work with our students.

NORTHWESTERN UNIVERSITY

Bienen School of Music
70 Arts Circle Drive
Evanston, IL 60208

Phone: (847) 491-3141
Website: music.northwestern.edu
Email: musiclife@northwestern.edu

Tuition: $$$
Campus student enrollment (undergraduate): 8,000

Degree(s): BM, BA, BS, dual degree and ad hoc degree options

Majors: Performance (jazz studies, piano, strings, voice and winds and percussion), Music Cognition, Composition, Music Education (choral, general, and instrumental tracks), Theory, Musicology (historical and ethnomusicology tracks)

Minors: Arts Administration, Commercial Music, Musicology, Music Cognition, Composition, Music Criticism, Music Education, Music Technology, and Theory

Audition requirement: Yes

Scholarships available: Yes

Number of faculty: 59 full-time, 115 part-time

Number of majors and minors: 450 undergraduates

Department activities: Bienen School of Music ensembles include Bienen Contemporary/ Early Vocal Ensemble, Chamber Music, Chamber Orchestra, Contemporary Music Ensemble, Symphonic Band, Symphonic Wind Ensemble, Symphony Orchestra, University Chorale, Alice Millar Chapel Choir, Baroque Music Ensemble, Concert Band, Guitar Ensemble, Jazz Orchestra and Small Ensemble, Philharmonia, University Singers, Women's Choir, and Wildcat Marching Band.

Prominent Alumni:

Matthew Annin (G00)—principal horn, Milwaukee Symphony Orchestra

Ryan Beach (G12)—principal trumpet, Alabama Symphony

Victor A. Benedetti (90, G92)—baritone

Ethan Bensdorf (07)—acting associate principal trumpet, New York Philharmonic

Karin Bliznik (G08)—principal trumpet, Saint Louis Symphony

Evan Boyer (07)—bass

Nicole Cash (98)—associate principal hornist, San Francisco Symphony

Paul Corona (06)—bass-baritone

Orbert Davis (G97)—jazz trumpeter; bandleader

Ross deLuna (91)—English hornist, San Francisco Symphony

John Engelkes (G80)—bass trombonist, San Francisco Symphony

Martha Gilmer—CEO, San Diego Symphony Orchestra

David Govertsen (G10)—bass-baritone

Giancarlo Guerrero (G92)—conductor; music director, Nashville Symphony

Nancy Gustafson (G80)—soprano

Sheldon Harnick (49)—lyricist

Wiley Hausam (80)—artistic and executive director, The Broad Stage

Tim Higgins (04)—principal trombone, San Francisco Symphony

William James (04)—principal percussion, Saint Louis Symphony

Amanda Majeski (06)—soprano

Michael Martin (07, G08)—Boston Symphony Orchestra

Andrew Mason (03)—founder and chief executive officer, Groupon

Matthew Muckey (06)—acting principal trumpet of the New York Philharmonic

Jacob Nissly (05)—principal percussionist, San Francisco Symphony

Timothy Owner (G06)—acting associate principal trombone, San Francisco Symphony

Guy Piddington (01)—trumpeter, San Francisco Symphony

Howard Reich (77)—arts writer, Chicago *Tribune*

Rufus Reid (71)—jazz bassist

Jonathan Ring (83)—hornist, San Francisco Symphony

Ned Rorem (44)—composer

Jason Snider (97)—Boston Symphony Orchestra

Jeffrey Strong (G08)—second trumpet, Saint Louis Symphony

Genevieve Thiers (G04)—founder, SitterCity.com, ContactKarma.com

Augusta Read Thomas (87)—composer

Jessica Valeri (G98, G99)—hornist, San Francisco Symphony

Gail Williams (G76)—principal horn, Grand Teton Music Festival Orchestra; former principal horn, Chicago Lyric Opera Orchestra

Steve Woomert (12)—associate principal trumpet, Toronto Symphony Orchestra

OBERLIN CONSERVATORY OF MUSIC

Admissions Office
39 W. College Street
Oberlin, OH 44074–1588

Phone: (440) 775-8413
Website: oberlin.edu/con/admissions
Email: conservatory.admissions@oberlin.edu

Tuition: $$$$
Campus student enrollment (undergraduate):
Conservatory: 580; College: 2,300

Degree(s): BM, BA, performance diploma, double-degree program (BM/BA), artist diploma
Concentrations: Composition, historical performance, keyboard studies, musicology, piano, organ, strings, harp, classical guitar, vocal studies, woodwinds, brass, percussion, jazz performance, jazz composition, vocal accompanying, electronic music, music education, conducting.
Audition requirement: Yes
Scholarships available: Yes
Number of faculty: 100
Department activities: 500 concerts on campus each year, including performances by the more than 25 student ensembles and performances and master classes by guest artists

Prominent Alumni:

Jeremy Denk (1990)—pianist, winner of a 2013 MacArthur Fellowship, the 2014 Avery Fisher Prize, and Musical America's 2014 Instrumentalist of the Year award
Robert Spano (1983)—music director of the Atlanta Symphony Orchestra and Grammy Award winner
Jennifer Koh (1997)—concert violinist, winner of Musical America's 2016 Instrumentalist of the Year award
Denyce Graves (1985)—mezzo-soprano

Marie Lenormand (1999)—Grammy-winning mezzo-soprano
Alek Shrader (2007)—tenor
Dashon Burton (2005)—Grammy-winning bass-baritone, member of Room Full of Teeth
Claire Chase (2001)—flutist and founder of the International Contemporary Ensemble, 2012 MacArthur Fellow
eighth blackbird—contemporary music ensemble formed at Oberlin, multi-Grammy winning ensemble
Miró Quartet members Daniel Ching (1995), violinist, and Joshua Gindele (1997), cellist

OHIO NORTHERN UNIVERSITY

Department of Music
525 S. Main Street
Ada, OH 45810

Phone: (419) 772- 2156
Website: onu.edu/music
Email: r-casey@onu.edu

Tuition: $
Campus student enrollment (undergraduate):
2,401

Degree(s): BA in music with concentrations in music history/literature, music theory/composition or applied studies; BM in performance or BM in music education
Audition requirement: Yes
Scholarships available: Yes. Music Talent Awards, Presidential Scholarships, Trustee Scholarships, Dean's Scholarships, and Faculty Scholarships at varying amounts.
Number of faculty: 10 full-time, 21 part-time (Fall 2015)
Majors: 65 majors, 20 minors
Percentage and number of applicants accepted into the department per year: 41%, acceptance of 20–25 new majors each year
Department activities: 18 performing groups:

Symphony Orchestra, Wind Orchestra, Symphonic Band, Marching Band, Jazz Ensemble, Woodwind, Brass, Percussion and String Ensembles, Composer's Workshop Ensemble, Athletic Band, Steel Drum Band, University Singers, Women's Chorus, Men's Chorus, Chamber Singers, a cappella ensembles, various chamber music groups, and Opera Workshop. Wind Orchestra, University Singers, Marching Band each tour internationally on a three-year rotation.

Prominent Alumni:
Robert Klotman (1940)—past president of MENC and the American String Teachers Association
Lloyd Butler (2000)—founding director of the Chicago Pops Orchestra
Mark Blowers (2013)—professional actor and New York City choreographer for Marilyn Exposed
Michael Oberhauser (2007)—composer, premiered at Kennedy Center for the Performing Arts
Dr. Gregory Decker (2005)—assistant professor of music theory at Bowling Green State University
Andrew Schultz (2006)—director of music programs at Defiance (Ohio) College
Lindsey Newlove (2010)—music teacher at Crestview (Ohio) Local Schools, recipient of the Ohio Music Education Association Outstanding Music Educator of the Year Award
Nathan Singer (2015)—double major in engineering and music at ONU, computer engineer at Cooper Tire & Rubber Company (Findlay, Ohio), and private piano studio instructor
Tyler Graves (2011)—freelance performer and educator in Cincinnati
Jeffrey Martin (2013)—full-time instructor of Steel Drum Bands at Clark Montessori School in Cincinnati

UNIVERSITY OF MICHIGAN

School of Music, Theatre & Dance
2290 Moore Building
1100 Baits Drive
Ann Arbor, MI 48109–2085

Phone: (734) 764-5112
Website: music.umich.edu
Email: music.admissions@umich.edu

Tuition: $$$$
Campus student enrollment (undergraduate): 28,312

Degree(s): BM, BMA, BFA, BS, BTA
Concentrations: BM: composition, music and technology, music education, music theory, musicology, performance and performance with teacher certification. BMA: multidisciplinary studies, performance. BFA: interarts performance, jazz and contemplative studies, jazz and contemporary improvisation, jazz studies, musical theater, performing arts technology, theater design and production, theater performance in acting or directing. BS: sound engineering.
Audition requirement: Yes
Scholarships available: Yes; merit-based, need-informed awards available in all areas at the freshman level except theater, from $1,500 to full tuition
Number of faculty: 176
Number of majors and minors: 800
Percentage of applicants accepted into the department per year: 30 percent
Department activities: More than 450 concerts, recitals and main stage productions.

Prominent Alumni: Alumni are found in nearly every major orchestra, opera company, and Broadway production. They are also prominent members of faculty at major universities and conservatories in the United States and abroad.

SAINT MARY'S UNIVERSITY OF MINNESOTA

Music Department
700 Terrace Heights #1460
Winona, MN 55987

Phone: (507) 457-1513
Website: smumn.edu/music
Email: jheukesh@smumn.edu

Tuition: $
Campus student enrollment: 1,758

Degree(s): BA, BA in Music and a Master of Arts in Instruction for students who intend to pursue a teaching licensure.
Concentrations: Music, music industry, music education (vocal, instrumental), music performance (instrumental, piano, strings, voice)
Audition requirement: Yes
Scholarships available: Yes; Street Cecelia Music Scholarships avg. $1,000 per year
Number of faculty: 4 full-time, 16 part-time
Number of majors and minors: 26 majors, 7 minors
Department activities: Chamber orchestra, concert band, wind ensemble, concert choir, chamber singers, women's choir, percussion ensemble, jazz ensemble, multiple jazz combos. Approximately 50 student, faculty, and ensemble performances per year, including domestic and international touring by performing ensembles.

TRINITY INTERNATIONAL UNIVERSITY

Music Department
2065 Half Day Road
Deerfield, IL 60015

Phone: (847) 317-7035
Website: tiu.edu/music
Email: music@tiu.edu

Tuition: $
Campus student enrollment (undergraduate): 793

Degree(s): BA
Concentrations: Music education/K–12; music with emphases in arts administration, contemporary music, music and missions, church music, piano pedagogy, performance, music and psychology, theory/composition.
Audition requirement: Yes
Scholarships available: Yes, $315–full tuition
Number of faculty: 3 full-time, 20 adjuncts
Number of majors and minors: 22 majors, 4 minors
Percentage and number of applicants accepted into the department per year: About 6 percent of the university is composed of music students. This includes all those on music scholarship. There are many other students involved in ensembles, lessons, etc., that are not part of the music department any other way. About 10 new students were added on scholarship to the music department this past year. About half of the students are actual majors. There is no set limit on number of applicants accepted per year.
Department activities: Symphonic band, concert choir, philharmonic orchestra, string ensemble, jazz ensemble, men's ensemble, guitar ensemble, string quartet, opera/music theater. Approximately 30 student, faculty, and ensemble performances per year, including domestic and international touring by performing ensembles.

UNIVERSITY OF MISSOURI–KANSAS CITY

Conservatory of Music and Dance
4949 Cherry Street
Kansas City, MO 64110

Phone: (816) 235-2900
Website: conservatory.umkc.edu
Email: cadmissions@umkc.edu

Tuition: $$
Campus student enrollment: 16,699

Degree(s): BA, BFA, BME, BM
Concentrations: Composition, jazz studies, music theory, performance, choral, instrumental, dance, music, music therapy, conducting, musicology, music education/music therapy
Audition requirement: Yes
Scholarships available: Yes
Number of faculty: Approximately 80
Number of majors and minors: Approximately 600 students
Percentage and number of applicants accepted into the department per year: Varies
Department activities: Dance company, orchestras, wind ensembles, chamber ensembles, choral ensembles, operas, jazz ensembles, percussion ensembles, string quartets, woodwind and brass quintets, musical theater.

WESTERN MICHIGAN UNIVERSITY

Department of Music
1903 W. Michigan Avenue
Kalamazoo, MI 49008

Phone: (269) 387-2572
Website: wmich.edu/music
Email: ask-wmu@wmich.edu

Tuition: $$$
Campus student enrollment (undergraduate): 18,567

Degrees: BA, BM, BM in Education
Concentrations: Instrumental, orchestral, and choral/general, music therapy, composition, performance (instrumental, keyboard, vocal, jazz studies)
Courses:
Choral music: choral music methods, choral conducting, classroom instruments, K–12 content literacy, human development

Composition: composition I and II, counterpoint, orchestration, 4-course sequence in electronic music, composition seminar
Instrumental music education: instrumental music methods, instrumental conducting, instrumental pedagogy, K–12 content literacy, human development
Jazz studies: Jazz improvisation, jazz arranging, jazz composition, jazz history and literature, jazz aural skills
Multimedia arts technology: 4-course sequence in recording technology, 4-course sequence in electronic music, computer music, digital video concepts, audio for video
Music therapy: 4-course sequence in clinical practicum, psychology of music, therapy activities for children and adults, clinical internship
Scholarships available: Yes
Acceptance rate: 1 in 3 applicants
Number of full-time faculty: 43
Number of majors and minors:
Composition: 23 students
Choral music education: 47 students
Instrumental music education: 83 students
Jazz studies: 35 students
Multimedia arts technology: 65 students
Music therapy: 65 students
Honors and awards: Over 150 student DownBeat awards since 1984, ranking WMU among the top three collegiate award winners in the nation since that time. Recent appearances: Gold Company (vocal jazz ensemble) at Choralies Festival, Advanced Jazz Ensemble at Monterey NextGen Jazz Festival

Prominent Alumni:
Jennifer Shelton Barnes—arranger and recording artist
April Arabian Tini—arranger and faculty, Wayne State University
Xavier Davis—Michigan State University faculty
Shawn "Thunder" Wallace—Ohio State University faculty
Greg Jasperse—recording artist, arranger, and Western Michigan University faculty

West

CALIFORNIA INSTITUTE OF THE ARTS

School of Music
24700 McBean Parkway
Valencia, CA 91355

Phone: (661) 253-7816
Website: calarts.edu
Email: info@music.calarts.edu

Tuition: $$$
Campus student enrollment (undergraduate): 1,471

Degrees offered: BFA
Programs: Composition, performer/composer, jazz, musical arts, voice arts, instrumental arts (winds/brass/strings/harp/piano/keyboard/guitar/percussion/voice); music technology: Interaction, Intelligence & Design (MTIID); world music performance (world music/African music and dance/Balinese and Javanese music and dance/North Indian music/world percussion).
Audition required: Yes
Scholarships available: Yes
Number of faculty: 75
Number of applicants: 475
Acceptance rate: 50%
Number of students: 280
Department activities: Over 250 concerts a year; jazz bands, orchestra, conducted ensembles, small ensembles, opera, world music performances, interdisciplinary projects.

Prominent Alumni:
Ralph Alessi
James Carney
Ravi Coletrane
Julia Holter

CORNISH COLLEGE OF THE ARTS

Music Department
1000 Lenora Street
Seattle, WA 98121

Phone: (800) 726-ARTS
Website: cornish.edu
Email: admission@cornish.edu or music@cornish.edu

Tuition: $
Campus student enrollment (undergraduate): 720

Degree(s): BM
Concentrations: Jazz, instrumental and vocal performance, and composition.
Audition requirement: Yes
Scholarships available: Yes,
Number of faculty: 37 music faculty
Number of majors/students in department: 99 (2015–16)
Number of applicants accepted into the department per year: Approximately 35 slots are open annually for new and transferring students.
Department activities: Student performers and composers are presented in noon concerts, studio labs, the Scores of Sound Music Marathon, end-of-semester presentations (juries), Junior and Senior recitals and other special performance activities. Additionally, many opportunities exist to represent Cornish in community-based performances and at local jazz clubs. Student composers also work with Dance, Film+Media, and Theater departments and music students may perform as part of exhibitions and performances mounted by the visual or performing arts departments.

Prominent Alumni:
Mary Lambert—songwriter/activist
Catherine Harris-White (aka SassyBlack)—singer/actor/hiphop artist
Eyvind Kang—jazz composer
Reggie Watts—musician

MILLS COLLEGE

Music Department
5000 MacArthur Boulevard
Oakland, CA 94612

Phone: (510) 430-2171
Website: mills.edu/undergrad
Email: admission@mills.edu

Tuition: $$
Campus student enrollment: 1,345

Degree(s): BA
Concentrations: Students majoring in music can choose from five areas of emphasis: performance; music and culture; theory and history; composition; or composition with an emphasis in media technology or electronic music.
Courses offered: The Music Department at Mills is internationally respected as a leader in electronic and computer music, the recording arts, and experimental music. Students delve into a wide variety of styles and repertory while exploring music in the broader context of global history and culture. Sample courses include:
African American Music: The Meaning and the Message; Classical and Romantic Music; Cross-Currents in Rock Music; Exploring Music: Performance, Creation, and Cultural Practice; Film Music: Mood and Meaning; Individual Instruction in Performance and Composition; Intermedia Collaborations; Introduction to Computer Music; Introduction to Electronic Music; Mills College Choir; Music Instrument Building; Musics of the World: The Pacific, Asia, and India; Sound Art; Sound Techniques of Recording; The World of Opera; Women, Gender, and Musical Creativity
Audition requirement: Applicants are not required to audition as part of the Mills undergraduate admission process. Students who wish to be considered for the Barbara Hazelton Floyd or Carroll Donner Scholarships in Music are required to complete an audition.
Scholarships available: Barbara Hazelton Floyd Scholarships in Music for up to $10,000. Carroll Donner Scholarships in Music for up to $8,000. Merit and need-based scholarships from Mills can total up to $26,000 for first-year students and up to $17,000 for transfer students. More than 80% of our incoming students receive some form of financial aid. Visit mills.edu/cost-and-aid for more information.

Number of faculty: 8
Number of majors and minors: 17 music majors, 2 music minors
Department activities: Gamelan ensemble, African drumming ensemble, early vocal music ensembles (2), early instrument ensembles (2), Music Improvisation Ensemble I, Vocal Jazz Improvisation Ensemble, the Mills Percussion Group and the Contemporary Performance Ensemble perform at least once per semester. All music students can also work at the Center for Contemporary Music at Mills, a world-renowned facility for electronic and computer music and recording facilities. The Performance Collective at Mills performs at least three times per semester. Additionally, performance students perform in two noon concerts and/or one Showcase Concert per semester. The student-run Thursday Night Special concerts are held every other week. Students are often asked to perform composition students' works several times per semester and are at times invited to perform in our Concert Series. A senior concert is required of performance majors at undergraduate level, and participation in the X Sound Undergraduate Festival is required of composers.

Prominent alumni:
Elinor Armer—composer, San Francisco Conservatory of Music
Steve Bissinger—film sound designer, sound effects editor
Julia Christensen—author, multidisciplinary artist
Jennifer Curtis—Juilliard graduate, violinist and mandolinist
Paul DeMarinis—multimedia artist
Janice Giteck—composer, Cornish Institute

Holly Herndon—composer, musician, and sound artist
Miya Masaoka—kotoist and conceptual artist
Rebeca Mauleón—musician, composer, author, and educator
Amy X Neuburg—composer, vocalist, live electronics performer
Steve Reich—Pulitzer Prize–winning composer
Tara Rodgers—author, award-winning composer and sound artist
Laetitia Sonami—electronic performer and sound installation artist
Morton Subotnick—electronic music pioneer
Willow Williamson—film composer

SAN FRANCISCO CONSERVATORY OF MUSIC

50 Oak Street
San Francisco, CA 94102

Phone: (415) 503-6231
Website: sfcm.edu
Email: admit@sfcm.edu

Tuition: $$
Campus student enrollment (undergraduate): 157

Degree(s): BM
Concentrations: Classical music performance, early music, composition, technology and applied composition
Audition requirement: Yes
Scholarships available: Yes
Number of faculty: 100+

Prominent Alumni:
Eleazar Rodriguez, tenor (2010)—IMG Artists
Gyan Riley (2001)—guitar
Elza van den Heever (2002)—soprano
Jeffrey Strong (2006)—second trumpet at St. Louis Symphony Orchestra
Teddy Abrams (2005)—music director/conductor of Louisville Orchestra

Achilles Liarmakopoulos (2005)—trombone, Canadian Brass Quintet
Hai-ye Ni (1992)—principal cellist at Philadelphia Orchestra

SAN DIEGO STATE UNIVERSITY

School of Music and Dance
5500 Campanile Drive
San Diego, CA 92182–7902

Phone: (619) 594-3061
Website: music.sdsu.edu
Email: musicdance@mail.sdsu.edu

Tuition: $
Campus student enrollment (undergraduate): 28,334

Degree(s): BA in music, BM in music
Concentrations: Performance, music education, jazz studies, composition, general music, professional studies—enterpreneurship & business, recording technology, and audio design
Audition requirement: Yes
Scholarships available: Yes, approximately $200,000 annually
Number of faculty: Full-time music: 15, part-time music: 30
Number of majors and minors: 255 music majors
Percentage of applicants accepted into the department per year: 65%

SCRIPPS COLLEGE

Music Department
1030 Columbia Avenue
Claremont, CA 91711–3948

Phone: (909) 607-3266
Website: scrippscollege.edu/departments/Music
Email: music@scrippscollege.edu

Tuition: $$$$
Campus student enrollment (undergraduate): 973

Degree(s): BA
Concentrations: (1) history, theory, composition, (2) ethnomusicology, (3) performance
Audition requirement: No
Scholarships available: Six scholarships totaling approximately $51,000 are available annually to music students with financial need based on the recommendation of the music faculty.
Number of faculty: 4 full-time, 7 part-time
Number of majors and minors: First Major = 5 students; Second Major = 4 students; First Minor =3 students; Second Minor = 0 students
Department activities: Concert choir, chamber choir, joint student faculty gala recitals, joint music-language department programs

Prominent Alumni:

Marsha Genensky—member, Anonymous 4, Grammy Award–winning medieval vocal group
Marjorie Merryman—Head of Theory and Composition, School of Music, Boston University
Linda Horowitz—resident conductor, State Theater, Kassel, Germany
Sharon Baker—vocal soloist, Boston Baroque, Handel and Haydn Society
Kazuko Hayami—concert pianist and recording artist

SOUTHERN METHODIST UNIVERSITY

Meadows School of the Arts
Division of Music
P.O. Box 750356
Dallas, TX 75275–0356

Phone: (214) 768-3680
Website: meadows.smu.edu
Email: music@smu.edu

Tuition: $$$$

Campus student enrollment (undergraduate): 6,391

Degree(s): BA, BM
Concentrations: Performance, music education, music therapy, composition
Audition requirement: Yes
Scholarships available: Yes. Academic merit scholarships available through SMU admissions process. Artistic merit scholarships available based on audition or portfolio evaluation. Scholarship amounts vary.
Number of faculty: 91
Number of majors and minors: 200
Percentage and number of applicants accepted into the department per year: 36%, 408 auditions
Department activities: Wind ensemble, symphony orchestra, opera, choral ensemble, jazz ensemble, world music; ensembles perform 4–12 times per year, guest artists, internships.

Prominent Alumni:

Alessio Bax (AC Piano, 1996, MM Piano, 1998)—Leeds Competition first prize, Lincoln Center; Chamber Music Society, performances with major symphony orchestras worldwide
Clifton Forbis (MM Voice, 1990)—tenor, Metropolitan Opera, San Francisco, Tokyo, Köln, Seattle Opera, Chicago Lyric, La Scala, Paris Opera, Brussels and other top U.S. and European opera companies and symphonies; voice professor, Southern Methodist University
Kimberly Grigsby (BM Piano, 1991)—Broadway musical conductor/director, *Spring Awakening, Grease, Caroline or Change, Spider-Man: Turn Off the Dark,* and Others
Michelle Merrill (BM Music Education 2006; MM Music Education and MM Conducting 2012)—Assistant Conductor, Detroit Symphony Orchestra

STANFORD UNIVERSITY

Department of Music, Braun Music Center
541 Lasuen Mall
Stanford, CA 94305–3076

Phone: (650) 725-1932
Website: music.stanford.edu
Email: ugmusicinquiries@stanford.edu

Tuition: $$$
Campus student enrollment (undergraduate):
6,994

Degree(s): BA
Concentrations: Performance; musicology/theory; composition; conducting; music, science and technology
Audition requirement: Not required, but strongly encouraged as a supplement to the application for students with extraordinary ability and experience in music composition, conducting, or performance.
Scholarships available: All financial aid at Stanford is need-based only. Students whose family income is $65,000/year or less are expected to pay nothing toward tuition, room, or board. Students whose family income is $125,000/year or less are expected to pay nothing toward tuition. Over 70% of Stanford undergraduate students receive financial aid.
Percentage and number of applicants accepted into the department per year: Students apply to the university, not to the Department of Music. Applicants for the class entering in 2016: 43,997. Applicants admitted for the class entering in 2016: 2,063. Admission rate: 4.69%.
Number of majors and minors: Average of 45 majors, 12 minors

UNIVERSITY OF ALASKA ANCHORAGE

Music Department
3211 Providence Drive
Anchorage, AK 99508

Phone: (907) 786-1766
Website: uaa.alaska.edu/music
Email: narose@uaa.alaska.edu

Tuition: $
Campus student enrollment (undergraduate):
19,487

Degree(s): BA with Emphasis in Music; BM with two tracks including Performance and Music Education
Audition requirement: Yes
Number of faculty: 20
Number of majors and minors: 157.
Department activities: Ensembles: Guitar Ensemble, Jazz Ensemble, Opera Ensemble, Percussion Ensemble, University Sinfonia, University Singers, Wind Ensemble.

UNIVERSITY OF CALIFORNIA, RIVERSIDE

Department of Music
Riverside, CA 92521

Phone: (951) 827-3343
Website: music.ucr.edu
Email: PAadvising@ucr.edu

Tuition: $$$$
Campus student enrollment (undergraduate):
18,607

Degree(s): BA
Concentrations: Composition, musicology, ethnomusicology, music education
Audition requirement: No
Scholarships available: Yes, Chancellor's Performance Award, up to $2,250

Number of faculty: 10 academic faculty, 14 lecturers, 23 instructors

Number of majors and minors: 40 majors, 15 minors

Department activities: More than 50 concerts per year.

UNIVERSITY OF OREGON

School of Music
Undergraduate Office
1225 University of Oregon
Eugene, OR 97493–1225

Phone: (541) 346-3761
Website: music.uoregon.edu
Email: SOMDAdmit@uoregon.edu

Tuition: $$
Campus student enrollment (undergraduate): 20,797

Degree(s): BA, BS, BM
Concentrations: Composition, music education, jazz studies, performance, history/literature, music theory, popular music studies, general music, music technology
Audition requirement: Yes
Scholarships available: Yes, $1,000 to $25,000
Number of faculty: 60
Number of majors and minors: 250 undergraduate majors, 230 undergraduate minors
Department activities: 200 musical events annually, including opportunities for nonmajors to perform.

UNIVERSITY OF SOUTHERN CALIFORNIA

Thornton School of Music
University Park Campus
Los Angeles, CA 90089–0851

Phone: (213) 740-8986
Website: music.usc.edu
Email: uscmusic@usc.edu

Tuition: $$$$
Campus student enrollment (undergraduate): 19,000

Degree(s): Bachelor of Arts (BA), Bachelor of Music (BM), Bachelor of Science (BS)
Concentrations: BA: Music, Jazz Voice, Choral Music
BM: Classical and Popular Music Performance (instrumental and vocal), Jazz Studies (instrumental only), Composition, Music Production
BS: Music Industry
Audition requirement: Varies by program (see website for details)
Scholarships available: Varies by program (see website for details)
Department activities: Instrumental Ensembles: USC Thornton Symphony, USC Thornton Wind Ensemble, Edge Contemporary Music Ensemble, Early Music Ensemble, Percussion Ensemble, Jazz Orchestra, ALAJE (Afro Latin American Jazz Ensemble), Guitar Ensemble, Chamber Ensembles. Vocal/Choral Ensembles: Chamber Choir, Concert Choir, Thornton Opera, Apollo Men's Chorus, Oriana Women's Choir, University Chorus, Vocal Jazz Ensembles, Vocal Chamber Ensembles.

Prominent Alumni:

Dale Warland—choral director and conductor
Michael Tilson Thomas—music director, San Francisco Symphony
Morten Lauridsen—composer
Marilyn Horne—soprano
Michelle Kim—assistant concertmaster, New York Philharmonic

Elizabeth Rowe—principal flute, Boston Symphony Orchestra

The Calder Quartet: Eric Beyers, Andrew Bulbrook, Benjamin Jacobson and Johnathan Moerschel

Andrew Lowy—second clarinet, Los Angeles Philharmonic

Sunny Yang—cellist, Kronos Quartet

UNIVERSITY OF WASHINGTON

School of Music
Box 353450
Seattle, WA 98195–3450

Phone: (206)543-1201
Website: music.washington.edu
Email: somadmit@u.washington.edu

Tuition: $$$
Campus student enrollment (undergraduate):
31,063

Degree(s): BA, BM
Concentrations: Composition, classical guitar, jazz, studies, orchestral instruments, organ, piano, strings, voice, music theory, music history, music education, ethnomusicology, American music studies.
Audition requirement: Audition required for all majors except ethnomusicology, composition, and American music studies. Ethnomusicology, Composition, and American Music Studies require prerequisite classes and application process.
Scholarships available: Yes
Number of faculty: 57
Majors: 130 undergraduate majors, 150 minors
Percentage of applicants accepted into the department per year: 53%
Department activities: Over 200 concerts and recitals are presented each year by the School of Music.

UNIVERSITY OF NORTHERN COLORADO

School of Music
Frasier Hall 108
Greeley, CO 80639

Phone: (970) 351-2993
Website: arts.unco.edu/music
Email: music@unco.edu

Tuition: $
Campus student enrollment (undergraduate):
9,424

Degree(s): BA, BM, BME
Concentrations:
BA (liberal arts emphasis)
BM (instrumental performance emphasis)
BM (composition emphasis)
BM (jazz studies emphasis)
BM (piano emphasis)
BM (vocal performance emphasis)
BM (business)
BME (instrumental music K–12 teaching emphasis)
BME (vocal, piano and general music K–12 teaching emphasis)
Music Technology Certificate
Audition requirement: Yes
Scholarships available: Yes, amounts vary
Number of faculty: 45 full-time, 29 part-time
Number of majors and minors: 532 music majors, 53 music minors
Percentage of applicants accepted into the department per year: 72%
Department activities: UNC/Greeley Jazz Festival, Western States Honor Orchestra Festival, Colorado All-State Band Festival, Colorado Piano Festival.

UNIVERSITY OF COLORADO AT BOULDER

College of Music
Campus Box 301
Boulder, CO 80309–0301

Phone: (303) 492-6352
Website: colorado.edu/music
Email: ugradmus@colorado.edu

Tuition: $$$
Campus student enrollment: 32,775

Degree(s): BA, BM, BME, certificate programs
Concentrations: classical performance; jazz performance; composition; music education; musicology; certificates in jazz studies, music technology, and music entrepreneurship
Audition requirement: Yes
Scholarships available: Yes
Number of faculty: 90
Number of majors and minors: 300 majors, no minors

Prominent Alumni:

Dave Grusin: (BM 1956)—Grammy and Academy Award–winning composer, arranger, and producer
Cynthia Lawrence (BM 1983; MM 1986)—professional opera singer, frequent duet partner of Luciano Pavarotti
Tim Cooper (MM, 1977)—Musical Director for the Excalibur and Luxor Hotels, Las Vegas
Leenya Rideout (BM, 1991)—Broadway

UNIVERSITY OF HAWAII AT MANOA

Music Department
2411 Dole Street
Honolulu, HI 96822

Phone: (808) 956-7756
Website: hawaii.edu/uhmmusic
Email: uhmmusic@hawaii.edu

Tuition: $$
Campus student enrollment (undergraduate): 14,126

Degree(s): BA, BM, BEd
Audition requirement: Yes
Scholarships available: Yes
Number of faculty: 22 full-time, 31 part-time
Number of majors and minors: 124 majors, 50 minors
Department activities: The Music Department at the University of Hawaii at Manoa offers a wide variety of performing classes. In addition to its large wind, orchestral, and vocal ensembles, there are many opportunities for students to enroll in classes that focus on scenes from opera and musicals, jazz, chamber literature, new music, guitar, brass, and saxophone.

The unique feature of this department is its wealth of performing ensembles representing cultures from Asia and the Pacific. Hawaii is strongly represented through classes in hula and chant, slack key guitar, choral singing, and "string band" (singing Hawaiian songs with ukulele and guitar). Pacific cultures are represented by the Samoan and Tahitian ensembles, and Asian cultures by the Chinese ensemble, Koto ensemble, Japanese Gagaku, Javanese Gamelan, Korean Ensemble, Okinawan Ensemble, and Asian Theatre Music (in support of Asian theater performances offered by the Department of Theatre and Dance).

Prominent Alumni:

Quinn Kelsey
Daniel Ho
Robert and Roland Cazimero

UNIVERSITY OF HOUSTON

Moores School of Music
120 School of Music Building
Houston, TX 77204–4017

Phone: (713) 743-3009
Website: uh.edu/class/music/
Email: MSM_undergrad.adm@uh.edu

Tuition: $$
Campus student enrollment (undergraduate):
33,404

Degree(s): BM in piano performance, organ performance, instrumental performance, vocal performance, music theory, music composition, elective studies; teacher certification, music business, music in religion; BA.
Concentrations: Flute, oboe, clarinet, bassoon, euphonium, trumpet, French horn, trombone, tuba, violin, viola, cello, double bass, piano, organ, harp, percussion, voice.
Audition requirement: Yes; portfolios for BM in composition
Scholarships available: Yes, from $500–10,000
Number of faculty: Approximately 32 full-time, 38 lecturers and affiliate artists
Number of majors and minors: 550
Percentage and number of applicants accepted into the department per year: 55%, approximately 110 students
Department activities: Symphony orchestra, multiple wind and choral ensembles, percussion ensemble, two jazz ensembles, contemporary music ensemble, and collegium. An opera program that produces four fully staged performances with orchestra each year.

Music Programs by State

Note: Programs with an asterisk (*) are accredited by the National Association of Schools of Music.

ALABAMA
Alabama State University*
Auburn University*
Birmingham–Southern College*
Faulkner University
Huntingdon College*
Jacksonville State University*
Judson College*
Oakwood University
Samford University*
Stillman College*
Troy University*
University of Alabama*
University of Alabama at Birmingham*
University of Alabama in Huntsville*
University of Mobile*
University of Montevallo*
University of North Alabama*
University of South Alabama*

ALASKA
University of Alaska Anchorage*
University of Alaska Fairbanks*

ARIZONA
Arizona State University*
Northern Arizona University*
University of Arizona*

ARKANSAS
Arkansas State University*
Arkansas Tech University*
Harding University*
Henderson State University*
Hendrix College*
John Brown University
Lyon College
Ouachita Baptist University*
Philander Smith College

Southern Arkansas University*
University of Arkansas*
University of Arkansas—Fort Smith*
University of Arkansas at Little Rock*
University of Arkansas at
   Monticello*
University of Arkansas at Pine Bluff*
University of Central Arkansas*
University of the Ozarks
Williams Baptist College

CALIFORNIA

Azusa Pacific University*
Biola University*
California Baptist University*
California College of the Arts
California Institute of the Arts*
California Lutheran University
California Polytechnic State
   University, San Luis Obispo*
California State Polytechnic
   University, Pomona
California State University,
   Bakersfield
California State University, Chico*
California State University,
   Dominguez Hills*
California State University, East
   Bay*
California State University, Fresno*
California State University,
   Fullerton*
California State University,
   Hayward
California State University, Long
   Beach*
California State University, Los
   Angeles*
California State University,
   Monterey Bay
California State University,
   Northridge*
California State University,
   Sacramento*

California State University, San
   Bernardino*
California State University, San
   Marcos
California State University,
   Stanislaus*
Chapman University*
Christian Heritage College
Claremont McKenna College
Colburn School*
Concordia University
Dominican University of California
Fresno Pacific University
Holy Names University
Humboldt State University*
La Sierra University*
Los Angeles College of Music*
Loyola Marymount University*
The Master's University*
Mills College
Mount Saint Mary's University
Musicians Institute*
Notre Dame de Namur University
Occidental College
Otis College of Art and Design
Pacific Union College*
Pepperdine University*
Pitzer College
Point Loma Nazarene University*
Pomona College
Saint Mary's College of California
San Diego State University
San Francisco Art Institute
San Francisco Conservatory of
   Music*
San Francisco State University*
San Jose State University*
Santa Clara University
Scripps College
Simpson University
Sonoma State University*
Stanford University
University of California, Berkeley
University of California, Davis

University of California, Irvine
University of California, Los
   Angeles
University of California, Riverside
University of California, San Diego
University of California, Santa
   Barbara
University of California, Santa
   Cruz
University of La Verne
University of Redlands*
University of San Diego
University of San Francisco
University of Southern California*
University of the Pacific*
Vanguard University of Southern
   California*
Westmont College*
Whittier College
William Jessup University

COLORADO

Adams State University*
Colorado Christian University*
Colorado College
Colorado Mesa University*
Colorado State University*
Colorado State University–Pueblo*
Fort Lewis College*
Metropolitan State University of
   Denver*
Naropa University
University of Colorado at Boulder*
University of Colorado Denver*
University of Denver*
University of Northern Colorado*
Western State Colorado
   University*

CONNECTICUT

Central Connecticut State
   University*
Connecticut College
Fairfield University

Southern Connecticut State
   University
Trinity College
University of Bridgeport
University of Connecticut*
University of Hartford/The Hartt
   School*
University of New Haven
Wesleyan University
Western Connecticut State
   University*
Yale University*

DELAWARE
Delaware State University
University of Delaware*

DISTRICT OF COLUMBIA
American University*
Catholic University of America*
George Washington University*
Howard University*
University of the District of
   Columbia

FLORIDA
Baptist College of Florida*
Barry University
Bethune-Cookman University
Broward College*
Eckerd College
Edward Waters College
Florida Atlantic University*
Florida College*
Florida Gulf Coast University*
Florida International University*
Florida Memorial University*
Florida Southern College*
Florida State University*
Jacksonville University*
Lynn University*
New World School of the Arts*
Palm Beach Atlantic University*
Rollins College*

Southeastern University
Stetson University*
University of Central Florida*
University of Florida*
University of Miami*
University of North Florida*
University of South Florida*
University of Tampa*
University of West Florida*

GEORGIA
Agnes Scott College
Albany State University
Armstrong State University*
Augusta State University*
Berry College*
Brenau University
Brewton–Parker College
Clark Atlanta University
Clayton State University*
Columbus State University*
Covenant College
Emmanuel College
Emory University*
Georgia College & State University*
Georgia Southern University*
Georgia Southwestern State
   University
Georgia State University*
Kennesaw State University*
LaGrange College
Mercer University*
Morehouse College*
Oglethorpe University
Piedmont College
Point University
Reinhardt University*
Savannah College of Art and
   Design
Savannah State University
Shorter University*
Spelman College*
Toccoa Falls College*
Truett McConnell University*

University of Georgia*
University of North Georgia
University of West Georgia*
Valdosta State University*
Wesleyan College*
Young Harris College*

HAWAII
University of Hawaii at Hilo
University of Hawaii at Manoa*

IDAHO
Albertson College of Idaho
Boise State University*
Brigham Young University–Idaho*
Idaho State University*
Northwest Nazarene University*
University of Idaho*

ILLINOIS
Augustana College*
Benedictine University
Blackburn College
Bradley University*
Chicago State University*
Columbia College Chicago
Concordia University*
DePaul University*
Eastern Illinois University*
Elmhurst College
Eureka College
Greenville College
Illinois Central College*
Illinois State University*
Illinois Wesleyan University*
Judson College
Knox College
Lake Forest College
Lewis University
Loyola University Chicago
MacMurray College
McKendree College
Millikin University*
Monmouth College

North Central College
North Park University*
Northeastern Illinois University*
Northern Illinois University*
Northwestern University*
Olivet Nazarene University*
Principia College
Quincy University*
Rockford College
Roosevelt University*
Southern Illinois University,
    Carbondale*
Southern Illinois University,
    Edwardsville*
Saint Xavier University*
Trinity Christian College
Trinity International University
University of Chicago
University of Illinois at Chicago
University of Illinois-Urbana
    Champaign*
VanderCook College of Music*
Western Illinois University*
Wheaton College*

INDIANA
Anderson University*
Ball State University*
Bethel College*
Butler University*
DePauw University*
Earlham College
Goshen College
Grace College and Theological
    Seminary
Hanover College
Huntington University
Indiana State University*
Indiana University Bloomington*
Indiana University–Purdue
    University Fort Wayne*
Indiana University–Purdue
    University Indianapolis*
Indiana University South Bend*

Indiana University Southeast
Indiana Wesleyan University*
Manchester University
Oakland City University
Saint Joseph's College
Saint Mary-of-the-Woods College*
Saint Mary's College*
Taylor University*
University of Evansville*
University of Indianapolis*
University of Notre Dame
Valparaiso University*
Wabash College

IOWA
Ashford University
Briar Cliff University
Buena Vista University
Central College*
Clarke College*
Coe College*
Cornell College
Dordt College
Drake University*
Graceland University
Grand View University
Grinnell College
Iowa State University*
Loras College
Luther College*
Morningside College*
Mount Mercy College
Northwestern College
St. Ambrose University
Simpson College*
University of Iowa*
University of Northern Iowa*
Waldorf University
Wartburg College*

KANSAS
Baker University*
Benedictine College*
Bethany College*

Bethel College
Emporia State University*
Fort Hays State University*
Friends University*
Kansas State University*
McPherson College
MidAmerica Nazarene University*
Ottawa University
Pittsburg State University*
Southwestern College*
Sterling College
Tabor College*
University of Kansas*
Washburn University*
Wichita State University*

KENTUCKY
Asbury University*
Bellarmine University
Berea College
Campbellsville University*
Centre College
Eastern Kentucky University*
Georgetown College
Kentucky State University*
Morehead State University*
Murray State University*
Northern Kentucky University*
Southern Baptist Theological
    Seminary*
Transylvania University
University of the Cumberlands
University of Kentucky*
University of Louisville*
Western Kentucky University*

LOUISIANA
Centenary College of Louisiana*
Dillard University
Grambling State University*
Louisiana College*
Louisiana State University*
Louisiana Tech University*
Loyola University New Orleans*

McNeese State University*
Nicholls State University*
Northwestern State University of
    Louisiana*
Southeastern Louisiana University*
Southern University and A&M
    College*
Tulane University
University of Louisiana at Lafayette*
University of Louisiana at Monroe*
University of New Orleans*
Xavier University of Louisiana*

MAINE

Bates College
Bowdoin College
Colby College
Maine College of Art
University of Maine*
University of Maine at Augusta
University of Southern Maine*

MARYLAND

Bowie State University
Frostburg State University
Goucher College
Hood College
Johns Hopkins University*
McDaniel College
Morgan State University*
Notre Dame of Maryland
    University
Salisbury University*
St. Mary's College of Maryland
Towson University*
University of Maryland*
University of Maryland, Baltimore
    County*
University of Maryland Eastern
    Shore
Washington Adventist University
Washington College

MASSACHUSETTS

Amherst College
Anna Maria College*
Atlantic Union College*
Bard College at Simon's Rock
Berklee College of Music
Boston College
Boston Conservatory
Boston University*
Brandeis University
Bridgewater State College*
Clark University
College of the Holy Cross
Eastern Nazarene College
Gordon College*
Hampshire College
Harvard University
Holyoke Community College*
Longy School of Music of Bard
    College
Massachusetts Institute of
    Technology
Mount Holyoke College
New England Conservatory of
    Music*
Northeastern University
Pine Manor College
Salem State University*
Simmons CollegeSmith College
Tufts University
University of Massachusetts
    Amherst*
University of Massachusetts Boston
University of Massachusetts
    Dartmouth
University of Massachusetts Lowell*
Wellesley College
Westfield State University*
Wheaton College
Wheelock College
Williams College

MICHIGAN

Adrian College
Albion College*
Alma College*
Andrews University*
Aquinas College
Calvin College*
Central Michigan University*
Concordia University
Cornerstone University*
Eastern Michigan University*
Ferris State University
Grand Valley State University*
Hope College*
Kalamazoo College
Madonna University
Marygrove College
Michigan State University*
Northern Michigan University*
Oakland University*
Olivet College
Rochester College
Saginaw Valley State University*
Siena Heights University
Spring Arbor University*
University of Michigan*
University of Michigan–Dearborn
University of Michigan-Flint*
Wayne State University*
Western Michigan University*

MINNESOTA

Augsburg College*
Bemidji State University*
Bethany Lutheran College
Bethel University
Carleton College
College of Saint Benedict and
    Saint John's University*
College of St. Scholastica
Concordia College*
Concordia University, St. Paul
Crown College
Gustavus Adolphus College

Hamline University*
Macalester College
McNally Smith College of Music*
Minnesota State University,
    Mankato*
Minnesota State University
    Moorhead*
North Central University
Northwestern College*
Saint Cloud State University*
Saint John's University
Saint Mary's University of
    Minnesota*
St. Catherine University
St. Olaf College*
Southwest Minnesota State
    University*
University of Minnesota Duluth*
University of Minnesota, Morris
University of Minnesota Twin
    Cities*
University of St. Thomas*
Winona State University*

MISSISSIPPI

Alcorn State University*
Belhaven College*
Blue Mountain College
Delta State University*
Jackson State University*
Millsaps College
Mississippi College*
Mississippi State University*
Mississippi University for Women*
Mississippi Valley State University*
Rust College
Tougaloo College
University of Mississippi*
University of Southern Mississippi*
William Carey College*

MISSOURI

Avila University
Baptist Bible College

Central Methodist University*
Central Missouri State University*
College of the Ozarks
Culver-Stockton College*
Drury University*
Evangel University*
Hannibal-LaGrange University
Lincoln University*
Lindenwood University
Maryville University of Saint Louis*
Missouri Baptist University*
Missouri Southern State University
Missouri State University*
Missouri Valley College
Missouri Western State University*
Northwest Missouri State
    University*
Saint Louis University
Southeast Missouri State
    University*
Southwest Baptist University*
Southwest Missouri State
    University*
Truman State University*
University of Missouri *
University of Missouri–Kansas
    City*
University of Missouri–St. Louis*
Washington University in St. Louis
Webster University*
William Jewell College*

MONTANA

Montana State University*
Montana State University Billings*
Rocky Mountain College
University of Montana, Missoula*
University of Montana Western

NEBRASKA

Chadron State College
Concordia University*
Creighton University
Doane College

Hastings College*
Midland Lutheran College
Nebraska Wesleyan University*
Union College
University of Nebraska at
    Kearney*
University of Nebraska–Lincoln*
University of Nebraska, Omaha*
Wayne State College
York College

NEVADA

Sierra Nevada College
University of Nevada, Las Vegas*
University of Nevada, Reno*

NEW HAMPSHIRE

Dartmouth College
Franklin Pierce College
Keene State College*
Plymouth State University
University of New Hampshire*

NEW JERSEY

Bloomfield College
Caldwell College
The College of New Jersey*
College of Saint Elizabeth
Drew University
Georgian Court University
Kean University*
Monmouth University
Montclair State University*
New Jersey City University*
Princeton University
Ramapo College of New Jersey
Rider University*
Rowan University*
Rutgers University–Camden
Rutgers University–New
    Brunswick*
Rutgers University–Newark
Rutgers, The State University of
    New Jersey*

Seton Hall University

Thomas Edison State College

William Paterson University of
New Jersey*

NEW MEXICO

College of Santa Fe

Eastern New Mexico University*

New Mexico Highlands University

New Mexico State University*

University of New Mexico*

Western New Mexico University

NEW YORK

Adelphi University

Alfred University

Bard College

Barnard College

Canisius College

Colgate University

College of Saint Rose*

Columbia University

Cornell University

CUNY, Baruch College

CUNY, Brooklyn College

CUNY, City College

CUNY, College of Staten Island

CUNY, Hunter College

CUNY, Lehman College

CUNY, New York City College of
Technology

CUNY, Queens College

CUNY, York College

Daemen College

Eastman School of Music/
University of Rochester*

Elmira College

Excelsior College

Five Towns College

Fordham University

Hamilton College

Hartwick College*

Hobart and William Smith
Colleges

Hochstein School of Music and
Dance*

Hofstra University

Houghton College*

Ithaca College*

The Juilliard School

Long Island University, Brooklyn

Long Island University CW Post
Campus

Manhattan School of Music

Manhattanville College

Marist College

Molloy College*

Nazareth College *

New York University

Rensselaer Polytechnic Institute

Roberts Wesleyan College*

Sarah Lawrence College

Skidmore College

St. Lawrence University

SUNY at Albany

SUNY at Binghamton*

SUNY at BuffaloSUNY Buffalo
State College

SUNY College at Brockport

SUNY Cortland

SUNY at Fredonia*

SUNY at Geneseo

SUNY at New Paltz*

SUNY at Old Westbury

SUNY at Oneonta*

SUNY at Oswego*

SUNY at Plattsburgh

SUNY at Potsdam*

SUNY Purchase College
Conservatory of Music

SUNY at Stony Brook

Syracuse University*

University of Rochester

Vassar College

Villa Maria College *

Wagner College

Wells College

Yeshiva University

NORTH CAROLINA

Appalachian State University*

Bennett College

Brevard College*

Campbell University

Catawba College

Chowan College*

Davidson College

Duke University

East Carolina University*

Elizabeth City State University*

Elon University

Fayetteville State University*

Gardner-Webb University*

Greensboro College*

Guilford College

Johnson C. Smith University

Lenoir-Rhyne University

Livingstone College

Mars Hill University*

Meredith College*

Montreat College

North Carolina A&T State University*

North Carolina Central University

North Carolina School of the Arts

Pfeiffer University*

Queens University of Charlotte*

Saint Augustine's University

Salem College*

Shaw University

University of Mount Olive

University of North Carolina at
Asheville

University of North Carolina at
Chapel Hill

University of North Carolina at
Charlotte*

University of North Carolina at
Greensboro*

University of North Carolina at
Pembroke*

University of North Carolina at
Wilmington*

Wake Forest University

Western Carolina University*
William Peace University
Wingate University*
Winston-Salem State University*

NORTH DAKOTA

Dickinson State University*
Jamestown College
Minot State University*
North Dakota State University*
Trinity Bible College
University of Mary*
University of North Dakota*
Valley City State University*

OHIO

Antioch College
Ashland University*
Baldwin Wallace College*
Bluffton University*
Bowling Green State University*
Capital University*
Case Western Reserve University*
Cedarville University*
Central State University*
Cincinnati Christian University*
Cleveland Institute of Music*
Cleveland State University*
College of Wooster*
Denison University
Heidelberg College*
Hiram College*
Kent State University*
Kenyon College
Lake Erie College
Malone University*
Marietta College*
Miami University*
Mount St. Joseph University*
Mount Vernon Nazarene
   University*
Muskingum University*
Oberlin College
Ohio Northern University*

Ohio State University*
Ohio University*
Ohio Wesleyan University*
Otterbein University*
Shawnee State University
University of Akron*
University of Cincinnati*
University of Dayton*
University of Mount Union*
University of Rio Grande
University of Toledo*
Wilberforce University
Wittenberg University*
Wright State University*
Xavier University*
Youngstown State University*

OKLAHOMA

Cameron University*
East Central University*
Langston University
Northeastern State University*
Northwestern Oklahoma State
   University
Oklahoma Baptist University*
Oklahoma Christian University*
Oklahoma City University*
Oklahoma Panhandle State
   University
Oklahoma State University*
Oklahoma Wesleyan University
Oral Roberts University*
St. Gregory's University
Southeastern Oklahoma State
   University*
Southern Nazarene University*
Southwestern Oklahoma State
   University*
University of Central Oklahoma*
University of Oklahoma*
University of Science and Arts of
   Oklahoma*
University of Tulsa*

OREGON

Eastern Oregon University
George Fox University*
Lewis & Clark College
Linfield College*
Marylhurst University*
Northwest Christian University
Oregon State University
Pacific University*
Portland State University*
Reed College
Southern Oregon University*
University of Oregon*
University of Portland*
Warner Pacific College
Western Oregon University*
Willamette University*

PENNSYLVANIA

Academy of Vocal Arts*
Albright College
Allegheny College
Bloomsburg University of
   Pennsylvania*
Bryn Mawr College
Bucknell University*
Cairn University*
Carnegie Mellon University*
Cedar Crest College
Chatham College
Cheyney University of
   Pennsylvania
Clarion University of
   Pennsylvania*
The Curtis Institute of Music*
Dickinson College
Drexel University
Duquesne University*
Eastern University
Edinboro University of
   Pennsylvania*
Elizabethtown College*
Franklin & Marshall College
Gannon University

Geneva College
Gettysburg College*
Grove City College
Haverford College
Holy Family University
Immaculata University*
Indiana University of
    Pennsylvania*
Kutztown University of
    Pennsylvania*
La Salle University
Lafayette College
Lebanon Valley College*
Lehigh University
Lock Haven University of
    Pennsylvania
Lycoming College
Mansfield University of
    Pennsylvania*
Marywood University*
Mercyhurst College*
Messiah College*
Millersville University*
Moravian College*
Muhlenberg College
Pennsylvania State University*
Rosemont College
Saint Joseph's University
Saint Vincent College
Seton Hill University*
Settlement Music School*
Shippensburg University of
    Pennsylvania
Slippery Rock University of
    Pennsylvania*
Susquehanna University*
Swarthmore College
Temple University*
University of Pennsylvania
University of Pittsburgh
University of Scranton
University of the Arts*
Washington & Jefferson College
West Chester University of

Pennsylvania*
Westminster College*
Wilkes University
York College Pennsylvania*

RHODE ISLAND
Brown University
Providence College*
Rhode Island College*
Salve Regina University
University of Rhode Island*

SOUTH CAROLINA
Allen University
Anderson University*
Bob Jones University
Charleston Southern University*
Claflin University*
Coastal Carolina University*
Coker College*
College of Charleston*
Columbia College*
Converse College*
Erskine College
Furman University*
Lander University*
Limestone College*
Newberry College*
North Greenville College*
Presbyterian College*
South Carolina State University*
University of South Carolina*
University of South Carolina Aiken*
Winthrop University*

SOUTH DAKOTA
Augustana College*
Black Hills State University*
Dakota Wesleyan University
Mount Marty College
Northern State University*
South Dakota State University*
University of Sioux Falls
University of South Dakota*

TENNESSEE
Austin Peay State University*
Belmont University*
Bryan College
Carson-Newman College*
Cumberland University
East Tennessee State University*
Fisk University*
Freed–Hardeman University
Lambuth University
Lane College
Lee University*
Lipscomb University*
Maryville College*
Middle Tennessee State University*
Milligan College
Rhodes College
Sewanee: The University of the
    South
Southern Adventist University*
Tennessee State University*
Tennessee Technological
    University*
Tennessee Temple University
Trevecca Nazarene University*
Union University*
University of Memphis*
University of Tennessee*
University of Tennessee at
    Chattanooga*
University of Tennessee at Martin*
Vanderbilt University*

TEXAS
Abilene Christian University*
Angelo State University*
Austin College
Baylor University*
Dallas Baptist University*
Del Mar College*
East Texas Baptist University*
Hardin–Simmons University*
Houston Baptist University
Howard Payne University*

Huston–Tillotson University

Lamar University*

Lubbock Christian University

McMurry University

Midwestern State University*

Odessa College*

Our Lady of the Lake University

Prairie View A&M University*

Rice University

Saint Mary's University *

Sam Houston State University*

Schreiner University

Southern Methodist University*

Southwestern Adventist University

Southwestern Assemblies of God
University

Southwestern Baptist Theological
Seminary*

Southwestern University*

St. Mary's University

Stephen F. Austin State University*

Sul Ross State University

Tarleton State University*

Texas A&M University

Texas A&M University–Commerce*

Texas A&M University–Corpus
Christi*

Texas A&M University–Kingsville*

Texas Christian University*

Texas College

Texas Lutheran University*

Texas Southern University

Texas State University *

Texas Tech University*

Texas Wesleyan University*

Texas Woman's University*

Trinity University

University of Dallas

University of Houston*

University of Mary Hardin–Baylor*

University of North Texas*

University of St. Thomas

University of Texas at Arlington*

University of Texas at Austin*

University of Texas at Brownsville*

University of Texas at El Paso*

University of Texas–Pan American

University of Texas at San
Antonio*

University of Texas at Tyler*

University of the Incarnate Word

Wayland Baptist University*

West Texas A&M University*

Wiley College

UTAH

Brigham Young University*

Southern Utah University*

University of Utah*

Utah State University*

Utah Valley State University

Weber State University*

VERMONT

Bennington College

Castleton State College

Johnson State College

Marlboro College

Middlebury College

Saint Michael's College

University of Vermont

VIRGINIA

Averett University

Bluefield College

Bridgewater College

Christopher Newport University*

College of William and Mary

Eastern Mennonite University

Emory and Henry College

George Mason University*

Hampton University*

Hollins University

James Madison University*

Liberty University*

Longwood University*

Lynchburg College*

Mary Baldwin University

Norfolk State University*

Old Dominion University*

Radford University*

Randolph–Macon College

Roanoke College

Shenandoah University*

Sweet Briar College

University of Mary Washington*

University of Richmond

University of Virginia

Virginia Commonwealth
University*

Virginia State University*

Virginia Tech*

Virginia Union University

Virginia Wesleyan College

Washington and Lee University

WASHINGTON

Central Washington University*

Cornish College of the Arts

Eastern Washington University*

Gonzaga University*

Northwest College

Pacific Lutheran University*

Saint Martin's College

Seattle Pacific University*

Seattle University

University of Puget Sound*

University of Washington*

Walla Walla University*

Washington State University*

Western Washington University*

Whitman College

Whitworth College*

WISCONSIN

Alverno College*

Beloit College

Cardinal Stritch University

Carroll College

Carthage College*

Concordia University Wisconsin

Edgewood College

Lakeland College

Lawrence University*

Marian University

Northland College

Ripon College

St. Norbert College

Silver Lake College*

University of Wisconsin–Eau
    Claire*

University of Wisconsin–Green
    Bay*

University of Wisconsin–La
    Crosse*

University of Wisconsin–Madison*

University of Wisconsin–
    Milwaukee*

University of Wisconsin–Oshkosh*

University of Wisconsin–Platteville*

University of Wisconsin–River
    Falls*

University of Wisconsin–Stevens
    Point*

University of Wisconsin–Superior*

University of Wisconsin–
    Whitewater*

Viterbo University*

Wisconsin Lutheran College

WEST VIRGINIA

Alderson Broaddus College

Bethany College

Concord University

Davis & Elkins College

Fairmont State University

Marshall University*

Shepherd University*

University of Charleston

West Liberty State University*

West Virginia University*

West Virginia Wesleyan College*

WYOMING

University of Wyoming*

Colleges for Writers

Creative writing is a liberating form of self-expression. It has the power to change the world, is lasting, and can teach generations for years to come. Because writing is a skill that is learned from an early age—a communication tool used by almost everyone—the masses are a captive audience. Writing appreciation is already ingrained in all of us, creating an environment in which future writers can enjoy lifelong fulfillment.

For students aspiring to find the writer within, there is no better time to study creative writing than in college. Creative writing has gained immense popularity on campuses over the past few decades. There are more programs than ever before, and as a result, more options to explore in your college search. When deciding whether you want to focus your college studies on creative writing, ask yourself these questions:

★ Why do I want to be a writer?
★ What kind of writer do I want to be?

These questions, in addition to research into different programs, will help you figure out where you ultimately want to study.

Types of Creative Writing Programs

Traditionally, creative writing programs have been part of English departments at colleges and universities across the country. But in recent decades, creative writing has expanded as a discipline and is now offered at many more institutions. Today, there are several different degree plans that a student can consider when seeking college training in creative writing.

The first is the most traditional route, which is declaring an English major and taking creative writing courses as part of that major. This usually means pursuing a bachelor of arts (BA) in English with a concentration or emphasis in creative writing.

A second option is a bachelor of fine arts (BFA) in creative writing. Fewer colleges offer this degree plan. The curriculum at these schools may still require a student to take literature courses, but they are often designed slightly differently than an English course offered in a traditional English department. Many times, the courses approach the studying of literature from a writer's perspective and teach how to use this knowledge to enhance students' writing. Creative writing programs offering the BFA sometimes are separate from English departments and usually have their own faculty.

KEVIN
COLGATE UNIVERSITY

Kevin wrote his first story in second grade, and so began his writing career! In fact, that first story was "published" on manila paper and laminated for Kevin as a keepsake.

In high school, Kevin continued writing and served as editor-in-chief of his high school's newspaper as well as editor of the literary magazine. Now attending Colgate University in upstate New York, he is a double major in economics and English with a creative writing emphasis.

Kevin chose Colgate knowing he wanted to double major. He was drawn to the liberal arts college atmosphere and one-on-one contact with professors. "I view them as a support network," confides Kevin.

"My visit day to the campus was the clinching factor," Kevin explains. "I sat in on a Shakespeare course that blew me away."

The Visiting Writers program also impressed Kevin immensely. Little did he know that once he enrolled at

Hot Tips from Kevin

→ Liberal arts colleges are great campus environments for creative writing students. What's special is the close personal attention with professors. This is especially important for writers who need individual feedback or help improving a piece.

→ Explore as many aspects of your interests as possible. For example, study more than creative writing. Another discipline can give you a different perspective and give your writing a unique flavor that can be refreshing to your reader.

Colgate, the Visiting Writers program would eventually have a profound impact on his writing for the long term.

During his junior year, Kevin had the opportunity to study in a short fiction seminar with renowned writer Sarah Towers, a visiting writer for two years. "She was amazing," declares Kevin. "But I say this in hindsight."

Kevin remembers that Towers "tore apart" the first paper he submitted for her class. "She took me aside and said she was going to challenge me."

In retrospect, Kevin realizes just how much he learned from her course.

"My prose became tighter. I started to write what I wanted to say. I found my voice," Kevin confesses.

Balancing life as a double major can be challenging, according to Kevin. He says that an English major with creative writing is "almost like a major and a half," and the double-major life can be especially hard during senior year if you have large projects to complete for both disciplines.

Primarily a fiction writer, Kevin's honors project for his English/creative writing major is a novel.

After Colgate, Kevin plans to apply to graduate school to both creative writing MFA programs and to master's programs in public policy. He is leaving his options open until it is time to decide what to do next. With a background in two disciplines, Kevin has doubled his options after graduation.

A few schools offer a combined BA in English and creative writing or literature and creative writing. The availability of such a degree plan often reflects a departmental philosophy of wanting to place equal importance on each part of the curriculum—writing *and* literature.

If you have other academic interests outside of creative writing, double majoring in another field is always an option. Because creative writing is an artistic discipline that is most closely aligned with academic studies (in other words, there is no performing requirement that involves rehearsals or time in an art studio), it's probably one of the more logical choices of disciplines that can be combined with other majors.

The most common tracks in creative writing programs are fiction and poetry, regardless of the degree offered. Many schools offer courses in creative nonfiction and screenwriting. A small number of colleges may offer a specific concentration in creative nonfiction or screenwriting at the undergraduate level, but it's more common to concentrate in these specific areas in graduate MFA programs.

If you are interested in journalism, some colleges that offer courses in creative nonfiction writing also group journalism classes within that program rather than in a separate journalism degree program. This is most common at liberal arts colleges and small universities.

Writing Portfolios

At most colleges and universities that offer a BA in English with a concentration or emphasis in creative writing, preparing a portfolio is usually not required for admission. However, some of these institutions may require a portfolio before you can declare a major for acceptance into the creative writing program. It is important to investigate the writing portfolio requirement at each school you are considering because it varies from school to school.

You may find that you do need to submit a creative writing portfolio for either admission to a BFA program or for acceptance into the creative writing program at a school where you've already been accepted. Normally, portfolio requirements include the submission of at least ten pages of your best work. The material you assemble for the portfolio should represent the genre you are most interested in studying. Of course, if you are interested in studying multiple genres, you may want to ask if it would be appropriate to submit a fewer number of samples from each genre.

DAY IN THE LIFE OF A CREATIVE WRITING MAJOR	
8:30 a.m.	Breakfast
9:10 a.m.	Class (History of the English Language)
10:30 a.m.–12:30 p.m.	Library to edit writing, write, or read
12:30–1:30 p.m.	Extracurricular meeting
2 p.m.	Lunch
2:30–6 p.m.	Library for more editing, writing, or reading
6 p.m.	Dinner
7–10 p.m.	Seminar (Poetry Manuscript Preparation)

Remember that once you start taking creative writing courses in college, honing your craft as a writer has only just begun. At some institutions, students must have a minimum grade to advance to the next level of creative writing workshops.

"We want to make sure students in creative writing workshops really want to be there," says Jim Daniels, director of the creative writing program at Carnegie Mellon University in Pittsburgh, Pennsylvania.

What to Expect in a Creative Writing Workshop

"What exactly is a workshop class?" you may ask. In college creative writing programs, intermediate and advanced-level classes are often called workshops because the students are involved in hands-on activities. Typically, most of the class time in these courses is spent reading and evaluating each student's writing. Classmates bring several copies of their writing assignment—whether it is a short story, collection of poems, a portion of a novel, an essay, or a play—to class on a specified date. The class assignment is then to read everyone's work and come to the next class prepared to discuss each student's writing and provide individual feedback.

Of course, sharing writing among other classmates can be intimidating at first. "You have a fearful opportunity to improve your writing," comments Danny Clifford, a senior creative writing student at the University of Arizona. "A lot of the work that is shared consists of your innermost thoughts."

Here are some ground rules to follow when taking your first college writers', workshop:

1. Treat others' work with respect.
2. Give other students comments about specific areas of their craft that are not working, rather than saying what you don't "like" about it. Individual tastes vary, so what you don't like is not appropriate feedback that should be shared out loud. A good critique means that you look for areas where the writing technique can be technically improved.
3. Try to take constructive criticism gracefully. People in the workshop care about writing, and like you, they want to improve their writing as well. Remember that many times you will walk away from the class with new ideas about how to improve your writing that you may have not previously considered.

Finding a Writing Community

It is important to find a sense of community in a creative writing program. Students in creative writing programs often form very close bonds because they share their innermost thoughts through the writing workshop review process. Students share parts of themselves through their writing, which requires a great deal of trust, an element that can become the foundation for deep friendships. Evaluating relationships between students and creative writing professors is also important.

There is no better way to find out if a writing community truly exists on a campus than visiting the school. A brochure can tout faculty members, literary conferences, and a visiting writers series, but this may not necessarily reflect what the writing life on campus is actually like.

"Things going on outside of the classroom often influence what goes on inside the classroom," explains Daniels, of Carnegie Mellon.

Evaluating Creative Writing Programs

After you've visited campuses, talked to faculty members and students at various schools and discussed college options with your parents, it's time to take a close look at each institution you are seriously considering. It may seem that many of the creative writing programs look alike from afar. Hopefully, the campus visits have revealed elements of the various programs that will help you narrow down which campus might be the best for you. Here are some questions to keep in mind when you are in the last stages of making your final choice. You may want to make a list and compare notes side-by-side for each school. The answers might reveal where you should ultimately enroll.

- *Coursework.* Whether you are looking at BA or BFA programs, consider how the major is structured. How many introductory and advanced writing courses will you take? How many different genres are offered? How many traditional English literature survey courses and seminars will you need to take? Are independent studies in creative writing available? Is a thesis required, and can it be a creative thesis like a novel, a play, or a collection of poems or short stories?

- *Faculty.* Are the faculty well-known writers? Will you be taught by them or by graduate assistants? Have faculty won writing awards? Do they have master's degrees in writing (MFA) or doctoral degrees? A few institutions in the country now offer PhDs in English with creative writing emphases, which is a somewhat new development in the discipline.

- *Visiting writers.* Do visiting writers teach on campus, or do they only give readings? Who has been a visiting writer? How often are they on campus?

- *Internship opportunities.* Does the department have connections with local newspapers, magazines, or publishing companies to help place students in internships for possible writing-related careers?

- *Publication opportunities.* What kinds of publication opportunities are available to students? Is there a student literary magazine or newspaper? Are there writing contests?
- *Alumni.* How many alumni have become published authors? Have they gone on to successful careers as writers or editors? Have they been successful in other fields like teaching, journalism, law, or higher education?

MATTHEW
UNIVERSITY OF NORTH CAROLINA AT WILMINGTON

Hot Tips from Matthew

→ Read the faculty's writing. If you can relate to their writing, they might be good teachers for you. If they have a similar perspective, it can enhance your experience in the program—they can bring out the best in your writing.

→ The hardest thing about writing is learning how to revise. The good news is that it gets easier the more you do it.

→ Not all teachers are created equal. Most teachers are great, but if you get one that is mediocre, don't get discouraged. You can still have a positive experience and learn something from that teacher even if he or she doesn't knock your socks off.

Why write?

"I get into the writing itself," says Matthew, a senior at the University of North Carolina at Wilmington. "Those moments of expression that are worth building the context of stories around...those emotions that you can put into words that you normally can't put into words."

SARAH
CARNEGIE MELLON UNIVERSITY

Growing up in rural Pennsylvania, Sarah was familiar with the science, engineering, and drama departments at Carnegie Mellon University. But she didn't discover the creative writing program until she met its director at the Pennsylvania Governor's School of the Arts one summer during high school.

Both a jazz musician and a poet, Sarah is now pursuing a double major in creative writing and English while minoring in music at the university.

Through Carnegie Mellon, Sarah has had several opportunities to enhance her knowledge of what it would be like to be a working writer after college.

"CMU has excellent career education," Sarah asserts.

One of Sarah's career education opportunities was an internship at CMU Press. She designed books and spent a couple of years reading poetry manuscripts. "These experiences lead easily into paying gigs," Sarah expounds. "And they show students how to operate in the writing world after college."

Sarah's education has already come in handy in getting a "paying gig" in writing. Last summer, she went back to the Pennsylvania Governor's School for the Arts—this time as a teaching assistant. Sarah is passionate about writing and teaching writing because, in her words, "With creative writing, you are studying a productive art; you show people an imagined vision you have on paper."

"I am kind of sad to see my undergraduate education come to an end," Sarah admits. "I feel privileged and am ridiculously happy in my program."

Sarah feels that she found the ultimate creative writing community at Carnegie Mellon. "We spend a lot of time together—both writing faculty and students," Sarah explains.

"It's a wonderful model of how to live the writing life."

Hot Tips from Sarah

→ Look for a vibrant writing community.

→ A lot of schools advertise famous teachers, but make sure you'll have the opportunity to take classes with them.

→ If you know whom you might want to study with, it can be a good way to select a creative writing program.

→ Visiting classes is critical. If you can observe a writing workshop, even better.

→ It is important to review the course catalogue to investigate which courses you might want to take.

→ Read books written by the faculty who teach at the college.

→ Talk to students on campus about the writing program.

Creative Writing and the "Real World"

Like other artistic disciplines, many people wonder what creative writing students will do with their degree once they get into the "real world." Some creative writing programs have connections to writing-related internships in which students may participate during their course of study.

For example, Carnegie Mellon is unique in that Carnegie Mellon University Press publishes more fiction and poetry than any other university press in the nation. Consequently, the university press relies on student interns to do a significant amount of work that requires a great deal of responsibility on their part. This gives students opportunities to gain experience in their craft as well as published work to include in their résumés when they graduate.

"A question a lot of people ask is, 'What am I going to do with a degree in creative writing?'" says Daniels. "The answer is 'Just about everything.' At Carnegie Mellon, our alumni have done everything from becoming a lawyer to being a rock star—everyone seems to be using writing in some way."

This is not at all surprising to Daniels because, in his view, "Every occupation needs people to communicate."

So to quench any fears about what you are going to do with that creative writing degree, remember that having good writing skills can help in almost any professional field. Also, most writers have day jobs (which could be writing-related or something completely different). It is likely you'll be using your writing in other ways besides writing the great American novel. The most successful writers, a small percentage, can rely on creative writing income alone but many writers find careers as professional writers or in professions that use writing skills.

PROFESSOR JIM DANIELS
THOMAS S. BAKER PROFESSOR OF ENGLISH AND DIRECTOR OF THE CREATIVE WRITING PROGRAM, CARNEGIE MELLON UNIVERSITY

How to Pick the Right Writing Program

★ *Look for faculty members who are actively publishing their work.*

★ *Seek a department that is committed to teaching creative writing at the undergraduate level, not just the graduate level.*

★ *Consider a program that is undergraduate only; sometimes a department with a graduate degree in creative writing may give priority to graduate students.*

★ *Investigate class size.*

★ *Find out how many courses are offered in a given semester—if there aren't enough classes, it may be hard to get into the class of your choice.*

★ *Research the kinds of writing-related extracurricular activities that exist on campus— you want to find a sense of community.*

★ *Ask if the college has an active visiting writers program.*

PROFESSOR CHRISTINE COZZENS
DIRECTOR OF THE CENTER FOR WRITING AND SPEAKING, AGNES SCOTT COLLEGE

Not All Creative Writing Programs Are the Same

Each creative writing program has a different approach. Some schools primarily emphasize creative writing coursework; some emphasize literature and have fewer creative writing courses focusing on both. Agnes Scott College in Georgia, for example, offers a bachelor's degree in English literature and creative writing.

"You really have to be a good reader to be a good writer," says Christine Cozzens, professor of English and director of the Center for Writing and Speaking at Agnes Scott College. "One forms the skeleton for the other."

Cozzens explains that the oral presentation of creative writing is important because "it develops the ear in listening to writing." Because of this, students should look for opportunities to read their work as an integral component of a creative writing program.

Overall, Cozzens emphasizes that creative writing courses can be beneficial for undergraduates regardless of their declared major.

"Creative writing is a fantastic emphasis for undergraduate students," she asserts. "Courses in creative writing can help students to think creatively and use their minds in any endeavor, whether it be in another arts discipline or the corporate world."

DANNY
UNIVERSITY OF ARIZONA

Right after high school, Danny joined the military, but he always knew he wanted to go to college. The service gave Danny the opportunity to see the world and then take advantage of the college funding that the military offers. After five years, Danny was ready to go back to school, and he enrolled in the University of Arizona as a double major in communications and creative writing. Before too long, Danny decided that he really wanted to focus on creative writing, and he is now earning a bachelor of fine arts.

A poet by craft, Danny isn't a long-winded writer. In fact, he attributes his attraction to poetry to this choice of style. "I like to write succinctly and get to the point," Danny shares.

As an adult student, Danny is older than most of his classmates and even older than one of his professors. However, Danny's writing epiphany came in an intermediate poetry class that was led by an instructor who was only twenty-three years old.

Danny recalls his first impression of the instructor, including his coming in with ripped jeans and sandals. But Danny soon got past his teacher's casual appearance. "What was so astonishing was the passion with which he taught," Danny comments. "The joy came through."

This young professor's teaching on Tony Hoagland, a midwestern poet, resonated with Danny in a most unusual way. "The way he translated Hoagland's work to our class really reached me, and being from the Midwest myself, it made me want to emulate Hoagland."

That class marked a significant turning point in Danny's college career. "It verified that I was doing the right thing by studying poetry," he confides.

Danny has found great friends in the writing program at the University of Arizona. "A few of my fellow classmates and I got along so well that we formed a poetry group," explains Danny. "We get together every Thursday to share our writing and encourage each other."

SAMPLE ADMISSIONS ESSAY

"Evaluate a significant experience, achievement or risk that you have taken and its impact on you."

Inspiration

Inspiration is a funny thing, isn't it? Like lightning, it strikes randomly, not playing by any rules of order, probability, or frequency. Sometimes months pass before it strikes, but when it does, it forces me into my seat and guides my pen. Those bursts of inspiration have made me who I am.

It was one of these bolts of inspiration that founded my little company named Conquer Ventures Inc. a few years ago. Its days of creation are still fresh in my mind...

Wall Street found its way into my blood. Before I knew what was happening, I was watching CNBC for hours upon end every day and reading countless books on the philosophies and theories behind the market. I woke up to that neverending ticker and went to bed with a printout of my personal list of the day's "hot stocks." The constant cycle of gaining knowledge satisfied me, at least until that one monumental night.

My eyes were slowly closing, heavy from a week of assignments, rules and regulations. I sat at my computer, printing out market data, when I started thinking. I thought of a newsletter, one that could spread my knowledge about the "pulse" of the market to people who could actually do something about it. So after more than three years of studying and obsessing over Wall Street, I became a part of it, in a sense, by doing something most talk about their entire lives, but never do: I executed. I spent that night typing up what would be the first piece of market literature I would ever write. It would only include a few carefully researched "Upgrades and Downgrades," but to me, it was one of the most momentous things I had ever done. I was off on a ride that everyone thought would end in a few months, but I knew would last far into the future.

The first issue was a minor success. My newsletter generated a mediocre response, which was enough to keep my spirits high while sailing into the next monthly issue. But Issue #2 gave me something that I had wanted my whole life, the ability to expand and improve upon my own work.

So in the second issue, I added my own voice to the mix, adding an ongoing editorial. The second issue went out, and to my delight, word spread and my subscriber base began to grow. I had accumulated over 500 subscribers, including stockbrokers and investors from across the country.

Over the coming winter months and into the spring, I taught myself how to make my time more useful, build an Internet site from scratch, and hold onto that very inspiration that started it all.

Through this experience of inspiration and hard work, I learned a number of important lessons, the most important of which was that one should never get a step ahead of the dream, lest he/she lose focus on the goal.

Supplemental Essay

"What three words best describe you, and why?"

Ambition, innovation, and creativity best describe me. These characteristics have been evident in the leadership roles I have assumed and will add to Colgate's mosaic like no other personality traits can.

Serving as an editor over the years for my high school's nationally recognized newspaper, *The Courant*, and now leading it as its editor-in-chief, I have picked up valuable writing and editing skills sure to enhance any college newspaper with which I am involved. My ambition and drive to make it to the top forced me to prove myself countless times to my peers and mentors, showing them that I could carry on their tradition of excellence. Being in my current position as the head of the paper, I have gained the long-sought ability to express myself creatively, utilizing *The Courant*'s style and words and my innovative skills to enhance our layout and gain a larger readership. I am also learning how to manage people, a skill necessary in most personal and career-related activities.

My submissions and participation in the construction of *Etchings*, our school literary magazine, allowed me to express and challenge my creative side through various writings that I was asked to submit. These writings, most of which were published, forced me to find the time to do what I love to do: write. The ability to express oneself through the written word is an art unparalleled. I only hope to be able to bring this talent I have to a medium where it can be appreciated and enjoyed.

Throughout my high school career I have had many experiences, such as the ones highlighted here, which have proven that these three words of ambition, innovation, and creativity make up an active part of who I am. I would love to share my abilities with Colgate University and add my piece to your very diverse and esteemed puzzle.

Sample Writing Résumé

Sarah B.

9TH GRADE (WINCHESTER THURSTON SCHOOL)

Plaid Literary Award (Awarded to a piece of fiction or poetry published in the literary magazine that is deemed outstanding by the English staff; for "The Perks of Being a Wallflower"*)

Poetry published in Plaid Literary Magazine ("The Perks of Being a Wallflower")

Finalist in Poetry Slam held by high school; guest poets included Christina Springer

10TH GRADE (WINCHESTER THURSTON SCHOOL)

Submissions editor of Plaid Literary Magazine

Published in Plaid Literary Magazine ("Dante's Address to his Long-Dead Beloved," "Untitled")

Participated in Poetry Slam; guest poets included Christina Springer

Wrote a two-act play in pentameter for AP European History final project

11TH GRADE (THE COLUMBUS ACADEMY)

Editor of Quest Literary Magazine

Published in Quest Literary Magazine ("Two Minutes on the Drive," "Ask the Dust")

Member of Creative Writing Club

Summer: Kenyon Young Writer's Workshop at Kenyon College in Gambier, Ohio. Two-week course with published authors in prose, poetry, and creative nonfiction

12TH GRADE (THE COLUMBUS ACADEMY)

Co-editor in Chief of Quest Literary Magazine

Work accepted into Quest Literary Magazine ("The Mimes Rehearse," "Nostalgia," "It Isn't Easy Being Green")

Member of Creative Writing Club

Enrolled in Creative Writing class offered second semester

Wrote and delivered speech for Red Carpet Fashion Show for eating disorder awareness

Senior Project (May 2005): independent creative writing, in an attempt to complete a manuscript of stories and poetry, mentored by an English teacher and a holder of a Poetry MFA

Submitted to Scholastics Writing Awards (Results pending...)

Sample Creative Writing Résumé

Skylar S.

EXTRACURRICULAR ACTIVITIES

Cross Country (10)

Film Society (10)

FOCUS (10–11)

Drama Society and fall play, *The Women*, (11)

It's Academic, academic superbowl team (11)

JV Tennis (11–12) captain (12)

Tidbit literary magazine, assistant editor (11) editor (12)

Dubious Dozen, a cappella singing group, (11–12)

Rarebit, yearbook, co-editor (12)

SUMMER EXPERIENCE

Camp Seafarer (9–10)

Mother Hubbard's Cupboard, food pantry for low-income families (9–10, 10–11) cashier

Duke Young Writers' Camp (10–11)

Sewanee Young Writers' Conference (11–12)

VOLUNTEER EXPERIENCE

YMCA: Adapted Aquatics for developmentally disabled children, Adapted Martial Arts, Race for the Cure marshal, Young Women's Health Fair (9)

Food Bank: monthly repack of food for families (9), Mother Hubbard's Cupboard (summer 9, 10)

Playing harp at holidays in retirement center and nursing homes

CREATIVE EXPERIENCE

Precollege harp program, 2009–2015

Private harp lessons, 2012–2016

Designed yearlong Independent Study in Creative Writing (12) exploring several genres; edited and polished work with creative writing teacher to produce 60 pages final portfolio

Writing portfolio, harp CD available upon request

Sample Résumé

Elisabeth D.

EDUCATION			
Solon High School	Graduated with Honors	Solon, Ohio	June 2017
Cleveland Institute of Art	Studied letterpress and digital printmaking	Cleveland, Ohio	Summer 2016

WORK EXPERIENCE			
Private Art Instructor	Created and implemented art lessons from drawing to sculpture. Met with one middle school student twice a week.	Solon, Ohio	(July 2015–August 2016)
Caricature Artist	Drew caricatures at Six Flags Worlds of Adventure, Aurora, Ohio.	Kaman's Art Shoppes, Chagrin Falls, Ohio	Summer 2016
Student Aide	Assisted American teachers instructing English as a second language to Polish students. Also lived with a Polish family.	American Educators for Poland, Stary Sacz Poland	2014 & 2015

EXTRACURRICULAR & VOLUNTEER ACTIVITIES			
Feature Editor & Columnist	Managed the Features section and copy edited articles in addition to writing a monthly opinion piece.	*The Courier*, Monthly Solon High School Newspaper	2015–2016
Co-Editor	Solicited, edited, and formatted student work for publication.	*Images*, Annual Solon High School Literary Magazine	2015–2016
Treasurer	Organized fundraising events and responsible for financial bookkeeping. Active member of drama club all four years, held the title role in fall 2016's production of *The Prime of Miss Jean Brodie*.	Solon High School Drama Club	2015–2016
Co-Director	Shared responsibilities in casting and directing the one-act play *The Lost Elevator*.	Solon High School One-Act Play Festival	Winter 2001

AWARDS & PUBLICATIONS	
The Alliance for Young Artists & Writers National Scholastic Awards	Spring 2001
Writing Portfolio Silver Key recipient	Spring 2001
National Council of Teachers of English Writing Awards	2000–2001
National writing award recipient	2000–2001
National Honors Society	2000–2001
Oddfellow's and Rebbekah's United Nations Pilgrimage for Youth	Summer 2000
Traveled to New York with students from across the country to observe the workings of the United Nations	Summer 2000

SKILLS	
Languages:	Conversational French
Computer Skills:	Windows XP, Microsoft Word, PowerPoint

SAMPLE CREATIVE WRITING CURRICULUM *

Carnegie Mellon University

Department of English

Creative Writing Program

English Department Core *Complete both courses.*	2 courses, 18 units

76–26x Survey of Forms (Fiction, Poetry or Screenwriting) *

76–294 Interpretive Practices

Creative Writing Core *Complete five courses.*	5 courses, 45 units
English Electives	4 courses, 36 units

This is presented as a two-year (junior-senior) plan for completing major requirements. Its purpose is to show that this program can be completed in as few as two years, not that it should or must be. In fact, as a department, we recommend beginning the major in the sophomore year if possible. Students in Humanities and Social Sciences may declare a

major as early as mid-semester of the spring of their first year and begin major requirements the following fall. Freshman may take a seminar in Creative Writing (offered each
fall) and Introduction to Creative Writing (two to three sections offered per year).

JUNIOR YEAR		SENIOR YEAR	
Fall	**Spring**	**Fall**	**Spring**
Survey of Forms 76–26x	Survey of Forms 76–26x	Creative Writing Workshop 76–3xx/4xx	Creative Writing Workshop 76–3xx/4xx
Interpretive Practices 76–294	Creative Writing Workshop 76–3xx/4xx	Creative Writing Workshop 76–3xx/4xx	English Elective 76–3xx/4xx
English Elective 76–2xx/3xx	English Elective 76–3xx/4xx	English Elective 76–3xx/4xx	Elective
Elective	Elective	Elective	Elective
Elective	Elective	Elective	Elective

*This sample curriculum is reprinted with permission. The course schedule shown here is representative of courses for a creative
writing major at most colleges and universities. Of course, each school has slightly different emphases and requirements, and
students are advised to investigate the curriculum at each program they apply to.

CREATIVE WRITING PROGRAMS

Profiles of Selected Programs

Northeast / 358

Southeast / 368

Midwest / 371

West / 379

Comprehensive List of Colleges with Creative Writing Programs

By State / 383

Northeast

BRANDEIS UNIVERSITY

Department of English and Creative Writing
415 South Street, MS 023
Waltham, MA 02454–9110

Phone: (781) 736-2130
Website: brandeis.edu/departments/english/
creativewriting/index.html
Email: chaucer@brandeis.edu

Tuition: $$$$
Campus student enrollment (undergraduate):
3,621

Degree(s): BA in creative writing
Courses offered: Fiction, poetry, screen writing
Writing portfolio requirement: Yes for the
thesis option, at the end of the sophomore year
Scholarships available: No department
scholarships
Number of faculty: 5
Number of majors and minors: 15–25
**Percentage and number of applicants
accepted into the department per year:**
Varies. Each workshop is by instructor's permission
following the submission of a manuscript. The thesis
option requires a separate application at the end of
the sophomore year.
Department activities: *Laurel Moon* literary
magazine (biannual), *Where the Children Play*
magazine, *Gravity* magazine, School of Night
Reading series (about every 3 weeks), student-
organized readings, jams, and reader events, 5–6
annual awards.

Prominent Alumni:
Ha Jin
Mary Leader

BROWN UNIVERSITY

Literary Arts
Box 1923
Providence, RI 02912

Phone: (401) 863-3260
Website: brown.edu/cw
Email: writing@brown.edu

Tuition: $$$$
Campus student enrollment (undergraduate):
6,133

Degree(s): AB in literary arts
Courses offered: Poetry, fiction, screenwriting,
digital language arts, cross-genre writing, literary
translation.
Writing portfolio requirement: Yes
Scholarships available: No (through university,
not through department)
Number of faculty: 15
Number of majors and minors: About 40
seniors graduate with this concentration each year.
Department activities: More than 50 events
per year; International Writers Project, several literary magazines.

Prominent Alumni:
Mark Amerika
Mary Caponegro
Nilo Cruz
Edwidge Danticat
Jeffrey Eugenides
Percival Everett
Gayle Jones
Ben Lerner
Ben Marcus
Ruth Margraff
Rick Moody
Marilynne Robinson
Sarah Ruhl
Joanna Scott
Kevin Young

CARNEGIE MELLON UNIVERSITY

Department of English
Baker Hall 259
5000 Forbes Avenue
Pittsburgh, PA 15213

Phone: (412) 268-2850
Website: english.cmu.edu/degrees/ba_cw/
Email: English-Undergrads@andrew.cmu.edu

Tuition: $$$$
Campus student enrollment (undergraduate):
6,362

Degree(s): BA in creative writing
Courses offered: Poetry, fiction, screenwriting, creative nonfiction
Writing portfolio requirement: Portfolio recommended
Scholarships available: Yes; Gladys Schmitt Creative Writing Scholarship, amount varies.
Number of faculty: 7 full-time
Number of majors and minors: 53
Department activities: Internships at Carnegie Mellon University Press, Adamson Student Writing Awards, Visiting Writers Series, Student Reading Series, Martin Luther King Jr. Day Writing Awards, The Hilary Masters Award for the Personal Essay, The Excellence in First-Year Writing Awards, High School Mentoring Program, Undergraduate Exchange with Sheffield Hallam University in Sheffield, UK Honors Thesis Program, Charles C. Dawe Memorial Award, Letterpress Program, Student Filmmaking Club, Ink Pot, creative writing program newsletter, *Minnesota Review* poetry editorial internship, *Oakland Review* literary journal, *Dossier*, literary supplement to campus newspaper, Sigma Tau Delta, Student Advisory Committee.

Prominent Alumni:
Elisabeth Finch—writer for *Grey's Anatomy*
Brittany McCandless—Associate Producer for *CBS This Morning*

Jewell Parker Rhodes—writer and professor, Colby College

COLBY COLLEGE

Department of English
Creative Writing Concentration
4800 Mayflower Hill Drive
Waterville, ME 04901–8852

Phone: (800) 723-3032
Website: colby.edu/cw/
Email: admissions@colby.edu

Tuition: $$$$
Campus student enrollment: 1,850

Degree(s): BA in English with creative writing concentration
Courses offered: Fiction, nonfiction, creative nonfiction, poetry, and annual genre courses (screenwriting, feature writing, or playwriting)
Writing portfolio requirement: No
Scholarships available: Yes. Scholarship aid at Colby is need-based, and financial aid is granted to ensure equal access and opportunity for students from all economic backgrounds. Financial aid is available to all students who apply for aid and demonstrate financial need. Colby meets 100% of calculated need as determined by the college and does not include loans in financial aid packages.
Number of faculty: 6
Number of majors and minors: 76 English majors (including the concentration in creative writing), 18 majors in the creative writing concentration, and 35 creative writing minors.
Percentage and number of applicants accepted into the department per year: 100% (not competitive—any student can declare this major or minor)
Department activities: *The Pequod*, a biannual literary arts magazine featuring short stories, poems and artwork by students.

Prominent Alumni:

E. Annie Proulx (1957)—Pulitzer Prize–winning novelist and short-story writer

Robert B. Parker (1954)—author of more than three dozen mysteries including the Spenser series

Doris Kearns Goodwin (1964)—Pulitzer Prize–winning historian

Alan Taylor (1977)—Pulitzer Prize–winning historian

COLUMBIA UNIVERSITY

Undergraduate Creative Writing Program
609 Kent Hall
New York, NY 10027

Phone: (212) 854-3774
Website: arts.columbia.edu/writing/undergraduate
Email: writingprogram@columbia.edu

Tuition: $$$$
Campus student enrollment (undergraduate): 8,102

Degree(s): BA
Concentrations: Poetry, Fiction, Literary Nonfiction
Courses offered: Fiction, literary nonfiction, poetry, dramatic writing, and screenwriting.
Writing portfolio requirement: Yes (writing sample required)
Number of faculty: 28
Department activities: Publishes annual *Columbia Journal*, creative writing lecture series; students can partake in readings, lectures, performances, and plays through Columbia's School of the Arts.

Prominent Alumni:

Jonathan Ames
Mary Jo Bang
Tina Chang
Kiran Desai
Stephen Dubner
Emily Fragos
Rivka Galchen

Philip Gourevitch
Dinaw Mengestu
Susan Minot
Sigrid Nunez
Gregory Orr
Beth Raymer
Karen Russell
Tracy K. Smith
Wells Tower
Adam Wilson

CORNELL UNIVERSITY

Department of English
250 Goldwin Smith Hall
Cornell University Ithaca, NY 14853–3201

Phone (department) (607) 255-6800
Website: english.arts.cornell.edu/creative/
Email: creativewriting@cornell.edu

Tuition: $$$$
Campus student enrollment (undergraduate): 14,315

Degree(s): BA in English
Concentrations: Creative writing, minor in creative writing for non-English majors
Courses offered: Fiction, poetry, introduction to creative writing, intermediate narrative writing, intermediate verse writing, and advanced creative writing.
Number of faculty: 10
Department activities: Each academic year, the Barbara and David Zalaznick Reading Series brings poets, fiction writers, essayists, and industry professionals to campus for readings and talks. Summer study abroad: Imagining Rome: Creative Writing Workshops in Italy. The award-winning national literary journal *Epoch* is published by the Department of English and the Creative Writing Program.

Prominent alumni:

John Cleese, Writer and Actor

Clifford Irving

Bill Maher

Lorrie Moore

Toni Morrison

Thomas Pynchon

Helen Schulman

Kurt Vonnegut

EMERSON COLLEGE

Department of Writing, Literature & Publishing

120 Boylston Street

Boston, MA 02116–4624

Phone: Undergraduate Admission: (617) 824-8600; WLP Department: (617) 824-8750; WLP Department: (617) 824-7856

Website: emerson.edu

Email: admission@emerson.edu

Tuition: $$

Campus student enrollment (undergraduate): 3,780

Degree(s): BA in Writing, Literature and Publishing, BFA in Creative Writing, BFA in Comedic Arts

Courses offered: Fiction, poetry, creative nonfiction, screenwriting, comedy writing, children's writing (occasional), magazine writing, book publishing, magazine publishing, editing, book and magazine design and production, desktop publishing.

Writing portfolio requirement: BFA: Senior Thesis

Scholarships available: Yes

Number of faculty: 49 full-time, 11 writers/publishers-in-residence, 73 part-time

Percentage of applicants accepted into the department per year: 58%

Department activities: Literary Journals: Award-winning *Ploughshares*, and *Ploughshares Solos*—digital-first long stories and essays.

Student Literary Magazines: *Gauge* (contemporary issues magazine), *Concrete* (literary magazine), *Developed Images* (photography magazine), *Stork* (fiction journal), *em* magazine (lifestyle), *The Emerson Review* (undergrad literary journal), *Your Magazine* (lifestyle).

Organizations: Undergraduate Writers Network, Writers' Block (a learning community in one of the College's residence halls), spec. (screenwriters club), emersonWRITES (opportunities to teach creative writing to high school student from the Greater Boston community).

Emerson Reading Series: Recent readings/events guests include Michael Cunningham, Victor Fowler Calzada, Pulizer Prize winner Megan Marshall (also a faculty member), Boston's Poet Laureate Danielle Legros Georges (also an alumna), Jon Papernick (senior writer-in-residence), Sara Novic (also alumna), Jabari Asim (also faculty), Matthew Salesses, Pamela Painter (also faculty member), Laura Van Den Berg.

Prominent Alumni:

Thomas Lux—poet and professor, Georgia State University

Ralph Pine—president, Drama Book Publishers

Don Lee—editor, *Ploughshares*

Barbara Layman—senior writer, Walt Disney Productions

Michael Andor Brodeur—writer/editor, *Both* magazine

Jack Gantos—author of *Rotten Ralph* series

Risa Miller—fiction writer

Lisa Jahn-Clough—writer, children's books

Susan Cannon—executive editor, *Freetime* magazine

Janet Tashijian—writer, young adult novels

Reed Foster—publisher, Hearst Publications

Genevieve Roth—*Details* magazine

Andre Mora—*Oprah* magazine

Astrid Sandoval—Harvard Business School Publishing

Jennifer Pieroni—Quick Fiction

FAIRLEIGH DICKINSON UNIVERSITY

College at Florham
Department of Literature, Language, Writing and Philosophy
285 Madison Avenue
Madison, NJ 07940

Phone: (973) 443-8711
Website: view2.fdu.edu/academics/becton-college
/literature-language-writing-philosophy/creative
-writing-ba/
Email: Chace@fdu.edu

Tuition: $
Campus student enrollment (undergraduate):
9,171

Degree(s): BA in creative writing
Courses offered: Introduction to Creative Writing: includes Fiction, Poetry, Creative Non-fiction. Fiction Writing, Advanced Fiction Writing. Creative Nonfiction Writing: Personal Essay, Memoir. Introduction to Poetry, Advanced Poetry. Playwriting and Dramatic Structure, Young Adult and Children's Writing, Screenwriting, Reading as Writers. Senior Writing Project I (fall of senior year), Senior Writing Project II (spring of senior year). Getting Published Creative Writing Internship World Literature I, II, or III, Advanced.
Writing portfolio requirement: Senior writing project.
Scholarships available: Yes, various university scholarships; most students receive financial aid.
Number of faculty: 5 full-time
Number of majors and minors: 64
Department activities:
Creative Writing Club
Words and Music Festival
Publishing Panels with professionals: Agents, Editors
Visiting Writers: Poetry, Fiction, Creative Nonfiction

Prominent Alumni:
Dave Wielgosz—Assistant Editor, DC Comics
Chee Gates—Editor, Health & Wellness at Sears

Holdings Corporation (formerly at *O* Magazine)
Marie Formica—Marketing Director, NJI Media, also has an MFA
Lisa Grgas (Voltalina)—poet and Regulatory Associate at Oregon Health & Science University (OHSU)
Gloria Beth Amodeo—Online Editor at TLR and Copy Supervisor at Corbett (Advertising)
Loni Venti—Style & Beauty Editor, *People* Magazine (formerly at *Cosmopolitan* Magazine)
Peter Florek—published award-winning book of poetry, *Splattervision*, ELJ Publications
Alexander Oliver—graduate assistant for CEHS Career Services at Montclair State University and short story writer
John Saavedra—Associate Editor Den of Geek U.S.; published articles in the NY *Times*
Gillian Kleiman—Reporter/Copyeditor New York *Post*
Frankie Lopes—short essay selected as Distinguished Story in *Best American Essays 2014.*
Emily Chamberlain—MFA Creative Writing Program at the New School, NYC (received National Fiction Prize)
Kaitlin McCleary—MFA Creative Writing Program at the New School, NYC
Cheryl Thompson—MFA Creative Writing Program at the New School, NYC
John Saavedra—MFA Creative Writing Program at the New School, NYC
Katarina Tonks (rising senior)—included in upcoming anthology of "Wattpad" authors pubished by Simon and Schuster, Gallery Books, Spring 2016. Has received numerous awards for her book *Death Is My BFF* from Wattpad, on online writing site.

GEORGE WASHINGTON UNIVERSITY

Department of English
Rome Hall 760
801 22nd Street NW
Washington, D.C. 20052

Phone: (202) 944-6180
Website: gwu.edu/~english/cw.htm
Email: engldept@gwu.edu

Tuition: $$$
Campus student enrollment (undergraduate):
10,240

Degree(s): BA with major in English, BA with major in Creative Writing & English, minor in English, minor in Creative Writing & English
Courses offered: Fiction, nonfiction, poetry screenwriting
Number of faculty: 34 full-time, 15 adjuncts
Department activities: The English department awards four prizes to undergraduate writers each year: the Vivian Nellis Memorial Prize, awarded to a graduating senior who has demonstrated excellence in creative writing during his or her years at GW; the Astere E. Claeyssens Prize in Playwriting; the Academy of American Poets College Prize and the Hasan Hussain Award, awarded to two graduating seniors in the English and creative writing major for excellence in thesis for either fiction or poetry. Undergraduates can also contribute to one university-sponsored literary magazine: *Wooden Teeth.*

GOUCHER COLLEGE

Department of English
Kratz Center for Creative Writing
Admissions Office
1021 Dulaney Valley Road
Baltimore, MD 21204

Phone: (800) 468-2437
Website: goucher.edu/cwpromo/kratz
Email: admissions@goucher.edu

Tuition: $$
Campus student enrollment (undergraduate):
1,478

Degree(s): BA in English with creative writing concentration and creative writing minor
Courses offered: Fiction, nonfiction, journalism, poetry, screenwriting and screenwriting adaptation.
Writing portfolio requirement: Depends on individual course requirement
Scholarships available: Yes
Number of faculty: 15 in the English department; 5 creative writing faculty
Majors: 59
Department activities: Numerous literary and campus magazines including *Goucher Review*, *Verge* magazine, and *Preface* magazine. Each year, the Kratz Center for Creative Writing at Goucher College offers writing fellowships for the summer. These awards range from between $1,000 to $3,000 and are open to all sophomores, juniors, and seniors who have taken a 200-level and a 300-level writing workshop at Goucher College. The fellowships fund worthy projects falling within the following areas: (1) travel and/or research connected to and culminating in a work of creative writing; (2) a writing-related internship at (for example) a literary magazine or book publisher; (3) attendance at a summer conference or workshop.

Prominent Alumni:
Jordana Frankel—author of *The Ward*
Laura Tims—author of *Please Don't Tell*
Andrew Ervin—author of *Burning Down George Orwell's House*
Jean Crowell—author of *Necessary Madness* and *Letting the Body Lead*
Darcey Steinke—award-winning novelist and professor at the New School University
John McManus—award-winning novelist
Eleanor Wilner—MacArthur "Genius" Fellow and award-winning poet

HARVARD UNIVERSITY

English Department
Barker Center
12 Quincy Street
Cambridge, MA 02138

Phone: (617) 495-2533
Website: english.fas.harvard.edu/undergraduate
/creative-writing/
Email: engdept@fas.harvard.edu

Tuition: $$$
Campus student enrollment (undergraduate):
10,225

Degree(s): BA in English
Courses offered: Fiction, poetry, nonfiction,
screenwriting, and playwriting.
Writing portfolio requirement: Yes, students
must submit writing samples for admission to partic-
ular courses.
Number of faculty: 11

HAMILTON COLLEGE

Literature and Creative Writing Department
198 College Hill Road
Clinton, NY 13323

Phone: (315) 859-4370
Website: hamilton.edu
Email: english@hamilton.edu

Tuition: $$$
Campus student enrollment (undergraduate):
1,850

Degree(s): Bachelor of Arts (concentration in
Literature or Creative Writing)
Courses offered: Fiction, poetry.
Writing portfolio requirement: No
Scholarships available: No merit scholarships.
All scholarships are need-based.

Number of faculty: 15, including four published
and award-winning creative writers
Number of majors and minors: 45 majors
(including 7 creative writing majors) and 15 minors
(including 5 creative writing minors)
Department activities: Senior Program includes
a seminar in creative writing. Many faculty are
published authors, including Jane Springer, recipient of the Whiting, Pushcart, and Beatrice Hawley
awards, among other honors; and Tina Hall,
winner of the 2010 Drue Heinz Literature Prize for
short fiction. Naomi Guttman (poetry) and Doran
Larson have also won awards for their writing.

Prominent Alumni:
Henry Allen (1963)—a Pulitzer Prize–winning
author
Terry Brooks (1966)—NY *Times* bestselling author
of the *Shannara*, *Landover* and *Word/Void* series
Deborah Forte Stone (1977)—President of Scholastic
Media
Sarah Maas (2008)—author of Young Adult
fantasy novels, e.g., *Throne of Glass*
Lauren Magaziner (2012)—author of Young Adult
novels
Peter Cameron (1982)—PEN/O. Henry Award–
winning fiction writer, e.g., *Coral Glynn*
Tom Meehan (1951)—Tony Award–winning
playwright, e.g., *The Producers*
Nat Faxon (1997)—actor, screenwriter, and
2012 Academy Award recipient for Best Adapted
Screenplay for *The Descendants*
Kamila Shamsie (1994)—award-winning author,
e.g., *Salt and Saffron, Kartography*
John Nichols (1962)—author of *The Sterile Cuckoo*
Stuart Kestenbaum (1973)—State of Maine Poet
Laureate
Peter Meinke (1955)—State of Florida Poet Laureate

HOFSTRA UNIVERSITY

Department of English
204 Calkins Hall
Hempstead, NY 11550

Phone: (516) 463-5454 or toll-free (800) HOFSTRA
Website: hofstra.edu/English
Email: engpmu@hofstra.edu

Tuition: $$
Campus student enrollment (undergraduate):
6,824

Degree(s): BA in English—areas of specialization include literatures, creative writing, publishing studies, and children's and young adult literature; BA in English education; BA and BA/MA in journalism (through the School of Communication). Minors are offered in creative writing, English, journalism (through the School of Communication), and writing studies.
Courses offered: Prose, poetry, drama, essays, screenwriting, children's literature.
Number of faculty: 27 full-time, 13 part-time
Department activities: *Font* magazine, a student literary magazine, the Hofstra Revels, *Leviathan: A Journal of Melville Studies*, the F. Scott Fitzgerald Society, *Twentieth-Century Literature*, and Hofstra Writers, a creative writing club.

ITHACA COLLEGE

Department of Writing
4th Floor, Smiddy Hall
953 Danby Road
Ithaca, NY 14850

Phone: (607) 274-3138
Website: ithaca.edu
Email: ddeweese@ithaca.edu

Tuition: $$
Campus student enrollment (undergraduate):
6,769

Degree(s): BA in writing
Concentrations: Optional concentrations in creative writing, nonfiction writing, feature writing and professional writing.
Courses offered: Fiction, poetry, creative nonfiction, feature writing, professional writing, science fiction and fantasy, children's literature, theory courses, selected topics, senior seminars, and senior projects of the students' own design.
Writing portfolio requirement: Recommended but not required
Scholarships available: Yes
Number of faculty: 30 full-time, 20 part-time
Number of majors and minors: Approximately 134 majors, 57 minors
Number of applicants accepted into the department per year: 35–40 students
Department activities: Distinguished Visiting Writers Series, Internship Program in Writing and Publishing, Annual Writing Contest, Stillwater Literary Magazine, Handwerker Reading Series, Writing Center, New Voices Literary Festival, Ithaca Writers Institute.

Prominent Alumni:

Graduates have been accepted by graduate programs at the University of Iowa and New York University, hired by publishers such as Random House, and published in major periodicals such as the New York Times and by major publishers such as Norton.

JOHNS HOPKINS UNIVERSITY

The Writing Seminars
81 Gilman Hall
Baltimore, MD 21218

Phone: (410) 516-6286
Website: writingseminars.jhu.edu
Email: See writingseminars.jhu.edu/people/

Tuition: $$$$
Campus student enrollment (undergraduate):
5,591

Degree(s): BA in The Writing Seminars
Courses offered: Fiction, poetry, non-fiction, science writing.
Writing portfolio requirement: Optional
Scholarships available: Yes
Number of faculty: 9 plus numerous visitors and adjunct faculty
Number of majors and minors: 194 majors
Department activities: Undergraduate reading series; numerous literary journals. Literary magazine, the *Hopkins Review*.

Prominent Alumni:

John Barth—novelist
Russell Baker—*New York Times* columnist
John Astin—actor
Ilene Rosensweig—author and designer of *Swell*
Kathryn Hart—television producer of *Pocoyo*

LESLEY UNIVERSITY

College of Liberal Arts and Sciences
29 Everett Street
Cambridge, MA 02138

Phone: (888) LESLEY-U or (617) 349-8300
Website: lesley.edu/bachelor-of-arts/creative-writing/
Email: admissions@lesley.edu

Tuition: $
Campus student enrollment (undergraduate): 1,982

Degree(s): BA, accelerated BA/MFA dual degree
Concentrations: Fiction, Nonfiction, Poetry, Script and Screenplay, Writing for Children and Young Adults.
Courses offered: Magazine production, poetry, scriptwriting, creative nonfiction, autobiographical writing, fiction, literature.

PRINCETON UNIVERSITY

Creative Writing Program
185 Nassau Street
Princeton, NJ 08544

Phone: (609) 258-4096
Website: arts.princeton.edu/academics/creative-writing/
Email: writing@princeton.edu

Tuition: $$$
Campus student enrollment (undergraduate): 5,100

Degree(s): A degree in creative writing is not offered, however students can earn a certificate in creative writing in addition to a degree in another area.
Courses offered: Fiction, poetry, translation.
Writing portfolio requirement: Writing sample for all writing courses
Scholarships available: No, financial aid is need-based
Number of faculty: 22
Department activities: Small workshop courses, averaging eight to ten students, provide intensive feedback and instruction for both beginners and advanced writers, and each year 25 to 30 seniors work individually with a member of the faculty on a creative thesis: a novel, a screenplay, or a collection of short stories, poems or translations. Writers of national and international distinction visit campus throughout the year to participate in the Althea Ward Clark W'21 Reading Series and to discuss their work. The Lewis Center's Performance Central series presents the biennial Princeton Poetry Festival drawing poets from around the world. An Emerging Writers series puts thesis students at the podium alongside a lineup of established guest writers curated by seniors in the program. The Leonard Milberg collections and Princeton's unparalleled library and archives also provide world-class opportunities for the study of contemporary literature.

Prominent alumni:
Madison Smartt Bell, novelist; finalist for the 1995 National Book Award and the 1996 PEN/Faulkner Award
Jane Hirshfield, poet
Branden Jacobs-Jenkins, award-winning playwright and MacArthur Fellow
Galway M. Kinnell, Pulitzer Prize and National Book Award recipient
Akhil Sharma, International Dublin Literary Award

WESLEYAN UNIVERSITY

English Department
294 High Street
Middletown, CT 06459

Phone: 860-685-2360
Website:
wesleyan.edu/writing/academics/creative.html
Email: admission@wesleyan.edu

Tuition: $$$$
Campus student enrollment (undergraduate):
2,895

Degree(s): BA in English with creative writing concentration. The Writing Certificate allows students from all majors to develop proficiency in creative writing (poetry, fiction, creative non-fiction, screenwriting, playwriting).
Courses offered: Fiction, poetry, nonfiction, playwriting, screenwriting, and writing for television.
Writing portfolio requirement: Admission in competitive to the creative writing concentration. Students have to submit writing samples to receive instructor permission for particular courses.
Number of faculty: 5
Department activities: Poets, essayists, journalists, and fiction writers visit the campus throughout the year, offering readings, workshops, colloquia, and informal discussions about writing. Writing prizes recognize exceptional student work and

support independent summer writing projects while students publish creative writing, journalism, and academic essays in more than a dozen student publications.

SARAH LAWRENCE COLLEGE

1 Mead Way
Bronxville, NY 10708

Phone: (914) 337-0700;
(914) 395-2510 (admissions)
Website: sarahlawrence.edu
Email: slcadmit@sarahlawrence.edu (admissions)

Tuition: $$$$
Campus student enrollment (undergraduate):
1,400

Degree(s): BA in liberal arts
Courses offered: Fiction, nonfiction, poetry.
Scholarships available: Merit-based aid as well as need-based aid
Number of faculty: 15 poetry, 18 fiction, 16 nonfiction
Department activities: More than 40 events per year.

Prominent Alumni:
Alan Gurganus
Ann Patchett
Alice Walker

Southeast

AGNES SCOTT COLLEGE

Department of English

141 E. College Avenue

Decatur, GA 30030

Phone: (404) 471-6000 or toll-free (800) 868-8602

Website: agnesscott.edu

Email: info@agnesscott.edu

Tuition: $

Campus student enrollment (undergraduate): 915

Degree(s): BA in English/Creative Writing

Courses offered: Poetry, fiction, creative nonfiction and dramatic writing.

Writing portfolio requirement: No

Scholarships available: Scholarships and need-based aid, up to full tuition and room and board.

Number of faculty: 10 full-time

Number of majors: 22–23

Percentage of applicants accepted into the department per year: (college) Fall 2015: 62% of applicants accepted

Department activities: Annual Writer's Festival, *Aurora* (literary journal).

Prominent Alumni:

Marsha Norman—Pulitzer and Tony Award–winning playwright

ECKERD COLLEGE

Department of Creative Writing

4200 54th Avenue South

St. Petersburg, FL 33711

Phone: (727) 864-8331 or toll-free (800) 456-9009

Website: eckerd.edu

Email: admissions@eckerd.edu

Tuition: $$

Campus student enrollment (undergraduate): 2,023

Degree(s): BA in creative writing

Courses offered: Fiction, poetry, playwriting, screenwriting, journal writing, the personal essay, journalism, publishing and the writing career.

Writing portfolio requirement: No

Scholarships available: Yes

Number of faculty: 3

Department activities: The *Eckerd College Review*, a student literary magazine. Annual Times Reading Festival. Most Writing Workshop majors spend a semester or January term abroad with an Eckerd professor at the Eckerd College London Study Centre located in the historic Bloomsbury district of London.

Prominent Alumni:

Dorothy Allison

James Hall

Dennis Lehane

EMORY UNIVERSITY

The Creative Writing Program

537 Kilgo Circle

N209 Callaway Center

Atlanta, GA 30322

Phone: (404) 727-4683

Website: creativewriting.emory.edu

Email: creativewriting@emory.edu

Tuition: $$

Campus student enrollment (undergraduate): 7,803

Degree(s): BA in English/creative writing

Courses offered: Fiction, poetry, playwriting, screenwriting, creative nonfiction.

Writing portfolio requirement: No
Scholarships available: No
Number of faculty: 7
Number of majors and minors: 98 majors
Percentage and number of applicants accepted into the department per year: Majors do not have to go through an application process. Students meet with faculty adviser before deciding.
Department activities: Creative Writing, Program Reading Series.

Prominent Alumni:

Holly Gregory—producer with Nickelodeon in New York City

Lauren Gunderson, award-winning Atlanta-based playwright, screenwriter, short story author and actor

Lorrie Hewett—who published her first novel in high school and attended the Iowa Writers Workshop after graduation from Emory

Anton DiSclafani—novelist and teacher

Gina Atwater—filmmaker

Adam Roberts—food writer

HOLLINS UNIVERSITY

Box 9707
7916 Williamson Road
Roanoke, VA 24020

Phone: (800) 456-9595
Website: hollins.edu/academics/majors-minors/english-creative-writing-major/
Email: huadm@hollins.edu

Tuition: $
Campus student enrollment (undergraduate): 639

Degree(s): B.A. in English with concentration in creative writing
Courses offered: Fiction, poetry, creative nonfiction, screenwriting, cinematic adaptation, expository writing, cross-genre and experimental writing, writing out of the multicultural experience, playwriting.
Writing portfolio requirement: No
Scholarships available: Yes
Percentage and number of applicants accepted into the department per year: All admissions at the undergraduate level are to the university, not to the department.
Department activities: Undergraduate writers publish poetry and fiction in the student periodical, *The Album*, the student literary journal, *Cargoes*, or the multicultural literary magazine, *Gravel*. The annual Lex Allen Literary Festival features the university's writers-in-residence and guest authors. Cash prizes are awarded in fiction and poetry to undergraduate college students. Approximately 12 readings a year by acclaimed published writers. During the Jackson Poetry Reading, held each April, nationally known poets read from their work.

Prominent alumnae:

Margaret Wise Brown
Annie Dillard
Elizabeth Forsythe Hailey
Cathryn Hankla
Sally Mann
Karen Osborn
Shannon Ravenel
Lee Smith
Jane Gentry Vance

UNIVERSITY OF NORTH CAROLINA AT WILMINGTON

Department of Creative Writing
601 South College Road
Wilmington, NC 28403–5938

Phone: (910) 962-7063
Website: uncw.edu/writers/
Email: adamsl@uncw.edu

Tuition: $

Campus student enrollment (undergraduate): 13,261

Degree(s): BFA in Creative Writing

Major tracks: Fiction, poetry, creative nonfiction, with limited courses in screenwriting and playwriting.

Writing portfolio requirement: Yes. Students are required to provide a writing portfolio for admission to the BFA program after they have completed 24 credit hours and certain creative writing prerequisites.

Number of faculty: 19

Department activities: Atlantis student literary journal, visiting writers, Writer's Week Symposium.

UNIVERSITY OF TAMPA

Department of English and Writing

401 W. Kennedy Boulevard

Tampa, FL 33606

Phone: (813) 253-6211 or toll-free (800) MINARET

Website: ut.edu

Email: admissions@ut.edu

Tuition: $

Campus student enrollment (undergraduate): 7,959

Degree(s): BA in writing and English

Courses offered: Fiction, nonfiction, poetry, dramatic writing and professional writing courses such as journalism, advertising, technical writing, writing for interactive media, writing for informational design.

Writing portfolio requirement: No

Scholarships available: Yes

Number of faculty: 30 total (12 teach in the writing major, though none exclusively)

Number of majors and minors: 139 total (46 writing, 47 journalism, 46 English)

Percentage and number of applicants accepted into the department per year: All university students are eligible to enroll in the department. University overall rate is 35%.

Department activities: Four student publications including a weekly student newspaper, yearbook, literary magazine, and honors journal.

Prominent Alumni:

Connie May Fowler

Amy Hill Hearth

UNIVERSITY OF VIRGINIA

Department of English

219 Bryan Hall

P.O. Box 400121

Charlottesville, VA 22904

Phone: (434) 924-6675

Website: creativewriting.virginia.edu/ugrad.html

Email: mpm3a@virginia.edu

Tuition: $$$

Campus student enrollment (undergraduate): 15,669

Degree(s): BA in English, Area Program in Poetry Writing; Area Program in Literary Prose

Courses offered: Fiction, creative nonfiction, poetry.

Writing portfolio requirement: Creative writing courses require students to complete a manuscript of fiction or poetry before registering for a course.

Department activities: The Poetry Writing Area Program, a two-year course of study, allows talented undergraduate writers to pursue serious study of the craft of poetry writing within the context of the English major. Students usually apply in the spring semester of their second year. The Area Program in Literary Prose follows the model of the Poetry Program, but in it students work on fiction, creative nonfiction, and hybrids.

Midwest

HOPE COLLEGE

Department of English
338 Lubbers Hall
126 East 10th Street
Holland, MI 49423

Phone: (616) 395-7620
Website: hope.edu/english
Email: english@hope.edu

Tuition: $
Campus student enrollment (undergraduate):
3,200

Degree(s): BA in English with writing emphasis
Courses offered: Fiction, poetry, nonfiction, playwriting, novels, graphic fiction, translation.
Writing portfolio requirement: No
Scholarships available: Yes, Distinguished Artist Award, $2,500
Number of faculty: 30 full- and part-time in the department, 10 of them in creative writing
Number of majors and minors: About 60 graduating per year
Percentage and number of applicants accepted into the department per year: Students admitted to the college will be accepted into the creative writing program.
Department activities: Visiting Writers Series (3 readings per semester); student-edited literary magazine (1 issue per semester)

KENYON COLLEGE

Department of English
Sunset Cottage
Gambier, OH 43022

Phone: (740) 427-5210
Website: kenyon.edu/academics/departments-programs/english/
Email: admissions@kenyon.edu

Tuition: $$$$
Campus student enrollment (undergraduate):
1,711

Degree(s): BA in English with a concentration in creative writing
Courses offered: Fiction, poetry, creative nonfiction.
Writing portfolio requirement: No
Scholarships available: No scholarships specifically for creative writers, but scholarships are available through the college
Number of faculty: 23 in English Department, 7 of them teach creative writing courses
Department activities: The *Kenyon Review*, a literary magazine. Students may apply to be *Kenyon Review* Student Associates and gain experience in editing and producing. The Kenyon Chapbook Series offers poets the opportunity to prepare their work for publication. The English Department also awards a series of prizes each year to its most talented student poets, fiction writers and literary critics. Several student-run journals and magazines publish student work and offer students opportunities to hone their editing and production skills. *Hika* is the oldest literary magazine at Kenyon; newer ones include *Persimmons* and the *Horn Gallery* magazine. Students have opportunities to read their work at the Horn Gallery, a student-run arts space. Kenyon hosts a great variety of visiting writers, more than 30 in a typical year. Students have the opportunity to study with and attend readings by internationally renowned poets and writers through the Richard L. Thomas Chair, which brings a different visiting writer to campus for one semester every year. The English Department has designed its own yearlong off-campus studies program—the Kenyon-Exeter Program—in which Kenyon students attend the University of Exeter in Devon, England, under the direction of a Kenyon English professor. The

Kenyon-Exeter program offers students an opportunity to study literature and deepen their knowledge of British culture.

Prominent Alumni:

Robert Lowell (1940)—Pulitzer Prize–winning poet (*Lord Weary's Castle, Life Studies*)

Peter Taylor (1940)—Pulitzer Prize–winning fiction writer (*A Summons to Memphis, The Old Forest*)

Robie Macauley (1941)—writer and editor (*Kenyon Review*, fiction editor of *Playboy*)

William Gass (1947)—National Book Award–winning writer (*Omensetter's Luck, The Tunnel*)

E. L. Doctorow (1952)—Pulitzer Prize–winning author of *Ragtime, Loon Lake, Billy Bathgate,* and many other novels

James Wright (1952)—Pulitzer Prize-winning poet (*The Green Wall, The Branch Will Not Break*)

Robert Mezey (1955)—poet (Lamont Award winner, *The Lovemaker*)

P. F. Kluge (1964)—writer (*Eddie and the Cruisers, Alma Mater, Biggest Elvis*)

Jay Cocks (1966)—Academy Award–winning screenwriter (*The Age of Innocence, Gangs of New York*)

Daniel Mark Epstein (1970)—poet and biographer (*Nat King Cole, Sister Aimee*)

David Lynn (1976)—editor of the Kenyon Review

Nancy Sydor Zafris (1976)—Flannery O'Connor Prize–winning author (*The People I Know*)

Caleb Carr (1977)—novelist (*The Alienist*)

Wendy MacLeod (1981)—playwright (*The House of Yes, Schoolgirl Figure*)

Allison Joseph (1988)—poet (*Imitation of Life*)

Laura Hillenbrand (1989)—author (*Seabisquit*)

Adam Davies (1994)—novelist (*The Frog Prince*)

Andrew Grace (2001)—poet (*A Belonging Field*)

KNOX COLLEGE

Program in Creative Writing
2 East South Street
Galesburg, IL 61401–4999

Phone: (309) 341-7195
Website: knox.edu/academics/majors-and-minors/creative-writing
Email: mberlin@knox.edu or emetz@knox.edu

Tuition: $$
Campus student enrollment (undergraduate): 1,420

Degree(s): BA in creative writing

Courses offered: Fiction, poetry, creative nonfiction, playwriting, screenwriting, translation workshops (beginning, intermediate, advanced levels); independent study in various fusion writing/arts forms; Senior Portfolio (book-length creative thesis completed by all senior creative writing majors); modern and contemporary literature, selected single-authors (often with travel options), dramatic literature, English, American, world literatures, journalism; Creativity (creative process seminar for firstyear students); London Arts Alive, Chicago Semester (ACM), Knox in New York, Green Oaks Term, numerous additional international programs.

Scholarships available: Yes (including achievement scholarships in creative writing and all arts fields)

Number of faculty: 12 (all widely published; winners of numerous national/international literary awards); college-wide student/faculty ratio: 12:1.

National recognition: Featured in *Poets & Writers* Magazine as 1 of 3 top undergraduate creative writing programs in U.S. Regional recognition: Top number of winners and finalists in annual Nick Adams Fiction Contest (over 35 years), sponsored by Associated Colleges of the Midwest (ACM, 13-college consortium)

Department activities: *Catch*, student literary magazine eight national/international awards); six additional student magazines (print and online)—*Cellar Door, Diminished Capacity, Third Level, Wynken, Blynken and Nod, Common Room, Folio; TKS* (student newspaper); WVKC (student radio station); two student theaters; writers' internships at professional Vitalist Theatre (Chicago); Writers' Forum, Off-Knox, "61401," Playwrights Workshop, Art-to-Art (student presentations of creative projects); numerous art gallery and music venues (from classical to jazz, folk, rock), Davenport Awards (annual student competitions in fiction, poetry, playwriting); numerous additional writing competitions; Caxton Club/Felowes Fund (visiting writers, artists, scholars series—averaging 20 per academic year); Carl Sandburg Days (literary festival, including competitive Poetry Slam); Dorothea Tanning Days (literary/art festival); Rootabaga Jazz Festival; student writing internships at Carl Sandburg Historical Site, Galesburg *Register Mail* (and others); numerous opportunities for collaborative projects between student creative writers and departments/programs of theater, art, music, dance, literature, journalism, etc.; Member AWP (since 1967)—U.S. largest creative writing organization.

Prominent Alumni:

Carl Sandburg—poet, three-time winner of the Pulitzer Prize

Dorothea Tanning—internationally acclaimed poet: *Coming to That*; painter; sculpture; theater designer

Edgar Lee Masters—author, *Spoon River Anthology*

S. S. McClure—founder, *McClure's* Magazine; investigative reporter

Eugene Field—journalist, author: *Wynken, Blynken and Nod*

George Fitch—humorist, journalist, Illinois State Representative, author: "Old Siwash" stories

Don Marquis—author, playwright: *Archie and Mehitabel*

John Huston Finley—editor, the *New York Times*; president, Knox College; president, City College of New York; president, State University of New York

Ismat Kittani—president, United Nations General Assembly

Jack Finney—novelist and screenwriter, *Invasion of the Body Snatchers*

Alex Kuo—author; winner, American Book Award

David Lunde—author; 2-time winner, Rhysling Award for science fiction poetry

Sally Arteseros—senior editor, Doubleday and Co.

Barry Bearak—journalist, the *New York Times*; winner, Pulitzer Prize

Richard Riddell—theater designer; winner, Tony Award

Michael A. Ryan—screenwriter, winner, Emmy Award

Dave Newbart—journalist, *Chicago Sun-Times*; winner, The Nation Award

Rod Barker—author: *And the Waters Turned to Blood*

Sherwood Kiraly—novelist, playwright, screenwriter, *Diminished Capacity*

Barbara Bean—author, *Dream House*; University Press of Colorado First Book Award

Wendy Saul—author; professor of education, University of Missouri–St. Louis

Ruth Katz—psychotherapist, Sternau & Associates

William Kowinski—author, *The Malling of America*

William Colby—attorney; author, *Long Goodbye: The Deaths of Nancy Cruzan*

Ander Monson—editor; author, *Other Electricities*; winner, Zacharis First Book Award, *Ploughshares* magazine

Sean Mills—editor, Random House

Alex Keefe—political reporter, NPR-WBEZ Chicago; winner: Best Newswriter Award, Illinois Associated Press

Michael Walsh—poet: *Dirt Riddles*; winner, Miller Williams Poetry Award; Thomas Gunn Poetry Award

Lara Moritz—award-winning News Anchor, KMBC Channel 9, Kansas City

William Boast—author, *Power Ballads*; winner, Iowa Short Fiction Award

Elizabeth VanSteenwyk—award-winning children's author

Brenda Butler—Senior Features Editor, *Chicago Tribune*

Norman Golar—chair, Department of English, Stillman College

Lucas Southworth—author, *Everyone Here Has a Gun*; winner, Grace Paley Award for Short Fiction

Mark Suchomel—President, Legato Publishers Group

Anna Leahy—editor; poet, *Constituents of Matter*; winner, Wick Poetry Prize

Donald Harmon—Senator, State of Illinois

Tony Etz—Senior Agent, Creative Artists Agency, Los Angeles

LORAS COLLEGE

Creative Writing
1450 Alta Vista
Dubuque, IA 52001

Phone: (563) 588-7536
Website: loras.edu
Email: admissions@loras.edu

Tuition: $
Campus student enrollment (undergraduate):
Approximately 1,600

Degree(s): BA
Courses offered: Fiction writing; advanced fiction writing; fantastic fiction; poetry writing; advanced poetry writing; creative nonfiction writing; nonfiction literature and workshop; nature writing; writing the Midwest landscape; screenwriting; revision, editing, and publishing; senior thesis seminar.
Writing portfolio requirement: No entrance portfolio required.
Scholarships available: No scholarships specific to creative writing, but scholarships are given through the college. Seniors may compete for the $1,000 Bauerly-Roseliep Award.
Number of faculty: 3 in creative writing, 8 in the full English program.
Number of majors and minors: 49 current majors in creative writing

Percentage and number of applicants accepted into the department per year: There is no application process separate from application/acceptance into the college.
Department activities: Campus literary magazine: *The Limestone Review*. Majors also edit a national undergraduate literary magazine, *Catfish Creek*.

Prominent Alumni: Recent alum Alison Balaskovits ('09) won grand prize in the 2015 Santa Fe Writers Project Literary Awards Program for her short story collection *Magic for Unlucky Girls*. Many alums have placed into MFA programs, law school, graduate schools for other programs, have entered into the publishing field, grant writing, nonprofits, teaching, general business, etc.

NORTHWESTERN UNIVERSITY

Department of English
University Hall 215
1897 Sheridan Road
Evanston, IL 60208–2240

Phone: (847) 491-7294
Website: english.northwestern.edu
Email: english-dept@northwestern.edu

Tuition: $$$
Campus student enrollment (undergraduate):
8,000

Degree(s): BA with English Major in Creative Writing
Courses offered: Fiction, poetry, creative nonfiction
Scholarships available: Yes
Number of faculty: 12
Number of majors and minors: 250 in the entire English department
Department activities: An Annual Writing Competition held in the spring to recognize student writing. Writers-in-Residence program features prominent writers every spring. The university-wide

Center for the Writing Arts hosts visitors, colloquia and new courses for an entire quarter. Student literary magazines *Prompt* and *Helicon*.

Prominent alumni:

Dan Chaon, author of *Await Your Reply* (Ballantine Books, 2009) *You Remind Me of Me* (Ballantine Books, 2005), *Among the Missing* (Ballantine Books, 2002), and *Fitting Ends* (Ballantine Books, 2003)

Leslie Pietrzyk, author of *A Year and a Day* (Avon Books, 2005), *Pears on a Willow Tree* (William Morrow, 1999), *This Angel on My Chest* (University of Pittsburgh Press, 2015)

Veronica Roth, *Divergent* (movie rights starring Shailene Woodley), *Insurgent*, and *Allegiant*

Karen Russell, *Swamplandia*, finalist for 2012 Pulitzer Prize

Heidy Steidlmayer, winner of Ploughshares' 2012 John C. Zacharis First Book Award for poetry

OBERLIN COLLEGE

Creative Writing Program
153 W. Lorain Street
Oberlin, OH 44074

Phone: (440) 775-6567
Email: creativewriting@oberlin.edu
Website: new.oberlin.edu/arts-and-sciences/departments/creative_writing/departments/creative_writing/

Tuition: $$$$
Campus student enrollment (undergraduate): 2,900

Degree(s): BA
Courses offered: Fiction, poetry, creative nonfiction, playwriting, and screen writing
Writing portfolio requirement: Yes
Scholarships available: Yes
Number of faculty: 4 full-time, 1 visiting writer each fall
Number of majors and minors: More than 65 majors

Percentage and number of applicants accepted into the department per year: 75–85 students apply for 36 spots in the introductory-level major workshop, which is mandatory for entrance to the major.
Department activities: Affiliation with Field and the Oberlin College Press.

Prominent Alumni:
Poets
Thylias Moss (MacArthur fellow)
Franz Wright (Pulitzer winner)
Fiction writers
Myla Goldberg
Thisbe Nissen
Peter Cameron
Paul Russell
Wendy Brenner
Tracy Chevalier
Alan Furst
Emma Straub
Nonfiction writers
James McBride
Sonia Shah

PURDUE UNIVERSITY

English Department in the College of Liberal Arts
500 Oval Drive
West Lafayette, IN 47907–2038

Phone: (765) 494-3740
Website: cla.purdue.edu/english/
Email: griff@purdue.edu

Tuition: $$
Campus student enrollment (undergraduate): 39,409 (total), 29,497 undergraduate

Degree(s): BA in creative writing
Courses offered: Fiction, drama, poetry
Writing portfolio requirement: No
Scholarships available: Yes
Number of faculty: 60

Number of majors and minors: Undergraduate Creative Writing Majors: 60 Undergraduate Creative Writing minors: 20
Department activities: Literary journals, Literary Awards, *Modern Fiction Studies, Sycamore Review, The Writing Instructor, World Englishes;* creative writing newsletter.

Prominent Alumni:

Stephanie S. Nolan

Elizabeth Stuckey-French

Chielozona Eze

Henry Hughes

Gretchen Steele Pratt

Fred Arroyo

Laura Pritchett

Martin Walls

Aaron Michael Morales

Mehdi Tavana Okasi

SIENA HEIGHTS UNIVERSITY

Department of English
1247 E. Siena Heights Drive
Adrian, MI 49221

Phone: (517) 263-7611
Website: sienaheights.edu
Email: mbarbeel@sienaheights.edu

Tuition: $
Campus student enrollment (undergraduate): 2,492

Degree(s): BA
Courses offered: Fiction, poetry, creative nonfiction, scriptwriting, editing and publishing.
Writing portfolio requirement: No
Scholarships available:
Prestige Scholarship (full tuition)
Trustee Scholarship ($7,000–12,000)
Presidential Scholarship ($6,000–10,000)
Dean Scholarship ($5,000–10,000)
Honor Scholarship ($2,500–8,500)

Fine Arts and Performance Scholarship (varies)
Campus Ministry Scholars Program (varies)
Athletic Scholarship (varies)
Siena Grant ($1,500–5,500)
Phi Theta Kappa Scholarship ($1,000)
Number of faculty: 2
Number of majors and minors: 25 majors, 10 minors
Number of applicants accepted into the department per year: 10–15 applicants
Department activities: *Eclipse* (literary journal), Lambda Iota Tau (international literary honor society), *Spectra* (school newspaper), Sigma Tau Delta (literary honor society), annual film and speaker series.

Prominent Alumni:
Charles Fort Jr.—poet, former Reynold's Chair in poetry at University of Nebraska at Kearney
Todd Marshall—author, professor of English at Gonzaga University, and 2016 poet laureate for the state of Washington

STEPHENS COLLEGE

Office of Admissions
1200 East Broadway
Columbia, MO 65215

Phone: (800) 876-7207
Website: stephens.edu
Email: apply@stephens.edu

Tuition: $
Campus student enrollment (undergraduate): 594

Degree(s): BA in English with emphasis in creative writing and BFA in creative writing
Courses offered: Students take courses such as "Starting with Story," "Women Writers," and "Introduction to Scriptwriting." They must continue to take at least one creative writing workshop each semester thereafter, in at least three genres to be selected from poetry, fiction,

creative nonfiction, playwriting, and screenwriting. Students may take additional workshops in any of these genres.

Writing portfolio requirement: No for admission, yes for scholarship consideration and for graduation

Scholarships available: Yes, merit- and need-based scholarships available; amount varies

Number of faculty: 2 full-time, 3 part-time, 2 visiting writers per year

Number of majors and minors: More than 40 majors and minors

Percentage and number of applicants accepted into the department per year: Students are accepted to the college, not to the department.

Department activities: *Harbinger* literary magazine, individual student chapbooks, Sigma Tau Delta Honor Society, Visiting Writers Series, internships with *The Missouri Review*, audio drama internship, annual scriptwriting contest and New Script Showcase.

Prominent Alumni:

Leslie Adrienne Miller

Diane Johnson

Janet Beiler Shaw

Amy Knox Brown

Alanna Nash

Ann Daniel Stone

Lyah Beth LeFlore

Jennifer Woods

UNIVERSITY OF EVANSVILLE

Department of English

1800 Lincoln Avenue

Evansville, IN 47722

Phone: (812) 488-2963

Website: evansville.edu/majors/creativewriting /creativewriting/

Email: rg37@evansville.edu

Tuition: $

Campus student enrollment (undergraduate): 2,495

Degree(s): BA, BFA in creative writing

Courses offered: Fiction, nonfiction, poetry, screenwriting

Number of faculty: 4

Number of majors and minors: 80

Department activities: The *Evansville Review*, an award-winning student-edited literary journal; internships with *Measure*, a faculty-edited poetry journal, the *Ohio River Review*, a student-edited journal of student writings; Harlaxton England semester abroad; Harlaxton Summer Writing Program in the English Midlands; the Coffee Hours, a visiting writers series; the Wahnita DeLong writing workshop; the Virginia Grabill literary awards; various off-campus internships.

WESTERN MICHIGAN UNIVERSITY

Department of English

1903 W. Michigan Avenue

Kalamazoo, MI 49008

Phone: (269) 387-2572

Website: wmich.edu/english/

Email: ask-wmu@wmich.edu

Tuition: $$$

Campus student enrollment (undergraduate): 19,478

Degree(s): BA with creative writing emphasis

Courses offered: Fiction, poetry, creative nonfiction, playwriting

Writing portfolio requirement: No

Scholarships available: Yes.

Number of faculty: 5 full-time creative writing faculty; 35 total full-time faculty

Number of majors and minors: More than 140 creative writing majors, 100 creative writing minors

Percentage and number of applicants accepted into the department per year: 80%, more than 100 students

Department activities: *Third Coast* Literary Magazine (national circulation); *The Laureate* (undergraduate journal); New Play Project (summer courses in English and theater leading to productions on campus); public student play readings each semester; annual writing competition (cash prizes, national judge); Gwen Frostic Reading Series (nationally distinguished authors); New Issues Poetry, Prose and Drama Series (publishing house with more than 60 titles published); English Studies Symposium (includes creative writing presentations by undergrads).

Prominent Alumni:

Howard Norman—several National Book Award nominations

Bonnie Jo Campbell—winner, AWP fiction collection competition

Lisa Lenzo—winner, Iowa Short Fiction Collection Competition

Naeem Murr—QPBC Fiction selection

Patricia Wesley—winner, *Crab Orchard Review* Poetry Competition

Anthony Butts—winner, William Carlos Williams Poetry Award

Chris Torockio—Pushcart Special Mentions

Ron Renauld—producer, *Dynasty*

Melinda Moustakis—2011 National Book Foundation 5 Under 35 Fiction Writer

UNIVERSITY OF MICHIGAN

Department of English
435 South State Street
3187 Angell Hall
Ann Arbor, MI 48109

Phone: (734) 764-1817
Email: undergrad.sec.eng@umich.edu

Tuition: $$$$
Campus student enrollment (undergraduate): 28,395

Degree(s): Bachelor of Arts
Concentrations: Subconcentration in Creative Writing (Department of English)
Minor in Creative Writing (Department of English)
Creative Writing and Literature Major (Residential College)
Courses offered: Introduction to creative writing, introduction to poetry writing, advanced poetry writing, narrations, advanced narrations, fiction writing workshop, poetry writing workshop, advanced fiction writing workshop, advanced poetry writing workshop.
Majors: English Department Subconcentrators: 14 English Department Minors: 80
Writing portfolio requirement: Yes
Number of faculty: 20+
Department activities: Helen Zell Reading Series, Hopwood Awards Program, several literary journals.

Prominent Alumni:
Residential College Alumni include:
Alyson Foster—author of *God is an Astronaut* and *Heart Attack Watch and Other Stories*
Matthew Rohrer—*Satellite, A Green Light, Rise Up, They All Seemed Asleep*
Megan Abbott—numerous novels
Davy Rothbart—*Found* Magazine
Anna Clark—editor of *A Detroit Anthology*
Dennis Foon—film and television
English Department Alumni include
Carlina Duan—poet
Will Dunlap—poet

West

COLORADO COLLEGE

Department of English
14 E. Cache La Poudre Street
Colorado Springs, CO 80903

Phone: (719) 389-6853
Website: coloradocollege.edu
Email: admission@coloradocollege.edu

Tuition: $$$$
Campus student enrollment (undergraduate):
11,668

Degree(s): BA in English with creative writing track
Courses offered: Fiction, poetry tracks; courses also offered in creative nonfiction, journalism, nature writing, etc.
Writing portfolio requirement: No
Scholarships available: No scholarships specific to the department, scholarships given through the college
Number of creative writing faculty: 4
Number of majors: 20 senior majors per year
Percentage and number of applicants accepted into the department per year: No restriction on English majors. About 20 students a year accepted in the creative writing track.
Department activities: *Leviathan* literary magazine. Visiting Writers Series brings guest writers including, in recent years, Alison Bechdel, Margaret Atwood, Peter Behrens, Diane Seuss, Martin Amis, Jess Walter, Madeleine Thien, Jim Moore, Teju Cole, and Amitava Kumar. Visiting writers sometimes teach advanced creative writing courses.

Prominent Alumni:
Neal Baer—executive producer for the NBC show *ER*
Richard Kilbride—managing director of ING Asset Management
Margaret Liu—senior adviser to the Bill and Melinda Gates Foundation
Mark McConnell—animator who has won Emmys for television graphics
Michael Nava—author of the Henry Rios detective novels
Anne Reifenberg—deputy business editor of the *Los Angeles Times*
Ken Salazar—former attorney general of Colorado, now U.S. senator
Thorn Shanker—Pentagon correspondent for the *New York Times*
Joe Simitian—named to the 2003 *Scientific American* list of the 50 most influential people in technology
Cynthia Lowen—coproducer and writer of the film *Bully*
Kaui Hart Hemmings—writer of the novel *The Descendants*, on which the film was based
Michael Dahlie—author of *The Gentleman's Guide to Graceful Living*, winner of the PEN/Hemingway Award for best first novel

LEWIS & CLARK COLLEGE

Department of English
Miller Center for the Humanities
0615 Palatine Hill Road
MSC 58
Portland, OR 97219
Website: college.lclark.edu/departments/english/
Email: english@lclark.edu

Tuition: $$$
Campus student enrollment (undergraduate):
2,209

Degree(s): BA
Courses offered: Fiction, nonfiction, poetry, playwriting
Scholarships available: Yes
Number of faculty: 11 full-time, 2 visiting
Department activities: *Lewis & Clark Literary Review*, a student literary journal. *Synergia*

publishes poems and stories with a focus on gender issues and appears as part of the annual Gender Studies Symposium. The Theatre Department journal, *Pause*, publishes one-act plays by student playwrights. The *Literary Review*, *Synergia*, and *Pause* solicit manuscripts from across campus for jurying and editing by their student editors and staffs. Visiting writers. Readings by visiting poets and fiction authors.

MILLS COLLEGE

English Department
5000 MacArthur Boulevard
Oakland, CA 94613

Phone: (510) 430-2135
Website: mills.edu/undergrad
Email: admission@mills.edu
Note: Mills is a women's college at the undergraduate level and coeducational at the graduate level.

Tuition: $$
Campus student enrollment (undergraduate): 1,345

Degree(s): BA
Concentrations: English majors can individualize their studies by pursing an emphasis in literature or in creative writing. Students also have the option of pursuing a minor in English or creative writing.
Courses offered: The Mills English Department provides students with introductory and advanced courses in creative writing and literatures in English from a wide variety of cultural and historical contexts. The undergraduate program culminates in a senior thesis either in literature or creative writing. Sample courses include:
Beginning Fiction for Children and Young Adults Workshop
Community Teaching: Literary Arts Education, Theory, and Pedagogy
Contemporary Fiction by Women

Craft of Creative Writing
Craft of Digital Storytelling (Nonfiction)
Introduction to Literary Studies
Memoir, Essay, and Other Creative Nonfiction Forms
Poetry Workshop
Poets of Color of the Twentieth and Twenty-First Centuries
Professional Survival for Writers
Social Action and the Academic Essay
Studies in Lesbian Writing
Survey of African American Literature
U.S. Literature and Social Change
World Roots of Literature
Scholarships available: Merit- and need-based scholarships from Mills can total up to $26,000 for first-year students and up to $17,000 for transfer students. More than 80% of our incoming students receive some form of financial aid. Visit mills.edu/cost-and-aid for more information.
Number of faculty: 26
Number of majors and minors: 77 English majors
Department activities: *The Walrus* (undergraduate literary magazine), senior thesis in creative writing or literature, writing contests, the *Campanil* (student-run campus newspaper), community teaching program, teaching English as a second language course, journalism and book art programs, Contemporary Writers Series.

Prominent alumnae:
Dorianne Laux—poet
Ariel Gore—writer and publisher
Laura Cucullu—CNET editor
Cynthia Cruz—poet
Romney Steele—chef and writer
Melissa Lozano—spoken word writer and artist

UNIVERSITY OF ARIZONA

The Department of English
445 Modern Languages
P.O. Box 210067
Tucson, AZ 85721

Phone: (520) 621-1836
Website: english.arizona.edu
Email: admissions@arizona.edu

Tuition: $$$
Campus student enrollment (undergraduate): 32,987

Degree(s): BA in creative writing
Courses offered: Poetry, creative nonfiction, fiction
Writing portfolio requirement: Yes
Scholarships available: Departmental scholarships available for eligible students with junior standing and above. New students are eligible for a variety of university-administered scholarships and aid programs at the time of application.
Number of faculty: 11
Number of majors and minors: 350 majors, 150 minors
Percentage and number of applicants accepted into the department per year: Students who meet the minimum GPA requirement are accepted into the undergraduate creative writing major or minor.
Department activities: *Persona* literary magazine, English and Creative Writing Club.

Prominent Alumni:
Sherwin Bitsui—author of *Shapeshift*
Carl Marcum—author of *Cue Lazarus* and 2000–2002 Wallace Stegner Fellow
Katharine Larson—2003–2004 Ruth Lilly Fellow and winner of the Yale Younger Poets Award

UNIVERSITY OF CALIFORNIA, RIVERSIDE

Creative Writing Department
1120 Hinderaker Hall
Riverside, CA 92521

Phone: (951) 827-3615
Website: creativewriting.ucr.edu/
Email: discover@pop.ucr.edu

Tuition: $$$$
Campus student enrollment (undergraduate): 18,607

Degree(s): BA
Courses offered: Poetry, fiction, nonfiction
Writing portfolio requirement: No
Scholarships available: Yes, Chancellor's Performance Award up to $2,250
Number of faculty: 16
Number of majors and minors: 260 majors, 10 minors
Department activities: Literary journals, writing competitions, awards, Writers Week.

Prominent Alumni:
Elizabeth George
Billy Collins—U.S. Poet Laureate

UNIVERSITY OF HOUSTON

Department of English
R. Cullen 205
Houston, TX 77204–3013

Phone: (713) 743-3004
Website: uh.edu
Email: cwp@uh.edu

Tuition: $$
Campus student enrollment (undergraduate): 34,716

Degree(s): The UH Department of English offers

the Bachelor of Arts in 3 concentrations—Literature, Creative Writing, and Linguistics.

Courses offered: Poetry, fiction

Writing portfolio requirement: Yes, for Creative Writing Students

Scholarships available:

Jimmie Katherine Morris Gentile Scholarship in Literary Criticism: two scholarships of up to $1,000 each.

Eligibility Requirements: English majors who have completed at least 9 hours of upper division English courses (with a minimum of 6 upper division hours on this campus), have a 3.25 GPA in English, and will be enrolled for the applicable academic year are eligible for this scholarship.

Creative Writing Prizes:

The Sylvan Karchmer Prize in Fiction

The Howard Moss Prize in Poetry

The Brian Lawrence Prize in Fiction

The Brian Lawrence Prize in Poetry

The Brian Lawrence Prize in Nonfiction

Number of faculty: 12 in creative writing

Number of majors and minors: 515 English majors, approximately 800 English minors

Percentage of applicants accepted into English Department: 64%

Prominent Alumni:

Donald Barthelme, author of *Snow White* (Atheneum Books, 1967), *The Dead Father* (Farrar, Straus and Giroux, 1975), *Paradise* (Putnam, 1986), and *The King* (Harper, 1990)

Jericho Brown, author of *The New Testament*, which won the Anisfield-Wolf Book Award and was named a finalist for the Lambda Literary Awards

Nina McConigley, author of *Cowboys and East Indians*, winner of the PEN/American Open Book Award and named one of *O* magazine's "best of the best" of award-winning books of 2014

Lacy Johnson, author of *The Other Side*, finalist for Dayton Peace Prize and National Book Critics Circle Award

David Stuart MacLean, author of *The Answer to the*

Riddle Is Me: A Memoir of Amnesia, named Best Memoir/Biography in the Midwest by the Society of Midland Authors

Barbara Duffey, Jessica Greenbaum, and Sean Hill awarded 2015 National Endowment for the Arts Creative Writing Fellowships

UNIVERSITY OF REDLANDS

Department of English

1200 E. Colton Avenue

P.O. Box 3080

Redlands, CA 92373–0999

Phone: (909) 793-2121

Website: redlands.edu

Email: admissions@redlands.edu

Tuition: $$$

Campus student enrollment (undergraduate): 3,493

Degree(s): BA in creative writing

Courses offered: Fiction, nonfiction, poetry, screenwriting

Writing portfolio requirement: Yes, students must complete a writing portfolio during their senior year.

Scholarships available: Yes

Number of faculty: 16

Number of majors and minors: 48 creative writing majors, 2 minors

Department activities: Literary magazine *Redlands Review* showcases student poetry, fiction, nonfiction, and art. In conjunction with the Academy of American Poets, the department sponsors the Jean Burden Prize in poetry. The department also sponsors an annual fiction contest.

UNIVERSITY OF WASHINGTON

Department of English
A101 Padelford Hall, Box 354330
Seattle, WA 98195–4330

Phone: (206) 543-2690
Email: engladv@u.washington.edu
Website: https://english.washington.edu/english-creative-writing-option

Tuition: $$$
Campus student enrollment (undergraduate): 31,063

Degree(s): BA in English
Concentrations: Creative writing
Courses offered: Verse, short story, novel, creative nonfiction, expository writing, literature.
Writing portfolio requirement: Yes, writing samples required
Number of faculty: 8
Department activities: Undergraduate students have the opportunity to work on the staff of *Bricolage*, the undergraduate literary magazine.

Writing Programs by State

Note: The programs listed here offer undergraduate degrees with a major, concentration or emphasis in creative writing, writing, or professional writing. An asterisk (*) indicates a program is an institutional member of the Association of Writers and Writing Programs (AWP).

ALABAMA

Auburn University*
Huntingdon College
Jacksonville State University
University of Alabama*
University of Alabama at Birmingham*
University of South Alabama
University of West Alabama

ALASKA

University of Alaska Fairbanks*

ARKANSAS

Arkansas Tech University*
Hendrix College*
University of Arkansas at Little Rock*

ARIZONA

Arizona State University*
Northern Arizona University*
University of Arizona*

CALIFORNIA

Antioch University Los Angeles*
Azusa Pacific University*
California College of the Arts*
California Lutheran University
California Polytechnic State University*
California State University, Chico
California State University, Fresno*
California State University, Hayward
California State University, Long Beach
California State University, Los Angeles*
California State University, Northridge*
California State University, Sacramento*

California State University, San
  Bernardino
Chapman University
Dominican University of
  California*
Glendale Community College
Humboldt State University
Loyola Marymount University*
Mills College*
Pitzer College
Point Loma Nazarene University*
Pomona College*
San Diego State University*
San Francisco State University*
San Jose State University*
Santa Clara University*
Sonoma State University
St. Mary's College of California*
Stanford University*
University of California, Davis*
University of California, Irvine*
University of California, Los
  Angeles*
University of California, Riverside*
University of California, San Diego
University of California, Santa
  Cruz
University of La Verne*
University of Redlands*
University of San Francisco*
University of Southern California*

COLORADO
Adams State University*
Colorado College*
Colorado Mesa University*
Colorado State University*
Metropolitan State University of
  Denver
Naropa University*
University of Colorado at Boulder*
University of Colorado Colorado
  Springs
University of Colorado Denver

University of Denver*
Western State Colorado
  University*

CONNECTICUT
Albertus Magnus College*
Central Connecticut State
  University*
Connecticut College*
Eastern Connecticut State
  University*
Fairfield University*
Southern Connecticut State
  University*
Trinity College
University of Bridgeport
University of Connecticut*
University of Hartford*
Western Connecticut State
  University*
Yale University

DISTRICT OF COLUMBIA
George Washington University*
Howard University

FLORIDA
Eckerd College*
Florida International University*
Florida State University*
Saint Leo University*
University of Central Florida*
University of Florida*
University of Miami*
University of South Florida*
University of Tampa*

GEORGIA
Agnes Scott College
Augusta State University*
Berry College*
Emory University*
Georgia College & State
  University*

Georgia Southern University*
Georgia State University*
Mercer University*
Savannah College of Art and
  Design*
Spelman College
University of West Georgia
Valdosta State University*
Young Harris College

HAWAII
University of Hawaii at Manoa*

IDAHO
The College of Idaho
Idaho State University
Lewis & Clark College
University of Idaho*

ILLINOIS
Augustana College*
Benedictine University
Bradley University*
Chicago State University
Columbia College Chicago*
DePaul University*
Dominican University
Eastern Illinois University*
Illinois State University *
Illinois Wesleyan University*
Knox College*
Lake Forest College
Lewis University*
Millikin University
North Central College
Northwestern University*
Roosevelt University*
Southern Illinois University,
  Carbondale*
University of Illinois-Urbana
  Champaign
Western Illinois University

INDIANA

Ball State University*
Butler University*
Calumet College of St. Joseph*
DePauw University*
Indiana State University
Indiana University East*
Indiana University Bloomington*
Indiana University–Purdue
    University Fort Wayne
Indiana University–Purdue
    University Indianapolis*
Indiana University South Bend
Purdue University*
Saint Joseph's College
Saint Mary's College
Taylor University*
University of Evansville*

IOWA

Drake University
Iowa State University*
Loras College
Morningside College
University of Iowa*
University of Northern Iowa
Waldorf University

KANSAS

Emporia State University*
Kansas State University*
Pittsburg State University
University of Kansas*
Washburn University
Wichita State University*

KENTUCKY

Morehead State University*
Murray State University*
Northern Kentucky University*
University of Kentucky*
University of Louisville*
Western Kentucky University*

LOUISIANA

Dillard University
Louisiana State University*
Loyola University New Orleans*
Tulane University*
University of Louisiana at
    Lafayette*
University of Louisiana at Monroe
University of New Orleans*
Xavier University of Louisiana

MAINE

Colby College
College of the Atlantic
University of Maine
University of Maine at Farmington*
University of Maine at Machias
University of Maine at Presque Isle

MARYLAND

Frostburg State University*
Goucher College*
Johns Hopkins University*
Loyola University Maryland*
Morgan State University
Salisbury University*
Towson University*
University of Baltimore*
University of Maryland, College
    Park*
Washington College

MASSACHUSETTS

Boston College*
Boston University
Brandeis University
Bridgewater State College*
Emerson College*
Hampshire College
Harvard University*
Massachusetts College of Liberal
    Arts
Massachusetts Institute of
    Technology*
Northeastern University
Pine Manor College
Salem State University*
Smith College
Suffolk University
Tufts University
University of Massachusetts
    Amherst
University of Massachusetts
    Dartmouth*
Wellesley College
Western New England University
Wheaton College
Williams College

MICHIGAN

Albion College
Central Michigan University*
Cornerstone University
Grand Valley State University*
Hope College*
Michigan State University*
Northern Michigan University*
Oakland University*
Siena Heights University
University of Michigan*
University of Michigan-Flint
Wayne State University
Western Michigan University*

MINNESOTA

Augsburg College
Bemidji State University
Bethel College
Concordia College*
Hamline University*
Macalester College
Minnesota State University,
    Mankato*
St. Catherine University*
Southwest Minnesota State
    University*
University of St. Thomas*
Winona State University*

MISSISSIPPI

Belhaven University
Delta State University
Mississippi State University
Mississippi University for Women*
University of Southern Mississippi*

MISSOURI

Central Missouri State University
Drury University
Lindenwood Univerity*
Lincoln University
Missouri Southern State University
Missouri State University*
Rockhurst University
Southeast Missouri State
   University*
Southwest Missouri State
   University*
Stephens College*
University of Missouri
University of Missouri–Kansas
   City*
Webster University*
Westminster College

MONTANA

University of Montana*

NEBRASKA

Creighton University*
Hastings College
Union College
University of Nebraska at Kearney
University of Nebraska Omaha*

NEVADA

University of Nevada, Reno*

NEW HAMPSHIRE

Colby-Sawyer College
Dartmouth College
Franklin Pierce University*
New England College*

Southern New Hampshire
   University*
University of New Hampshire*

NEW JERSEY

Bloomfield College
Fairleigh Dickinson University*
Kean University
New Jersey City University*
Princeton University
Rowan University*
Rutgers University–Camden*
Seton Hall University
Stockton University
William Paterson University of
   New Jersey

NEW MEXICO

Institute of American Indian Arts*
New Mexico State University
Santa Fe University of Art and
   Design*
University of New Mexico

NEW YORK

Adelphi University*
Bard College
Canisius College*
Clarkson University
Colgate University
College of Mount Saint Vincent
College of Saint Rose*
College of Staten Island
Columbia University*
Cornell University*
CUNY, Baruch College
CUNY, Brooklyn College*
CUNY, Hunter College
CUNY, Lehman College
Dowling College
Fordham University*
Hamilton College*
Hofstra University*
Houghton College

Ithaca College*
Keuka College
Lehman College
Le Moyne College
Manhattanville College
Medaille College*
New York University*
Pace University*
Pratt Institute
Queens College, City University of
   New York
Rochester Institute of Technology
Sarah Lawrence College*
Skidmore College*
St. Lawrence University*
Saint Thomas Aquinas College
SUNY at Binghamton*
SUNY College at Brockport*
SUNY Buffalo State College
SUNY at Buffalo*
SUNY at Geneseo*
SUNY at Oswego*
SUNY at Potsdam*
SUNY Purchase College
The New School*
University of Rochester
Villa Maria College

NORTH CAROLINA

Appalachian State University*
Catawba College
Davidson College*
East Carolina University*
Elon University*
Methodist College
North Carolina State University*
Queens University of Charlotte*
St. Andrews University
Salem College
University of Mount Olive
University of North Carolina at
   Asheville*
University of North Carolina at
   Chapel Hill

University of North Carolina at
  Charlotte
University of North Carolina at
  Greensboro *
University of North Carolina at
  Pembroke
University of North Carolina at
  Wilmington*
Wake Forest University*
Warren Wilson College*
Western Carolina University

NORTH DAKOTA
Dickinson State University
University of North Dakota*

OHIO
Antioch University Midwest*
Ashland University*
Bluffton University
Bowling Green State University*
Capital University
Case Western Reserve University*
Cleveland State University*
Denison University*
Hiram College*
John Carroll University
Kent State University*
Kenyon College*
Malone University
Marietta College
Miami University*
Oberlin College
Ohio Northern University
Ohio State University*
Ohio University*
Ohio Wesleyan University
Otterbein University
Tiffin University
University of Akron
University of Cincinnati*
University of Findlay
University of Mount Union
University of Toledo*

Wittenberg University
Wright State University
Youngstown State University

OKLAHOMA
Oklahoma Baptist University
Oklahoma State University*
Southeastern Oklahoma State
  University
Southwestern Oklahoma State
  University
University of Central Oklahoma*
University of Oklahoma
University of Tulsa

OREGON
Corban University
Eastern Oregon University*
Lewis and Clark College
Linfield College
Marylhurst University*
Oregon State University
Pacific University*
Reed College
Southern Oregon University*
University of Oregon
Willamette University

PENNSYLVANIA
Allegheny College*
Arcadia University*
Bloomsburg University of
  Pennsylvania*
Bucknell University*
Cabrini University
Carlow University*
Carnegie Mellon University*
Cedar Crest College*
Eastern University
East Stroudsburg University of
  Pennsylvania
Edinboro University of
  Pennsylvania
Franklin & Marshall College*

Gannon University
Geneva College
Gettysburg College
King's College
Kutztown University of
  Pennsylvania*
La Salle University
Lafayette College*
Lock Haven University of
  Pennsylvania*
Lycoming College*
Mercyhurst College
Misericordia University
Moravian College
Pennsylvania State University*
Pennsylvania State University, Penn
  State Altoona
Penn State Erie, The Behrend
  College*
Point Park University
Saint Joseph's University*
Saint Vincent College
Seton Hill University
Shippensburg University of
  Pennsylvania*
Slippery Rock Univrsity of
  Pennsylvania*
Susquehanna University*
University of the Arts*
University of Pennsylvania*
University of Pittsburgh*
University of Pittsburgh at
  Bradford*
University of Pittsburgh at
  Greensburg*
University of Pittsburgh at
  Johnstown*
University of Scranton*
Washington & Jefferson College*
Waynesburg College
West Chester University of
  Pennsylvania
Widener University*

RHODE ISLAND

Brown University*
Providence College
Rhode Island College*
Roger Williams University*

SOUTH CAROLINA

College of Charleston*
Columbia College
Converse College*
Francis Marion University
University of South Carolina*
Winthrop University*
Wofford College

TENNESSEE

Austin Peay State University*
Belmont University
Bryan College
Christian Brothers University*
Fisk University
Lipscomb University
Rhodes College*
Sewanee: The University of the
   South
University of Memphis*
University of Tennessee at
   Chattanooga*
University of Tennessee, Knoxville*
Vanderbilt University

TEXAS

Baylor University*
Hardin–Simmons University*
Lamar University*
McMurry University
Sam Houston State University*
Southern Methodist University*
Stephen F. Austin State University*
St. Edward's University
Texas A&M University*
Texas State University*
Texas Tech University*
Trinity University*

University of Houston*
University of Mary Hardin–Baylor*
University of North Texas*
University of Texas at Dallas*
University of Texas at El Paso*
University of Texas at San
   Antonio*
University of Texas Rio Grande
   Valley

UTAH

Brigham Young University*
University of Utah*
Weber State University*
Westminster College

VERMONT

Champlain College
Goddard College*
Green Mountain College
Johnson State College
Marlboro College
Middlebury College
Southern Vermont College
Vermont College of Fine Arts*

VIRGINIA

Christopher Newport University
College of William & Mary
Emory and Henry College
George Mason University*
Hollins University*
James Madison University*
Longwood University*
Lynchburg College*
Marymount University*
Norfolk State University
Old Dominion University*
Radford University
Randolph College*
Regent University
Roanoke College*
Sweet Briar College*
University of Mary Washington*

University of Richmond
University of Virginia*
Virginia Tech*
Virginia Wesleyan College
Washington and Lee University

WASHINGTON

Central Washington University
Eastern Washington University*
The Evergreen State College
Seattle Pacific University*
Seattle University
University of Puget Sound
University of Washington
University of Washington Bothell*
Walla Walla University*
Washington State University
Western Washington University*

WEST VIRGINIA

Alderson Broaddus University
Marshall University
West Virginia University*
West Virginia Wesleyan College*

WISCONSIN

Beloit College*
Cardinal Stritch University*
Carroll College
Lakeland College*
Marian University
Marquette University*
Mount Mary College*
University of Wisconsin–Green
   Bay
University of Wisconsin–Madison*
University of Wisconsin–
   Milwaukee*
University of Wisconsin–Superior*
University of Wisconsin–
   Whitewater*

CHAPTER

8

The Next Step

Congratulations! You've researched the schools, found the one that best meets your goals, and have more direction about how the arts will fit into your future. You've made your final college choice and are getting ready for your freshman year—or you may already be on campus. Now what? Well, your college journey has just begun. Here is some advice on how you can make the most of it.

Making the Most of Your Creative College Experience

Being a freshman can be daunting. It's a pretty fast learning curve once you are on campus, and, of course, you want to make the best impression you can—especially in your department. If you have good study habits and organizational skills, these will definitely help you in college. It may seem obvious, but basic things like being on time, always having 100 percent of your attention focused on the material in class, and doing assignments to the best of your ability and handing them in on time really do matter.

You will want to make yourself known to faculty members and students in your school or department. Good relationships are the key to having a good college experience. Go out of your way to introduce yourself quickly to faculty members. You never know—you may just find a mentor. If there are graduate students on campus, you may want to get to know one or two of them as well. Because graduate students have been right where you are, they can give you advice on courses, direct you to the best professors, give guidance on particular assignments, and provide general advice. And maybe you can learn from their mistakes!

Exploring the Local Arts Community

It may seem like the college campus you attend is your entire world—don't forget that it isn't. While most of your time will be devoted to your studies and your life on campus, be aware that you can also find ample opportunities in the creative arena off campus. This is especially true if you attend college in a metropolitan area or a very creative college town.

As you think through extracurricular opportunities, ask yourself these questions:

- **For actors and theater graduates:** Can you participate in any local or regional productions?
- **For artists:** Can you exhibit in local exhibitions or get involved in local arts organizations?
- **For dancers:** Can you perform in any local dance companies or teach in local dance studios?
- **For musicians:** Can you perform in any local symphonies or bands or at specific venues, or teach music?
- **For writers:** Can you get published in a local newspaper or magazine?

Making connections in the arts world outside the university can give you insight on what professional life after college will be like. In addition, it can give personal connections that may come in handy when you are seeking an internship or a job after graduation.

Study Abroad Opportunities

Sometime during your sophomore year, you may want to start looking into opportunities for studying abroad. Many college campuses offer programs that allow certain students the privilege of studying in a foreign country. Educational placements such as these usually last a semester or a year.

Students who participate in college programs for studying abroad normally do so during their junior or senior year. While opportunities for studying abroad are more common at colleges and universities, some conservatories offer options for foreign studies, sometimes for periods shorter than university programs.

Studying the arts abroad may provide an interesting educational perspective that you wouldn't get in the United States. Such studies have certainly been known to broaden students who participated in many creative aspects. Studying abroad can be rewarding both personally and educationally. An added bonus is the financial equity of some programs—it can actually cost the same amount as the regular tuition, and some plans even offer spending money as part of the package! You can essentially travel to a new place and gain credits toward your degree without paying more than you would studying at home.

If your school doesn't participate in programs for studying abroad, you can try to attend a program through another school and transfer the credits back to your home institution. Butler University is one institution that is known for extensive opportunities to study abroad. Don't limit yourself to only the programs that your school offers. With a little research, you may find the perfect opportunity through another institution.

Internships

Internships are experience-based opportunities for students to work in their field of study. To maximize the chances of obtaining the internship of your choice, you will want to start investigating possibilities during your sophomore year of college These work times are usually scheduled during semester breaks or the summer, and students can receive credit hours or even scholarship funds for their participation. Internships can be valuable to you in other ways as well, including the following:

1. You can gain practical, real-world experience in your field.
2. You can learn what you like about your field—and possibly what you don't like.
3. You can use your internship experience as a résumé builder that can enhance your career opportunities after graduation.

You'll want an internship during summer break whenever possible so you have enough time to learn something and get as much as you can out of the experience. The summers between your sophomore and junior years and between your junior and senior years are both good options. Some internships are paid, and some are not. Of course, it is nice to make money while interning, but if your dream internship doesn't pay, you might not want to pass it by. A little sacrifice could go a long way if you can apply that experience later to get other opportunities. You may want to talk with your career services office, professors, seniors, and recent graduates about different internship opportunities to ensure that the internship you choose is reputable. Recommendations from other students about which internships were the most valuable to them professionally may help steer you toward the best internship opportunities.

While you are an intern, take the time to learn as much as you can. Try to arrange interning in multiple roles within the organization to learn what you like and dislike about the field. For example, if you intern at an arts organization, you may want to ask to spend some time in programming, communications, and fundraising. That way, you'll have a sense of what type of job you might seek if you don't pursue the professional arts path. Also, learning about marketing and fundraising in the arts can be very useful even if you pursue a perfroming as a career because you will need to know how to promote yourself, and if you seek artistic grants, learning about fundraising and writing grant applications will likely provide to be valuable skills for your career. You also may find that a career in arts administration is a good option for you when you learn about all of the different roles within an arts organization. Consider another scenario, at a publishing company. You might want to divide your time between acquisitions, editorial, marketing, and publicity to see what area you like best.

Exploring Career Choices after Graduation

By the time you are a senior, you will begin to think about your next step after college. You may still want to become a professional actor, artist, dancer, musician, or writer—or you may have changed your mind about the specifics of your field and the jobs related to it. You may have even started to look into other options or might consider graduate studies.

Each creative discipline has unique intricacies that intertwine in the planning of a professional career. Actors might want to jump into the professional acting scene right away to maximize their chances of success. Artists can make art forever, but it is important to establish a reputation as soon as possible so that they can start earning a living. Dance has a timeline that is shorter than other artistic disciplines, and dancers often decide to embark on a professional career immediately after graduation, since they've already postponed it by being in college. Some instrumentalists quickly find jobs, while others move overseas, where there are more professional openings than in the United States. Singers may have to wait before beginning professional careers, because their voices don't mature for a few more years after they graduate. Because of this, some singers attend graduate school or enroll in a postgraduate training program at a conservatory. Writers may want to submit short stories or poems for publication immediately after their senior year, or try their hand at a writing career like journalism or a related career in publishing, or they may want to consider graduate school.

If you think a a career as a performer, professional artist, or novelist might not be what you ultimately want, there are plenty of alternative creative career fields worth considering. An arts career often follows paths you may not have considered, and your training may qualify you for related disciplines. Perhaps you'll want to think about some of these other professions:

For Actors and Other Theater Professionals

* Drama teacher or professor
* Talent agent
* Casting agent
* Set designer
* Costume designer
* Stage manager
* Producer

For Artists and Designers

* Animator
* Art teacher or professor
* Arts administrator
* Dramatic art director
* Drama/movie sets creator
* Graphic designer
* Illustrator
* Industrial designer (furniture designer, toy designer, footwear designer, etc.)
* Interior designer
* Web designer

For Dancers

* ★ Arts administrator
* ★ Dance teacher or professor
* ★ Dance therapist

For Musicians

* ★ Arts administrator
* ★ Music teacher or professor
* ★ Music therapist

For Writers

* ★ Book publicist
* ★ Editor
* ★ Journalist
* ★ Public relations officer
* ★ Reporter

The college career office at your school most likely has a library of books that can help you delve further into career possibilities. Your alumni office may have a list of people working in certain fields that you can contact as well. Many make themselves available for informational interviews. Faculty members in your department may also have personal contacts with whom you can speak about career choices. Make sure you use your campus resources to the fullest—that is what they are there for.

No matter what you do after you finish your degree, you can take pride in the fact that you've made a commitment to having the arts as an integral part of your education and your life. And always, you will be an artist wherever you go and no matter what you choose to do.

Appendix

General Information

Visual and Performing Arts College Fairs
National Association for College Admission Counseling
1050 N. Highland Street, Suite 400
Arlington, VA 22201
Phone: (800) 822-6285
Website: nacacnet.org

Magazines
College Bound Teen
College Magazine
Next Step U Magazine

Online Chat
College Confidential Message Board
talk.collegeconfidential.com

Websites
collegeboard.com
collegebound.net/
collegemagazine.com
collegenet.com
collegeweeklive.com
commonapp.org
creativecollegesandcareers.com
nextstepu.com
students.gov

Financial Aid
Free Application for Federal Student Aid
Phone: (800) 4-FED-AID
Website: fafsa.ed.gov

RESOURCES FOR ACTORS

Publications
The College Theatre Directory (*Dramatics* Magazine's
annual guide)
Website: collegedirectory.schooltheatre.org/
Dramatics magazine, published by the Educational
Theatre Association

Organizations
Educational Theatre Association
2343 Auburn Avenue
Cincinnati, OH 45219
Phone: (513) 421-3900
Website: edta.org
National Association of Schools of Theatre
11250 Roger Bacon Drive, Suite 21
Reston, VA 20190–5248
Phone: (703) 437-0700
Fax: (703) 437-6312
Website: nast.arts-accredit.org
Email: info@arts-accredit.org

RESOURCES FOR ARTISTS AND DESIGNERS

Events

National Portfolio Days
National Portfolio Days Association
For more information, visit portfolioday.net

Organizations

National Association of Schools of Art and Design (NASAD)
11250 Roger Bacon Drive, Suite 21
Reston, VA 20190–5248
Phone: (703) 437-0700
Fax: (703) 437-6312
Website: nasad.arts-accredit.org
Email: info@arts-accredit.org

RESOURCES FOR DANCERS

Organizations

American College Dance Association
326 N. Stonestreet Ave., Suite 204
Rockville, MD 20850
Phone: (240) 428-1736
info@acda.dance
National Association of Schools of Dance
11250 Roger Bacon Drive, Suite 21
Reston, VA 20190–5248
Phone: (703) 437-0700
Fax: (703) 437-6312
Website: nasd.arts-accredit.org
Email: info@arts-accredit.org
National Dance Education Organization
8609 Second Ave, Suite #203B
Silver Spring, MD 20910
Phone: (301) 585-2880
Website: ndeo.org
Email: info@ndeo.org

Publications

Dance Magazine College Guide
Dance
Dance Spirit
Pointe

RESOURCES FOR MUSICIANS

Website

majoringinmusic.com

Publications

Directory of Music Faculties in Colleges and Universities in the U.S. and Canada (CMS Publications)
Music Scholarship Guide (Music Educator's National Conference)
School Band and Orchestra

Organizations

National Association for Music Education (NAfME)
1806 Robert Fulton Drive
Reston, VA 20191
Phone: (703) 860-4000
Toll-free: (800) 336-3768
Fax: (703) 860-1531
Website: menc.org
National Association of Schools of Music (NASM)
11250 Roger Bacon Drive, Suite 21
Reston, VA 20190–5248
Phone: (703) 437-0700
Fax: (703) 437-6312
Website: nasm.arts-accredit.org
Email: info@arts-accredit.org

RESOURCES FOR WRITERS

Publications
AWP Official Guide to Writing Programs
Poets & Writers

Organization
The Association of Writers and Writing Programs
(AWP)
George Mason University
4400 University Drive Mail Stop 1E3
Fairfax, VA, 22030–4444
Phone: (703) 993-4301
Fax: (703) 993-4302
Website: awpwriter.org
Email: services@awpwriter.org

Index

A

Actors, 8, 24–103, 393, 395
  auditions, 32–33, 35, 48–49
  concentrations in, 27–28, 32
  degrees/programs, types of, 24–27
  evaluating programs, 37
  film and television, 28, 32
  musical theater, 28, 32
  portfolios, 34
  production and design, 28, 34, 40–42, 49–51, 53–57
  program philosophy, 34, 36
  programs, lists of, 58–103
  sample admission essay, 42–43
  sample application questions and answers, 44–46
  sample curriculums, 52–57
  sample résumé, 46–48
  tips and personal stories, 25–26, 29–32, 35–40, 48–49
  typical college day, 33
ACT/SAT tests, 3–4, 14–15
Admissions process. *See* College admissions process
Artistic résumés. *See* Résumés, admission
Artists and designers, 8, 104–190, 393, 396
  concentrations in, 107–108
  degrees/programs, types of, 106–107
  evaluating programs, 118–119, 121–122
  "exploring" *vs.* "focused" students, 104–105
  freshman "foundation" year, 108–109
  graphic/digital design, 111–116, 131–134
  portfolios, 109–111, 116–118, 119, 127–128
  program philosophy, 107
  programs, lists of, 136–190
  sample artist statement, 123–125
  sample curriculums, 130–135
  sample essays, 125–127, 128
  sample introduction for art portfolio, 127–128
  sample résumé, 129
  tips and personal stories, 105–106, 109–111, 119–123
  typical college week/day, 118, 122
Artist's statement, 18–19, 123–125, 276–277
Arts community, local, 390
Auditions, 2, 3
  for actors, 32–33, 35, 48–49
  admissions process and, 11–12, 15–16
  for dancers, 196–202, 210
  financial aid and, 20–21
  for musicians, 259–262, 263, 265–266, 268–274

C

Campus visits, 3
Career paths, 22–23, 392–394
Cinema, 28, 32

College admissions process, 1–2
  See also specific arts discipline
  artistic résumés, 19–20
  artist's statement/essay, 18–19
  auditions/portfolios, 11–12, 15–16, 20–21
  standardized tests, 3–4, 14–15
  student interviews, 17
  teacher recommendations, 17–18
  traditional *vs.* arts colleges, 10–11
Colleges, arts *vs.* traditional, 10–11, 21–23
Colleges, choosing, xiii, 2–3, 12–14, 21–23
Commitment, 12–13
Costs. *See* Financial aid and college costs
Curriculums, sample, 52–57, 130–135, 206–207, 284–287, 355–356

D

Dancers, 9, 191–254, 394, 396
  auditions, 196–202, 210
  dancing without a dance major, 195
  degrees/programs, types of, 191–195
  evaluating programs, 209–211
  programs, lists of, 219–254
  sample application questions and answers, 203–205
  sample curriculums, 206–207
  sample essay, 202–203
  sample résumés, 212–218
  tips and personal stories, 192–193, 196–198, 200–201, 205, 207–209
  typical college day, 199
Design, theater, 28, 34, 40–42, 49–51, 53–57
Digital design, 111–116, 131–134
Double majors, 9, 197–198, 278–279, 339–340, 344–345
Drama students. *See* Actors

E

Employment, part-time, 8–9

Employment after graduation, 22–23, 392–394
Essays, admission, 18–19, 42–43, 125–128, 202–203, 278–279, 349–351

F

FAFSA (Free Application for Federal Student Aid), 5–6
Film, 28, 32
Financial aid and college costs, 4–9, 20–21
Foreign studies, 390–391

G

Graphic/digital design, 111–116, 131–134

I

Illustration, 120–121
Industrial design, 134–135
Internships, 41, 391–392
Interviews, student, 17

J

Jazz auditions, 272–274
Jobs, part-time, 8–9
Jobs after graduation, 22–23, 392–394

M

Majors, academic, 9–10, 205
Majors, double, 9, 197–198, 278–279, 339–340, 344–345
Musical theater, 28, 32
Musicians, 9, 255–337, 394, 396
  auditions, 259–262, 263, 265–266, 268–274
  concentrations, admission requirements for, 274–275
  degrees/programs, types of, 255–259

evaluating programs, 263–265, 268

programs, lists of, 288–337

sample application essay, 278–279

sample artist statement, 276–277

sample curriculums, 284–287

sample repertoire list, 279–280

sample résumé, 281–283

tips and personal stories, 256–258, 260–263, 265–268, 276

typical college day, 264

Music therapy, 256–258

N

National Portfolio Days, 118

P

Parents, 5, 6, 22–23

Part-time work, 8–9

Photography, 105–106

Portfolios, 2, 3

admissions process and, 15–16

for artists and designers, 109–111, 116–118, 119, 127–128

for music composition, 274

for theater design and production, 34

for writers, 341

Production, theater, 28, 34, 40–42, 49–51, 53–57

R

Recommendations, teacher, 17–18

Résumés, admission, 19–20, 46–48, 129, 212–218, 281–283, 352–355

S

SAT/ACT tests, 3–4, 14–15

Scholarships, 7, 20–21

Standardized tests, 3–4, 14–15

Statement, artist's, 18–19, 123–125, 276–277

Studying abroad, 390–391

T

Teacher recommendations, 17–18

Television, 28, 32

W

Writers, 9, 338–388, 394, 397

career prospects, 346

community for, 342–343

creative writing workshops, 341–342

degrees/programs, types of, 338–341

evaluating programs, 343–344

portfolios, 341

programs, lists of, 357–388

sample admission essay, 349–350

sample curriculums, 355–356

sample résumés, 352–355

sample supplemental essay, 350–351

tips and personal stories, 339–340, 344–345, 347–349

typical college day, 341

About the Author

Photo by Michael Cairns

Elaina Loveland has been a professional writer and editor for nearly twenty years. Raised in upstate New York, she discovered her two greatest passions in life—dance and writing—at an early age. A dancer since age five, Loveland performed in several classical ballets and musicals as a teen. She also started writing short stories at age eleven, prompting her starting in ninth grade to search for the perfect college that had both writing and dance programs. Her search led her to study English and dance at Goucher College in Baltimore, Maryland.

Loveland began her career in the Washington, D.C., metropolitan area and worked for several nonprofit national and international education organizations. She has served as editor of the *Journal of College Admission* and *International Educator* magazine. Loveland also was the editor of *The Orff Echo*, a quarterly journal for The American Orff-Schulwerk Association, a professional organization of educators dedicated to the creative music and movement approach developed by Carl Orff and Gunild Keetman.

Since earning a master's degree in English at George Mason University, Loveland has taught college-level English courses as an adjunct instructor at several institutions in the Washington, D.C., area. She also has taught ballet to children and taken opera lessons and studied sculpture to expand her artistic palate.

Loveland's articles on dance and higher education have been published in numerous publications, including *Adjunct Advocate*, *American Careers*, *Dance Teacher*, *Dance Studio Life*, *Dance Spirit*, *Hispanic Outlook on Higher Education*, *International Educator*, the *Journal of College Admission*, *Northern Virginia*, *Pointe*, *University Business*, and the *U.S.News & World Report's Annual College Guide*, among others. *Creative Colleges* has earned recognition in the *College Bound Teen*, the *Washington Post*, the *San Francisco Gate*, and *U.S.News and World Report's Annual College Guide*. Loveland has spoken at the Independent Educational Consultants Association, the University of the Arts, as well as several high schools about college admission for creative students.

Loveland also provides college and career counseling services to students, families, and recent college graduates. For more information, visit elainaloveland.com and creativecollegesandcareers.com.